THE RIGHT NOT TO BE CRIMINALIZED

Dedicated To
Mrs. Mildred Cherry

The Right Not to be Criminalized
Demarcating Criminal Law's Authority

DENNIS J. BAKER
King's College, University of London, U.K.

LONDON AND NEW YORK

First published 2011 by Ashgate Publishing

2 Park Square, Milton Park, Abingdon, Oxon OX14 4RN
711 Third Avenue, New York, NY 10017, USA

Routledge is an imprint of the Taylor & Francis Group, an informa business

First issued in paperback 2016

Copyright © 2011 Dennis J. Baker

Dennis J. Baker has asserted his right under the Copyright, Designs and Patents Act, 1988, to be identified as the author of this work.

All rights reserved. No part of this book may be reprinted or reproduced or utilised in any form or by any electronic, mechanical, or other means, now known or hereafter invented, including photocopying and recording, or in any information storage or retrieval system, without permission in writing from the publishers.

Notice:
Product or corporate names may be trademarks or registered trademarks, and are used only for identification and explanation without intent to infringe.

British Library Cataloguing in Publication Data
Baker, Dennis J.
  The right not to be criminalized : demarcating criminal
law's authority. -- (Applied legal philosophy)
  1. Criminal law--Philosophy. 2. Criminal justice,
Administration of--Moral and ethical aspects.
  I. Title II. Series
  345'.001-dc22

Library of Congress Cataloging-in-Publication Data
Baker, Dennis J.
  The right not to be criminalized : demarcating criminal law's authority / by Dennis J. Baker.
    p. cm. -- (Applied legal philosophy)
  Includes bibliographical references and index.
  ISBN 978-1-4094-2765-0 (hardback) -- ISBN 978-1-4094-2766-7 (ebook)
  1. Criminal law--Philosophy. 2. Law and ethics. 3. Criminal liability--Philosophy. 4. Criminal justice, Administration of--Moral and ethical aspects. I. Title.
  K5018.B34 2011
  345.001--dc22

2010048244

ISBN 978-1-4094-2765-0 (hbk)
ISBN 978-1-138-27372-6 (pbk)

Contents

Series Editor's Preface		*vii*
Preface		*ix*
Acknowledgments		*xiii*
1	Unprincipled Criminalization	1
2	Taking Harm Seriously as a Criminalization Constraint	37
3	The Limits of Remote Harm and Endangerment Criminalization	101
4	The Harm Principle vs. Kantian Criteria for Ensuring Fair Criminalization	141
5	The Moral Limits of Consent as a Defense to Criminal Harm-Doing	173
6	The Morality of Criminalizing Conventional Wrongs	195
7	Conclusion	245
Bibliography		*259*
Index		*285*

Series Editor's Preface

The objective of the Applied Legal Philosophy series is to publish work which adopts a theoretical approach to the study of particular areas or aspects of law or deals with general theories of law in a way which focused on issues of practical moral and political concern in specific legal contexts.

In recent years there has been an encouraging tendency for legal philosophers to utilize detailed knowledge of the substance and practicalities of law and a noteworthy development in the theoretical sophistication of much legal research. The series seeks to encourage these trends and to make available studies in law which are both genuinely philosophical in approach and at the same time based on appropriate legal knowledge and directed towards issues in the criticism and reform of actual laws and legal systems.

The series will include studies of all the main areas of law, presented in a manner which relates to the concerns of specialist legal academics and practitioners. Each book makes an original contribution to an area of legal study while being comprehensible to those engaged in a wide variety of disciplines. Their legal content is principally Anglo-American, but a wide-ranging comparative approach is encouraged and authors are drawn from a variety of jurisdictions.

Tom Campbell
Series Editor
Centre for Applied Philosophy and Public Ethics
Charles Sturt University, Canberra

Preface

This book is aimed at legislators, as clearly even liberal courts such as The Warren Court (The Supreme Court of the United States between 1953 and 1969), will find themselves hamstrung by some of the technicalities imposed by our ancient constitutional texts. But it is hoped that the courts will continue to do what they can, as the United States Bills of Rights and also the European Convention for the Protection of Human Rights and Fundamental Freedoms, to a large extent, constitutionalize the moral right not to be criminalized. Nevertheless, much more needs to be done. It is time for twenty-first-century legislatures to push for constitutional reform. Our existing charters have not kept pace with social change, and this has been exacerbated by a lack of innovation in our higher courts. Of course courts cannot usurp the role of the legislature, but they should not go too far the other way either. The piecemeal innovations of Warren Court have largely been read down by later courts. The Bill of Rights needs to be amended to make it easier for judges to apply it to modern problems, as the current text leaves too much discretion to the judges—discretion which is not always used wisely. It means that rights are contingent on the makeup of the court; then on the makeup of the next court and so forth.

The Warren Court expanded civil rights liberties and judicial powers in an extraordinary way, but in recent decades the pendulum has been swinging against human rights; unless the rights violation has involved high profile terrorists and people of a similar ilk. If the media is present, then so too are the human rights lawyers. Everyday citizens are by and large ignored by those who make a living by promoting human rights. We all know that it is wrong to send a person to jail for 50 years for shoplifting, but such a sentence is possible in America. Alas, we ask China and other countries to follow our standards, but in doing so we must surely be asking the international community to follow some draconian practices.

If the Supreme Court is legally and constitutionally bound to read down rights so as to allow a person to go to jail for 50 years for shoplifting, then it is time for the legislature to take an active role to bring our rights into line with the expectations of people living in the twenty-first century. Senator Jim Webb of Virginia has sponsored legislation that would create a commission to look at the state of criminal justice in America. (It is hoped that the government of the United Kingdom will do the same.) That legislation arose in large part from the Senator's knowledge of criminal justice and his concern about the great number of criminal statutes in the United States and the extensive incarceration of individuals in United States prisons. The legislation has passed the House of Representatives and will most likely clear the Senate before this book goes to press.

In this book, I try to ascertain what external constraints are available for ensuring that criminal laws are just. The legitimacy and justice of criminalization is an area that has been largely overlooked by criminal law theorists, politicians and criminal justice and human rights practitioners. In the 1960s, Sanford Kadish referring to a list of victimless crimes complained of a 'crisis of overcriminalization.' Douglas N. Husak has conceptualized the problem as one of both 'overcriminalization' and 'unjust criminalization.' In this book, I treat the problem as a 'crisis of unjust criminalization,' as the number of criminal laws is not an issue so long as those laws are a just, proportionate and necessary legislative response to a genuine social problem. Criminalization should serve some kind of legitimate social purpose, as criminal laws are effectively the majority of a given community making claims on the freedom of individuals within that community.

The State is merely society as a collective and we need to know why the commands of the collective as expressed in criminal laws have authority over us as individuals. In this book, I argue that this is predominantly explained by pointing to an offender's culpability and the badness and harmfulness of his or her acts/actions. The harm might be indirect and thus attack the preservation of the community (State) by diminishing the good results that flow from communal cooperative living, as is the case with crimes such as bribery and perjury; or the harm might be directly victimizing as is the case with murder, theft, rape, and so forth. The issue of indirect or collective harm is controversial as it could include any activity that causes social conflict and disagreement of a kind that would attack the harmonious balance of the given community. For example, exhibitionism is not inherently harmful, but it does flout social customs and decriminalizing it suddenly might cause conflict and cooperation problems between various sectors within a plural community. That is, if masses were to change their social practice of wearing clothes, which is not likely. Social norms seem a sufficient regulator. However, in some cases the social custom will involve treating a minority as less than full members of the community and rapid change will be necessary, as was the case with the decriminalization of many sexual morality offenses.

In this book we will see that many activities that are deemed bad, and often as harmful, by the State (the collective) involve little more than someone flouting a social custom, as is the case with exhibitionism or with wearing a burqa. The French plan to ban the burqa, and exhibitionism is already an offense: but are not prohibitions against such practices merely laws telling us how to dress? In this book, I attempt to explain the legitimacy of just criminalization. I argue that certain acts/actions are deserving of the crime label because they produce bad consequences (or risk producing bad consequences as is the case with attempts, endangerment, *etc.*) of an avoidable (avoidable in that the wrongdoer culpably aimed for the bad consequences and could have chose otherwise) for others. It is the gravity of the wrongness of certain actions that make criminalizing them justifiable. Justified criminal laws have authority over us as they protect our genuine human interests in socialized, cooperative, plural societies. More significantly, I argue that the right not to be criminalized is not merely a cardinal human right found in morality, but is also a constitutional right. In this book, I reinterpret a number of existing constitutional and international rights to demonstrate that these texts incorporate a constitutional right not to be criminalized. The limits of asking the courts to do all the work are obvious, so greater advances will require the legislators to get involved, but legislators often lack the temerity to tackle the problem.

Dennis J. Baker
King's College,
University of London

Acknowledgments

This book pulls together and adds to the theories that I have developed in a number of essays to provide an evocative and compelling explanation of the morality of good criminalization and of the normative foundations of the cardinal right not to be criminalized.

Large sections of some of my earlier essays have been incorporated into this book. Therefore, I would like to acknowledge a number of publishers for allowing me to reuse parts of that material here. I acknowledge the Journal *Criminal Justice Ethics*, John Jay College, New York for allowing me to incorporate large sections from 'Constitutionalizing the Harm Principle,' (2008) 27(2) *Criminal Justice Ethics* 3; the Regents of the University of California, California University Press for allowing me to incorporate large sections from 'The Moral Limits of Consent as a Defense in the Criminal Law,' (2009) 12(1) *New Criminal Law Review* 93; Taylor & Francis Group Publishing for allowing me to incorporate an extensive part of 'Collective Criminalization and the Constitutional Right to Endanger Others,' 28(2) *Criminal Justice Ethics* (2009); and the *Australian Journal of Legal Philosophy* for allowing me to reuse 'The Harm Principle vs. Kantian Criteria for Ensuring Fair, Principled and Just Criminalization,' (2008) 33 *Australian Journal of Legal Philosophy* 66.

I am especially grateful to Professor Andrew von Hirsch LL.D. for reading several earlier drafts of this book. It was his inspiring lectures in the philosophy of punishment that aroused my interest in this topic. In particular, I would like to thank him for the immense effort he put into directing the earlier stages of this project during my time working with him at the University of Cambridge. His input helped me to conceptualize and analyze the issues with greater logicality, convincingness and consistency. The numerous discussions I had with Andrew stimulated my thinking and provided me with many original ideas. I am also grateful to Professor Michael Tonry, Mrs. Nicola Padfield and Mr. Peter Glazebrook for their assistance during my time in Cambridge. I am also immensely grateful to Dr. Xia Zhao for her support during the course of this project. I also acknowledge Mr. Charles Oh, Professor Geoff Harcourt A.O., Laurie Baker and Jason Baker.

If you have ten thousand regulations you destroy all respect for the law.

Sir Winston Churchill

It is quite easy to state what may be right in particular cases (*quid sit juris*), as being what the laws of a certain place and of a certain time say or may have said; but it is much more difficult to determine whether what they have enacted is right in itself, and to lay down a universal Criterion by which Right and Wrong in general, and what is just and unjust, may be recognized. All this may remain entirely hidden even from the practical Jurist until he abandon his empirical principles for a time, and search in the pure Reason for the sources of such judgments, in order to lay a real foundation for actual positive Legislation. In this search his empirical Laws may, indeed, furnish him with excellent guidance; but a merely empirical system that is void of rational principles, is like the woodenhead in the fable of Phaedrus, fine enough in appearance, but unfortunately it wants brain.

Immanuel Kant[1]

---

1 Immanuel Kant, *The Philosophy of Law: An Exposition of the Fundamental Principles of Jurisprudence as the Science of Right*, translated from the German by William Hastie, *The Philosophy of Law* (Edinburgh: T. & T. Clark, 1887) at p. 44.

Chapter 1
Unprincipled Criminalization

There is a vast array of literature on the moral limits of the criminal law. In this book my goal is not merely to discuss the moral limits of the criminal law. Instead, the focus is on the legal limits of the criminal law. This book takes a different approach by trying to show how the moral criteria for constraining unjust criminalization can and have been incorporated into constitutional human rights and thus provide us with a legal right not to be unfairly criminalized. The aim of the book is to set out the constitutional limits of the substantive criminal law. As far as specific constitutional rights operate to protect *specific freedoms* (free speech, freedom of religion, privacy, *etc.*), the right not to be criminalized has proved to be a rather powerful justice constraint in the U.S. The general right not to be criminalized has not been fully embraced in either the U.S. or Europe, but it does exist. In this book, I set out the legal foundations of that right and the criteria for determining when the state might override it.

In the period since publication of J.S. Mill's Harm Principle, constitutional courts in North America and Europe have taken critical steps toward the decriminalization of sexual activities, abortion, begging, marijuana use and so on. I devote a substantial degree of attention to this subject; indeed, the pattern of decisions in favor of the decriminalization of such offenses is so pronounced that anyone writing within the Millsian tradition would of course feel substantial pride in the impetus that Mill provided for judicial conclusions along these lines. But presenting the right not to be criminalized as a legal rather than as a mere moral right requires caution, in part because the constitutional texts (in particular, the Canadian Charter of Rights and Freedoms, the American Bill of Rights, and the European Convention on Human Rights) are worded differently, and also because the courts interpreting these have taken different approaches even to largely similar textual terms. Everyone has a constitutional right not be criminalized without good reason, but different courts will adopt different interpretive strategies depending on the exegetical traditions of constitutional law in the given jurisdiction to identify it. This means that in some jurisdictions the courts are better equipped to enforce such a right, whereas in others constitutional reform may be required to make the right more effective. Nonetheless, it is undeniable that the U.S., European and Canadian courts are more open to considering persuasive precedents from other jurisdictions than they once were.

Culpable harm-doing provides the core justification for overriding a person's right not to be criminalized. But as we will see, harm is a very wide concept. Some scholars have tried to provide objective accounts of harm, but much more work is needed. If the constitutional right not to be criminalized is going to succeed in ensuring that people are only criminalized when they deserve it, then we need a fairly clear picture of harm. We need reasonably objective accounts of harm; otherwise any harm claim could be used to justify overriding a person's right not to be criminalized. The right's constitutional effectiveness depends on proper accounts of harm being put forward. The problem is that harm is conventionally contingent. This poses a real difficulty when it comes to soft harms or acts which cause umbrage such as exhibitionism. But even where the act does in fact cause harm, a given community might be willing to tolerate it for some conventional reason. For instance, in London (or at least in fashionable parts of the city) foxes are deemed worthy of protection and fetuses are not; in many regional parts of England, fetuses are deemed worthy of protection and foxes are not. I confess to deep skepticism about even the possibility of advancing a convincing theory that does any more than reinforce the preferences of these different communities; and I further confess to a misgiving that the theory-creating classes will almost always be convinced by a protracted argument that supports their preferences (in this instance, foxes/yes; fetuses/no). Throughout this book, I try to set a framework for identifying sound harm claims, because the constitutional right not to be criminalized is only useful if the argument used to override it is a good one.

The Problem: Unprincipled Criminalization

In positivistic terms a crime is any act that is labeled as criminal.[1] In a purely legal sense it is wrong to engage in any conduct that has been labeled as criminal, even if the conduct is not morally wrong. In this book, I argue that people have a general right not to have their choices restricted by criminalization. The right is not only about having the freedom do as one chooses so long as it does not wrong others, but also about not being subjected to the harmful consequences that flow from unfair criminalization (detention, penal fines, conviction, stigmatization, *etc.*). Criminalization has harmful consequences for those who are labeled as criminals and therefore people have a right not to be criminalized unless it is fair to override their right. I aim to set out criteria for identifying when the right may be overridden in order to justify criminalization.

---

1   Henry M. Hart, 'The Aims of the Criminal Law,' (1958) 23 *Law & Contemporary Problems* 401 at p. 404.

The detrimental side effects of criminalization are well documented.[2] The overcriminalization phenomenon and its causes are also well documented.[3] I do not intend to survey that literature in this work. Instead my aim is to address the problem identified in the literature by developing checks for constraining unjust criminalization. The bulk of the literature addressing the overcriminalization problem merely discusses the case for decriminalizing crimes that are usually victimless.[4] Numerous writers have produced instrumental arguments for decriminalizing crimes such as law enforcement costs, but few have developed arguments for ensuring that criminalization decisions accord with the constitutional requirements of fairness and justice.[5] Richards[6] notes: 'Certainly, if there are good

---

2   Nigel Walker, *Punishment, Danger and Stigma* (Oxford: Basil Blackwell, 1980) at pp. 142 *et seq.*; Jonathon Schonsheck, *On Criminalization* (London: Kluwer Academic Publishers, 1994) Chapter 1; Hilary Metcalf *et al., Barriers to Work for Offenders and Ex-Offenders* (London: Department of Work and Pensions, Research Report 155, 2001); Anthony E. Bottoms and Roy Light, *Problems of Long-Term Imprisonment* (Aldershot: Gower, 1987).

3   For a comprehensive and excellent overview of some of the causes of the current overcriminalization phenomena, see Douglas Husak, *Overcriminalization: The Limits of the Criminal Law* (New York: Oxford University Press, 2008). Husak argues that the cause of the overcriminalization phenomena is multifaceted. It stems from mislabeling morally innocuous acts as criminal, from prosecution discretion, from overcharging, and from law schools failing to teach or conduct research in the criminalization area. The problem is no less acute in England, see Andrew Ashworth, 'Is the Criminal Law a Lost Cause,' (2000) 116 *The Law Quarterly Review* 225.

4   Sanford H. Kadish, 'The Crisis of Overcriminalization,' (1967) 374 *The Annals of the American Academy of Political and Social Science* 157; Herbert L. Packer, *The Limits of the Criminal Sanction* (Stanford: Stanford University Press, 1968); Sanford H. Kadish, 'More on Overcriminalization: A Reply to Professor Junker,' (1971–1972) 19 *U.C.L.A. Law Review* 719; Jerome H. Skolnick, 'Criminalization and Criminogenesis: A Reply to Professor Junker,' (1971–1972) 19 *U.C.L.A. Law Review* 715; Norval Morris and Gordon Hawkins, *The Honest Politician's Guide to Crime Control* (Chicago: Chicago University Press, 1970); Arval A. Morris, 'Overcriminalization and Washington's Revised Criminal Code,' (1972–1973) 48 *Washington Law Review* 5; and John M. Junker, 'Criminalization and Criminogenesis,' (1971–1972) 19 *U.C.L.A. Law Review* 697. See also the symposium papers on 'Overcriminalization: The Politics of Crime' in the 2005 volume of the *American University Law Review*.

5   The exception is Joel Feinberg. Feinberg wrote four groundbreaking volumes on the topic of criminalization in the 1980s. See Joel Feinberg, *The Moral Limits of the Criminal Law: Harm to Others* (New York: Oxford University Press, Vol. I, 1984); Joel Feinberg, *The Moral Limits of the Criminal Law: Offense to Others* (New York: Oxford University Press, Vol. II, 1985); Joel Feinberg, *The Moral Limits of the Criminal Law: Harm to Self* (New York: Oxford University Press, Vol. III, 1986); and Joel Feinberg, *The Moral Limits of the Criminal Law: Harmless Wrongdoing* (New York: Oxford University Press, Vol. IV, 1988).

6   David Richards, 'Drug Use and the Rights of the Person: A Moral Argument for Decriminalization of Certain Forms of Drug Use,' (1980–1981) 33 *Rutgers Law Review* 607 at p. 614.

moral reasons for criminalizing certain conduct, quite extraordinary enforcement costs will be borne.' In practice, high costs have had little bearing on criminalization and punishment decisions. Notwithstanding the injustices and disproportional fiscal costs involved in implementing populist punitive policies such as three strikes and you-are-out,[7] politicians and legislatures have clutched such policies with alacrity.[8] Instrumental (the costs and benefits of enforcement and so on) arguments would not outweigh the compelling costs of trying and sentencing a murderer. Efficiency arguments are something to be considered at an instrumental level once there is a *prima facie* moral justification for criminalization. Such arguments are likely to tip the scales in cases where the conduct only involves trivial criminality.

An obvious moral basis can be found for criminalizing non-borderline conduct that clearly involves moral wrongdoing and serious harm such as theft, rape, murder, terrorism and so on. A more complex moral analysis is required for ascertaining the fairness and justice of criminalizing borderline wrongdoing such as exhibitionism, fox hunting,[9] *etc*. At the other end of the scale, it is not clear why the crime label has been applied to range of apparently innocuous activities such as passive begging,[10] feeding the homeless,[11] fornication,[12] possessing sex toys,[13] homosexuality,[14] possessing marijuana for personal use,[15] and attending live strip shows.[16] The majority in some societies may not approve of homosexuality,

---

7   Peter W. Greenwood *et al.*, *Three Strikes and You're Out: Estimated Benefits and Costs of California's New Mandatory-Sentencing Law* (California: Rand, 1994).

8   Anthony E. Bottoms, 'The Philosophy and Politics of Punishment and Sentencing,' in Christopher M.V. Clarkson and Rod Morgan, *The Politics of Sentencing Reform* (Oxford: Clarendon Press, 1995) at pp. 39–40.

9   Hunting Act 2004 (U.K.).

10   The free speech right has been used to decriminalize begging in the United States. See *Benefit v. Cambridge*, 424 Mass. 918 (1997). Cf. *Loper v. New York City Police Dept.*, 802 F. Supp. 1029, 1042 (S.D.N.Y. 1992). It is worth noting that in jurisdictions such as England, old anti-begging laws are still in force and have been enforced vigorously by the Blair/Brown governments to crack down on passive begging. See section 3 Vagrancy Act 1824 (U.K.).

11   Randal C. Archibold, 'Las Vegas Makes It Illegal to Feed Homeless in Parks,' (New York: *New York Times*, 28 July 2006).

12   See for example, *Lawrence v. Texas*, 539 U.S. 558 (2003) at pp. 586; 592–594 per Scalia J.

13   *Williams v. Pryor*, 240 F. 3d 944 (2001) at p. 949.

14   *Lawrence v. Texas*, 539 U.S. 558 (2003).

15   *Malmo-Levine* [2003] S.C.C. 74.

16   *Barnes v. Glen Theatre, Inc.*, 501 U. S. 560 (1991) at pp. 574–575 per Scalia, J. His Honor noted that: '[T]he dissent confidently argues, that the purpose of restricting nudity in public places in general is to protect non-consenting parties from offense ... Perhaps the dissenters believe that "offense to others" ought to be the only reason for restricting nudity in public places generally, but there is no basis for thinking that our society has ever shared that Thoreauvian "you-may-do-what-you-like-so-long-as-it-does-not-injure-someone-else" beau ideal—much less for thinking that it was written into the Constitution ... Our society

prostitution, marijuana use or homelessness, but majority mores do not tell us why it is fair to criminalize such conduct. Why are those who engage in such activities deserving of criminal censure? If lawmakers want to criminalize this type of conduct then they have to demonstrate that there are objective moral[17] justifications for doing so. The objectivity of justifications for criminalization can be tested by subjecting them to the inter-subjective scrutiny of communally situated moral agents. Such a process allows stakeholders to question non-genuine justifications (unreasoned harm arguments *etc.*) for criminalization.

> What it is rational for one person to do, to believe, or to value will thereby also of necessity be equally rational for the rest of us who might find ourselves in the same circumstances. For rationality is inherently 'objective': it does not reconfigure itself to meet the idiosyncratic predilections of particular individuals. To be sure, objectivity will have *to take context into account*, seeing that different individuals and *groups confront very different objective situations*. Rationality is universal, but it is circumstantially universal—and objectivity with it. ... The contextuality of good reasons can be reconciled with the universality of rationality itself by taking a hierarchical view of the process through which the absolutistic (and uniform) conception of ideal rationality is brought to bear *context-differentially on the resolution of concrete cases and particular situations.*[18]

Inter-subjectively, members of even the most advanced societies are not so rational that they can identify objective truths or universal standards. Nonetheless, we can scrutinize the harm, badness and wrong claims by drawing on our deep conventional understandings of harmfulness, badness, wrongness and so on. This level of objectivity is not of the indefeasible kind envisaged by Kant and other moral realists, but it may be all we have.

What objective criteria are currently used for ensuring fair and principled criminalization? The concepts that the edifice of the criminal law was built upon are multifaceted and complex. It is clear that outside of the basic constitutional prerequisites (which are predominantly procedural) there is no principled content or composition that the substantive criminal law must have. Ashworth notes

---

prohibits, and all human societies have prohibited, certain activities not because they harm others but because they are considered, in the traditional phrase, "*contra bonos mores,*" *i.e.,* immoral.'

17 Complete objectivity is impossible, but the reasons put forward for criminalization must be scrutinized by moral agents who are communally situated via an inter-subjective deliberation process—as far as that is possible in Western political systems. See Chapter 6 *infra*.

18 Nicholas Rescher, *Objectivity: The Obligations of Impersonal Reason* (Notre Dame, IL: University of Notre Dame Press, 1997) at p. 3. 'Objective judgments are those that have a cogency compelling for everyone alike (or at least all normal sensible people), independently of idiosyncratic tendencies and inclinations.' *Id.* at p. 7.

that, '[t]he contours of … criminal law are "historically contingent"—not the product of any principled inquiry or consistent application of certain criteria but largely dependent on the fortunes of successive governments, on campaigns in the mass media, on the activities of various pressure groups, and so forth.'[19] This unprincipled and politicized approach to criminalization is a major cause of the current unjust criminalization crisis in Britain and the United States. More than 8,000 criminal offenses now exist in England and Wales.[20] Many of these offenses criminalize activities that do not involve moral turpitude. In the United States there are 4,000 Federal offenses, and a comparable number of criminal offenses in the individual states.[21] Likewise, in the U.S.A. there is also a third stratum of criminalization at the local level.[22]

Governments eager to capitalize on the political advantages of engaging in penal populism have developed a plethora of politicized and unprincipled policies about what to criminalize.[23] The media also plays a major role in populism inspired criminalization by inculcating members of the public '[w]ith a powerful set of ideological images of immorality, heroism, evil, efficiency and justice. The political values and interests integral to the censure of crime in television crime drama daily reinforce State definitions of crime, the value of censure and punishment, and the importance of State violence for our comfort and safety.'[24] Criminal laws do not just appear out of thin air, someone has to provide the stimulus for their enactment. This is especially so with harmless conduct. But even when the conduct is objectively harmful, '[t]he harm must be discovered and pointed out. People must be made to feel that something ought to be done

---

19   Ashworth, *op. cit. supra*, fn. 3 at p. 226.
20   *Ibid*.
21   See John S. Baker, *Measuring the Explosive Growth of Federal Crime Legislation* (Washington, D.C.: Federalist Society for Law and Policy Studies, Crime Report, 2004); John S. Baker, 'Jurisdictional and Separation of Powers Strategies to Limit the Expansion of Federal Crimes,' (2005) 54 *American University Law Review* 545 at p. 548 *et seq*. Luna estimates a similar number of offenses in the individual states. See Erik Luna, 'The Overcriminalization Phenomenon,' (2005) 54 *American University Law Review* 703 at pp. 718 *et seq*. See also Paul H. Robinson and Michael T. Cahill, 'Can a Model Penal Code Second Save the States from Themselves?,' (2003) 1 *Ohio State Journal of Criminal Law* 169.
22   See for example, the *Las Vegas Municipal Code*, which prohibits mobile soup kitchens or members of the public from feeding the homeless. These misdemeanors carry fines and jail terms.
23   Julian V. Roberts *et al*., *Populism and Public Opinion: Lessons from Five Countries* (Oxford: Oxford University Press, 2003). The authors argue that politicians are more interested in capitalizing on the public fear of crime than they are in seeking workable solutions—they exploit anxiety for political advantage.
24   'Censures are revealed as quite complex compositions of images of personal deviance and images of political priority.' Colin Summer, *Censure, Politics and Criminal Justice* (Milton Keyes: Open University Press, 1990) at pp. 8–9.

about it. Someone must call the public's attention to these matters, supply the push necessary to get the law enacted.'[25]

A recent political campaign emphasizing the alleged harmfulness of homeless people was used in Las Vegas to justify the enactment of an ordinance, which makes it a crime for members of the public and charitable organizations to feed homeless people in the city's parks. This is a stark example of unprincipled criminalization. The Las Vegas City Council argues that the criminal law is needed to prevent people from feeding homeless people, because feeding homeless people allegedly lures them to the public parks. This apparently 'led to complaints by residents about crime, public drunkenness and litter.'[26] The ordinance bans members of the public and mobile soup kitchens from providing food or meals to indigent people in the city's parks. The law carries a maximum penalty of $1,000 and a six-month jail term. The Mayor has argued that the crackdown was necessary as families were allegedly too scared to use the park.[27]

If the public are fearful of some perceived harm, politicians tend to enact laws in response without considering whether the conduct is in fact harmful. Such a response materializes into votes at the ballot box. Professors Kelling and Wilson[28] authored the broken windows thesis, which holds that conduct such as street prostitution and begging are harmful because these activities are allegedly a part of a self-perpetuating cycle of decay dragging more serious crime into neighborhoods. Recently, the British government[29] used the broken windows thesis to justify a crackdown on begging in England and Wales. It referred to the broken windows type of harm to emphasize the harmfulness of homelessness; and has adopted 'zero tolerance policing.'[30] The espousal of such policies with an emphasis on the harmfulness and intolerableness of so-called nuisance behavior has resulted in the criminal law in that jurisdiction being extended through the use of the civil law. The Crime and Disorder Act 1998 (U.K.) and the Anti-Social Behaviour Act 2003 (U.K.) have been used in tandem to indirectly extend the scope of prohibitions backed by the criminal law. These Acts allow the police and local authorities to seek civil injunctions and Anti-Social Behaviour Orders (hereinafter ASBOs), which are effectively civil injunctions, to bar people from

---

25   Howard S. Becker, *Outsiders* (Glencoe, IL: The Free Press, 1963) at p. 162. See also Joseph R. Gusfield, *Symbolic Crusade* (Urbana: University of Illinois Press, 2nd ed. 1986).

26   Randal C. Archibold, *op. cit. supra*, fn. 11.

27   *Ibid*.

28   James Q. Wilson, and George Kelling, 'Broken Windows: The Police and Neighborhood Safety,' (1982) *Atlantic Monthly* 29.

29   *Respect and Responsibility—Taking a Stand Against Anti-Social Behaviour* (London: Home Office, White Paper Cm 5778, 2003) at paragraphs 1.8, 3.40–3.44. The broken window thesis has also had a substantial influence on policing practices. Debra Livingston, 'Police Discretion and the Quality of Life in Public Places: Courts, Communities, and New Policing,' (1997) 97 *Columbia Law Review* 551 at p. 584.

30   *Ibid*.

engaging in both criminal and non-criminal conduct.[31] Contravening an ASBO may result in as much as a five-year jail term. This is a way to bring more people within the reach of the criminal law.[32]

Bernard Harcourt[33] has argued that the Harm Principle has lost much of its clout as a restraining principle, because of the increasing use of populist harm arguments. He argues that harm arguments have become so prevalent that the Harm Principle has become an empty concept as far as restraining criminalization is concerned.[34] Nonetheless, it has not been objective conceptualizations of harm that have been the stimulus for the unjust criminalization crisis. The types of harm arguments that Harcourt refers to are not in fact harms, as many of them cannot be objectively described as genuine harms. Lawmakers are not too interested in determining whether the alleged harm does in fact cause harm. The Harm Principle requires that the conduct in fact cause harm to others. Both the moral analysis and the empirical data would have to demonstrate that the wrongdoer acted with moral culpability and caused some kind of objectively harmful consequence, before it could be criminalized under the Harm Principle. The Harm Principle is a cogent principle for limiting criminalization. As we will see, its main limitation is that it has no legal force. It has not been developed as a meaningful constitutional constraint in the way that other rights such as free speech and privacy have.

In this book, the Harm and Offense Principles, *inter alia*, are examined, their core elements set forth, and the legitimacy of criminalization evaluated in light of them. I rethink the concept of harm to make it a workable objective criterion for limiting unjust criminalization—and for explaining when it is appropriate to override a person's right not to be criminalized. I aim to demonstrate that people have a constitutional right not to be subjected to harmful prison terms (even a day in jail is harmful), unless their actions have caused (or risked) a proportional level of harm for others. Harm to others is not the only justification for overriding a person's right not to be criminalized, but it is the only moral justification of sufficient weight to outweigh a person's right not to be jailed.

I also critique Feinberg's Offense Principle and dismiss it as a constraint for ensuring fair criminalization. I argue that offense is a vacuous concept that does not provide legislatures with a sound objective justification for criminalizing many *legitimately unwanted* harmless wrongs. In its place, I provide other justifications

---

31   See generally, Evidence to House of Commons Home Affair Committee, Parliament of the United Kingdom, *Anti-Social Behaviour*, 19 January 2005, Stationery Office Ltd., HC-80-II: London at paragraphs 7–11.

32   John C. Coffee Jr., 'Does "Unlawful" Mean "Criminal"?: Reflections on the Disappearing Tort/Crime Distinction in American Law,' (1991) 71 *Boston University Law Review* 193. See also William J. Stuntz, 'The Pathological Politics of Criminal Law,' (2001–2002) 100 *Michigan Law Review* 505.

33   Bernard E. Harcourt, 'Collapse of the Harm Principle,' (1999–2000) 90 *Journal of Criminal Law and Criminology* 109.

34   *Id.* at p. 113.

for outlawing *harmless* wrongdoing such as the umbrage caused by exhibitionism. Notably, exhibitionism and privacy violations can have bad consequences that are sufficient to override the offending exhibitionist's right not to be criminalized, but because the bad consequences are of a harmless nature this type of criminalization has to be enforced with fines rather than jail terms.

Unfair and unjust criminalization flows from a number of practices[35] including the mislabeling of innocuous conduct as criminal; eliminating the *ex post* culpability requirement without moral justification (strict and vicarious liability for crimes that result in a conviction and/or imprisonment); eliminating the *ex ante* 'imputability of blame for remote harm' requirement without justification (*i.e.*, criminalizing people for being a mere 'but for' cause of harm caused by the intervening choices of others: remote harms);[36] imposing disproportional punishments;[37] and through the circumvention of human rights and due process protections by, for example, blurring the civil and criminal law. From the *ex ante* criminalization perspective the lawmaker has to consider a number of factors including what can be fairly labeled as criminal; the sentences that should be set for various offenses; and the structure that the criminal law will take to ensure that criminal liability will only be visited on those who are deserving of criminal censure.

The Right Not to be Criminalized

The right to not to be criminalized is a basic human right that aims to protect individuals from unwarranted state interference of a penal nature. In particular, the right is geared towards protecting individuals from being unjustly criminalized. The right is a basic moral right, but it is also a fundamental legal right. It is formed by a number of specific protections as well as the more general protections found in the Fifth and Eighth Amendments of the U.S. Constitution,[38] and the corresponding rights concerning deprivation of liberty and fair punishment as set

---

35   See generally Husak, *op. cit. supra*, fn. 3.

36   Dennis J. Baker, 'The Moral Limits of Criminalizing Remote Harms,' (2007) 10(3) *New Criminal Law Review* 370; Dennis J. Baker, 'Collective Criminalization and the Constitutional Right to Endanger Others,' (2009) 28(2) *Criminal Justice Ethics* (forthcoming) and Andrew von Hirsch, 'Extending the Harm Principle: "Remote" Harms and Fair Imputation,' in Andrew P. Simester and A.T.H. Smith, *Harm and Culpability* (Oxford: Clarendon Press, 1996) at pp. 259 *et seq*.

37   See *Harmelin v. Michigan*, 501 U.S. 957 (1991); *Locker v. Andrade*, 538 U.S. 63 (2003). See generally, Andrew von Hirsch and Andrew Ashworth, *Proportionate Sentencing: Exploring the Principles* (Oxford: Oxford University Press, 2005).

38   Constitution of the United States 1787. The nucleus of human rights generally is the preservation of human dignity and well-being—and more generally the flourishing of citizens in civilized states. See generally, James Griffin, *On Human Rights* (Oxford: Oxford University Press, 2008); Richard Kraut, *What is Good and Why: The Ethics of Well-Being* (Cambridge MA: Harvard University Press, 2007).

out in Articles 3, 5 and 8 of the European Convention[39] and Articles 7, 9, and 12 of the Canadian Charter of Rights and Freedoms.[40] While the core rights that have been codified in various domestic constitutions and international conventions have a similar purpose and scope, the exact compass of a given right will vary slightly depending on the textual nature of the right and the limits that the given text puts on the judges who are to interpret it. The various courts around the world use different standards of interpretation, but the differences are more formal than substantive. A careful analysis (that is, an examination that avoids dispensing with an analysis of the prudential and historical factors that typically inform judicial determinations of the rights individuals have in a given jurisdiction) of the personal autonomy and fair punishment type provisions found in the various constitutions demonstrates that these types of rights, however differently worded and however differently interpreted in the past, contain a general right not to be criminalized.

The 'evolutive interpretation' method used to determine rights in Europe allows the courts there to acknowledge that concepts can change over time and requires the courts to consider the E.C.H.R. in light of social and economic evolutions.[41] The 'margin of appreciation' doctrine allows courts take into account that the E.C.H.R. will be interpreted differently in different countries, but it should not permit the Strasbourg Court to endorse interpretations that would result in human rights abuses, such as allowing a person to be criminalized and jailed for engaging in innocuous activities or allowing a person to be sent to prison for 40 years for shoplifting and so forth. Allowing someone to be jailed for 40 years for shoplifting contravenes our deeply held conventional (Western) standards of justice—the very same standards that we ask non-Western states to comply with.

I argue that the Due Process Clause and the Eighth Amendment (and their international counterparts) contain a general right not to be criminalized.[42] These rights can be distinguished from specific constitutional rights because they protect the autonomy of individuals generally. The right to avoid arbitrary detention, to be free to make private decisions concerning personal matters that do not affect others and not to be subjected to disproportionate punishment forms a more general right that allows people to engage in any conduct they like so long as it does not *wrong* others. *Per contra*, specific rights protect specific freedoms such

---

39 European Convention for the Protection of Human Rights and Fundamental Freedoms, 4 November 1950, 213 U.N.T.S. 222 (entered into force generally on 3 September 1953).

40 Part 1, section 2(b), Constitution Act 1982 (Can.). See also the corresponding rights in Articles 1, 3, 4, 5, 9, and 12 of Universal Declaration of Human Rights, GA Res. 217 A (III), U.N. Doc. A/810 (1948).

41 See Eva Brems, *Human Rights: Universality and Diversity* (The Hague: Martinus Nijhoff Publishers, 2001), at p. 396. Cf. Howard Charles Yourow, *The Margin of Appreciation Doctrine in the Dynamics of European Human Rights Jurisprudence* (The Hague: Martinus Nijhoff Publishers, 1995). Cf. *Lawrence v. Texas*, 539 U.S. 558 (2003).

42 See Dennis J. Baker, 'Constitutionalizing the Harm Principle,' 27(2) *Criminal Justice Ethics* 3 (2008).

as the right to free speech. Specific rights do not provide a person with a general right to do whatever she likes so long as it does not *wrong* others. When specific rights are involved the criminal law must violate an exercise of that specific right. For example, the decriminalization of passive begging in open places in some states in the United States[43] and Canada[44] was possible only because it was held to involve an exercise of the *specific* right that protects *freedom of speech*. The courts in the U.S. and Europe have not made a concerted effort to identify a more general liberty protection nor have they taken the proportionate punishment-type provisions seriously.

An important issue that needs to be resolved concerns the criterion of harm: what makes it so special? Is harm merely a label that is applied inter-subjectively to conduct that is viewed as harmful in a given state at a given time? If harm-doing is the justification for overriding D's right not to be criminalized, then do we need a trans-cultural account of harm? When might Australia, Britain, Botswana, China, Japan, the Republic of Guinea, the United States and so on legitimately override a given citizen's right not to be criminalized? Is it possible to identify objective criteria for constraining similar criminalization decisions in different states? Determining when an individual has wronged others is not a simple matter in international contexts. The common approach for determining whether a person has wronged others is to examine the *harmfulness* of his or her acting, and his or her level of *culpability*. But what is harm? Can harm and culpability work as criteria for determining the proportionality and fairness of criminalization decisions in all nations and in all contexts? This is an important question, because of the level of plurality in modern societies. This issue can only be resolved if we can produce a reasonably objective account of harm. Criminally wrongdoing involves more than culpable harm-doing, since harm is not the only bad consequence that can be culpably brought about for others. In Chapter 6, I examine the objectivity of badness claims concerning harmless acts/consequences.

I examine the objectivity of harm claims, because it can only be used by courts to constrain unjust criminalization if a reasonably robust account of the criminalized conduct's harmfulness is provided. It is not enough to claim something is harmful if it is not in fact harmful. To do so would make the harm criterion effectively useless as a constitutional guide for gauging the justice of criminalization decisions. I argue that reasonably objective accounts of harm and culpability can be identified; and can be used to limit disproportionate criminalization decisions. The formula for determining the justice of a particular punitive response might go as follows: bad act (BA) plus culpability (C) = wrong (W). The gravity of a given wrong would be determined by the formula: $BA \times C$. Conduct should be labeled as criminal and punished in accordance with this formula. Criminality should be labeled according

---

43   *Loper v. New York City Police Dept.*, 802 F. Supp. 1029, 1042 (S.D.N.Y. 1992); *Benefit v. Cambridge*, 424 Mass. 918 (1997).

44   *Federated Anti-Poverty Groups of British Columbia v. Vancouver (City)* [2002] B.C.S.C. 105.

to the gravity of the culpability involved (intention, recklessness, *etc.*) and the gravity of the bad act/consequence involved. The act/consequence involved in causing mere umbrage would not be as serious as those which result in physical or economic harm. In most cases the bad acts/consequences involved will involve harm or a threat of harm. But as we will see, even factual harm is *culturally and conventionally contingent*. Why is it a crime to feed homeless people in some conventional contexts; and reasonable to jail a person for life without the option of parole for uttering a no account check for $100 in other conventional contexts?[45] It is reasonable to suggest that most people in Western society would object to the criminal law being invoked in either case.

In the next few paragraphs, I outline the legal basis of the general right not be criminalized as it currently exists and the way in which harm and other bad acts/consequences work as criteria for determining the proportionality and justice of decisions that override an exercise of that right. Objectifying bad consequences such as harm only provides a part of the solution, because there is still a further legal barrier that prevents culpability, harm and other bad consequences from being taken seriously as yardsticks for measuring the fairness of criminalization decisions. How might the objective criteria provided by bad consequences such as harm and culpability be transplanted into legal systems? The objective criteria are important if constitutionalized rights are going to work as justice constraints against unwarranted criminalization. The right not to be unfairly criminalized already exists and is a fundamental legal right in both international law and in a number of domestic constitutions. It is the interpretations that have evolved in the domestic courts that have the most promise for developing this right.

It is not a crime to feed homeless people in China or Britain, but it is in some parts of the U.S. Europe and the U.S. commit human rights abuses as measured by their own standards, but continue to label non-Western states as human rights abusers. Objective criteria such as culpability and bad consequences can only be taken seriously as a check on unfair criminalization if lawmakers are forced to consider them. There are two core ways in which the concepts of harm (and harmless bad acts/consequences) and culpability could be made legally binding as justice constraints in most jurisdictions. Firstly, they could be used as objective criteria for measuring the proportionality of punishment pursuant to the Eighth Amendment of the U.S. Constitution and Article 3 of the *European Convention for the Protection of Human Rights and Fundamental Freedoms*. The jail sentence should be proportionate with the harmfulness of the conduct being punished. Objective harm is an appropriate measuring stick for determining the proportionality of jail sentences, because jail *harms* the prisoner. Proportionality requires any jail term to be proportionate with the offender's culpability and the harmfulness of her wrongdoing.

The second way in which the right not to be criminalized could be posited or constitutionalized is through the general *personal autonomy* (Due Process)

---

45 *Solem v. Helm*, 463 U.S. 277 (1983).

right, which derives either from deprivation of liberty right or privacy right; and sometimes from a reading of both depending on the jurisdiction.[46] In this sense proportionality is about considering the seriousness, badness and intolerableness of the unwanted acts/consequences and their implications for society and its individual members. According to this standard it would be unfair to impede a person's freedom to do act *x*, unless act *x* results in (or risks) bad consequences of a kind that make it appropriate to criminalize it. In *R. v. Malmo-Levine*,[47] Justices LeBel and Deschamps considered the *general* proportionality of criminalizing a person for possessing marijuana for private use under section 7 of the *Canada Charter* (which protects life, liberty and security of the person).[48] The learned judges expounded:

> [T]he harm that marihuana consumption for personal use may cause seems rather mild on the evidence we have. In contrast, the harm and the problems connected with the form of criminalization chosen by Parliament seem plain and important ... Jailing people for the offense of simple possession seems consistent with the perception that the law, as it stands, amounts to some sort of legislative overreach to the *apprehended problems* associated with marihuana consumption ... Moreover, besides the availability of jail as a punishment, the enforcement of the law has tarred hundreds of thousands of Canadians with the stigma of a criminal record. The fundamental liberty interest has thus been infringed by the

---

46   In Canada these rights can also be read in conjunction with the disproportionate punishment provision to produce a rather wide personal autonomy protection. For instance in *R. v. Malmo-Levine* [2003] S.C.C. 74, at para. 169 the court held that the proportionality at issue was wider than mere disproportionality of penalty. It held that: 'interaction by an accused with the criminal justice system brings with it a number of consequences, not least among them the possibility of a criminal record. We agree that the proportionality principle of fundamental justice ... is not exhausted by its manifestation in s. 12.'

47   [2003] S.C.C. 74, at para. 280. Their honors went on to note: 'For the state to be able to justify limiting an individual's liberty, the legislation upon which it bases its actions must not be arbitrary. In this case, the legislation is arbitrary. First, it seems doubtful that it is appropriate to classify marihuana consumption as conduct giving rise to a legitimate use of the criminal law in light of the Charter, since, apart from the risks related to the operation of vehicles and the impact on public health care and social assistance systems, the moderate use of marihuana is on the whole harmless. Second, in view of the availability of more tailored methods, the choice of the criminal law for controlling conduct that causes little harm to moderate users or to control high risk groups for whom the effectiveness of deterrence or correction is highly dubious, is out of keeping with Canadian society's standards of justice. Third, the harm caused by prohibiting marihuana is fundamentally disproportionate to the problems that the state seeks to suppress. This harm far outweighs the benefits that the prohibition can bring.'

48   Notably the European Human Rights Convention deals with this type of activity under Article 8 which deals with privacy, but also protects personal autonomy more generally. *Dudgeon v. United Kingdom* (1981) 4 E.H.R.P. 149.

adoption and implementation of a *legislative response* which is disproportionate to the *societal problems at issue* and therefore arbitrary, and in breach of s. 7 of the *Charter*.

In Canada and Europe[49] the privacy right, the right not to be arbitrarily detained, and the right not to be disproportionately punished could be read in conjunction as a general personal autonomy right—*i.e.*, as a right to do whatever one likes so long as it does not wrong others. Coupled with this, the other the specific rights such as the right to freedom of speech and freedom of conscience could be read in sum where necessary to constrain unjust criminalization. If lawmakers want to criminalize conduct then they have to produce empirical evidence to explain not only how it wrongs others, but also to explain why criminalization is a *proportionate state response*. To satisfy the proportionality constraint when criminalizing *harmless* conduct such as exhibitionism, the courts might point to the general societal problems that would be caused, such as cooperation issues concerning the ethical use of public spaces to justify using penal fines to deter it. The general standard of proportionality means that legislative responses must be proportionate for dealing with the social problem in question (in the U.S. the general proportionality of the criminal law would be considered by considering whether the state has a compelling interest in criminalizing the conduct—this standard, despite the difference of wording, could only be satisfied by showing that the criminal law is a proportionate and necessary state response given the interest at stake). If the consequences are not *prima facie* bad, then there will be no case for criminalization. If they are *prima facie* bad, then the criminal law response would have to be a proportionate response.

In the United States the personal autonomy right has been interpreted as existing in the Due Process clause. The right of personal autonomy delineated in *Griswold v. Connecticut*[50] was not an enumerated right; rather, it was constructed from the privacy interests that are implicit in the First, Third, Fourth, Fifth and Ninth Amendments. In *Roe v. Wade*[51] the court said that the 'right of privacy, whether it be founded in the Fourteenth Amendment's concept of personal liberty and restrictions upon state action, as we feel it is, or, as the District Court determined, in the Ninth Amendment's reservation of rights to the people, is broad enough to encompass a woman's decision whether or not to terminate her pregnancy.' The

---

49 The Canadian courts have tended to read section 7 of the Charter as containing a personal autonomy right. In Europe Articles 5 and 8 of the European Convention could be read together as providing a broad autonomy right.
50 381 U.S. 479, 484 (1965).
51 410 U.S. 113, 153 (1973).

personal autonomy constraint has been used to protect *personal* decisions relating to marriage,[52] child rearing and education,[53] contraception,[54] and so forth.

The U.S. courts have often referred to criteria such as harm when interpreting the fairness of decisions that have overridden the right not to be criminalized in the privacy context.[55] The privacy right in the U.S. has been given a fairly broad interpretation to allow a person the freedom to make personal choices in many areas. It has been used to decriminalize a range of conduct including homosexuality,[56] private marijuana use,[57] abortions, and so forth. For instance, in *Ravin v. State*[58] a law against private marijuana use was struck down for breaching the petitioner's privacy rights (*i.e.*, privacy in this sense refers to personal autonomy more generally, as the only thing that is private about the personal choice to use marijuana is that it does not produce bad consequences for *others*—it merely involves a personal lifestyle choice—a choice that does not impact the lifestyles of others). The court held that the privacy protection is absolute only 'when private activity will not endanger or harm the general public.'[59] Other courts have noted that the right to privacy derives primarily from 'the long-standing importance in our Anglo-American legal tradition of personal autonomy and the right of self-determination.'[60] The majority in *Wisconsin v. Yoder* held that there is no longer an assumption 'that today's majority is "right" and the Amish and others like them are "wrong." A way of life that is odd or even erratic but interferes with no rights or interests of others is not to be condemned because it is different.'[61]

---

52 *Loving v. Virginia*, 388 U.S. 1 (1967).
53 *Prince v. Massachusetts*, 321 U.S. 158 (1944); *Pierce v. Society of Sisters* 268 U.S. 510 (1925).
54 *Griswold v. Connecticut*, 381 U.S. 479 (1965); *Eisenstadt v. Baird*, 405 U.S. 438 (1972).
55 See *Armstrong v. State*, 989 P. 2d 364, 372–374 (1999) (in which it was noted that: 'John Stuart Mill recognized this fundamental right of self-determination and personal autonomy as both a limitation on the power of the government and as principle of preeminent deference to the individual. He stated: "[T]he only purpose for which power can be rightfully exercised over any member of a civilized community, against his will, is to prevent harm to others."' See also *Moran v. MGH Institute of Health Professionals*, 15 Mass. L. Rptr. 417; *The Matter of Conservatorship of Groves*, 109 S.W. 3d 317, 328 (2003); and *Richards v. State*, 743 S.W. 2d 747, 751 (1987) (in which Levy, J. dissenting, quoted Mill before concluding that: 'if we uphold the authority of the State to punish one's failure to use a seatbelt, we are one more step on our way to an Orwellian society in which the State can punish merely for smoking cigarettes, for not brushing one's teeth, or for being foolish.'
56 *Lawrence v. Texas*, 539 U.S. 558 (2003).
57 *Ravin v. State*, 537 2d 494 (Alaska 1975).
58 537 P. 2d 494 (Alaska 1975).
59 *Ravin v. State*, 537 2d 494 (Alaska 1975). See also *Cruzan v. Harmon*, 760 S.W. 2d 408, 417 (1988).
60 *Thor v. Superior Court*, 855 P. 2d 375, 380 (1993); *Commonwealth v. Bonadio*, 415 A. 2d 47, 96–98 (1980).
61 406 U. S. 205, 224 (1972).

In *Commonwealth v. Bonadio*[62] a state court invoked the personal autonomy and absence of harm to others justification to strike down a law criminalizing homosexuals. The court, quoting J.S. Mill, said:

> [T]he harm principle requires liberty of tastes and pursuits; of framing the plan of our life to suit our own character; of doing as we like, subject to such consequences as may follow: without impediment from our fellow creatures, so long as what we do does not *harm* them, even though they should think our conduct foolish, perverse, or wrong. [F]rom this liberty of each individual, follows the liberty, within the same limits of combination among individuals; freedom to unite, for any purpose not involving *harm to others*.[63]

> With respect to regulation of morals, the police power should properly be exercised to protect each individual's right to be free from interference in defining and pursuing his own morality but not to enforce a majority morality on persons whose conduct does not *harm others*. 'No harm to the secular interests of the community is involved in atypical sex practice in private between consenting adult partners. This philosophy, as applied to the issue of regulation of sexual morality presently before the court, or employed to delimit the police power generally, properly circumscribes state power over the individual.'[64]

In *Lawrence v. Texas*[65] the United States Supreme Court interpreted the privacy right as protecting atypical sex practices in private between consenting adult partners. In that case, the majority overruled *Bowers v. Hardwick*[66] and held that: 'It is a promise of the Constitution that there is a realm *of personal liberty*, which the government may not enter.'[67] The majority held that the consensual conduct at issue (homosexual relations) was covered by that liberty. The majority did not use the typical strict scrutiny standard to interpret the liberty interest involved as a fundamental liberty. Instead, it applied a standard that falls somewhere between the *strict scrutiny* and the *rational basis review* standards. In the U.S. a law that punishes a person for exercising a fundamental liberty is upheld only where it can be shown that it is narrowly tailored (necessary) to achieve its policy goal (that is, narrowly tailored to achieve a *compelling* government purpose). Under the rationally related test, a challenged law will be upheld if it is substantially related

---

62 415 A. 2d 47, 96–98 (1980).
63 415 A. 2d 47, 50–51(1980).
64 415 A. 2d 47, 49–50 (1980).
65 539 U.S. 558 (2003). While the judges in these cases do not always turn their minds to the distinction between objective and positive morality, they do seem to be engaging in a deliberative process that in many cases has allowed them to reach a conclusion that is reconcilable with fairness and justice.
66 478 U.S. 186 (1986).
67 *Lawrence v. Texas*, 539 U.S. 558, 578 (2003).

to a legitimate government purpose. 'The legitimate government purpose need not be the actual objective of the legislation—only its conceivable objective. Since only those laws that lack a conceivable legitimate purpose will fail this test, courts almost never find a law to be unconstitutional when non-fundamental liberties are burdened.'[68]

In *Lawrence v. Texas* the majority stated that: '[t]he Texas statute furthers no legitimate state interest which can justify its intrusion into the personal and private life of the individual.'[69] It also applied a rational basis test (legitimate governmental interest test) with the traditional fundamental privacy right in mind, but it did not apply a strict scrutiny test (compelling state interest test).[70] It held that the petitioner's threshold liberty interest could be overridden only if the legislature could show that it would further a legitimate state interest. *Lawrence* was a case where the court rightly interpreted (by drawing on evolving standards of justice) that the activities involved fell within the purview of the privacy right, and where the court also found that the state could not demonstrate that it had a substantial interest in having the exercise of that right overridden. The critical approach taken by the courts in some cases[71] cannot be overstated, because the current bench of the U.S. Supreme Court is dominated by judges who tend to read down rights in a way that is often contrary to the requirements of constitutional justice.[72]

In this country, many courts have held that a governing majority's belief that sexual immorality is unacceptable is sufficient to override liberty interests.[73] In many cases in the U.S. the right to privacy has proved to be rather hollow, because unprincipled political considerations have been used to satisfy the lower standard that is invoked where the courts have held that the right only involved a mere liberty as opposed to a fundamental liberty. If the exercise of a given right is construed as merely involving a mere liberty interest, then the protection offered is practically nothing. The exercise of a fundamental liberty is sufficient, however, to make some kind of proportionality analysis mandatory. In such cases, the courts should consider whether the relevant law is narrowly tailored to protect a *compelling state interest* (this surely means the state would have to show that the criminalization will in fact prevent real harm from transpiring)—which in effect asks whether

---

68 Douglas Husak, 'Limitations on Criminalization,' in *Criminal Law Theory: Doctrines of the General Part*, ed. Stephen Shute and Andrew P. Simester (Oxford: Oxford University Press, 2002) at pp. 17–25.
69 *Lawrence v. Texas*, 539 U.S. 558, 578 (2003).
70 *Lawrence v. Texas*, 539 U.S. 558 (2003).
71 In the Eighth Amendment context, the courts have tried to achieve objectivity and justice by applying an 'evolving standards of decency that mark the progress of a maturing society' standard. See *Trop v. Dulles*, 356 U.S. 86 (1958) and *Solem v. Helm*, 463 U.S. 277 (1983). Even though the Supreme Court is currently dominated by originalists, this approach was approved by the majority in *Kennedy v. Louisiana*, 554 U.S. 407 (2008).
72 See for example, *Harmelin v. Michigan*, 501 U.S. 957 (1991); *Locker v. Andrade*, 538 U.S. 63 (2003).
73 *Lawrence v. Texas*, 539 U.S. 558, 589 (2003) per Scalia J.

the state's response is necessary for dealing with the problem at hand. The harm criterion is important, as it prevents governments from effectively arguing that the criminalized conduct merely involves a mere liberty, because the criminalized party is able to point to the criminalization itself as a violation of the fundamental right not to be criminalized. It means the government has to demonstrate the criminalizability (its harmfulness) of the conduct that has been outlawed.[74] It is not good enough merely to claim something is harmful, it must be demonstrated that it is in fact harmful. One court held that criminalizing those who attend strip clubs furthered 'a substantial government interest in protecting order and morality.'[75] In *Williams v. Pryor*[76] the law banning the sale of sex toys was upheld because the court held that it was substantially related to the legitimate government purpose of protecting public morality. These erroneous decisions were only possible because the courts did not conduct a harm or proportionality analysis. It is submitted that the Canadian approach, of looking at the overall proportionality of using criminalization as a response for dealing with the particular social problem, is instructive as a mechanism for determining whether the right not to be criminalized should be overridden. The strict scrutiny standard works in a similar fashion since it requires the state to demonstrate that it has a compelling interest in retorting to criminalization to deal with the particular social problem.

The core of the general right not to be criminalized is the proportionate punishment provision found in the Eighth Amendment. In Chapter 2, I provide a deep analysis of this right and argue that it covers not only capital punishment and fines, but also jail terms and thus offers a powerful check for constraining unjust criminalization. The harm and culpability criteria are the most appropriate criteria for determining the proportionality of criminalization, because criminalization harms the offender. 'Even one day in prison would be a cruel and unusual punishment for the "crime" of having a common cold.'[77] Although the approach taken in the privacy/personal autonomy cases is welcome, it should be supplemented with the core right not to be unfairly punished. As we will see in Chapter 2, in the United States, unlike the personal autonomy provision, the proportionate punishment constraint has been interpreted almost out of existence. This was not always the case, however. For instance, in *Solem v. Helm*,[78] the respondent was convicted for uttering a dud check for $100. The usual maximum punishment for that crime would have been five years' imprisonment and a $5,000 fine. But the respondent was sentenced to life imprisonment without the option of parole under South Dakota's recidivist statute, because he had a number of prior

---

74 Cf. *Sherman v. Henry*, 928 S.W. 2d 464 (Tex. 1996).
75 *Barnes v. Glen Theatre Inc.*, 501 U. S. 560, 569 (1991).
76 240 F. 3d 944 (2001), 949. Notably, similar rights have been overridden in Canada and Europe to uphold positive morality. See, for example, *De Wilde, Ooms Versyp v. Belgium* (1971) 1 E.H.R.R. 373 at para. 68.
77 *Robinson v. California*, 360 U.S. 660, 667 (1962).
78 463 U.S. 277 (1983).

convictions. The Supreme Court held that the 'Eighth Amendment's proscription of cruel and unusual punishments prohibits not only barbaric punishments, but also sentences that are disproportionate to the crime committed.'[79] However, in *Harmelin v. Michigan*,[80] the court held that the Eighth Amendment allowed a state to impose a life sentence without the possibility of parole for the possession of 672 grams of cocaine. In Chapter 2, I argue that a careful reading of the Constitution demonstrates that this is a cardinal right that exists in law, not only in the U.S., but also in Europe. I aim to demonstrate that it forms a large part of the legal right not to be criminalized.

The Eighth Amendment cases demonstrate that Western courts are willing to allow gross human rights abuses to go unchecked. What is clear is that modern America often pays no attention to fair labeling and proportionate punishment. Britain too,[81] only pays lip service to the idea of proportionate punishment. In *Weeks v. United Kingdom*,[82] a 17-year old man was given a life sentence for robbing a store with a starter pistol. The robbery merely involved a sum of 35 pence, which was eventually found on the shop floor. The defendant went to a pet shop with a starting pistol loaded with blank cartridges, pointed it at the owner and demanded the contents of the till. After committing the robbery he telephoned the police station and confessed and gave himself up. It emerged that he carried out the robbery because he wanted to pay back £3, which he owed his mother. Earlier that day his mother had threatened to evict him. Nevertheless, the European Court held that the life sentence was not contrary to Article 3 of the *European Convention for the Protection of Human Rights and Fundamental Freedoms*. In a line of other cases, the European Commission of Human Rights has erroneously held that the convention does not contain a 'general right to call into question the length of a sentence imposed by a competent court.'[83]

The right not to be criminalized cannot be *enforced* until the courts recognize that there is such a right. This right is found in the personal autonomy and proportionate punishment provisions in a number of international human rights documents. It also permeates nearly every other constitutionalized human right. It is a fundamental right and it is time that courts started to take it seriously. Once the courts recognize the right, it will then be necessary to undertake the task of determining when that right should be overridden. At the international level this will be no easy task, as many bad consequences are conventionally and culturally

---

79   *Solem v. Helm*, 463 U.S. 277, 284–290 (1983).

80   501 U.S. 957 (1991).

81   Article 3 of the *European Convention for the Protection of Human Rights and Fundamental Freedoms*, 4 November 1950, 213 U.N.T.S. 222 (entered into force generally on 3 September 1953) is analogous to the Eight Amendment of the *U.S. Constitution* and is binding in Britain.

82   (1988) 10 E.H.R.R. 293.

83   See Michael Tonry and Richard S. Frase, *Sentencing and Sanctions in Western Countries* (Oxford: Oxford University Press, 2001) at p. 363.

contingent, as is the case with Western notions of the wrongness and badness of exhibitionism. In Chapter 6, I argue that at the center of the harm dartboard there is greater agreement about what is objectively harmful, because of the primitive nature of core harms such as those involving physiological pain and physical damage as is the case with murder, rape, starvation, amputation, torture and so on. These harms impact humans more or less in the same way regardless of the culture or context. But once we move away from the primitive-type harms to more conventionally contingent harms, the case for punishment and criminalization is more difficult to identify.

The harmfulness of many acts is dependent on convention and socialization. If x were to paint a bright yellow stripe across the Mona Lisa her conduct would be classified as gross criminal vandalism,[84] but unless we consider the underlying social norms it is not possible to comprehend the wrongness, badness or harmfulness[85] of intentionally painting a bright yellow stripe on an old painting. Some might argue that the additional stripe is art in itself and thus adds to the aesthetics of the original painting, if they have not been socialised into perceiving it as a cultural artefact. Painting a stripe on it would not diminish anyone's essential or primitive-type survival resources in the way that destroying a remote tribe's only source of water and food would. There is something much more universal about the latter harm, because suffering severe dehydration and starvation would impact all humans in the same way. The objective wrongness of conventional harms and umbrages can only be ascertained by considering contextual, circumstantial, social and empirical factors.

The conventional contingency of many bad consequences means that achieving proportionality is a complex matter indeed. The great challenge for lawmakers will be in identifying the objectivity of the *bad consequences* given that many of them are culturally contingent. In Chapter 6, I outline how a reasonably common ground might be found. A fairly robust analysis will be required to determine whether a particular criminal law or penal sentence is a disproportionate response. Not only will it be rather difficult to determine when a penal punishment is disproportionate, but it will also be difficult to determine when a criminal law is generally a disproportionate response for dealing with a particular social problem. But the case for decriminalization will be obvious in some cases. For instance, the innocuous nature of feeding homeless people, attending strip shows, begging, ingesting trans fats, and so on is obvious. As for the harm involved in ingesting trans fats, it is self-harm, and paternalism does not provide a sound basis for criminalization let alone a justification for sending people to prison. Jail is a form of *serious harm* so it makes sense no to inflict

---

84 This would be an offense under the *Criminal Damage Act 1971* (U.K.).

85 Husak argues that the Harm Principle even belongs to the General Part of the Criminal Law. Douglas N. Husak, 'Limitations on Criminalization,' in Stephen Shute and Andrew P. Simester, *Criminal Law Theory: Doctrines of the General Part* (Oxford: Oxford University Press, 2002) at pp. 13–46.

further harm on self-harmers. The type of disproportionate criminalization and punishment mentioned above clearly involves human rights abuses and should be given much more attention than it has received in recent decades. Human rights abuses involving non-Western countries and those involving terrorism suspects in Western states receive enormous scholarly and media attention, but everyday abuses in Western states seem to go unnoticed.

The Retributive Foundations of Individualized Criminalization

The moral justification for individualized criminalization rests on retributive norms. The general aim of the criminal law is to deter wrongdoing to others, but mere deterrence does not provide a moral justification for overriding the individual right not to be criminalized. The fairness of overriding a person's right not to be criminalized is satisfied by demonstrating that the offender's past wrongdoing warrants punishment. The general aim of the institution of criminalization is utilitarian: harm prevention for the benefit of the greater good.[86] The moral justification for individualized criminalization cannot be justified by pointing to the independent consequential aims of criminalization. These *aims* are instrumental and incidental to the *moral* justification for overriding the right not to be criminalized. The justification for individualized criminalization is that the agent wrongs others when she intentionally aims to bring about bad consequences for them.[87] Using the punitive institution of criminalization to deter unwanted conduct is only justified when there are objective reasons to support the claim that it is necessary to override the wrongdoer's right not to be criminalized.

Hart[88] argued that it would be unfair to criminalize a wrongdoer merely because the majority of the community claims that her actions are harmful (injurious, wrongful) without a reasoned justification to substantiate their harm claims. Fairness in the criminalization domain is about producing reasoned justifications to demonstrate certain *bad acts/consequences* are worthy of criminal condemnation. If a person culpably commits a bad act that has been labeled as a crime she is

---

86   H.L.A. Hart, *Punishment and Responsibility: Essays in the Philosophy of Law* (Oxford: Clarendon Press, 1968) at pp. 8–9.

87   See Andrew von Hirsch, *Censure and Sanctions* (Oxford: Oxford University Press, 1993) at p. 6. See also J.R. Lucas, *On Justice* (Oxford: Clarendon Press, 1980). I draw on desert theory to demarcate the boundaries of fair criminalization. Honoré notes: 'By a corollary it may be said that desert can equally depend on demerit, on bad conduct, in that the principle of justice according to desert includes also the principle that those who have behaved badly or harmfully should be punished according to the extent and character of their wrongdoing.' Tony M. Honoré, 'Social Justice,' in Robert S. Summers, *Essays in Legal Philosophy* (Oxford: Basil Blackwell, 1968) at p. 72. See also Joel Feinberg, *Doing and Deserving* (Princeton, NJ: Princeton University Press, 1970).

88   H.L.A. Hart, *Law, Liberty and Morality* (London: Oxford University Press, 1963) at p. 17.

ultimately labeled as a criminal—is censured and punished. It is not the crime label *per se* that causes an offender to suffer, but rather it is the penal consequences flowing from being labeled as a criminal wrongdoer.[89] The structure of the justification for criminalization (or for overriding the right not to be criminalized) is one where crime prevention is checked by the requirement that only those whose activities are deserving of criminalization are criminalized. Coupled with this, the degree of criminalization should be determined according to desert. The moral basis of a retributive-type justification for overriding a wrongdoer's right not to be criminalized can be explained in the following terms:[90]

> Because the wrongdoer is rebelling against the authority of morality, she knows that *prima facie* she is subject to it. Insofar as we repudiate her rebellion, we say that she should have acted otherwise not only from our standpoint but also from her standpoint, because we think that she, like us, has reason to be moral. Her action does not show her to be making any simple-minded mistake about what she ought to do; on the contrary, she knows exactly what she ought to do. Instead, we criticize her because we see her as mistaken in thinking she can successfully overthrow moral injunctions and live solely as she chooses.

Criminalization is about holding an actor accountable for his or her wrongful choices. We do not criminalize robots that might be used to harm others or dogs that have savaged humans, because robots and dogs are not responsible agents. Criminal condemnation is about censuring and punishing a person's culpable acting when it has brought about (or unreasonably risked) bad consequences for others. The wrongdoer is not punished for mere accidents but for her culpable and responsible choice to bring about bad consequences for others. By wronging others the wrongdoer chooses to have her right not to be criminalized overridden. A desert theory of criminalization not only requires that the conduct be *prima facie* deserving of criminalization, but also ensures that crimes are labeled in proportion with the wrongdoer's culpability and the badness or harmfulness of the consequences involved. Grading offenses is clearly an important *ex ante* matter

---

89 As Husak rightly notes: '[T]he notorious difficulty of justifying punishment is closely connected to the problem of defending a theory of criminalization. We cannot hope to justify punishment without attending to what individuals are punished *for*. Since persons who commit crimes become subject to punishment, and punishment must satisfy a stringent standard of justification, the State must be cautious before enacting a criminal offense.' Douglas Husak, 'Malum Prohibitum and Retribution,' in R.A. Duff and Stuart P. Green, *Defining Crimes: Essays on the Special Part of the Criminal Law* (Oxford: Oxford University Press, 2005) at p. 68. Or as Odujirin puts it: 'The scope of penal law is regarded as coterminous with criminal law. Hence, criminal liability is defined as liability to penal or punitive sanction.' Adekemi Odujirin, *The Normative Basis of Fault in Criminal Law: History and Theory* (Toronto: University of Toronto Press, 1998) at p. 140.

90 Jean E. Hampton 'The Nature of Morality,' (1989) 7(1) *Social Philosophy and Policy* 22 at pp. 41–42.

that has to be considered as a part of the criminalization process, because fair criminalization requires the conduct to be labeled according to its seriousness. It also means that appropriate sentence tariffs have to be put in place at the *ex ante* criminalization stage to give judges guidance at the *ex post* sentencing stage. It is about appropriately distributing the burden of having a harm prevention system in place.

What are the main types of criminalization? The lawmaker has to also consider, among other things,[91] the nature of the wrongdoing to determine whether it is worthy of individual criminal condemnation, *regulatory* criminal condemnation, or a private law response. Personal criminalization is based on an agent's culpable *choice* to bring about bad consequences for others. In the case of corporate wrongdoing penal censure for *culpable* wrongdoing is not possible, since a corporation cannot deliberate. Therefore, corporations are penalized in a regulatory sense. Regulatory criminalization is criminalization that involves criminal punishment other than imprisonment and it does not censure an individual. It censures a collective of individuals *indirectly* for their collective wrongdoing. The fictitious entity is labeled a criminal thereby allowing its executives, personnel, and shareholders to avoid direct stigmatization and punishment. It is a form of criminalization that does not censure or blame an individual as opposed to a collective of individuals in a very indirect way, since it is the fictitious entity (the company) that bears the direct stigma, censure and punishment.

In practice, the term *regulatory* in the criminalization domain is often used to describe offenses that do involve individualized conviction and jail time. But in this book the term is used as a convenient label for distinguishing criminalization that results in a personal conviction, personal stigma and personal punishment for individual wrongdoing from that which merely labels a *thing* (a company is an intangible thing) as a criminal. Corporate liability shelters the governing minds of a corporation from direct censure, stigmatization and imprisonment.

The term regulatory is used in this book to refer to censuring responses to unwanted behavior that do not (and cannot) result in a personal conviction or in an individual being jailed (*i.e.*, it is not possible to jail a company/government). Regulatory criminalization also catches those petty offenses where an individual is blamed, but does not receive a conviction or risk jail time for her wrongdoing as is the case with littering offenses, parking fines, *etc*. Regulatory criminalization is best explained as involving a lower level of censure,[92] where it is not possible to fairly impute the harmful wrongdoing to a particular moral agent such as a company director as opposed to her company or where the wrongdoing is too

---

91 See the discussion in the next chapter.
92 Littering offenses are regulatory even though they involve individualized blame for personal wrongdoing, because in most jurisdictions such offenses would not result in a criminal *conviction* or a *jail* term. In this context, the offenses are more a form of quasi-criminalization because the harm-doing involved is not sufficient to warrant the full censuring force of the criminal law.

trivial to warrant a criminal conviction. In many cases, corporate criminalization is used as a backup penalty, but in reality it works as little more than a cost of doing business. It is often a toothless tiger. This is especially so when the directors are too far removed from the actual harm to be blamed for it in an individualized sense. While reforms in Britain have made it easier to get a corporate manslaughter conviction,[93] such a conviction is no substitute for labeling the human agents responsible as criminals.

The criminalization of a fictitious legal entity does not have the same censuring and retributive impact as criminalizing a human agent for her wrongful choices. It might have an *indirect* impact (*i.e.*, a penal fine and corporate conviction might affect the directors and shareholders indirectly as the company would bear the costs of the fine and the cost of its stock being devalued by any bad publicity following a corporate conviction, but these losses are borne collectively and indirectly—not directly). Furthermore, the penal fine is not borne collectively when a government department is involved, because the taxpayers would bear the burden of any fine. Convicting a company is somewhat different from convicting an individual. An individual can feel shame, the effects of prison, and so forth. A company may suffer bad publicity when it is convicted, but the penalties are usually limited to fines and a revocation of license, *etc*.

It is important not to confuse collective corporate criminalization with white-collar wrongdoing—that is, offending that involves an agent acting outside the scope of his or her employment such as public officials who take bribes. In the case of bribe-taking, the individual gets her just deserts for her criminal choice. Likewise, in some cases company directors will be sufficiently connected to a remote harm to be held personally accountable. The only common element in *full* criminalization and *regulatory* criminalization is that in both cases the lawmaker is aiming to prevent certain unwanted (usually harmful) consequences from transpiring, but regulatory censure does not result in individualized criminal condemnation.

If we focus on culpability and the imputability of harm to a moral agent, we are able draw a crude line between full criminalization, regulatory criminalization and, to a lesser extent, private law regulation. There is no clear line, but it might be said that the high ground is the typical *malum in se* forms of criminality. The middle ground involves those cases where a criminal law response is appropriate, but where it is not possible to impute the harmful consequence to a human agent, even though the overall behavior of a collective of agents (a company or other entity) is sufficiently reprehensible to warrant a penal response.[94] The middle

---

93　The *Corporate Manslaughter and Corporate Homicide Act 2007* (U.K.) created a new offense that allows for the prosecution of companies and other organizations where a gross failing throughout the organization, regarding the management of health and safety, results in fatalities.

94　See for example, Celia Wells, *Corporations and Criminal Responsibility* (Oxford: Oxford University Press, 2nd ed., 2001) at pp. 107–126.

ground also includes those petty offenses that are proscribed to protect our collective interests such as littering offenses. At the lower end of the scale we have private law responses where the state is not compelled to use the criminal law as opposed to private law regulation. The private law is used to regulate many harmful wrongs, but harm is only a sufficient condition for criminalization. The state is not compelled to criminalize every harmful wrong, because in many cases the private law will provide adequate protection.[95]

In this book it is acknowledged that many forms of non-criminal regulation are coercive and often unjustly impinge the freedom of those affected. J.S. Mill was concerned with the legitimacy of all state coercion, but I limit my discussion to an examination of state coercion of a criminal kind. Civil laws and administrative regulations can restrict a person's freedom, but do not result in penal censure and thus are not my concern in this book. My focus simply concerns the proper scope of the criminal law. I am not concerned with unjust coercion of a civil/administrative or non-criminal regulatory nature such as rules that prohibit children from wearing jewelry in government funded schools. These forms of state coercion might affect the freedom of those regulated, but do not result in serious penal consequences. However, this does not mean a more general right not to be subject to coercive state power does not exist. Such a right does exist and it may be enforced by appealing to the general proportionality standard outlined above or by invoking specific rights. For instance, in Britain the administrative courts[96] have ruled that a school could not suspend a Sikh girl for wearing a bracelet which she wanted to wear for cultural reasons. Arguably, the atheists in the school would also have a right to wear bracelets, so long as it could be shown that regulating such conduct is a disproportionate response for dealing with a genuine social problem, and thus an arbitrary violation of their *freedom of conscience*. The disproportionality of the coercive state response might be demonstrated by arguing that wearing bracelets in schools does not harm or wrong others.

This type of administrative regulation is distinguishable from borderline criminal regulation as it does not result in a criminal conviction or penal consequences. I am only concerned with the limits of the criminal law. I do not also consider whether borderline activities that are not criminalizable might be fairly regulated to prevent a genuine nuisance. Nor do I consider the more general right not to be subject to coercive state power with respect to activities that can be the subject of such power even in the absence of criminalization.

---

95 I discuss this in greater detail in the next chapter.
96 *Singh v. The Governing Body of Aberdare Girls' High School and Others* [2008] EWHC 1865.

Principled Criminalization

The issue of what objective reasons there are to justify criminalization decisions is a huge philosophical question. I do not aim to outline every possible type of bad act/consequence beyond harm and privacy losses (*i.e.*, personal autonomy violations in public contexts) that might be sufficiently serious to warrant a criminal law response. I delineate the core prerequisites that must be present to justify invoking the criminal law in all cases. Those prerequisites are: (i) that the agent's actions result in or aim for objectively bad consequences of a kind that are sufficiently serious to make her deserving of criminal condemnation; and (ii) that the agent knowingly (culpably) chose to bring about (aimed or attempted) those bad consequences even though she knew her actions would adversely affect the interests of others. It is these elements that make a person deserving of criminalization. I argue that harm will be the objective bad consequence in most cases, but there will be other bad acts/consequences such as privacy losses. But the latter might be described as soft harm or conventional harm.

Justice and fairness are not established by merely referring to culpable harm, as some *harmless* consequences are objectively bad and a person who aims for such consequences would be worthy of criminal condemnation in certain circumstances. The lawmaker would need to demonstrate that the conduct is not only wrongful (this is largely satisfied by referring to moral culpability—an intention to wrong others), but has bad consequences that are deserving of criminalization. Mere wrongdoing such as false promising would not be sufficient for invoking the criminal law, because not all false promising risks consequences for others that are sufficiently serious to justify a criminal law response. This approach gives the legislature guidance about what it can criminalize and how to punish it fairly.

I have already emphasized the importance of looking for objective justifications for invoking the criminal law. I have argued that harm to others is the predominant justification available. Hart[97] took a similar view 45 years ago.[98] Arguably, culpable harm-doing provides the most far-reaching objective criterion for invoking the criminal law, because it is harm that is being criminalized in most cases. Preventing harm in both the primitive (basic survival rights) and conventionally contingent sense (for example, painting stripes on the Mona Lisa would be a conventionally contingent harm: its harmfulness is shaped by conventional and social norms about art—some people might consider the yellow stripes as enhancing the

---

97 Hart's theory is 'strongly associated with a specific conception of morality as a uniquely true or correct set of principles—not man made, but awaiting discovery by the use of reason ... [Whereas legal moralism] is associated with a relativist conception of morality, which has no rational or other specific content.' H.L.A. Hart, 'Social Solidarity and the Enforcement of Morality,' in *Essays in Jurisprudence and Philosophy* (Oxford: Clarendon Press, Oxford, 1983) at pp. 248 *et passim*.

98 H.L.A. Hart, *The Morality of the Criminal Law* (Oxford: Oxford University Press, 1965) at pp. 31 *et seq*.

painting, whereas others might view the yellow stripe as outright vandalism of a classic painting), provides an objective basis for criminalization in cooperative societies.[99]

The Harm Principle holds that 'the sole end for which mankind are warranted, individually or collectively, in interfering with the liberty of action of any of their number, is self-protection. That the only purpose for which power can be rightfully exercised over any member of a civilized community, against his will, is to prevent harm to others.'[100] J.S. Mill's Harm Principle played an influential role in criminalization debates in earlier times. It permeates section 1.02(1)(a) of the American Law Institute's Model Penal Code, which holds that one of the purposes of the criminal law is 'to forbid and prevent conduct that unjustifiably and inexcusably inflicts or threatens substantial harm to individual or public interests.' In 1957 the Wolfenden Committee,[101] referring to the Millian ideology, argued for the decriminalization of homosexuality and prostitution. The Committee's recommendations sparked the now famous debate between Patrick Devlin and Herbert Hart.

Devlin argued that positive morality was a sufficient reason for criminalizing conduct. He alleged that private vice had the potential to cause both physical and spiritual (tangible and intangible) harm to society.[102] Devlin sums up his tangible harm argument in his social disintegration thesis: 'It is obvious that an individual may by unrestricted indulgence in vice so weaken himself that he ceases to be a useful member of society. It is obvious also that if sufficient numbers of individuals so weaken themselves, society will thereby be weakened ... A nation of debauchees would not in 1940 have responded satisfactorily to Winston Churchill's call to blood and toil and sweat and tears.'[103] Devlin alleges that vice should be criminalized to protect society from disintegration. His contention is not objective and is not supported with sound moral reasoning or credible empirical data.[104] Devlin's positive morality type 'harm' argument is a variant of his extreme thesis,[105] which advocates that conduct is criminalizable so long as it breaches the majority's moral code.[106]

---

99   Rescher, *op. cit. supra*, fn. 18 at pp. 129–130.

100   J.S. Mill, *On Liberty and Other Essays* (Oxford: Oxford University Press, 1991) at p. 14.

101   *Report of the Committee on Homosexual Offenses and Prostitution* (London: Home Office, Cmd. 247, 1957) at paragraphs 13 and 61.

102   Patrick Devlin, *The Enforcement of Morals* (Oxford: Oxford University Press, 1965) at p. 111.

103   *Ibid.*

104   See Hart, *op. cit. supra*, fn. 86 at pp. 53–55.

105   *Id.* at p. 54.

106   Devlin, *op. cit. supra*, fn. 100 at p. 25.

The objectivity of justifications for criminalization cannot hinge on idiosyncratic preferences.[107] It would be inequitable to criminalize conduct just because the majority claims that it is harmful, injurious and/or offensive. Positive morality is majority sanction, with the public being the 'great sophist now as truly as in the times of Plato.'[108] The majority is usually only interested in what appears to be persuasive, not in what is rigorously rational (sound moral arguments that are susceptible to reason).[109] In the current zero tolerance of crime climate the majority are often persuaded by non-objective harm arguments. A reasoned justification for overriding a person's right not to be criminalized is found by referring to 'publicly accepted and rationally criticizable standards of argument.'[110] The state could not justify criminalizing lesbians and homosexuals merely because of their status, because this type of criminalization would not withstand the inter-subjective scrutiny of moral agents communally situated.[111]

Criminalization addresses the victim, potential wrongdoers and the individual perpetrator. The fairness constraint means that the lawmaker must be able to explain to the wrongdoer why she deserves to be criminalized.[112] Intentionally aiming to bring about harm to others is deserving of criminalization and it is possible for

---

107 Cf. Ronald Dworkin, *Taking Rights Seriously* (King's Lynn: Duckworth, 1977) at p. 22 *et seq*.

108 Harold N. Lee, 'Morals, Morality, and Ethics: Suggested Terminology,' (1928) 38(4) *International Journal of Ethics* 450 at p. 465.

109 See also Jean E. Hampton, *The Authority of Reason* (Cambridge: Cambridge University Press, 1998); and Jonathan Dancy, *Normativity* (Oxford: Blackwell Publishers, 2000).

110 David Wiggins, *Needs, Values, Truth* (Oxford University Press, Oxford 1998) at p. 101.

111 'If I can argue for my own position only by citing the beliefs of others ("everyone knows homosexuality is a sin") you will conclude that I am parroting and not relying on moral conviction of my own. With the possible (though complex) exception of deity, there is no moral authority to which I can appeal and so automatically make my position a moral one. I have reasons, though of course I may have been taught these reasons by others.' Dworkin, *op. cit. supra*, fn. 105 at p. 250.

112 Rescher, *op. cit. supra*, fn. 18 at p. 16. The Oxford moral philosopher, J.R. Lucas notes that: '[I]n order to justicize an action, we have to show not only that we had to bear hardly on someone but that it had to be the offender. Only then will he see that we were not acting with wanton disregard of his rights and interests, but, in spite of manifest reluctance to do him down, we still had no alternative but to decide as we did. For that to be the case our reasons have to be of a special kind ... They must be based on facts about him, not exclusively but enough to justify, even to him if he is reasonable, not simply our reaching an adverse decision, but its being adverse to him. We have to structure the argument so that it can be seen from his point of view, as well as that of anybody else in danger of being done down. We therefore need to operate in terms of a rationality that sees things primarily from the agent's own point of view.' Lucas, *op. cit. supra*, fn. 85 at p. 45.

communally situated agents[113] to understand the wrongness of wantonly harming others. The disagreement will be over what is in fact harmful in a given context.

The Structure of this Book

In Chapter 2, I start with an extensive examination of the Harm Principle. Hart[114] made specific mention of the Harm Principle as a fairness constraint, but he did not attempt to develop harm as a criterion for constraining unjust criminalization. Feinberg reformulated the Harm Principle to make it a more effective criterion for limiting criminalization. But Feinberg did not look at the constitutional implications of using the harm standard to measure the proportionality of punishments under the Eighth Amendment or under the personal autonomy right. Feinberg's approach was too far removed from law and thus failed to show that the harm constraint forms part of a *constitutional right* not to be unfairly criminalized/punished.

I vigorously defend the Harm Principle, but I reformulate it to make it a much more useful criterion. Feinberg's formulation of the Harm Principle differs from Mill's in that it is not an exclusive ground for criminalizing conduct. He supplements the Harm Principle with a further moral principle, which holds that it would also be fair for wrongful 'offense to others' to be criminalized in certain circumstances.[115] In his *magnum opus* on criminalization, he argues that under a liberal scheme for criminalization 'the Harm and Offense Principles, duly clarified and qualified, between them exhaust the class of good reasons for criminal prohibitions.'[116] In his two later volumes he asserts that 'legal moralism' and 'legal paternalism' are insufficient grounds for criminalizing conduct,[117] but does not embrace the conventionally contingent nature of offense doing and of soft harms. Feinberg's principles have received widespread academic approval,[118]

---

113 Cf. Gerald Postema, 'Objectivity Fit for Law,' in Brian Leiter, *Objectivity in Law and Morals* (Cambridge: Cambridge University Press, 2001) at p. 121.
114 Hart, *op. cit. supra*, fn. 86 at pp. 1–20.
115 Feinberg, Vol. II, *op. cit. supra*, fn. 5 at p. 1.
116 Feinberg was aware of the Harm Principle's limitations. Feinberg, Vol. IV, *op. cit. supra*, fn. 5 at pp. 323–324.
117 Feinberg, Vol. III, *op. cit. supra*, fn. 5.
118 Husak recently stated: 'Despite my failure to provide substantive theories of rights or of wrongdoing, I simply note that Feinberg's views have enormous potential to retard the growth of the criminal law.' Husak, *op. cit. supra*, fn. 3 at p. 72. Smith cites a list of cases and scholarly works that have cited Mill's Harm Principle with approval. See Stephen Douglas Smith, 'The Hollowness of the Harm Principle,' Paper 17, *Public Law and Legal Theory Research Paper Series*, No. 05-07 (University of San Diego School of Law, 2004) at pp. 2–4. See also Claire Finkelstein, 'Positivism and the Notion of an Offense,' (2000) 88 *California Law Review* 335 at pp. 371 *et seq*; Hamish Stewart, 'Harms, Wrongs, and Set-Backs in Feinberg's Moral Limits of the Criminal Law,' (2001–2002) 5 *Buffalo Criminal Law Review* 47; *Consent in the Criminal Law* (London: Law Commission of

but in practice they have had little to no impact on the unjust criminalization phenomena. In this book, I do not deal directly with the issue of paternalism, as I believe that Feinberg has covered that topic sufficiently.[119]

Why defend the harm criterion rather than invent some new criterion? The harm criterion is worth defending and developing because in the real world most criminal laws target genuine harm. When criminal laws aim to prevent harm, it makes sense to use culpable harm as the criteria for determining fairness. It would be nonsensical to refer to some other abstract notion of wronging such as a loss of freedom,[120] when it is in fact harm that is being targeted by the criminal law. Harm is an *actual* bad consequence that can be used to give the legislature guidance about whether it is necessary to invoke the criminal law. It is not some abstract notion, but is factual and can be identified. Harm prevention lies at the very heart of morality and the aim of protecting basic human interests and needs. 'And this issue of human needs and benefits, of people's real interests, such as their physical and psychological well-being, is not a matter of subjective reaction. What is in our interest—what is advantageous for our long-term, overall physical and psychological well-being, given the sorts of creatures we are—is a large measure of factual issue capable of empirical inquiry that lies open to general, public investigation.'[121]

Feinberg's formulation of the Harm Principle has a number of shortcomings, which I aim to address in this book. The core problem is that wrongful harm only provides a principled justification for criminalizing obviously harmful activities. If the conduct is *harmless* then it cannot be criminalized under Feinberg's scheme. Feinberg also argues that offensive conduct could be criminalized. *Per contra*, I argue that the concept of offense is *vacuous*. Offending others does not provide a principled justification for criminalization. Conduct can only be criminalized when it is wrongful and has *objective bad consequences* of a nature that is deserving of criminal censure and offense to others does not meet this test. In the final chapter, I argue that there are other bad acts (privacy violations) that are criminalizable, even though the consequences may not always result in tangible harm.

Harm can only be taken seriously as a fairness constraint if we distinguish objective harm from non-objective harm, compel lawmakers to criminalize serious harm, constitutionalize the harm criterion and incorporate an account of

---

England and Wales, Consultation Paper No. 139, H.M.S.O., 1995). A number of leading criminal law texts have also cited the Harm Principle with approval: see for example, Andrew Ashworth, *Principles of Criminal Law* (Oxford: Oxford University Press, 4th ed. 2003) at pp. 32 *et passim*.

119   See also Russ Shafer-Landau, 'Liberalism and Paternalism,' (2005) 11(3) *Legal Theory* 169.

120   I have in mind the deontological constraint proposed by Ripstein, which does not consider actual moral consequences at all. Arthur Ripstein, 'Beyond the Harm Principle,' (2006) 34(3) *Philosophy & Public Affairs* 215.

121   Rescher, *op. cit. supra*, fn. 18 at pp. 128–129.

the culpableness of wantonly harming animals. I argue that harm to others is the only good reason for depriving a person of his or her liberty through *imprisonment*. Such an approach leaves the state with ample discretion to enact a wide range of other regulatory offenses regardless of harm, but prevents it from using jail terms to enforce these offenses. I also argue that the courts might not be able to determine harmfulness claims with exact precision, but that they can do enough to make recognizing the harm criterion as a constitutional criterion worthwhile. Determining the objective harmfulness of a particular act is no different than trying to ascertain whether conduct involves an exercise of privacy or freedom of expression. In the current climate of penal populism the harm criterion has to be taken out of the academic literature and constitutionalized, if it is to be taken seriously.

In Chapter 3, I draw on secondary liability theory in an attempt to outline the moral limits of criminalizing people for merely influencing the criminal choices of others. A person cannot be held responsible for someone else's harm-doing. A person can only be held responsible for harm, if that harm can be fairly imputed to her because of something she did. This is an area that Feinberg's formulation of the Harm Principle completely neglects. A person's act is a *remote harm* when it is harmless *but for* the fact that it encourages another independent party to commit a harmful criminal act (a primary harm). For example, the broken windows thesis holds that minor offending (such as passive begging) is a precursor to more serious crime. Passive begging allegedly sends a signal to criminals that the broken windows area is un-policed and is an easy target for crime. The beggars are criminalized to deter independent parties from committing crimes in the broken windows area. In Chapter 3, I object to this kind of criminalization because it contravenes the requirements for *individual* responsibility. It aims to punish people for the inadvertent and very remote consequences of their actions. I argue that a person should only be held responsible for another's criminal harm when she is culpably involved in it.

What is needed are moral reasons for stating from an *ex ante* perspective that it will be fair to hold x morally responsible for s when it causes y to do harm n. If this requirement is satisfied then there will be a *prima facie* case for criminalization. I argue that a person is culpably involved in another's crime when she recklessly assists or intentionally encourages that crime. In addition, a person can become culpably involved in another's criminal harm by underwriting it. I also argue that the fairness constraint should only be overridden as a matter of necessity to prevent harm of an extraordinarily grave kind. I conclude that begging does not meet this test, but firearm possession might and examine when it might be criminalized as a form of endangerment. I outline the fundamental right not be criminalized for another's wrongdoing with reference to the gun possession exemplar and ask whether there are moral grounds for trumping the *individual responsibility* constraint for the collective good.

In Chapter 4, I defend my decision to use harm as the core criterion for ensuring principled criminalization. I argue that the harm criterion not only meets the challenges put forward by Dan-Cohen and Ripstein, but provides superior criteria for determining the fairness of criminalization decisions. Dan-Cohen[122] argues that the Harm Principle should be replaced with what he calls the *dignity principle*, that is, 'the main goal of the criminal law should be to defend the unique moral worth of every human being': treat humanity as an end in itself. I argue that Dan-Cohen's principle of respect for persons is not feasible, because it would allow mere deontological wrongness to be criminalized (*i.e.*, it would be unfair to criminalize mere false promising). This type of criminalization would contravene the fairness constraints as laid down in this book. Meanwhile, Ripstein[123] draws on Kant's concept of freedom that is specific to the *Doctrine of Right*[124] to postulate that violations of equal freedom provide a superior criterion than harm for ensuring that criminalization decisions meet the requirements of fairness. Because the harm constraint is a central feature in my scheme for ensuring fair and just criminalization, it is necessary for me to examine the critique put forward by Dan-Cohen and Ripstein. I conclude that chapter by examining how the Harm Principle might be reformulated to cover harm to animals.

Dan-Cohen and Ripstein argue that *covert* harms cannot be criminalized under the Harm Principle, because these types of harms are harmless in that the victim never discovers them. I demonstrate that conduct such as covert rape and trespassing is conduct that falls within the purview of the wrongful harm justification for criminalization. More generally, I argue that Kant's deontological theory emphasizing moral autonomy and respect for persons does not provide us with adequate criteria for carrying out a proportionality analysis of many unjust criminalization decisions. It would not be fair to criminalize all violations of dignity and moral freedom (*e.g.*, false promising, a harmless trespass to goods *etc.*). I briefly outline the core elements of Kant's idea of human dignity and freedom as laid down in the *Groundwork*[125] and in the *Principle of Universal Right*. I do this in order to demonstrate that neither Dan-Cohen nor Ripstein develops independent normative principles from Kant's metaphysics of morals, but rather they apply Kant's deontology to a social problem (criminalization decisions) that it was not designed to deal with. These criteria have the potential to increase unfair criminalization, because they do not consider the badness and gravity of any consequences or risks that transpire from the wrongdoing. It is essential to consider the social impact of harms on individuals otherwise we would not be able to provide lawmakers with guidance about what to criminalize and about how

---

122 Meir Dan-Cohen, 'Defending Dignity,' *Boalt Working Papers in Public Law* (University of California, Berkeley, Paper 99, 2002) at p. 1.

123 Arthur Ripstein, *op. cit. supra*, fn. 118 at p. 216.

124 Immanuel Kant, *Metaphysics of Morals* (1797), translated from the German by Mary J. Gregor, *Practical Philosophy: The Cambridge Edition of the Works of Immanuel Kant* (Cambridge: Cambridge University Press, 1999).

125 Immanuel Kant, *Groundwork of the Metaphysics of Morals*, 1785, translated from the German by Herbert James Paton, *The Moral Law* (London: Hutchinson University Library, 1972).

much punishment is required. Nor would we be able to fairly label the proscribed conduct according to its seriousness. Ripstein's equal freedom criterion does not even allow the legislature to distinguish a harmless trespass from a harmful trespass. Both are criminalizable in Ripstein's scheme.

Dan-Cohen also argues that the Harm Principle could not be used to provide a moral justification for criminalizing slavery in those cases where the slave consents. In Chapter 5, I argue that the wrongness of *grossly harming* human beings cannot be annulled through consent. Consent cannot be used to annul wrongdoing and harm in all cases. Consent has its moral limits. I argue that sadomasochism and gladiatorial battles are criminalizable because of the gravity of the harm involved. A person cannot alienate the right to be protected from these types of gross harms. I use Dan-Cohen's provocative critique to further explore the dimensions of harm as a criterion for measuring the justice of criminalization decisions. In doing this, I conclude that it does not adequately explain why it is fair to criminalize consensual harm-doing. I examine the objective limitations of consent as a defense and argue that the idea of consent is in itself an objective reason for justifying wrongful harms, but conclude that it can be overridden by other objective considerations of greater importance. Consent does not excuse or justify inflicting irreparable harm of an extraordinary kind on others. I also conclude that a weaker argument is available for limiting consent in those cases where the conduct involves repeated, purposeless harm of a grave kind.

I examine the relatively controversial English cases of *R. v. Brown*[126] (where the majority rejected consent as a defense to intentionally causing actual bodily harm) and *R. v. Konzani*[127] (where the majority argued that fully informed consent could have provided the *reckless* H.I.V. transmitter with a defense) to examine the limits of consent. Once there is a proper *prima facie* case of criminalizable harm, consent could be sufficient to provide a defense in certain circumstances. In the defense context, the harm-doer raises consent as a defense when she is being prosecuted for criminally harming the consenter. I accept that consent annuls wrongdoing when the conduct causes trivial harm or where it changes the nature of the conduct. For example, when a person consents to sexual intercourse she converts what otherwise would be a criminal harm into a harmless and desirable activity.[128] But if a person consents to having her hands amputated with a chainsaw, her consent cannot convert what otherwise would be a serious harm into a harmless or justifiable activity. I am concerned with consent in the context of serious harm-doing to others (*e.g.*, where the harm-doer breaks the bones of the consenter, blinds the consenter, kills and eats the consenter, and so forth).

Consent provides an objective reason for allowing a person to make choices that might involve consenting to harm, but consent is not absolute. Consent

---

126 [1994] 1 A.C. 212.
127 [2005] EWCA Crim. 706.
128 George P. Fletcher, *Basic Concepts of Legal Thought* (New York: Oxford University Press, 1996) at p. 109.

protects personal autonomy, but it does not allow a person to degrade or destroy the human dignity of the consenting party. The cardinal value of human dignity as recognized in Western society differs from the secondary value envisaged by the concept of personal autonomy, as it only allows 'one set of principles which people can rationally legislate and they are the same for all. Nobody can escape their rule simply by being irrational and refusing to accept them. Personal autonomy, by contrast, is essentially about the freedom of persons to choose their own lives.'[129] Respecting personal autonomy is fundamentally different from respecting human beings as ends in themselves. I argue that a person cannot alienate her right to be treated with a *minimum* degree of respect as a human being merely by being irrational.[130]

In Chapter 6 I argue that the Offense Principle is vacuous because umbrage/disgust *per se* does not provide an objective justification for criminalization. Offense is dependent on subjective sentiment and human socialization, so it is a fairly empty concept for the purpose of providing an objective criterion for guiding criminalization decisions. I argue that all crimes are human inventions. Criminalization is a process of labeling certain actions as wrong and thus punishable in order to solve social conflicts (cooperation problems) that arise in complex plural societies. Nonetheless, this does not mean that the criminalization of all harmless wrongs lacks a moral foundation.

Many criminalization decisions are just and fair because they are reconcilable with objective principles of justice such as the harm/bad consequence constraint, the equal respect constraint, the autonomy constraint, the culpability constraint and so on. These constraints are objective because they serve ends that are intersubjectively sharable by all agents as communally situated. Their objectivity does not extend beyond our deep conventional understandings of right and wrong and of good and bad. It is possible to make strong objectivity claims when the harm is of a primitive nature, because such accounts are supported not only by our deep conventional understandings of harm, but also by our scientific and biological understandings of harm. I examine the critical moral/relativism distinction in criminalization ethics and argue that even if there is a clear distinction, that criminalization decisions have to be guided by relativistic conventions since wrongs are conventionally contingent. I argue that the narrow formulation of objective morality that is grounded in realism has a very limited role to play.

Realism and critical morality have to be rejected as providing guidance in the criminalization ethics domain, because the wrongness and badness of the consequences that flow from certain social interactions are circumstantially and conventionally contingent. For instance, exhibitionism is not inherently wrong

---

129 Joseph Raz, *The Morality of Freedom* (Oxford: Clarendon Press, 1986) at p. 371.
130 Onora O'Neill, *Constructions of Reason: Explorations of Kant's Practical Philosophy* (Cambridge: Cambridge University Press, 1989) at pp. 53–54, 66; and Onora O'Neill, 'Public Health or Clinical Ethics: Thinking Beyond Borders,' (2002) 16(2) *Ethics & International Affairs* 35 at pp. 36–37.

or bad. Unlike being punched, seeing an exhibitionist cannot result in physical pain or harm. The proposition that exhibitionism is truly wrong in a critical *transcultural* sense is not convincing. In the final sections of Chapter 6, I use the idea of privacy/anonymity loss to demonstrate the conventional contingency of the badness and wrongness of certain harmless activities such as gross privacy violations. The criminalization of harmless wrongs is only justifiable when the wrong has some independent bad consequence that can be objectively defined as unacceptable (objectively defined by those who are socially situated—meaning objectivity does not equal truth or absolute rightness or wrongness). We cannot rely on the objective concept of harm, because the offensive acts that Feinberg had in mind are not harmful when measured against our deeply held conventional conceptualizations of harm. I critique Feinberg's Offense Principle and argue that mediating factors such as the magnitude, intensity, and avoidability of the offense, on the one hand, and the reasonableness of the offender's conduct, on the other, are not ultimately very helpful in determining its criminalizability.

The wrongness of some offensive acts can be defined in conventional terms because of the psychological damage the victim suffers because of his or her socialization. For instance, when x films up y's skirt and then uploads it onto the Internet, y might suffer genuine psychological distress because of the way in which she has been socialized to need privacy. In a different culture such a violation might not even be noticed. Nonetheless, it is a genuine wrong and is worthy of regulation. Privacy violations such as those involved when a person spies on others in a locker room has bad consequences of a conventionally contingent nature, but these consequences are objectively bad to the extent that there is deep agreement about the wrongness of such behavior. In Chapter 6, I examine the interconnections between contexts, convention and inter-subjectively acceptable principles of justice and the way in which these factors can be drawn on to explain the fairness of criminalizing certain harmless wrongs.

As far as proportionality is concerned, even if there is an absolute truth about the wrongness of certain actions or the amount of punishment that a particular wrong warrants, the range of possible truth conclusions would be too narrow to identify a wide range of objective *bad consequences* for the purpose of guiding punishment and criminalization decisions in international and plural contexts. Claims about the truth and universalizability of certain *harms* is probably limited to a few harms of the most primitive kind such as physical pain and suffering, starvation, a lack of shelter, dehydration, *etc.*), as it is not possible to demonstrate that many conventionally contingent bad consequences such as the disturbance caused by exhibitionism are truly bad in a universal sense. Primitive harms such as starvation and blinding are in the bull's eye of the inter-subjectively conceptualized bad-consequence-dartboard, and as the lawmaker moves concentrically away from the bull's eye the harms become more conventionally contingent. The more conventionally contingent a wrong, the greater will be the case for labeling it as a less serious crime and for punishing it proportionally less.

Chapter 2
Taking Harm Seriously as a Criminalization Constraint

Harm and Wrongdoing

Indisputably, one of the major aims of the criminal law over the centuries has been to prevent culpable harm-doing to others.[1] Hall[2] notes that: '[I]n penal theory, harm is the focal point between criminal conduct on the one side, and the punitive sanction on the other. In relation to criminal conduct, harm [a bad consequence] is essential as the relevant effect, the end sought. Without an effect or end [a *bad* risk/action/act/consequence], it is impossible to have a cause or means, and everything in penal law associated with causation and imputation would be superfluous.' *Blackstone's Commentaries* states that in all cases, a crime involves 'an injury; every public offense is also a private wrong, and somewhat more; it affects the individual, and it likewise affects the community.'[3] In *Dei delitte e delle pene* (1764), Beccaria stated that: 'the true measure of crimes is the *injury* done to society.'[4] Meanwhile Sir James Fitzjames Stephen[5] wrote that: 'In different ages of the world injuries to individuals, to God, to the gods, or to the community, have been treated as crimes, but I think that in all cases the idea of crime has involved the idea of some definite, gross, undeniable injury to some one.'

However, Stephen defined harm in loose conventional terms.[6] For Stephen, lesbianism, passive begging and so forth would clearly have involved 'some definite, gross, undeniable injury' to others, even though these types of activities clearly do

---

1   The older literature refers to many activities as being gravely harmful, but many of these activities were defined as harmful according to the relativist standards of the day, not according to sound objective argument.

2   Hall dedicates an entire chapter to the concept of harm. See Jerome Hall, *General Principles of Criminal Law* (Indianapolis: Bobbs-Merrill Co., 2nd ed., 1960) at pp. 212–246.

3   *Blackstone's Commentaries* (London: Sweet & Maxwell, Vol. 4, 21st ed. 1844), at p. 6. See also Richard Epstein, 'The Harm Principle —And How it Grew,' (1995) 45(4) *Toronto Law Journal* 369; and the literature review in *R. v. Malmo-Levine* [2000] B.C.C.A. 335.

4   Cesare Beccaria, *On Crimes and Punishments* (Indianapolis: Hackett Publishing, 1986) p. 17.

5   James Fitzjames Stephen, *A History of the Criminal Law in England* (New York: Burt Franklin, Vol. II, 1883) at pp. 78–79.

6   James Fitzjames Stephen, *Liberty, Equality, Fraternity* (London: Smith, Elder, & Co., 1873).

not result in consequences that could be described as objectively harmful. If harm is to work as a criminalization constraint, then the wrongdoing has to risk or produce bad consequences that can be described as harmful in objective terms.[7]

In this chapter, I defend and develop the harm criterion, because it meets the requirements of justice and provides the legislature with a criterion for ensuring that criminalization is fair and proportionate in a very wide range of situations. Feinberg has provided the most notable formulation of harm. According to Feinberg's[8] formulation of the Harm Principle: 'It is always a good reason in support of penal legislation that it would probably be effective in preventing (eliminating, reducing) harm to persons other than the actor (the one prohibited from acting) and there is probably no other means that is equally effective at no greater cost to others.' Feinberg argues that a responsible legislature should only apply the crime label to conduct that wrongfully harms or offends others.[9] I generally support Feinberg's formulation of the Harm Principle, but my use of harm differs to Feinberg's in two core respects. Firstly, I incorporate a fuller account of culpability in order to demonstrate its role as a core element of wrongness. Secondly, I demonstrate that the harm criterion is a constitutional yardstick for measuring the proportionate justice of criminalization decisions that carry jail terms.

I do not argue that wrongful harm to others is the only objectively bad consequence that might be available for justifying criminalization decisions. There are bound to be other bad consequences that might justify criminalization, but it is not my aim to identify all the possibilities and to consider every possible counterexample. If the conduct does not result in wrongful harm or a wrongful privacy loss,[10] then the lawmaker will have to produce other similarly compelling objective justifications to demonstrate that the actions that are to be criminalized have the potential to produce consequences that are factually bad and thus make the wrongdoer deserving of criminalization. The justice constraint will be satisfied in most cases by demonstrating that the conduct results in wrongful harm, but we cannot rule out the possibility of other wrongs that cannot be explained by wrongful harm or privacy losses. What can safely be said is that the above criteria should always be satisfied, that is, the agent's *culpable* actions should result in (or risk) a *bad consequence*. If either element is missing, then there will be no basis for invoking the criminal law.

In this chapter, my aim is limited to outlining and defending the harm constraint, and more importantly developing an account of why it should be

---

7   J.S. Mill would have favored an objectivity restriction had he clearly comprehended it.

8   Joel Feinberg, *The Moral Limits of the Criminal Law: Harm to Others* (New York: Oxford University Press, 1984) at p. 26. See also Herbert Packer, *The Limits of the Criminal Sanction* (Stanford: Stanford University Press, 1968).

9   Joel Feinberg, *The Moral Limits of the Criminal Law: Offense to Others* (New York: Oxford University Press, Vol. II, 1985).

10 See the discussion on privacy in Chapter 6.

recognized as a the objective standard for determining whether jail terms are excessive pursuant to the Eighth Amendment. I also note that justice can only be satisfied in the harm context when objective harm is properly identified. '[The harm] label is applied inappropriately when it is attached to any harmless act or when it is not attached to seriously harmful acts ... If the label is not applied appropriately, it is sensible to assume that it is applied for reasons that lie with the decision makers and not in the realm of objective dangers.'[11] Feinberg[12] holds that wrongful harm is only a sufficient condition for criminalization and therefore the lawmaker is not compelled to criminalize all forms of harm-doing. Nevertheless the *sufficient condition* requirement does need some qualification, because the normative implications of serious harm-doing would allow victims to demand that the criminal law be invoked to protect their basic welfare interests. The public can only have confidence in a criminal justice system that produces consistent and fair results.

A criminal justice system that disproportionately criminalizes trivial street offenses (*e.g.*, passive begging, *etc.*), while using non-criminal[13] and obscure legal mechanisms[14] to keep serious harm-doing (*e.g.*, corporate harm-doing and tax evasion) outside the realm of the criminal law, will cause the public to lose confidence in the criminal law.[15] Feinberg's harm as a *sufficient condition*[16] limitation plays an important role, but it does not mean that the lawmaker would not be morally compelled to act to prevent bad actions/acts/consequences in cases where it would not be fair to expect the victim to take proceedings on her own responsibility to prevent serious harm-doing (marital rape was criminalized for this reason).[17] It is important that the legislature take grave harm-doing seriously, even in those cases where it is not possible to hold an individual responsible because the wrongful harm cannot be imputed to a moral agent (*i.e.*, in the corporate harm-doing context it is not always possible to fairly impute the harm and blame for

---

11   Reiman, *The Rich Get Richer and the Poor Get Prison* (Boston: Allyn & Bacon, 4th ed. 1995) at p. 7.

12   Feinberg, Vol. I, *op. cit. supra*, fn. 8 at p. 10.

13   On regulation and criminalization, see Nicola Lacey, 'Criminalization as Regulation: The Role of Criminal Law,' in Christine Parker *et al.*, *Regulating Law* (Oxford: Oxford University Press, 2004).

14   Celia Wells, *Corporations and Criminal Responsibility* (Oxford: Oxford University Press, 2nd ed. 2001) at pp. 146 *et seq*.

15   A criminal justice system that produces unjust and inconsistent results achieves disutility as opposed to utility. See generally Paul H. Robinson, 'The Criminal–Civil Distinction and Dangerous Offenders,' (1993) 83(4) *The Journal of Criminal Law and Criminology* 693. Such a system loses its moral credibility and preventive force. See David Beetham, *The Legitimation of Power* (Basingstoke: Macmillan, 1991) at p. 22.

16   Feinberg, Vol. I., *op. cit. supra*, fn. 8 at p. 10.

17   If the criminal justice system is to maintain public legitimacy then '[i]t is important that the victim sees that the state has taken the wrong against him or her seriously.' See J.R. Lucas, *Responsibility* (Oxford: Clarendon Press, 1993) at p. 104.

the harmful consequences to a particular moral agent). This does not mean that it would be unfair to use regulatory criminalization, which can be backed up with hefty deterrent penalties, to prevent collective harm-doing in those cases where blame cannot be individualized.[18] The just deserts justification has a completely different dimension in this context, as no individual is being censured. The deterrent punishment would still have to be proportionate with the corporation's collective culpability[19] and the harmfulness of the bad consequence that it has negligently brought about. Slightly heftier deterrent penalties for corporate wrongdoing could be reconciled with justice, because no individual is being directly penalized or stigmatized. The harshness of the penalty is reduced by the fact that it is borne collectively.

As we will see in the next section, a serious problem for the harm justification is that it is misused to justify criminalizing conduct that is not objectively harmful. This is due to the fact that lawmakers frequently rely on unprincipled harm claims, often inspired by penal populism, rather than on objective accounts of harm. A further problem with Feinberg's Harm Principle is that it does not catch some conduct that is clearly being criminalized because of its harmfulness (*e.g.*, harm to animals). When a person kills an elephant for ivory she damages (harms) the elephant in an objective sense, but Feinberg's Harm Principle (which only criminalizes culpable harm to humans—setbacks to human interests) does not explain how or if the elephant has also been wronged. Hence, the theory of wrongdoing (which is human interests oriented) found in Feinberg's Harm Principle does not explain the wrongness of harming animals. When the criminal law is invoked to prevent *harm* to animals, surely the bad consequence of harm has to be part of the reason for invoking the criminal law. I argue that the justification for criminalization can catch harm to animals, so long as we have an account of why humans have duties not to wantonly harm animals;[20] and an account of why harm to animals (inflicting biological pain on sentient creatures) is a bad consequence for those creatures.

I conclude that a properly formulated harm constraint has the potential to prevent a plethora of activities from being unfairly criminalized. It also has sufficient reach to protect animals and potential victims of corporate harm-doing. It does not supply the only objective criterion for measuring the proportionality and justice of criminalization, but it has the widest reach for ensuring that criminalization decisions meet the requirement of justice. Since we are able to identify morally indefensible (unjustifiable) setbacks to human interests (harms that violate their rights), it is possible to make Feinberg's account of wrongdoing work with respect

---

18   Wells rightly points out that: 'Deterrent arguments may not be open to the same objections when applied to corporations as to individuals.' Wells, *op. cit. supra*, fn. 14 at p. 20.

19   *Id.* at pp. 155 *et seq.*

20   I invoke Raz/Kramer type *interest theory.* See Joseph Raz, *The Morality of Freedom* (Oxford: Clarendon Press, 1986) at Chapter 7. Matthew H. Kramer, *Rights, Wrongs and Responsibilities* (Chippenham, Wiltshire: Palgrave, 2001) at pp. 28 *et seq.*

to harm to humans without too much modification. I argue below that the bad act of harming animals and the non-correlative duties that humans owe to animals show that the harm justification for criminalization (which is the parallel of the harm constraint against criminalization) has a more expansive reach than Feinberg envisaged.

A properly formulated account of criminalizable harm only provides a part of the solution, because there is still a further legal barrier that prevents the harm constraint from being taken seriously as a restraint against unfair criminalization. The harm criterion can only be taken seriously as a check on unfair and unprincipled criminalization if lawmakers are forced to consider it. I not only extend the concept of harm to delineate its proper reach,[21] but also demonstrate that it is a criterion that has to be considered when interpreting proportionality of state punishments pursuant to the personal autonomy type provision and more specifically under the Eighth Amendment of the Constitution of the United States 1787.[22] In what follows, the elements of harm and wrongdoing are set forth, and the justice of criminalization evaluated in light of them.

Feinberg's Account of Objectively Wrongful Harm

What is meant by objective harm? Let us unpack Feinberg's concept of harm. Feinberg[23] expounds harm in three senses: (i) harm as damage, (ii) harm as a setback to interests, and (iii) harm as wrongdoing. Harm as used in Feinberg's theory is an

---

21 See Dennis J. Baker, 'The Moral Limits of Criminalizing Remote Harms,' (2007) 10(3) *New Criminal Law Review* 370; and Andrew von Hirsch, 'Extending the Harm Principle: "Remote" Harms and Fair Imputation,' in Andrew P. Simester and A.T.H. Smith, *Harm and Culpability* (Oxford: Clarendon Press, 1996) at pp. 259 *et seq*.

22 In this book, I draw predominantly on American law and examples, but the discussion is not jurisdiction specific, as the right not to be unfairly punished is a universal objective right. It has not only been enshrined in the United States Constitution, but also in a number of other human rights documents. See sections 2, 7 and 12 of the Canadian Charter of Rights and Freedoms, Part 1, section 2(b), Constitution Act 1982 (Can.), Articles 2, 3, 5 and 8 of the European Convention for the Protection of Human Rights and Fundamental Freedoms, 4 November 1950, 213 U.N.T.S. 222 (entered into force generally on 3 September 1953). Depending on the jurisdiction, the right is upheld by referring to the *unusual and cruel* punishment-type provision or alternatively under the deprivation of liberty-type provision. However, some documents contain broader express provisions that refer to liberty, process, proportionality and harm. See Articles IV and V of The French Declaration of the Rights of Man and of the Citizen 1789. These rights have also received universal constitutional recognition in Articles 12, 18 and 19 of the Universal Declaration of Human Rights, GA Res. 217 A (III), U.N. Doc. A/810 (1948). However, the Universal Declaration has no effect in signatory states such as Australia, because it has not enacted a bill of rights or domestic legislation to give such rights binding force.

23 Feinberg, Vol. I, *op. cit. supra*, fn. 8 at p. 215.

amalgamation of senses (ii) and (iii). Harm must be caused by *wrongful* conduct to be a candidate for criminalization. Thus, a person's actions are criminalizable when they are culpably designed to set back the interests of others.[24] The concept of harm as used by Feinberg represents 'the overlap of senses two and three: only setbacks of interests that are wrongs, and wrongs that are setbacks to interests, are to count as harms in the appropriate sense.'[25] The term interest when used in this way refers to a stake that a person has in his or her well-being. According to Feinberg, one's interests taken as a whole consist of all those things that one has a stake in. In the singular, one's personal interest 'consists in the harmonious advancement of all one's interests in the plural.'[26] These interests, or as Feinberg puts it, 'the *things* these interests are in, are distinguishable components of a person's well-being: s/he flourishes or languishes as they flourish or languish.'[27]

The trichotomy of interests delineated by Feinberg includes welfare interests and those security and accumulative interests that cushion our welfare interests.[28] Welfare interests are at the core of Feinberg's scheme. They are interests of a kind shared by almost everyone 'in the necessary means to [their] more ultimate goals, whatever the latter may be, or later may come to be.'[29] Welfare interests include our interest in prolonging the continuance of our life for a foreseeable period of time, preserving our physical health and security, maintaining minimum intellectual acuity and emotional stability, being able to engage in social intercourse and to benefit from friendships, sustaining minimum financial security, sustaining reasonable living conditions, avoiding pain and grotesque disfigurement, preventing unjustified anxieties and resentments (intimidation), and being free from unwarranted coercion.[30] They are those interests in goods and conditions that we all need independent of our individual life plans. Everyone has a necessary stake in these kinds of interests, as they are the requisites of our well-being.[31]

Feinberg's objective account of harm is strengthened because he distinguishes important welfare interests from those interests that merely concern a person's more ulterior aims.[32] Our ulterior aims might include the goal to own a dream house, to have a prominent career as a movie star or as a politician, *etc.*[33] A person's more ultimate goals and wants (*e.g.*, building a dream house, gaining a political

---

24   *Id.* at pp. 33–34.
25   *Id.* at p. 36.
26   *Id.* at p. 34.
27   Ibid.
28   *Id.* at pp. 37, 207.
29   *Id.* at p. 37.
30   Ibid.
31   Ibid.
32   Ibid.
33   'But in respect at least to welfare interests, we are inclined to say that what promotes them is good for the person in any case, whatever his beliefs or wants may be. … [T]here may be correspondence between interest and want, but the existence of the former is not dependent upon, nor derivative from, the existence of the latter.' *Id.* at p. 42.

or professional position, solving some vital scientific question, raising a family, achieving spiritual grace, *etc.*) are not directly protected by the law.[34] 'If I have an interest in making an important scientific discovery, creating valuable works of arts, or other personal achievements, the law will protect those aspirations by guarding my welfare interests that are essential to it. But given that I have my life, health, economic adequacy, liberty, and security, there is nothing more that the law (or anyone else, for that matter) can do for me; the rest is entirely up to me.'[35]

Ulterior interests that extend elements of welfare beyond minimal levels are also protected, however.[36] The law against burglary not only protects the welfare of the indigent person who might face ruin if burgled, but it also protects the billionaire whose welfare might not be directly affected by the theft of one of her Caravaggio paintings which she had forgotten she owned.[37] Even though certain types of harm only have a trivial impact on the interests of certain individuals, they can have an accumulative impact. It is not only the ulterior interests of billionaires that are protected, 'but also their interests in liberty (the interest in being the person who decides how the accumulated funds are to be spent) and security (even his welfare interests might be threatened by the act that invades his financial interest, especially if the invasive act employs force or coercion, or seems likely to be frequently repeated).'[38] Coupled with this, even minor setbacks to the financial interests of others 'threaten ... the general security of property, and the orderliness and predictability of financial affairs in which everyone has an interest, however small.'[39] Those security interests that cushion our welfare interests are protectable.[40] For instance, common assaults are criminalized to protect our elementary sense of security.[41] In a similar vein, our accumulative

---

34 *Id.* at p. 62.

35 'In my highest pecuniary accumulation as such, or in such uses of wealth as the purchase of a yacht or a dream house, the law can protect that interest indirectly by protecting me from burglary and fraud, but it cannot protect me from bad investment advice, personal imprudence, the unpredictable dependencies of others, the lack of personal diligence or ingenuity, and so on.' *Ibid.*

36 '[U]lterior interests are only indirectly invadable. The usual way of harming one of another person's ulterior interests is by invading one of the welfare interests whose maintenance at a minimal level is a necessary condition for the advancement of any other interests at all ... At least one class of ulterior interests are directly vulnerable: those that consist of the extension of welfare interests to transminimal levels. The rich man is wronged by indefensible acts of theft just as much as the poor man is, though he will not be harmed as much.' *Id.* at p. 112.

37 *Id.* at p. 63.

38 *Ibid.*

39 *Ibid.*

40 *Id.* at p. 207.

41 'Beyond the bare minimum of health and economic well-being required to pursue his aims, a person requires a certain additional safety margin. Without that margin, that person may be able to function, but only barely so—and with much reason for apprehension.'

interests are those non-essential interests that we have in 'the various good things in life.'[42] The theft of a billionaire's yacht or Caravaggio would not necessarily deprive her of her livelihood or of her margin of security above the minimum, but it would invade her accumulated resources.[43] If left unchecked, it would also destabilize the entire property system in which we all have an interest.

Feinberg distinguishes mere wants from cognizable interests. It would be implausible to classify strong wants as interests. For example, Lucy, a devoted fan of England, may have a fervent desire to see England win the World Cup, but that alone would hardly ground a case for claiming an interest in an English victory.[44] Feinberg argues that: 'Some of our most intense desires then are not of the appropriate kind to ground ulterior interests since (like a sudden craving for an ice cream cone) they are unlinked to our longer range purposes, or they are insufficiently stable and durable to represent any investment of a stake.'[45] The harm constraint is a measure that helps protect personal autonomy.[46] A person is harmed when his or her opportunities for enjoying or pursuing the good life are thwarted or diminished.[47] Harm occurs when a person's personal or proprietary resources are impaired, because our resources are needed to enable us to realize our other opportunities.[48] Simester and von Hirsch,[49] citing Raz,[50] rightly note that such impairments are harmful because of their eventual implications for our well-being.

Andrew von Hirsch, 'Injury and Exasperation: An Examination of Harm to Others and Offense to Others,' (1985–1986) 84 *Michigan Law Review* 700 at p. 703.

42 *Ibid.*
43 *Id.* at p. 704.
44 Feinberg, Vol. I, *op. cit. supra*, fn. 8 at p. 42.
45 *Id.* at p. 43.
46 'Such a rationale explains why a minimum of political liberty is a welfare interest. It is not that one cannot subsist without liberty. It is instead, that one cannot formulate, select, and pursue one's own purposes where there is excessive outside interference with one's choices, associations, and expressions.' Von Hirsch, *op. cit. supra*, fn. 41 at p. 705.
47 Andrew P. Simester and Andrew von Hirsch, 'Rethinking the Offense Principle,' (2002) 8(3) *Legal Theory* 269 at p. 281.
48 *Ibid.*
49 'A broken arm is an impaired arm, one which has (temporarily) lost its capacity to serve a person's needs effectively, and in virtue of that impairment, its possessor's welfare interest is harmed.' *Id.* at p. 281.
50 'Respect for the autonomy of others largely consists in securing for them adequate options, *i.e.*, opportunities or the ability to use them. Depriving a person of opportunities or of the ability to use them is a way of causing him harm. Both the use-value and the exchange-value of property represent opportunities for their owner. Any harm to a person by denying him the use or the value of his property is a harm to him precisely because it diminishes his opportunities. Similarly, injury to the person reduces his ability to act in ways which he may desire. Needless to say a harm to a person may consist not in depriving him of options but in frustrating his pursuit of the projects and relationships he has set upon.' Raz, *op. cit. supra*, fn. 20 at p. 413.

Our interests can be blocked or defeated by events impersonal in nature or by inadvertent misfortune. But only the intentional unjustifiable/inexcusable behavior of a human agent can harm our interests in a (wrongful) criminalizable sense. A person's genuine welfare interests are invaded or set back in an objective sense by the culpable choices of other human agents.[51] But interests may be set back in a non-wrongful sense, to a great degree, by a tsunami, earthquake, plague, famine, *etc*. For example, if *x* becomes the victim of a crocodile attack whilst wandering around in a national park in the north of Australia, her interests will be set back. Nonetheless, she could not claim that she had been wronged. If *x* goes swimming in a crocodile infested creek at night because a malicious tour guide tells her it is safe to do so, she will be harmed and wronged by the wicked guide. Her interests are set back by the morally wrongful actions of a human agent. A person is harmed in a objective *wrongful* sense when a fellow moral agent invades his or her interests, but obviously the random crocodile attack would cause him or her great harm in the ordinary sense.[52]

The objectivity constraint prevents the victim's subjective preferences and judgments being used as criteria for identifying harm and ultimately determining criminality. Some people might claim that lesbianism/homosexuality is harmful, but this does not mean such conduct is objectively harmful. Feinberg argues that we do not have an interest in avoiding mere *hurts* and *offenses* for the purposes of criminalization. Criminalization is only available to protect those interests that are typically shared by all human beings. Those who are offended by homosexuals and lesbians would have to show that it causes a *wrongful* setback to genuine interests. The setback would have to *objectively* lessen their options for enjoying or pursing a good life. They would have to show that their interests were put in a worse condition than they would otherwise have been in had they not been invaded.

More significantly, because criminalizing a person violates her right not be subjected to harm (that is, the harm that results from jail terms, stigmatization and so forth) no plausible justification for criminalization could be constructed without also considering how the wrongdoer's actions affected the genuine rights of others. Every human being has a right not be subjected to wanton and deliberate harm-doing by another human agent. This right is possessed by all human beings in virtue of their humanity, it is a basic moral right that not only protects human dignity, but also enhances personal autonomy and ultimately the flourishing and well-being of individual agents (animals do not have rights by virtue of their humanity, but humans have non-correlative duties not to wantonly harm animals because humans have sufficient rationality and empirical knowledge to understand that wantonly inflicting pain on sentient creatures is cruel and thus a bad and wrong thing to do).[53]

---

51   Feinberg, Vol. I, *op. cit. supra*, fn. 8 at p. 34.
52   *Ibid.*
53   See generally, James Griffin, *On Human Rights* (Oxford: Oxford University Press, 2008); Richard Kraut, *What is Good and Why: The Ethics of Well-Being* (Cambridge MA: Harvard University Press, 2007); Joel Feinberg, 'In Defence of Moral Rights,' (1992) 12(2)

The criminal law communicates to those who wantonly harm animals that animals feel pain in the same way as humans (as both share the same sensory system that allows pain to be felt), and because we know that this is a bad experience. As intelligent rational agents, humans have a duty not to wantonly harm animals, because they are able to understand the wrong involved in doing so.

But survival of the fittest means that we do allow people to be harmed in societies that are underwritten with competitive economic systems. The idea is that competition brings out the best in people and increases productivity, so people cannot expected to be protected from legitimate competition. Stronger players can harm weaker players for self-gain in many competitive contexts. For example, one might harm another by putting that other person out of business by offering a more competitive service such as working for less and so forth. In such cases the harmed party would have to demonstrate that her right was superior to that of her fellow competitor. The criminal law should not be invoked unless the fellow competitor acted wrongly (*i.e.*, the competitor might have engaged in fraud, blackmail, monopolistic practices and so forth). Unless the competitor has acted wrongly rather than merely unfairly, no one has been *wrongfully harmed* as opposed to harmed (it might be unfair when a small firm has to compete against a large multinational corporation because the latter has an accumulated competitive strength, but it would not be wrong for it to use its accumulated strength). In cases where each party has an equal right, there will be no wrongful violation. Take Herbert Hart's example of two people who are walking down the street when they both notice a ten-dollar bill.[54] The bill is at an equal distance away from each of them when they notice it and there is no clue about who originally lost the money. 'Neither of the two are under a "duty" to allow the other to pick it up. Of course there may be many things which each has a "duty" not to do in the course of the race to the spot—neither may kill or wound the other—and corresponding to

---

Oxford Journal of Legal Studies 149. As we will see below, animals do not have rights by virtue of being human, so we need some other account of why it is wrong for a human to wantonly harm animals. Drawing on Raz's 'interest theory,' I will argue that a rational agent knows that it is wrong to wantonly harm animals and the type of wrongdoing involved is *prima facie* criminalizable. See generally Raz, *op. cit. supra*, fn. 20 at Chapter 7. See also Larry Alexander, 'When are We Rightfully Aggrieved,' 11(3) *Legal Theory* 325 (2005).

54   H.L.A. Hart, 'Are There Any Natural Rights,' (1955) 64 *The Philosophical Review* 175 at p. 179. See also Feinberg, Vol. I, *op. cit. supra*, fn. 8 at pp. 218–220. In a perfectly competitive market none of the competitors would treat others unfairly, but there is no such thing as a perfectly competitive market. See generally, David Gauthier, *Morals By Agreement* (Oxford: Clarendon Press, 1986) at pp. 84 *et passim*. See also Albert O. Hirschman, 'Rival Interpretations of Market Society: Civilizing, Destructive, or Feeble?' (1982) 20 *Journal of Economic Literature* 1463; Rogene A. Buchholz, 'The Protestant Ethic as an Ideological Justification of Capitalism,' (1983) 2(2) *Journal of Business Ethics* 51. For a discussion on the thinking behind co-operative decision making in the market economy, see Ernst Fehr and Klaus M. Schmidt, 'A Theory of Fairness, Competition, and Cooperation,' (1999) 114(3) *The Quarterly Journal of Economics* 817.

these "duties" there are rights to forbearances. The moral property of all economic competition implies this minimum sense of "a right" in which to say that "x has a right to" means merely that x is under no "duty" not to.'

While both parties stand to benefit if they acquire the 10-dollar bill, neither has a right to it, it is not a proprietary resource in which either has a normative claim or existing interest. Thus, the loser cannot claim that her interests have been wrongfully harmed, because the 10-dollar bill is not one of her personal or proprietary resources: she has no greater stake than the next person. Similarly, the runner-up at Wimbledon might claim that the winner has harmed her, but she could not claim she had a right not to be harmed in this context (*i.e.*, she could not assert that harm-doing was *wrongful*). Other competitive practices raise more complex issues concerning wrongfulness. For instance, if Wal-Mart follows reasonable rules of competition, but puts a small corner store out of business by constructing a superstore in the same street, does it violate the proprietor's right not to be *culpably* harmed? The proprietor of the corner store might be in a weaker bargaining position, but this alone does not give the proprietor a right not to be harmed by competitive practices in a market economy. Planning and competition laws might be used to prevent Wal-Mart from monopolizing the market or overusing its *accumulated* bargaining strength. Furthermore, the criminal law could be used to prevent it from violating the smaller competitor's right not to be *wrongly* harmed as might be the case if it dishonestly gained an unfair advantage from price fixing, selling goods below cost, making counterfeit and substandard and dangerous products, stealing trade secrets, violating patent and copyright laws, using false and misleading advertising and so forth. Wal-Mart would be under no general duty to refrain from engaging in competitive practices (practices that are not culpably designed to harm others as opposed to causing harm as a mere side-effect of genuine competition) in a market economy.

The rights violation will be wrongful if moral and epistemic culpability is present—market players have special knowledge and their expertise means that it will be possible to explain to them that price fixing, misleading and deceptive conduct and certain other sharp practices are not only unfair but also wrong. In the above example, Wal-Mart does not *aim* to bring about bad consequences for anyone. Any bad consequence is a mere side-effect of legitimate competition. Wal-Mart merely aims to compete and benefit from the market that is available for all persons to make use of. It creates jobs and its economies of scale allow it to make goods available to many who might not normally be in a position to purchase. It is arguable that society has more to gain from reasonably robust and honest competition than it does from protective practices that aim to distort market efficiency;[55] and this is why anti-competition laws such as those that prevent price

---

55 The moral foundations of capitalism arguably rest on individual rights and liberty. '[A] right, for it is our rights that define our moral and legal relationships with each other and with the state: rights and the obligations correlative to them tell us and the state what the boundaries of behavior are.' Roger Pilon, 'Capitalism and Rights: An Essay Toward

fixing and monopolies are justifiable. Wal-Mart would not violate the corner store proprietor's rights by genuinely and honestly outcompeting her, but only a theory of the nature of wrong and right competition could tell us when competitive practices become wrong and thus criminalizable rather than merely unfair. Of course, an organization such as Wal-Mart has an enormous accumulated competitive strength, but beyond criminalizing culpable anti-competitive practices (rights-violating practices) the criminal law has no role to play. A fuller discussion of the various types of competition that might be right or wrong is beyond the scope of this book, but the prerequisites of wrongful competition will be culpability plus harm. The difficulty will be in determining when a particular competitive practice involves culpable harm rather than a legitimate competitive harm.

It is illogical to focus on unfairness rather than wrongness in this context, because the former would not provide much guidance about when to invoke the criminal law given that inequity is a biological fact and is the stimulus for market efficiency.[56] For example, it is not clear why a professor who has discovered DNA in a Cambridge laboratory is unable to earn patent fees equivalent to the type of copyright fees earned by airhead celebrities, given the professor's higher skill levels and the usefulness of what he has produced. Many simple-minded celebrities are able to use copyright laws (laws that others have invented), which only the celebrity's lawyer understands, to sell the same bit of effort or work over and over thereby earning excessively more than merit would warrant if the entertainer was merely paid for her original contribution. Footballers and celebrities are often paid fees that have no link with individual effort and merit. A robust market economy should distribute wealth in proportion to merit, but beyond punishing tax evasion the criminal law is not necessarily equipped to tackle all the inequities that arise in life. A windfall tax could be applied to target those who earn sums *vastly* beyond *merit*, but it would have to be fine-tuned to allow risk takers and genuine innovators to be rewarded significantly for their efforts.[57]

Determining the justice of competitive practices within a market economy or the proper boundaries of economic activity is beyond the scope of this book. What is clear is that a criminalizable harm has to result from something more than genuine competition. If Wal-Mart's aim was merely to destroy small businesses,

---

Fine Tuning the Moral Foundations of the Free Society,' (1982) 1(1) *Journal of Business Ethics* 29 at p. 30. See also Friedrich A. von Hayek, *The Constitution of Liberty* (Chicago: University of Chicago Press, 1978).

56   Cf. Jeffrey G. Williamson, *Did British Capitalism Breed Inequality?* (London: Routledge, 2005).

57   For an explanation of the normative and societal functions of the market economy, see Luigino Bruni and Robert Sugden, 'Fraternity: Why the Market Need Not Be a Morally Free Zone,' (2008) 24 *Economics and Philosophy* 35. For an alternative that attempts to demarcate a more merit oriented system, see Peter A. Corning, '"Fair Shares": Beyond Capitalism and Socialism, or the Biological Basis of Social Justice,' (2003) 22(2) *Politics and the Life Sciences* 12.

then it would be culpably violating the rights of those firms (epistemic and moral responsibility would be present, because as experts in the commercial community the wrongdoers would understand the wrongness of deliberately destroying other competitive players), but when its aim is merely to exploit the market economy there is no clear-cut case of wrongness. There is a large gray area between right and wrong competition where criminal and non-criminal regulation may be justifiable,[58] but demarcating those boundaries is beyond the scope of the present discussion.

A person may also be wronged without being harmed. Wrongs that do not set back our interests are not criminalizable[59] unless they have some bad consequence that warrants regulation. An example provided by Feinberg is where a wrongly broken promise redounds by fluke to the promisee's advantage.[60] The promisee has been wronged even though she has not been harmed. This conduct is not criminalizable, because it does not harm the promisee. A bad consequence of sufficient seriousness is needed to explain the criminalizableness of intentional wrongdoing. A bad consequence alone does not explain wrongness as opposed to the badness of a state of affairs. What's more, mere wrongdoing does not give the legislature sufficient guidance as to why a particular act is deserving of criminalization. We need an account of wrongdoing plus some bad consequence to give the legislature proper guidance.

Let us now consider Feinberg's use of *moral culpability*, as an explanation of the wrongness of harming others. The second element of the wrongful harm justification for criminalization requires the harm to be brought about by the culpable (*i.e.*, a person is responsible because she understands the wrongness of her actions) actions of a human agent. According to Feinberg, conduct is wrongful when it is intentionally designed to violate the moral rights of others.[61] Violations

---

58 '[B]y the same token there is no room for the view, that perfectly competitive markets, if any existed, would be a "morally free zone". If under certain conditions there is no moral objection to pursuit of profit at another's expense, that is not because under those conditions morality does not apply but because under those conditions morality permits what would otherwise be immorality.' John Gardner, 'Nearly Natural Law,' (2007) 52 *The American Journal of Jurisprudence* 1 at p. 5. For a discussion about the inherent unfairness of accumulated bargaining power, see Norman E. Bowie and Robert L. Simon, *The Individual The Political Order* (New York: Rowman and Littefield, 1998) at pp. 51 *et seq.*

59   Cf. Joel Feinberg, *The Moral Limits of the Criminal Law: Harmless Wrongdoing*, (New York: Oxford University Press, Vol. IV, 1988) at pp. 323–324.

60   Feinberg, Vol. I, *op. cit. supra*, fn. 8.

61   Feinberg argues that: 'Welfare interests most certainly are grounds for moral claims against others if any interests are. If we speak of moral rights at all, then, each of us has a moral right to life, minimal health, economic sufficiency, political liberty and so on … Welfare interests then are grounds for valid claims against others (moral rights) *par excellence.*' *Id.* at p. 112. See also J.R. Lucas, *On Justice* (Oxford: Clarendon Press, 1980) at pp. 20–34.

of the right not to be harmed are central to Feinberg's Harm Principle. Feinberg[62] states that an invasion of an interest (*i.e.*, a setback to a personal or proprietary resource that someone has a stake or interest in) is always a violation of another's rights. Everyone has a general claim against others as far as their interests are concerned—except, of course in those situations where the setback is justified because the other party has a superior interest. Criminalizable harm is dependent not only on 'interests' but also on pre-existing moral rights. Harm is about culpably setting back, thwarting or defeating the interests of others.[63] Feinberg argues that a setback to an interest only counts as harm when it is wrongfully inflicted—that is, when it is intentionally inflicted by an agent who has sufficient knowledge to know it will violate the rights of her victim not to be harmed.[64] One person wrongs another by violating her rights and thereby wrongfully setting back her interests. Feinberg puts a limit on harm by making it dependent on moral wrongdoing, which is in turn is dependent on an indefensible violation of pre-existing rights. He uses moral rights rather than legal rights to avoid circularity, as we cannot know what constitutes wrongful harm without knowing what rights people have, and we cannot know what rights we have without knowing what constitutes harm. Feinberg argues that the circularity is unavoidable if the rights invoked to classify what interests can be the subject of harm are legal rights, but suggests that this conflict can be overcome by specifying that the rights to be used to classify interests are 'merely moral rights.'[65]

Feinberg argues that 'any *indefensible invasion* of another's *interest* (excepting of course the sick and wicked interests) is a wrong, and hence an infringement of a moral right.'[66] Wrongness in Feinberg's scheme is about showing that the unjustifiable/inexcusable right-violating actions of the offender caused the harm. Feinberg's theory of moral wrongness is conceivable with respect to harm against human interests, but his use of doctrines (unjustifiably/inexcusably) that are traditionally used to explain legal fault from the *ex post* trial perspective requires some clarification. Feinberg fails to explain why these concepts have a moral basis that explains wrongness from the *ex ante* criminalization perspective. He argues that a wrongful invasion is an *indefensible* (inexcusable and unjustifiable) invasion.[67] Feinberg not only uses terms such as unjustifiable and inexcusable, but also refers to culpability terms such as intention, negligence, recklessness and even the term 'fault,' which are traditionally used to consider guilt from the

---

62   *Ibid.*
63   *Id.* at p. 33.
64   *Id.* at pp. 109–114.
65   *Id.* at p. 111. See also Hamish Stewart, 'Harms, Wrongs, and Set-Backs in Feinberg's Moral Limits of the Criminal Law,' (2001–2002) 5 *Buffalo Criminal Law Review* 47 at p. 53.
66   *Id.* at pp. 111–112.
67   *Id.* at pp. 105–108.

ex post trial perspective. For instance, Feinberg states that *A* wrongfully invades *B*'s welfare interest when:[68]

a. A acts ...
b. In a manner which is defective or faulty in respect to the risks it creates to B, that is, with intention of producing the consequences for B that follow, or similarly adverse ones, or with negligence or recklessness in respect to those consequences; and
c. A's acting in that manner is morally indefensible, that is, neither excusable nor justifiable; and
d. A's action is the cause of a setback to B's interests, which is also
e. a violation of B's right.

Let us look at the objectivity of moral culpability as an element of the moral justification for criminalization and penal detention. I use the term *wrongfulness* to refer to broad moral culpability and the term *wrongness* to refer to moral impermissibility.[69] According to the harm justification it is culpability accompanied with harmful consequences (or attempted harm and/or risked harm) that explains wrongness—that is, the criminal impermissibility or the criminalizableness of the action that causes the harm. After all, we do not criminalize and punish harmful accidents,[70] because bad consequences alone do not constitute wrongness. As Nagel notes:[71]

> But the essence of evil is that it should *repel* us. If something is evil, our actions should be guided, if they are guided at all, toward its elimination rather than toward its maintenance. That is what evil means. So when we *aim* at evil [harm-doing] we are swimming head-on against the normative current. Our action is guided by the goal at every point in the direction diametrically opposite to that which the value of that goal points. To put it another way, if we *aim* [to harm others] we make what we do in the first instance a positive rather than negative function of it. At every point, the *intentional function* is simply the normative reversed, and from the point of view of the agent, this produces an acute sense of moral dislocation.

---

68 *Id.* at pp. 105–106.
69 Moral culpability is the fulcrum of moral evil (acts/actions that are designed to have bad consequences such as murder, rape, etc.), and natural evil such as the devastation caused by malaria and so forth.
70 See generally, Itzhak Kugler, *Direct and Oblique Intention in the Criminal Law: An Inquiry into Degrees of Blameworthiness* (Aldershot: Ashgate, 2002) at pp. 1–57.
71 Thomas Nagel, *The View From Nowhere* (New York: Oxford University Press, 1986) at p. 182. See also Ronald D. Milo, *Immorality* (New Jersey: Princeton University Press, 1984).

Moral culpability is sufficient to explain the objective wrongness of intentional/reckless harm-doing, because the communally situated moral agent knows that it is wrong to *aim* to bring about bad consequences (harm) for one's fellow humans.[72] The same cannot be said about intentionally aiming to bring about good or neutral consequences. Intentional harm-doing provides a sound objective justification for using penal detention so long as the further justice requirements of fair labeling and proportional punishment[73] are also taken into consideration, that is, the crime should be labeled and punished according to its seriousness.[74] It is fair to punish those who deliberately harm others because harm-doing produces factually bad consequences for those who are harmed. It violates the genuine rights of the victims. The harm-doer aims for bad consequences and it can be explained to her in rational terms that her harm-doing was wrongful, bad and deserving of proportional punishment which may include jail time in the right circumstances.[75]

Even though culpability or more generally *intentionality* helps to explain both moral wrongness and legal fault, it alone does not equal moral wrongness. Firstly, merely thinking evil would not be criminalizable unless it is combined with an attempt to do harm. Secondly, if lawmakers enacted an offense prohibiting lesbians from kissing in public places, this would not mean that intentional lesbian kissing in public places is *morally wrong* in any objective sense. If a couple of lesbians decided to kiss in public to protest the law, they would culpably break the law in legal terms because they intentionally chose to kiss in public knowing that it was a criminal offense to do so. But they would not be morally blameworthy, because such a law is not reconcilable with the requirements of justice, as lesbian kissing does

---

72 The wrongness of intentional harm-doing is essentially self-evident to well-informed rational deliberators. See Christine M. Korsgaard, The Sources of Normativity (Cambridge: Cambridge University Press, 1996) at pp. 131–166. See also W.D. Ross, *The Right and the Good* (Oxford: Oxford University Press, 1930) at p. 29. Charles Fried notes that: 'harming an innocent person is wrong. Whatever may be the problems about intention in other contexts, intention as the mode of application clearly complements the substantive content of the norm.' That choosing to harm others 'should be subject to this norm also works to explain the logic of the norm, its categorical force.' Charles Fried, *Right and Wrong* (Cambridge, MA: Harvard University Press, 1979) at p. 31. See also Georg Henrik von Wright, *Norm and Action: A Logical Enquiry* (London: Routledge & Kegan Paul, 1963).

73 See Andrew von Hirsch and Andrew Ashworth, *Proportionate Sentencing: Exploring the Principles* (Oxford: Oxford University Press, 2005) at p. 4. With respect to fair labeling more generally, see Dennis J. Baker, 'Constitutionalizing the Harm Principle,' (2008) 27(2) *Criminal Justice Ethics* 3 at pp. 4–10.

74 Feinberg uses a balancing process to decide whether the harm is ultimately of a kind that warrants a criminal law response. See Feinberg, *op. cit. supra*, fn. 8 at pp. 215–217.

75 H.L.A. Hart, *Punishment and Responsibility: Essays in the Philosophy of Law* (Oxford: Clarendon Press, 1968) at pp. 181–182.

not produce inherently bad consequences.[76] The wrongness requirement cannot be satisfied by merely satisfying the intentionality requirement. It can be satisfied by intentional harm-doing, because harm is *prima facie* a bad consequence, whether it is brought about by the intentional action of a moral agent or by an accident or natural disaster. When a person deliberately aims to harm others or recklessly brings about harm for others, it can be said that she deserves normative reproach and criminal condemnation for her wicked intentions and for any resulting or risked harm. It is her moral culpability that makes her bad act a *wrong* act, since the wrongdoer not only intentionally aims for a bad consequence but knows that she is doing so. The same cannot be said about a person who aims to bring about a good or neutral consequence such as the lesbians who shock and enlighten the bigot by exercising their right to be treated as equals.

The rule *actus non facit reum nisi mens sit rea* does not merely explain why a person is legally liable for a particular bad consequence from the *ex post* trial perspective, but also helps to explain the moral wrongness of certain activities from the *ex ante* criminalization perspective. In the above example, the kissing lesbians are legally culpable to the extent that they intentionally violated the law that banned lesbian kissing knowing that it was a crime to do so. But they are not morally condemnable[77] as opposed to being responsible for bringing about an illegal consequence, because they did not aim to harm others. In such a case, all the lawmaker can say is that they are legally liable for kissing in public because they chose to break the law and did in fact break the law. This is no different from enacting a law to prohibit young men from helping little old ladies onto public buses with their shopping. If a young man helps a little old lady onto the bus with her shopping, he would not only be morally responsible for assisting her, but also legally liable under such a law. Nonetheless, since he is responsible for a good consequence—assisting the elderly—he should receive moral praise not moral condemnation for his actions. Aiming for good or neutral consequences is not worthy of normative reproach or criminal condemnation.

There is a difference between being responsible for bringing a consequence about and being morally culpable[78] and condemnable for the particular consequence

---

76 See Georg Henrik von Wright, *The Varieties of Goodness* (London: Routledge & Kegan Paul, 1963) at pp. 114–135.

77 Jean Hampton notes: 'Our anger at [culpable wrongdoers] is a function of the fact that we see them as knowingly aligning themselves against morality. We despise their allegiance. It is their knowledge which makes them culpable. Our anger, however, is defused if we discover that their action did not arise out of this hateful allegiance, *e.g.* if it was performed in ignorance of the prohibition against it, or by accident.' Jean E. Hampton, 'The Nature of Morality,' (1989) 7(1) *Social Philosophy and Policy* 22 at p. 42.

78 'In a nutshell, the view is that a culpable agent is one who chooses to defy what she knows to be an authoritative moral command in the name of the satisfaction of one or more of her wishes, whose satisfaction the command forbids. She is disobedient in the face of *knowledge that obedience is expected*, and a rebel in the sense that she is attempting to establish something more to her liking as authoritative over her decision-making, rather

that was brought about. Furthermore, aiming for bad consequences of a *harmless* kind will not be sufficient for jailing people, even though such conduct could be regulated with penal fines in the right circumstances. The justice constraints on penal detention require that the consequences flowing from the actions that are to be criminalized be harmful (the objective harm constraint); that those bad consequences be brought about culpably (the objective wrongfulness constraint); and that the harm be sufficiently serious to warrant the type of penal penalty used (the proportionate punishment constraint). Clearly identifying the harmfulness of the potential consequences is important, because in the real world it is consequences (or potential consequences) that give the legislature guidance about whether certain actions warrant criminal condemnation and whether that condemnation should involve a jail term.

Duff[79] has argued that Feinberg's test for identifying the wrongness of harm-doing conflates the *ex post* legal culpability inquiry (that is, the *ex post* determination of guilt of a particular defendant) with the *ex ante* determination of moral wrongness that should precede criminalization decisions (that is, the requirement that the lawmaker demonstrate that a particular harmful act is wrongful before criminalizing it). Duff argues that: '[W]hat is at stake is not whether the wrong can be attributed to this agent as something for which he can be held criminally liable. To build inexcusability into the criteria of criminalization, as Feinberg does, thus conflates wrongdoing with culpability.'[80] But Duff overlooks the fact that wrongdoing involves culpability—harming others cannot be *wrong* unless some moral agent culpably chose to bring it about. Feinberg's approach is plausible once we consider the points I raised above concerning the wrongness of aiming for bad consequences. It should also be kept in mind, that from the *ex ante* criminalization perspective the lawmaker is merely stating in advance that those who intentionally aim to harm others will face criminal censure, because communally situated (rational) *knowers* have the capacity and sufficient empirical information to understand that bringing about (culpable) avoidable bad consequences for others is wrong.[81] The lawmaker is making a putative claim about culpability as an aspect of wrongness for the purposes of justifying *ex ante* criminalization decisions. It is clearly plausible to consider putative culpability as an aspect of wrongness—

---

than these moral commands.' Jean E. Hampton, 'Mens Rea,' (1990) 7(2) *Social Philosophy & Policy* 1 at p. 15.

79   R.A. Duff, 'Harms and Wrongs,' (2001–2002) 5 *Buffalo Criminal Law Review* 13 at p. 19. Duff seems to overlook the role of intentionality/culpability as an element of *ex ante* wrongness. This suggests that an earthquake could wrong others as opposed to merely harming them, but such a conclusion would be nonsense on stilts.

80   Ibid.

81   In Chapter 6 I discuss the normativity of just criminalization by drawing on inter-subjectively identifiable normative criteria. On inter-subjectivity more generally, see Christine M. Korsgaard, 'The Reasons We Can Share: An Attack on the Distinction Between Agent-Relative and Agent-Neutral Values,' (1993) 10(1) *Social Philosophy and Policy* 24.

the lawmaker makes an *ex ante* generalization that morally culpable harm-doing ought to be the business of the criminal law, because this type of harm-doing is wrongful in a way that unintentional harm-doing is not.[82] Generalizing from this proposition, lawmakers are able to label certain putative consequences as crimes in advance on the basis that it is wrongful for any person to aim to bring about those types of bad consequences.[83]

The lawmaker states in advance that if *x* intentionally rapes *y* without excuse or justification he will wrongfully harm his victim and thus there should be laws in place to make this a crime. It is for the courts to determine whether a particular individual has met the culpability requirements from an *ex post* perspective. The legislature merely assumes from an *ex ante* perspective that a culpable rape would be wrongful, harmful and should be criminalized. It does not presume that a particular individual is blameworthy, as individual guilt is determined by a court according to the facts of the case from an *ex post* perspective. The police might justifiably shoot dead a terrorist if they believe it will stop him from blowing up a train.[84] Likewise, *x* might kill *y* in self-defense. Whether she did is not the legislature's concern, but if she did so justifiably then there should be an appropriate defense available. It is important not to understate the dual and distinct functions that concepts such as intention, excuse and justification have both in determining *ex ante* moral wrongdoing (a general function) and *ex post* blameworthiness (a very specific and technical legal function). A bad consequence is nothing without moral culpability.[85] Intention is necessary in the elucidation of wrongness. In sum it is the union of harm and intention that makes the end consequences (or bad consequences that the agent attempted or risked bringing about) wrongful consequences rather than merely bad consequences. In the harm context, culpableness is the fulcrum between bad consequence and criminalization. From the *ex ante* or constitutional review perspective culpability is an objective criterion, which should be used along with harm as a measuring stick for determining the proportionate fairness of criminalization decisions.

---

82   'It is a noteworthy asymmetry between moral goodness and moral badness that the first presupposes that some good should be intended and, moreover, intended for its own sake, whereas the second only requires that some bad should be foreseen to follow from the act.' See Georg Henrik von Wright, *op. cit. supra*, fn. 76 at p. 130. See also Fried, *op. cit. supra*, fn. 72 at p. 41.

83   'The application of this ethical rationale to intentional harm doing is obvious. Intention implies some degree of pre-meditation; hence the maxim culpability is represented in the intentional commission of harm.' Hall, *op. cit. supra*, fn. 2 at pp. 133–134.

84   Kurt Baier, *The Moral Point of View* (Ithaca: Cornell University Press, 1964) at p. 194.

85   'A first approximation of the domain of categorical norms is the domain of actions. It is a good start to see what is condemned as wrong is not some consequence, some state of affairs (a dead man, a false belief—these things are bad, not wrong) but the action which includes its morally relevant features within the description of the action itself.' Fried, *op. cit. supra*, fn. 72 at p. 16.

Wronging Non-human Animals

If we are going to take harm seriously it is necessary to make sure that the wrongful harm justification for criminalization is formulated to catch all those acts that are being criminalized because of their harmfulness (especially in cases where harm provides the best objective guidance for ascertaining why the criminal law should be invoked). Feinberg's formulation of harm does not explain the criminalizableness of wantonly destroying non-human animals. Harm is a particularly useful objective concept, not only because it can be conceptualized and understood by judges, politicians and members of the public, but because it has the widest reach as an objective justification for invoking the criminal law. In most cases the criminal law is being invoked to prevent some kind of perceived harm, even if it is not always of an objective nature. If a criminal law has been enacted to prevent objective harm, then the harm criterion ought to be used to explain the fairness of the decision to criminalize. It makes no sense to resort to other abstract philosophical explanations[86] that could leave legislators and judges totally bewildered, if the less problematic concept of harm is available and it is harm that is being criminalized.

If the harm constraint is to reach its full potential as a useful check on unfair criminalization, then it needs to be reformulated to protect non-human subjects from objective harm. A major shortfall of Feinberg's formulation of the Harm Principle is its narrow theory of wrongness. Feinberg's theory of wrongness only explains the wrongness of intentionally (unjustifiably/inexcusably) setting back human interests. Non-human animals do not have moral rights as defined in Feinberg's formulation of the Harm Principle.[87] The Harm Principle could be applied in those situations where humans have an interest in preserving animals such as farm animals that form a part of their property or a collective interest in preserving the environment,[88] but Feinberg's formulation of criminalizable harm is only feasible when a moral connection can be drawn between the harm and some tangible *human interest*.[89] It applies where there is a clear connection between the

---

86   Arthur Ripstein, 'Beyond the Harm Principle,' (2006) 34(3) *Philosophy & Public Affairs* 215. See also the elaborate filtering process proposed in Jonathan Schonsheck, *On Criminalization* (London: Kluwer Academic Publishers, 1994). Most judges and legislators would struggle to gain guidance from Ripstein's theory of freedom, as it does not consider bad consequences. Tangible consequences are measurable in a way that freedom is not. For an irrelevant sense in which freedom is measurable, see Ian Carter, *A Measure of Freedom* (Oxford: Oxford University Press, 1999).

87   Feinberg states welfare interests are the requisites of a human's well-being and invasions of those interests 'are grounds for valid claims against others (moral rights) *par excellence*.' Feinberg, Vol. I, *op. cit. supra*, fn. 8 at p. 112.

88   *Id.* at pp. 227–232.

89   Feinberg postulates that the notion of proxies can be invoked to give animals rights in the same way as infants have rights. Joel Feinberg, 'The Rights of Animals and Unborn Generations,' in William T. Blackstone, *Philosophy and Environmental Crisis* (Athens: University of Georgia Press: 1974) at p. 51. But this argument is less than convincing, because

harm-doer's actions and a setback to human interests. It would not be difficult to show that our collective interests are wrongfully set back by environmental crimes, such as dumping toxic waste into waterways.[90] However, humans do not have an interest in protecting animals that are commonly regarded as pests, such as foxes.[91] It is difficult to see how foxhunting sets back the collective or individual interests of human agents.[92] It is doubtful that we would have an interest in prohibiting foxhunting, dog fighting or bullfighting. Foxes are often culled for the benefit of other species and bulls are killed in large numbers to provide pet meat. Foxhunting and bullfighting do not amount to a wrongful setback to our collective or individual interests, as we do not have a stake or interest in protecting foxes or bulls.

Under Feinberg's scheme non-human animals would not be protected from harm, as they have no right not to be harmed. Likewise, harming non-humans does not necessarily result in harm for humans. For instance, humans are neither wronged nor harmed by bullfighting or foxhunting. Feinberg calls this type of harm a free-floating evil because it is an evil that does not impact on our interests.[93] Feinberg argues that free-floating evils are inherently evil 'despite the fact that they have no adverse effects on anyone's well-being.'[94] He describes the extinction of a species as a free-floating evil.[95] Feinberg acknowledged that his account of wrongful harm could not be used to explain the fairness or unfairness of all criminalization decisions in this context. According to Feinberg, free-floating evils are hardly ever worthy of criminalization. 'The qualifying words "hardly ever" and "perhaps never" reflect the conscientious liberal's inevitable wavering in the face of the legal moralist's strongest counterexamples ... however, we can define liberalism cautiously as the view that as a class, harm and offense prevention are far and away the best [critical moral] reasons that can be produced in support of criminal prohibitions, and the only ones that frequently outweigh the case for liberty.'[96] So what is wrong with wiping out a species and or using unnecessary cruelty to destroy common pests such as foxes?

---

equal rights for animals would be over-expansive. Notably, Feinberg does not develop this theory in his *Harmless Wrongdoing* volume. Cf. Christopher Heath Wellman, 'Feinberg's Two Concepts of Rights,' (2005) 11(3) *Legal Theory* 213. See also George W. Rainbolt, 'Two Interpretations of Feinberg's Theory of Rights,' (2005) 11(3) *Legal Theory* 227.

90   Feinberg, Vol. I, *op. cit. supra*, fn. 8 at pp. 227–232.
91   The *Hunting Act 2004* (U.K.) criminalized foxhunting.
92   'In the primary sense of harm, only beings with interests can be harmed, and that account excludes mere things, artifacts and lower animals.' Feinberg, Vol. IV, *op. cit. supra*, fn. 59 at pp. 22–23.
93   *Id.* at 20.
94   *Ibid.*
95   For example, Feinberg claims that our interests would not be set back by the extinction of the Colorado cave fish, which has existed almost unchanged for millions of years in the dark isolation of their shallow cavern pools. *Id.* at p. 24.
96   'The other principles state considerations that are at most sometimes (but rarely) good reasons, depending for example on exactly what the non-grievance is ... Indeed there

We do not yet know what role each species plays or which keys the various species hold for ensuring our own survival on the earth. Arguably, allowing a species to become extinct would produce bad consequences for the future of humanity as well as for the fine balance found in the various ecosystems which we all have an interest in maintaining. It would not be too controversial to argue that we have a collective interest in maintaining the various species that continue to exist on the planet. However, reducing fox numbers does not fall within this category. Foxhunting seems to be a free-floating evil. Feinberg does not explain why it would be fair to invoke the criminal law to prevent free-floating evils.[97] Feinberg's departure from harm in the endangered species/animal context is incongruous because clearly the wrongness of wantonly harming animals has to have something to do with the actual harm-doing involved. A departure from the harm criteria may be necessary to explain the objective criminalizableness of exhibitionism,[98] but I am of the view that the fairness of criminalizing *wanton* harm to animals can be explained within the wrongful harm paradigm. We have deep conventional understandings about wanton cruelty and there is no need to resort to critical morality to explain the wrongness of wantonly torturing animals.

Sentient creatures such as animals have basic interests[99] as do humans when it comes to avoiding death and gross pain and their instincts are geared towards harm avoidance. The zebra does not sit and wait for the lion to pounce, but rather it desperately tries to evade the lion's attack. Feinberg would agree that subjecting a cow to unnecessary electric shocks would harm it, but he would conclude that the cow does not have a moral *right* not to be harmed.[100] Does wantonly harming animals constitute an objectively bad consequence? In Chapter 6, I argue that objective harms cannot be identified by drawing on so-called realist or critical moral theories, but it may be possible to identify conduct that is objectively harmful in a culturally contingent sense. Objectivity can be determined in a rough fashion through a public deliberation process that focuses 'on normatively relevant evidence, reasons, arguments and standards of the merit of them.'[101] What might

---

are some extraordinary, and up to now only hypothetical examples of non-grievance evils (neither harms nor offenses, nor right-violations of any kind) that are so serious that even the liberal ... will concede that the prevention would be a good reason for criminalization.' *Id.* at p. 323.

97 *Id.* at p. 324.
98 See the discussion in Chapter 6.
99 See generally David DeGrazia, *Taking Animals Seriously: Mental Life and Moral Status* (Cambridge: Cambridge University Press, 1996).
100 Feinberg, Vol. IV, *op. cit. supra*, fn. 59 at pp. 22–23.
101 'The process is objective to the extent that reasons, evidence, and arguments that are deliberated upon and that bring participants to judgment are the relevant ones ... The project is to justify one's judgment to others, showing them that the judgments are reasonable and responsible in terms one sincerely believes all can recognize and affirm. Normative deliberation is regarded as a process of publicly offering public reasons—reasons which are not merely reasons *I personally* find persuasive, nor reasons I believe that *you* would

such a process establish with respect to unnecessarily harming animals? Wiggins notes that Bertrand Russell once wrote: 'I cannot see how to refute the arguments for the subjectivity of ethical values, but I find myself incapable of believing that all that is wrong with wanton cruelty is that I don't like it.'[102] Wiggins argues that the wrongness of cruelty is that it does not warrant liking given our actual *collectively scrutinized responses*. 'Those responses are directed at cruelty, and at what cruelty itself consists in on the level of motive, intention and outcome.'[103] Public deliberation in accordance with the dictates of reason would allow us to objectively conclude that intentionally subjecting animals to *unnecessary* cruelty is wrong. We could also reason that the outcome of which the harm-doer is fully aware and knowingly aims to bring about has objectively bad consequences for the affected animals. Animals may not be the bearers of rights, but humans, in light of the above analysis, would have non-correlative duties not to *intentionally* harm animals without justification.

Raz's[104] interest theory holds that non-human animals may not have rights as such, but that humans have certain duties *vis-à-vis* non-human animals. Animals are clearly harmed in an objective sense when they are killed and tortured and they are wrongfully harmed because humans have a moral duty[105] not to wantonly torture or destroy animals. It is because the harmer knows that her harm-doing will result in a bad and avoidable consequence for a helpless animal, that it can be explained to her that it is wrong to do so. Intentionally violating duties not to harm wantonly harm animals is wrong, and this account fills the *lacuna* in Feinberg's rights-oriented theory of criminalizable harm. The non-correlative duty theory deals with the narrowness of the Feinberg's theory, which is influenced by the Hohfeldian correlativity thesis between rights and duties. The Raz/Kramer interest-type theory explains the wrongness of breaching the duties we have not to

---

find persuasive (but I could not endorse), but reasons *we share*, or after conversation and argument, we *could come to share*.' Gerald J. Postema, 'Objectivity Fit for Law,' in Brian Leiter, *Objectivity in Law and Morals* (Cambridge: Cambridge University Press, 2001) at pp. 118–119.

102 David Wiggins, *Needs, Values, Truth* (Oxford: Clarendon Press, 3rd ed. 1998) at p. 185 citing Bertrand Russell, 'Notes on Philosophy January 1960,' (1960) 35 *Philosophy* at pp. 146–147.

103 'To be sure, we should not care about these things, these things would not impinge as they do upon us, if our responses were not there to be called upon. In the presence of a good reason to call them in question, we should not be able to trust them or take them too much for granted about the well-foundedness of the properties they are keyed to. But, in total absence of such reason, it will be question-begging for Russell simply to remind himself as thoroughly and vividly as he can of just what it is that he dislikes, abhors, detests … about cruelty and its ancient and hideous marks.' *Id.* at pp. 210–211.

104 Raz, *op. cit. supra*, fn. 20 at Chapter 7.
105 *Ibid.*

unnecessarily harm animals.[106] As Marmor[107] notes, 'According to the Hohfeldian tradition, acknowledging A's duty towards B, entails the correlative right of B. Hence the embarrassing question arises, whether animals or endangered species have rights? No such question necessarily arises, however, under the interest theory. The latter is compatible with the view which accords us duties towards creatures or entities that are incapable of having rights.'

We cannot just dismiss harm as an element of the justification for criminalizing wanton harm to animals, given that harm prevention is the aim of the criminal law in such cases. But animals are not entitled to the same consideration as humans.[108] Farming that does not involve unnecessary cruelty would be permissible. Likewise, there is no reason why scientists could not use animals in experiments so long as the animals are not subjected to torture or other unnecessarily cruel experiments. Researchers should take reasonable steps to avoid causing unnecessary pain to the animals that are being used for experimental purposes. Bullfighting clearly involves wanton cruelty and therefore would not be permissible as its purpose is less than compelling. As for foxhunting, it is a way of culling a common pest and to the extent that it serves that purpose it would be permissible, so long as it could be shown to be an efficient and compassionate form of extermination. If the scientific evidence demonstrated that fox numbers were too high and that the use of hounds was not a cruel form of extermination, then there would be no grounds for criminalizing foxhunting. However, the evidence would have to demonstrate that using a gun would not be a more efficient and compassionate way of exterminating foxes.

The complexities of determining the type of animals that should be protected would be a major project, which I do not wish to explore here. Clearly, we would not want to criminalize a little boy for jumping on ants.[109] My aim has been merely to demonstrate that the harm criterion can be used to criminalize the bad consequence of unnecessarily torturing and mistreating animals. I do not intend to

---

106 Kramer notes: 'The Interest Theory leads to quite a different stance. Its focus is on the preservation of well-being rather than on the exercise of choice, which enables it to leave open the possibility of ascribing rights to animals and dead people and mentally incapacitated people.' See Kramer, *op. cit. supra*, fn. 20. We would have a duty to avoid setting back various aspects of their well-being.

107 Andrei Marmor, 'On the Limits of Rights,' (1997) 16(1) *Law and Philosophy* 1 at p. 6.

108 Cf. Peter Carruthers, *The Animal Issue: Moral Theory in Practice* (Cambridge: Cambridge University Press, 1992).

109 See DeGrazia, *op. cit. supra*, fn. 99. I am not totally convinced by DeGrazia's distinction between higher order animals such as dolphins and apes and lower order animals such as insects and rats. I am of the view that the focus needs to be on the type of overall damage involved and whether it involves a good or bad purpose, that is, the necessary extermination of a pest as opposed to wanton destruction. It is one thing to cull kangaroos to prevent them from starving and something entirely different to wantonly smash up 50 beehives belonging to a rare kind of honeybee.

apply it to countless individual cases. I limit my analysis to noting that the criminal law involves censure and hard treatment and should only be used to prevent grave cruelty that is totally unnecessary. Legitimate harm-doing such as culling, farming and so forth would be permissible so long as the least cruel means were used to achieve these types of legitimate goals. The cruelty would have to involve a fairly grave kind of purposeless harm-doing to warrant a criminal law response. We would not want to criminalize a cowboy for putting a hot brand on a few calves or for castrating the bull calves without anesthetic. Farming arguably prevents famine for animal species and thus the problems that Malthus envisaged with respect to unchecked human population growth. In the end, it is a matter of evaluating the harmfulness of the bad consequence in the individual categories of mistreatment and the purpose it aims to serve. If its purpose were to deliberately subject an animal to cruelty, then the criminal law would be an appropriate response.

Non-objective and Objective Conceptions of Harm

If lawmakers are going to take the harm criterion seriously, then they should only be influenced by objective accounts of harm. Non-objective harm arguments are claims of harm that do not in fact result in actual harm. In recent years lawmakers, motivated by the political advantages of engaging in penal populism,[110] have used various harm arguments to support criminalizing harmless activities. For example, in both the United States and United Kingdom[111] passive beggars have been targeted, even though this type of activity does not cause any tangible harm to passers-by. After all, we are talking about passive begging in open places, not aggressive begging near ATMs, *etc.*[112] The United Kingdom government has relied on a number of non-objective harm arguments in its crackdown on begging, but it has made no attempt to demonstrate that passive begging does in fact cause wrongful harm. Other examples of innocuous activities that have been dressed up as harmful in the United States include feeding homeless people,[113] fornicating,[114] possessing sex toys,[115] possessing marijuana for personal use,[116] attending strip shows,[117] *etc.*

---

110 Julian V. Roberts *et al.*, *Populism and Public Opinion: Lessons from Five Countries* (Oxford: Oxford University Press, 2003).
111 *Respect and Responsibility—Taking a Stand Against Anti-Social Behaviour* (London: Home Office, White Paper Cm 5778, 2003) at paragraphs 1.8, 3.40–3.44.
112 *Together, Action Plan* (London: Home Office, 2003) at p. 10.
113 Randal C. Archibold, 'Las Vegas Makes it Illegal to Feed Homeless in Parks,' (New York: *New York Times*, 28 July 2006).
114 See for example, Associate Justice Scalia's support for the retention of such crimes in *Lawrence v. Texas*, 539 U.S. 558 (2003) at pp. 586 and 592–594.
115 *Williams v. Pryor*, 240 F. 3d 944, 949 (2001).
116 *Malmo-Levine* [2003] S.C.C. 74.
117 *Barnes v. Glen Theatre, Inc.*, 501 U. S. 560, 575–576 (1991).

Interestingly, the Devlin-type non-objective harm argument also surfaced recently in Hong Kong where it was used to justify invoking the criminal law to protect *consenting* adults from the so-called dangers of viewing obscene photos on the Internet. It is difficult to see how a person who willingly views photos of naked people harms herself in an objective sense. The Hong Kong case provides us with a good example of a non-objective harm argument. The Devlin-type of non-objective harm argument permeates the Hong Kong *Control of Obscene and Indecent Articles Ordinance*.[118] Section 10 of that enactment holds that: 'In determining whether an article is obscene or indecent or whether any matter publicly displayed is indecent ... a Tribunal should have regard to: (a) standards of morality, decency and propriety that are generally accepted by reasonable members of the community.' Who are these reasonable members of the community? The young, the old, the poor, the expatriates, the middle class, the artists, the academics; it is not clear. In Hong Kong, the anachronistic reasoning found in the old English case law [119] is used to interpret and define obscene and indecent.[120] '"Obscenity" is not confined to a tendency to depravity and corruption of a sexual nature. It encompasses material that tends to induce violence.'[121] The courts have held that the dictionary meaning of obscenity and indecency can be employed to determine obscenity and indecency: *i.e.*, 'disgusting, filthy, lewd, loathsome, repulsive or shocking for "obscene"; and unbecoming, in extremely bad taste, unseemly, offending against propriety or delicacy, or immodest for "indecent."'[122]

In *HKSAR v. Hiroyuki Takeda* [1998] 1 HKLRD 48, the Court held that a harsh deterrence sentence was appropriate for an offender who had published obscene

---

118 See, for example, the recent scandal in Hong Kong, where obscene photos of celebrities were taken from a star's computer that had been sent for repair. The photos were subsequently uploaded onto the World Wide Web, which led to a hasty prosecution where the defendant was denied bail on the basis that the offense was of a very serious nature. Dennis J. Baker, 'The Sense and Nonsense of Criminalizing Transfers of Obscene Material,' (2008) 26 *Singapore Law Review* 126. See also Keith Bradsher, 'Internet Sex Video Case Stirs Free-Speech Issues in Hong Kong,' (New York: *New York Times*, February 13, 2008).

119 See *R. v. Gibson* [1991] 1 All E.R. 649, where the defendant was convicted for outraging public decency by displaying earrings made out of human fetuses in an art gallery.

120 The legislation is also interpreted with reference to a number of anachronistic conceptions of public morality as set down in English and New Zealand case law. It is noted in the Hong Kong Archbold manual that: 'The English statutory definition is partially incorporated under Hong Kong law and certain provisions of the Hong Kong legislation were modeled after the *New Zealand Indecent Publications Act 1965* (N.Z.).' See Archbold Hong Kong, *Criminal Law, Pleading, Evidence and Practice* (Hong Kong: Sweet & Maxwell Asia, 2007), at p. 1820.

121 *Id.* at p. 1822.

122 *Id.*

materials because such a sentence reflected the 'abhorrence of society.' The English cases also put a particular emphasis on using indecent and obscene materials to corrupt others. In the United States in *Stanley v. Georgia*[123] the Supreme Court summed up the most basic argument against the corruption of public morals contention: 'the State may no more prohibit mere possession of obscene matter on the ground that it may lead to antisocial conduct than it may prohibit possession of chemistry books on the ground that they may lead to the manufacture of homemade spirits.' Criminalizing innocent activities merely because it might help to prevent consenting others from being corrupted is not an account of objective harm.[124] It is worth noting that most of those who were outraged and offended by the recent scandal involving nude photos of celebrities in Hong Kong never saw the photos. Society's so-called majority was offended by the bare knowledge that others were choosing to download such images for their own use.

A plethora of these types of non-objective harm arguments also permeate criminalization decisions in the United States. Consequently, a leading scholar Bernard Harcourt[125] has concluded that the liberal Harm Principle no longer plays a dominant role in Anglo-American criminalization debates. Harcourt notes that during the 1960s and 1970s the Harm Principle was fairly influential, but that by the 1990s it was being used to support a proliferation of conservative harm arguments.[126] Many of these non-objective harm arguments are based on poorly

---

123   394 U.S. 557 (1969) at p. 567.

124   The English cases justify criminalization by holding that the offensive material might corrupt others (lead them to self-depravity). *R. v. Calder and Boyars Ltd.* [1969] 1 Q.B. 151; *Knuller (Publishing, Printing and Promotions) Ltd. v. DPP* [1973] A.C. 453. There are four core reasons why such arguments can be dismissed. Firstly, such a claim is a remote harm argument and will only be valid if a normative link can be drawn between the influencer's activities and the ultimate harm that is likely to be brought on the corrupted party: it would be unjust to hold x responsible for merely influencing y's potential (paternalistic) self-harming choices (for example, where x uses a book sold to her by y, which advocates drug-taking; it is x's independent choice that causes any resulting harm). Cf. *John Calder (Publications) Ltd. v. Powell* [1965] 1 Q.B. 509. Secondly, there is no empirical connection to support such claims (*i.e.*, it has not been shown that merely supplying information about drug use is a but-for cause of addiction, or that nude photos and sex videos cause widespread promiscuity). Thirdly, selling pornographic movies with adult actors, nude photos of adults, a lady's directory, *etc.* to *consenting adults* is harmless and inoffensive because those who seek such products consent to receiving the material. Fourthly, such arguments are paternalistic (they aim is to protect people from their own autonomous choices). I deal with remote harm criminalization in the next chapter. For a compelling account of the wrongness of using paternalism as a justification for criminalization see Joel Feinberg, *The Moral Limits of the Criminal Law: Harm to Self* (New York: Oxford University Press, Vol. III, 1986).

125   Bernard E. Harcourt, *Illusion of Order, The False Promise of Broken Windows Policing* (Cambridge, MA: Harvard University Press, 2001) at pp. 185 *et seq.*

126   *Id.* at p. 184.

scrutinized empirical claims and anecdotal evidence.[127] By turning to conservative harm arguments lawmakers have been able to label disadvantaged people as dangerous people. Those people who were in earlier times considered to be the unfortunate in society (a nuisance to some but unthreatening)—such as vagrants, beggars, drunks, drug addicts, loiterers and so forth—are now 'considered the agents of crime and neighborhood decline.'[128] The principal justification for criminalization is no longer offense or immorality, but harm—the harm that these misdemeanors [allegedly] ... cause.'[129] For the purposes of criminalization it should be shown that the conduct causes harm in an objective sense. Harcourt[130] suggests that the Harm Principle has collapsed, but this is an erroneous claim. The Harm Principle has not collapsed, but lawmakers have never made a distinction between *objective* and *non-objective* harm and have recently failed to give the former any meaningful consideration. Coupled with this, there is no evidence to suggest that non-objective harm arguments were not as prevalent in previous decades and centuries.

At the other end of the scale seriously grave objective harms often go unchecked. An issue that has been focused on by philosophers and penal theorists for some decades is the disproportional criminalization of crimes committed by the disadvantaged in society. Some take the view that a class-based political system dominated by populist penal rhetoric is one reason why the activities of the socially deprived in society account for the bulk of all criminal offenses. It has been claimed that lawmakers tend to overemphasize the harmfulness of crimes committed by the poor and are inclined to label corporate harm as a regulatory wrong rather than as a criminal wrong.[131] Reiman argues that crime is an artificially constructed social reality, which is controlled by the powerful in society to protect their interests at the expense of the less fortunate in society. The nucleus of his thesis is summed up in the following passage:[132]

> [T]he criminal justice system fails to reduce crime while making it look as if crime is the work of the poor. It does this in a way that conveys the image that the real danger to decent, law-abiding people comes from below them, rather than from above them, on the economic ladder. This image sanctifies the *status quo* with its disparities of wealth, privilege, and opportunity and thus serves the interests of the rich and powerful—the very ones who could change criminal justice policy if they were really unhappy with it.

---

127 Bernard E. Harcourt, 'Collapse of the Harm Principle,' (1999–2000) 90 *Journal of Criminal Law and Criminology* 109.
128 Ibid.
129 Ibid.
130 Id. at p. 110.
131 Reiman, *op. cit. supra*, fn. 11 at p. 123.
132 Id. at 7.

Reiman acknowledges that the public need to be protected from harms committed by the poor (*e.g.*, shoplifting, mugging, robbery and so forth), but argues that these crimes are not the only source of serious harm. He cites a comprehensive set of American statistics to support his claim that there is a greater chance of being disabled, injured, maimed or killed in a workplace accident or by shoddy emergency medical[133] services than by aggravated assault or homicide.[134] Reiman notes that such acts are generally not listed in the FBI's index of serious crimes. He notes that the public loses 'more money from price fixing and monopolistic practices and from consumer deception and embezzlement than from any property crimes in the FBI's Index combined.'[135] Some of the corporate mismanagement which caused the Credit Crunch provides a contemporary example. Corporations and governments make numerous decisions that they know or suspect will result in death or harm, but criminalization has been disproportionately aimed at the disadvantaged. Scores of unscrupulous decisions made knowingly and recklessly by both corporations and governments have exposed employees to horrendous dangers and have caused many deaths. For example, many people have lost their lives from 'asbestos, thalidomide; use of soldiers to test mustard gas or effects of atomic bomb radiation,' mining and construction disasters, *etc.*[136] It is not so much that these harms are labeled as harmless, but rather it is that they are labeled as accidents. It will not always be possible to fairly impute blame for these types of harms to individual agents, but that does not prevent a robust regulatory form of criminalization being invoked to prevent corporate and governmental harm-doing.[137] In the next chapter, I argue that vigorous efforts should be made to impute blame to those who are sufficiently connected to the harm-doing.

The aforementioned injustice is exacerbated by prosecutorial practices that target certain wrongdoers vehemently, while using *second chance mechanisms*[138] that allow certain wrongdoers to pass through a filtering process where the criminal law is used as a last resort. Objective harms such as petty larceny are prosecuted vehemently whilst corporate harm-doing is often couched in terms that

---

133 In England medical negligence would come within the purview of the criminal law. See *R. v. Adomako* [1995] 1 A.C. 171. However, it is it is not clear whether medical negligence is readily detected and prosecuted.

134 Reiman, *op. cit. supra*, fn. 11 at p. 55.

135 *Id.* at pp. 1–20. See also James Gobert and Maurice Punch, *Rethinking Corporate Crime* (London: Butterworths LexisNexis, 2003).

136 Katherine S. Williams, *Textbook on Criminology* (Oxford: Oxford University Press, 2001) at p. 21.

137 Wells, *op. cit. supra*, fn. 14 at pp. 146 *et seq.*

138 I use this term to refer to those mechanisms that allow a tax evader and others to receive a warning or a civil penalty before the criminal law is even considered. This allows such offenders to play the system knowing that the criminal law will only be used after they have used up their first chance: their warning or civil penalty.

make it difficult to get a prosecution off the ground.[139] Ashworth lists a number of alternatives to prosecution that are available to avoid criminalization. For example, he notes that: 'the Inland Revenue brings only a few hundred prosecutions each year, relying chiefly on *warnings* and on its power to impose civil penalties on tax-evaders. No warnings are available to provide common thieves with a chance or an option to avoid criminalization in the first instance. Similarly, inspectors working for the Health and Safety Executive issue far more enforcement notices than they initiate prosecutions—in the U.K. in 1998–1999, 10,844 notices compared with 1,797 prosecutions.'[140] In these kinds of cases 'the criminal law is very much in the background, and the criminal process is experienced by relatively few of those caught breaking the law.'[141]

A recent Australian example of prosecutorial discretion being used to allow a wealthy and influential individual to avoid charges of insider trading can be seen in the Vizard[142] case. In that case, Vizard allegedly profited from engaging in insider trading. Arguably, his crime would have caused greater economic harm to those affected than the average pickpocket causes to her victims. There was no clear justification for the prosecuting authority's preference to proceed under the civil penalty provisions rather than via criminal prosecution. It was suggested that there was insufficient evidence to mount a criminal prosecution, because a key witness refused to testify against Mr. Vizard. However, this does not explain why a subpoena could not have been issued compelling the witness to testify, and why the prosecuting authorities could not have applied to cross-examine the witness under section 38 of the *Evidence Act 1995* (Cth.). Goldsmith *et al.* argue that, 'Vizard should have been prosecuted for the criminal offense of insider trading, but was able to escape criminal charge.'[143]

In an earlier Australian case, Peter Reith, a senior government minister in the Federal government let his son run up AU$50,000 worth of phone calls on a telephone account that was provided to the Minister for ministerial purposes.[144] The Minister claimed that he gave his son the phone-card and the pin number

---

139 Andrew Ashworth, *Principles of Criminal Law* (Oxford: Oxford University Press, 4th ed. 2003) at p. 38.

140 *Ibid.*

141 *Ibid.*

142 *Australian Securities and Investments Commission v. Vizard* [2005] F.C.A. 1037.

143 Andrew Goldsmith *et al.*, *Crime and Justice: A Guide to Criminology* (Sydney: Thomson Lawbook Co., 3rd ed. 2006) at pp. 162–163.

144 Margo Kingston, 'More on the Reith Telecard Affair,' (Sydney: *Sydney Morning Herald*, Monday 30 October 2000). See also Patrick Barkham, 'Australian Government Rocked by Phonecard Sleaze Row,' (London: *Guardian Unlimited*, Monday 30 October 2000). Recently, in Britain, there has been a parliamentary expense scandal involving around 200 MPs claiming approximately £500,000 for expenses such as *personal* mortgages that did not exist, and more bizarrely, for having a moat cleaned around an MP's castle. It was obvious to all concerned that many of the claims were dishonest and fraudulent as they had no connection with the genuine expenses involved in working as an MP, but to date no

for the card, and that it was his son and his son's friends who misused the card. The Minister offered to pay the money back in lieu of being charged for criminal wrongdoing. The prosecution did not bother to charge the Minister or his son for theft or fraud.[145] It is doubtful that a common shoplifter or a car thief would avoid prosecution so easily. Clearly, these types of serious harms come within the purview of Feinberg's definition of objectively wrongful harm. The Harm Principle cannot be taken seriously unless it acts as more than a sufficient condition when serious harm-doing is involved. Serious (intentional/unjustifiable/inexcusable) harm-doing should be criminalized and prosecuted consistently otherwise the public will lose respect for the criminal law. A criminalization process that allows some offenders to circumvent criminalization for serious harm-doing, while criminalizing others for trivial harm-doing, would not only be unfair and unjust, but would also bring the criminal law into disrepute.[146] The focus in this book is on the justice of the justifications that are used to justify criminalization decisions. I do not want to explore the literature on the litany of practices that conspire to produce the unjust criminalization phenomena that we are currently experiencing.[147] However, the brief overview provided above tells us the focus must be on objective harm and on the mechanisms that should be used to fairly impute that type of harm to individual or corporate wrongdoers when it is fair and necessary to do so. There also needs to be parity between labeling and enforcement in the various categories of criminality.

Constitutionalizing the Harm Principle

In the foregoing sections I have outlined objective harm and its potential reach as a criterion for determining the fairness of criminalization. In this section, I present the central thesis of this chapter, which is that a constitutionalized *harm criterion* could ensure that people are not jailed unless they deserve it. Harm provides a general objective standard for determining the proportional fairness of criminalizing various activities. The harm criterion is particularly apt for considering the proportionality of criminal punishments, because punishment harms those who are punished. Unlike criminalization generally, wrongful harm-doing provides the only moral and constitutional justification for criminalization that carries jail terms. Imprisonment harms prisoners in a grave way, so people should not be imprisoned unless they have caused proportionate harm to others.

---

charges have been laid against any of those involved. See Sarah Lyall, 'British MPs Say Speaker Has Lost Moral Authority,' (*New York Times*, May 19, 2009, on page A12).
    145   Goldsmith *et al.*, op. *cit. supra*, fn. 143.
    146   See generally Beetham, *op. cit. supra*, fn. 15.
    147   For an excellent discussion of the miscellany of ways in which the criminal law's reach has been extended in the United States, see Douglas Husak, *Overcriminalization: The Limits of the Criminal Law* (New York: Oxford University Press, 2008).

The sufficient conditions for sending an offender to jail are culpability somewhere on the culpability continuum[148] and a bad action/act/consequence of a harmful or dangerous kind. The lawmaker would need to demonstrate from the *ex ante* perspective that proposed offenses carrying jail sentences are a proportionate and fair way of dealing with the wrongs involved. Since jail (including short sentences of a few days) involves hard treatment (seriously harmful consequences for the prisoner) harm to others would be the only bad consequence of sufficient weight to justify a jail sentence. Jailing people for wrongful behavior that has harmless consequences would be an unjust and disproportionate response.[149]

The purpose of constitutionalizing the harm criterion is not only to ensure that it is used as a yardstick for measuring the proportionality of criminalization (is the criminal law a proportionate response for the given societal problem being tackled), but also to provide a constitutional constraint for measuring the fairness of sentences that are attached to *prima facie* legitimate criminal laws. In this section, I argue that the harm criterion should be recognized as a constitutional constraint against disproportionate punishment. It could be used to prevent the government from jailing offenders for engaging in harmless wrongdoing. My discussion in the remainder of this chapter focuses on the legitimacy of criminalization that is enforced with *jail sentences* rather than on the wider issue of the legitimacy of criminalization. I argue that intentional/reckless harm-doing to others provides an objective justification for sending a wrongdoer to jail. Jailing a person who harms others can be reconciled with justice and fairness so long as she has caused objective harm and the harm is sufficiently serious to warrant penal detention. I also aim to demonstrate that the courts are equipped to ascertain the harmfulness of conduct for this purpose. Coupled with this, I attempt to show that the U.S. Supreme Court has in the past recognized the proportionate punishment requirement as a constitutional principle of justice. Future courts could use objective criteria such as harm and moral culpability to determine proportionality.

---

148 Somewhere on the gross negligence, recklessness and purpose continuum, *etc.*

149 The relevant fairness constraint here is proportionality in punishment. See generally, von Hirsch and Ashworth, *op. cit. supra*, fn. 73. The United States Supreme Court has recognized the proportionality fairness constraint for close to a century in both non-capital and capital punishment cases, see *Weems v. United States*, 217 U.S. 349 (1910); *Robinson v. California*, 360 U.S. 660 (1962) and *Solem v. Helm*, 463 U.S. 277 (1983). Cf. *Harmelin v. Michigan*, 501 U.S. 957 (1991) where the majority erroneously refused to follow a century of precedent. The principle has also been taken seriously in a number of capital punishment cases, see *Woodson v. North Carolina*, 428 U.S. 280 (1976); *Coker v. Georgia*, 433 U.S. 584 (1977); and *Kennedy v. Louisiana*, 554 U.S. 407 (2008).

Wrongful Harm as a Normative Justification for Penal Detention

Retribution in the penal detention context works as a constraint against unbridled punishment. Although the general aim of the criminal law is to deter and prevent wrongdoing to others, deterrence through the communication[150] of censure supplies only a prudential reason for obedience. More importantly, it does not supply an objective justification for individualized criminalization and punishment. The moral justification for labeling a wrongdoer's actions as criminal and for sending her to jail when her actions have sufficiently harmful consequences is that she deserves to be punished when her actions aim for bad consequences for others. The fact that she and others like her may be deterred from engaging in similar wrongdoing is an incidental *aim* or *function* of the institution of punishment and criminalization rather than a *moral justification* for *personalized* punishment for personal wrongdoing. The instrumental[151] crime prevention function of criminalization and punishment is fair and just to the extent that it is necessary to have institutions and mechanisms such as the police, the courts, the criminal law, and prison sentences to protect genuine human interests.[152] This may explain the legitimacy of having a system of criminalization and punishment, but it does not explain when that system should be used and to what extent it should be used. To determine whether it is fair to criminalize conduct or to use a jail sentence to enforce an instance of criminalization, the lawmaker has to consider why a given activity is worthy of criminalization and punishment.

Tasioulas argues that von Hirsch's theory of punishment is a hybrid theory incorporating both consequential (crime prevention) and retributive (just

---

150 Andrew von Hirsch, *Censure and Sanctions* (Oxford: Oxford University Press, 1993). See also Lucas, *op. cit. supra*, fn. 61.

151 The general consequential forward-looking justification (crime prevention) for having an institution of punishment and criminalization is not an objective moral justification for *individualized* criminalization and punishment. However, it does provide a liberal democracy with a general justification for having a system of criminalization and punishment. This general utilitarian forward-looking justification, while inherently good because it generally aims at preserving human well-being, is distinct and independent from the *objective moral* justification for individualized criminalization and punishment, which is based on individual wrongdoing: that is, the backward-looking justification concerning just deserts (from the *ex ante* perspective the backward-looking process is only putative, as the lawmaker asks what if *x* brings about consequence *y*). Moore argues that retributive punishment in itself is inherently good regardless of whether it also prevents crime. See Michael Moore, *Placing Blame: A General Theory of the Criminal Law* (Oxford: Clarendon Press, 1997), pp. 83–188. *Per contra*, I am of the view that retributive punishment is not inherently *good*, but rather it is inherently *right and fair* (*right* not *good*) to inflict proportionate retribution on those who have wronged others.

152 On the goodness of preventing harm to humans, see generally Nicholas Rescher, *Objectivity: The Obligations of Impersonal Reason* (Notre Dame, IL: University of Notre Dame Press, 1997).

deserts) elements and thus is not a workable theory.[153] However, the correct reading of von Hirsch's theory is that it uses consequential and retributive theories independently to *explain* and *justify* distinct aspects of the institution of punishment. Consequentialism as used by von Hirsch merely *explains* the legitimacy of having a general system of harm prevention—it is about showing why it is necessary to have a system of criminalization and punishment in place. The retributive constraint (just deserts for individual wrongdoing) adopted by von Hirsch, Moore[154] and myself *justifies* individualized punishment in objective terms: it provides an objective *justification* for criminalization and punishment at the individual level. Von Hirsch argues that it is the offender's past wrongdoing that provides the justification for invoking the institution of punishment in individual cases.[155] Inflicting individual just deserts on wrongdoers might indirectly achieve the prudential aim of convincing others not to engage in similar wrongdoing, but it is individual wrongdoing that justifies individualized punishment.

The lawmaker can demonstrate that criminalization and punishment is a fair response by pointing to the wrongfulness and harmfulness of an offender's actions. It is the *potential* harmfulness of certain bad consequences that flow from agents' intentional actions that make it fair to prohibit agents from doing such actions and also for stating in advance that those who do so may go to jail. This approach gives the legislature guidance about what it can fairly criminalize and how to grade or label that criminalization. The lawmaker might satisfy the bad actions/act/consequences constraint by referring to harm/endangerment or to other objectively bad consequences (that is, wrongful privacy violations, and so forth, that might not necessarily result in harm) to demonstrate that it is fair to invoke the criminal law. Nonetheless, if the legislature wants to underwrite its criminalization decisions with harmful jail sentences, it will have to demonstrate that the potential bad consequences would be of a harmful kind.

I argue below that exhibitionism can have bad consequences in that it can violate a non-consenting person's right not to be forced to receive non-public information in public places.[156] When a person culpably aims to copulate in a public bus knowing (or recklessly indifferent to the fact) that it will bring about the bad consequence of invading the other passengers' rights to be let alone and to avoid receiving unwanted intimate information in confined public spaces, an objective justification is available to demonstrate that it is fair to invoke the criminal law. Since the bad consequence does not result in harm, it would not be fair to allow the state to use *penal detention* to punish it. The appropriate response would be to use penal fines or community service orders. As we will see below, the same applies to trivial harms such as littering. The proportionality and

---

153 John Tasioulas, 'Punishment and Repentance,' (2006) 81 *Philosophy* 279 at pp. 285–291.
154 Moore, *op. cit. supra*, fn. 151.
155 See generally, von Hirsch, *op. cit. supra*, fn. 150.
156 See Chapter 7. See also Baker, *op. cit. supra*, 118.

justice of criminalizing harmless wrongs should be considered under the personal autonomy right as found in the Due Process Clause, as the punishment will often not be sufficient for an Eighth Amendment analysis.

If x intentionally rapes y, criminalization and punishment through imprisonment can be explained to x in terms that can be reconciled with fairness and justice, because x deserves to be punished for his harmful choice.[157] The objective reasons we can offer to x to explain why it is just and fair to send him to jail for raping y are: that he deserves hard treatment for *choosing* to inflict hard treatment (*harm*) on his victim by raping her and because he knew (or was recklessly indifferent to the fact) that he was bringing about bad consequences of a harmful kind for her, and the gradation of that offense as a serious crime can be dialectically defended in rational discussions with both him and his victim. If the public is to have confidence in the criminal justice system, the victim's rights must be taken seriously, which means the offender must be subjected to proportionate hard treatment by way of penal detention.

Fairness also means that it is important that harm and culpability arguments accord with objectivity.[158] This can be done when lawmakers are able to point to objectively bad consequences such as privacy violations flowing from exhibitionism or other actions that result in (or risk) harm. If x shoots (or attempts to shoot) y, this can be empirically ascertained and its actual harmfulness (or potential harmfulness in the case of attempts) can be assessed in objective terms. Coupled with this, because the bad consequence is of a harmful kind, attaching a jail sentence to the offense would be a proportionate response. Clearly, intentionally aiming to bring about harm to others is behavior that is deserving of criminalization and it is possible to explain its wrongness in a public dialectical process to those being criminalized in terms that they would be hard put to deny.[159] Claims about the objective wrongness of intentionally or recklessly[160] harming

---

157 See Lucas, *op. cit. supra*, fn. 17 at p. 284.

158 See the discussion in Chapter 6 concerning the distinction between realism and inter-subjectively derived objectivity as used in this book.

159 'In cultivating objectivity ... We enter (even if merely hypothetically) into a public forum of discussion (of dialectics if you will) where we must see it as incumbent on ourselves to put what we maintain in a way that others (insofar as reasonable) would be hard put to deny.' Rescher, *op. cit. supra*, fn. 152 at p. 16.

160 Some commentators argue that invented human concepts such as the culpability doctrine, which is instantiated in our social world, exists in the world outside of human thought and conceptualization in a strongly mind-independent sense. See also Matthew H. Kramer, *Objectivity and the Rule of Law* (Cambridge: Cambridge University Press, 2007) at pp. 11–99. I disagree, because the concept of culpability originated from human thought and reflection and even though it then became instantiated in the world, it still requires human knowers to know that they are wronging others in an individual sense by culpably harming them. A mind is needed for intentional action and to make an ultimate ethical determination of wrongness.

others can be justified with maximally supportive arguments that derive from the public deliberative process.[161]

Distinguishing Criminal Harm from Private Law Harm: Culpability and Collective Enforcement

Does the above discussion mean that all intentional harms should carry jail terms? Kleinig[162] notes that harm *per se* does not really explain why some forms of harm-doing are criminalizable while others are not. He suggests that moral culpability could play an important role in drawing a distinction between criminalizable wrongs and other wrongs, but notes that in some cases (such as intentionally breaching a contract) intentional harm-doing is remedied through the use of the private law.[163] Glanville Williams once said that he was not able to distinguish crimes from other types of legal wrongs. Williams concluded that: '[a] crime is an act capable of being followed by criminal proceedings having a criminal outcome.'[164] There are various moral overlaps between crimes and torts.[165] It is not the degree of harm (or other objectively bad consequence) alone that determines whether conduct should be criminalized rather than regulated through private law. Some torts involve greater harm than criminal conduct. The negligent train driver is likely to cause greater harm than someone who deliberately drives her car over a single pedestrian. Similarly, the negligent banker[166] would cause more harm than 1,000 pickpockets.[167] The lawmaker has to consider the degree of moral blameworthiness involved to determine whether the activities are sufficiently serious to warrant penal condemnation or a private law response.

There will always be some overlaps. The private law also aims to prevent certain unwanted (usually harmful) bad consequences but compensates the

---

161 Postema, *op. cit. supra*, fn. 101 at p. 121.
162 John Kleinig, 'Criminally Harming Others,' (1986) 5 *Criminal Justice Ethics* 3.
163 *Id.* at p. 6.
164 Glanville L. Williams, 'The Definition of a Crime,' (1955) 8 *Current Legal Problems* 107 at p. 130.
165 To some extent this is attributable to the way in which the criminal and civil law evolved out of a single body of law. For a convenient and compendious overview of the criminal law's historical development and its relation to tort law, see Carleton Kemp Allen, *Legal Duties* (Oxford: Clarendon Press, 1931) at pp. 221–252; J.A. Jolowicz, *Lectures on Jurisprudence* (London: Athlone Press, 1963) at pp. 344–358.
166 For example, James Gobert and Maurice Punch note that: 'Before its collapse, Barings Bank was sending sums of money to Nick Leeson in Singapore for amounts that in some instances exceeded both the bank's assets as well as the limits set by the Bank of England.' James Gobert and Maurice Punch, *Rethinking Corporate Crime* (London: Butterworths LexisNexis, 2003) at p. 19.
167 Allen, *op. cit. supra*, fn. 165 at p. 255.

wronged party.[168] Although a perfect line cannot be drawn, civil wrongs are distinguishable from crimes primarily because of the degree of culpability involved. Hampton,[169] like von Hirsch,[170] and Ashworth,[171] argues that the degree of moral culpability accompanying the harm-doing is important for drawing a distinction between torts and crimes. Torts usually involve negligent harm-doing, whereas crimes involve intentional, reckless or grossly negligent harm-doing. Nevertheless, the degree of harm and culpability involved in some private wrongs could be sufficient to ground a case for criminalization (intentional defamation, intentional breaches of contracts without excuse or justification, and so forth), but wrongful harm does not necessarily have to be criminalized. It is important to note that wrongful harm provides a necessary condition for criminalization, but the state is not compelled to criminalize every from of wrongful harm-doing.[172] The fact that some harmful intentional wrongs are dealt with through the civil law helps to reduce the extent of criminalization. Ensuring that criminalization decisions meet the requirements of fairness is not about telling the lawmakers what they *should* criminalize, but what they *may* criminalize.[173] The criminal law should be used only as a last resort to prevent reasonably grave wrongs.

If lawmakers want to use the criminal law rather than a civil law response, then they have to show why the conduct is worthy of criminal condemnation. Having said that, it is important to note that in some cases, the case for criminalization will be so compelling that the state will be *morally obliged* to invoke the criminal law to protect the legitimate interests of its citizens. For example, in the 1990s lawmakers were morally compelled to criminalize marital rape.[174] It is the gravity

---

168 Kleinig, *op. cit. supra*, fn. 162.

169 Jean E. Hampton, 'Liberalism, Retribution and Criminality,' in *In Harm's Way: Essays in Honor of Joel Feinberg*, ed. Jules L. Coleman and Allen Buchanan (Cambridge: Cambridge University Press, 1994) at pp. 176 *et seq*.

170 See von Hirsch, *op. cit, supra*, fn. 150 at p. 10.

171 '"Result-crimes," and many other crimes, impose liability on the basis of conduct which is preliminary to the infliction of harm, merely because of the intention with which the person acted.' Andrew Ashworth, 'Taking the Consequences,' in *Action and Value in Criminal Law*, eds Stephen Shute, John Gardner and Jeremy Horder (Oxford: Clarendon Press, 1993) at p. 116.

172 'It is important to point out that these proposed coercion-legitimizing principles do not even purport to state necessary and sufficient conditions for justified state coercion. A liberty-limiting principle does not state a *sufficient condition* because in a given case its purportedly relevant reason might not weigh heavily enough on the scales to outbalance the standing presumption in favor of liberty. That presumption is not only supported by moral and utilitarian considerations of a general kind; it is also likely to be buttressed in particular cases by appeal to the practical costs.' Feinberg, *op. cit. supra*, fn. 8 at pp. 10, 187–190.

173 *Id.* at pp. 4, 10.

174 Marital rape was criminalized in some jurisdictions only in the 1990s. See *R. v. R.* [1991] 4 All E.R. 481. See also the discussion in Nicola Lacey, Celia Wells, and Oliver Quick, *Reconstructing Criminal Law* (London: LexisNexis, 3rd ed. 2003) at pp. 487 *et seq*.

and character of the badness and harmfulness of intentional marital rape that makes it a moral issue that cannot be left to the parties concerned to resolve, especially in a humane society that cares for its members.[175] Furthermore, these types of serious harms require a criminal law response rather than a private law response because 'it would not be reasonable to expect one person to take proceedings on [her] own responsibility to put a stop to it, but ... it should be taken on as the responsibility of the community at large.'[176] Historically, publicness and the idea of the community being harmed have been used for identifying crimes. This approach is not valid for distinguishing crimes from torts, because it is clear that many private wrongs also harm the community.[177] The focus should be on whether the state has an obligation to use the criminal law because of the gravity and character of the harm involved, and the degree of culpability involved. In less serious cases, wrongful harm is only a sufficient condition for invoking the criminal law and penal detention.

The damage caused by a negligent train driver is every bit as grave as the harm caused by a single rape, but unless the harm has been caused by at least gross negligence, its gravity alone will not be sufficient to justify a criminal law response. Furthermore, the harmfulness of the consequences that flow from intentional defamation or from breaches of contractual duties means that such wrongs could be criminalized, but the nature/badness of the harm is not sufficient to *compel* the state to criminalize these types of wrongs. It would not be fair to ask a person to commence proceedings on her own account to seek retribution for being raped (not only because it affects us all indirectly, but also because of the unequal bargaining position between the rapist and the victim), whereas it would be reasonable to ask a person to commence proceedings on her own account to seek compensation for losses flowing from a breach of contract. In the end, only a crude line can be drawn.

Marshall and Duff[178] discuss the overlap between harm to individuals and harm to the community. They suggest that punishment should be considered in

---

175   'It makes a great difference to the victim whether the community takes his wrong seriously, or passes it off as of no consequence. If he sees the man who cared nothing for him go scot-free, he is given to understand that society cares nothing for him either. But if the wrongdoer is made to see the error of his ways, the man to whom the wrong was done sees his rights vindicated, and is assured that society cares for him, even if one of its members does not, and will uphold his rights in face of assault and injury.' Lucas, *op. cit. supra*, fn. 17 at p. 104.

176   This is Lord Denning's test for ascertaining public nuisances. See his judgment in *Attorney-General v. PYA Quarries* [1957] 2 Q.B. 169.

177   The current credit crunch exemplifies the public damage that can flow from private wrongs. The taxpayers will be paying for bailouts for corporations that have been mismanaged for decades. Clearly, the 'negligent mismanagement of a company's affairs brings about a widespread and severe calamity.' See Peter Brett, *An Inquiry into Criminal Guilt* (London: Sweet & Maxwell Ltd., 1963) at pp. 6–7.

178   S.E. Marshall and R.A. Duff, 'Criminalization and Sharing Wrongs,' (1998) 11 *Canadian Journal of Law and Jurisprudence* 7 at pp. 20–21.

the context of the wrongdoer's relationship with the wider community as well as with the individual victim. By making the wrong done to a 'rape victim "ours," rather than merely "hers"; in thus understanding it as an attack on "our" good, not merely on her individual good: we do not turn our attention *away* from the wrong that she has suffered, towards some distinct "public" good. Rather, we share *in* the very wrong that she has suffered: it is not "our" wrong *instead of* hers; it is "our" wrong *because* it is a wrong done to her, as one of us—as a fellow member of our community whose identity and whose good is found within that community.'[179] Likewise, C.K. Allen[180] is essentially correct in holding that: 'Crime is crime because it consists in wrongdoing which directly and in *serious degree* threatens the security or well-being of society, and because it is not safe to leave it *redressable only by compensation* of the party injured.' Wrongful harm criteria only provide a sufficient condition for criminalization, but in some cases the legislature will be compelled to act because of the serious nature of the harm involved.

Distinguishing wrongs that *ought* to be criminalized from those that *may* be criminalized is a matter of drawing a line somewhere along the continuum of culpability and the continuum of *the nature and seriousness of the harm*. There is also a continuum of *fairness of enforcement*, because in some cases as a matter of justice and/or practicality it would be unfair to ask individuals to take action to police harm that affects our collective interests more than it does our personal interests. The *practicality* constraint is especially relevant in the case of collective harms, such as littering. Littering may not be harmful in isolation, but in aggregate widespread littering would cause more harm to a city the size of New York than a few incidences of other serious individualized harms such as homicide.[181] Because littering impacts our collective interests it would not be reasonable to expect one person to commence proceedings on her own initiative to put a stop to it, as it would be unfair randomly to impose the burden of harm prevention on individuals. Instead, the community at large (by means of public institutions, such as the police, courts, government—and public mechanisms, such as criminal law and punishment) is responsible for protecting our collective interests (preventing littering, tax evasion, and so forth).

The Moral Dimensions of Constitutional Rights

In this book, I argue that everyone has a constitutional right not to be criminalized. I assert *has*, because I take the view the legal right already exists in various constitutions and international conventions. An advanced reading of the inventory of rights that form the general right not to be criminalized shows that this right

---

179 Id.
180 Allen, *op. cit. supra*, fn. 165 at pp. 233–235.
181 I discuss these types of harms further *infra*.

exists. My primary focus is on the U.S. Bill of Rights. The existing provisions in the U.S., Canada and Europe have not been interpreted as incorporating an express right not to be criminalized. Canada has gone further than the U.S. or Europe in recognizing an express right not to be criminalized, but has not gone all the way. Unfortunately, in the U.S. the personal autonomy (privacy) right has been applied in an *ad hoc* and arbitrary manner (to abortion, contraceptive use, and medical treatment cases and private sexual relations, but has not been applied to many other innocuous activities); and the proportionate punishment provision has been interpreted narrowly to allow gross punishments to be inflicted for minor crimes. Everyone has a right not to be criminalized, which *ought* to be recognized by the constitutional courts wherever they may be situated when interpreting the personal autonomy and proportionate punishment rights, however differently worded and however differently interpreted in the past.

In this book, I do not advocate that the examination of the existing constitutional rights should dispense with an analysis of the prudential and historical factors that typically inform judicial determinations of the rights individuals have. Instead, I argue that given that there is sufficient precedent in the U.S. to demonstrate a person has a right not to be subject to disproportionate punishments, the right exists and should be recognized. The abortion cases support a more general right—that is, that one should not be criminalized at all unless her actions interfere with the freedom of others. The U.S. 'evolving standards of decency' standard or the Strasbourg Court's 'evolutive interpretation' standard allows courts some flexibility and it was this *margin of reasonable judicial discretion* standard that allowed the Warren Court to interpret rights according to contemporary standards of justice without dispensing with an analysis of the prudential and historical factors that typically inform judicial determinations. Contemporary standards of justice cannot be ignored when interpreting the inventories of rights that form the cardinal right not to be criminalized, because to do so would be to approve abuses that are contrary to our deeply held conventional understandings of human rights. The U.S. and other Western nations cannot deride countries such as China as human rights abusers and at the same time interpret the Eighth Amendment (and the corresponding provisions in Canada and Europe) as permitting a man to go to jail for 50 years for stealing $100.

How might harm work as a constitutional constraint? The Harm Principle can be distinguished from constitutional rights in a number of ways. The most important differences for present purposes are twofold. Firstly, the Harm Principle proposes a broad right to freedom to engage in any conduct that does not harm others, whereas constitutional rights protect specific freedoms such as the right to free speech. A constitutional right is not as broad as the general moral claim to freedom found in the Harm Principle. If the conduct does not involve the exercise of one of the specific freedoms found in the relevant constitutional document, then it will not be protected from criminalization. The decriminalization of passive begging in open places in the United States[182] and Canada[183] was possible only because it was held to involve an exercise of the specific freedom of speech right. Secondly, constitutional rights have legal force. Constitutional rights bind legislatures and can be used to strike down substantive criminal laws that interfere with specific freedoms such as the right to privacy and free speech. The constitutional *right not to be criminalized* hinges on the moral right that every human should be free to do whatever she likes so long as it does not wrong others. Harm is merely a criterion for determining when the right not to be criminalized can be fairly overridden. It is an important constitutional constraint, as it is one of the core criteria for measuring the justice and proportionality of criminalization decisions.

Generally, constitutional rights have to be interpreted in a way that is reconcilable with deeply held conventional understandings of justice. Otherwise, it would be meaningless to enact such rights. Such rights can only be reconciled with justice, if they are interpreted in a way that achieves the general moral purpose or aim that the right was intended to serve. Providing a full theory of how constitutions should be read is beyond the scope of this book. Rather, I draw on the ideas presented by Dworkin[184] over the last 40 years. Dworkin holds that constitutional rights have to be interpreted by considering not only history and precedent but also the underlying moral explanations for having the right. I make specific reference to a number of cases that have achieved justice by adopting such an approach.[185] Hermeneutically, Dworkin has provided a convincing explanation as to why it is necessary and fair to refer to moral principles when interpreting constitutional rights.[186]

The cardinal rights that have been constitutionalized in the United States, Europe and Canada are objective rights that bind legislatures.[187] Such rights can

---

182 *Loper v. New York City Police Dept.*, 802 F. Supp. 1029, 1042 (S.D.N.Y. 1992); *Benefit v. Cambridge*, 424 Mass. 918 (1997).

183 Federated Anti-Poverty Groups of British Columbia v. Vancouver (City) [2002] B.C.S.C. 105.

184 See generally, Ronald Dworkin, *Freedom's Law: The Moral Reading of the American Constitution* (New York: Oxford University Press, 1996). See also Scott Hershovitz, *Exploring Law's Empire: The Jurisprudence of Ronald Dworkin* (New York: Oxford University Press, 2006).

185 The relevant examples for present purposes include: *Solem v. Helm*, 463 U.S. 277 (1983); *Robinson v. California*, 360 U.S. 660, 667 (1962); the Canadian case, *R. v. Malmo-Levine* [2000] B.C.C.A. 335; and *Kennedy v. Louisiana*, 554 U.S. 407 (2008).

186 Dworkin focuses on the core human rights, but moral and evaluative judgments clearly permeate constitutional interpretation more generally. See Michael C. Dorf, 'Truth, Justice, and the American Constitution,' (1997) 97 *Columbia Law Review* 133.

187 Rights such as free speech, the right not be subjected to unusual and cruel punishment, privacy, due process and equality under the law clearly have a objective basis. The rights found in constitutions such as that of the United States are constitutionalized (or codified) conventional understandings of justice. Cf. Ronald Dworkin, *A Matter of Principle* (Cambridge, MA: Harvard University Press, 1985), p. 33 *et seq*. See also Onora

only be taken seriously if objective reasons of great weight are produced to justify overriding them. For instance, a beggar's right to express freely her condition of poverty by sitting passively in an open street with a hat in front of her is not absolute, but it should not be overridden unless there is an objective justification that outweighs her constitutionalized right to freedom of expression.[188] Something other than a mere non-objective claim of harm is needed to justify overriding fundamental rights that have been constitutionalized. Constitutionalized rights such as the right to free speech, the right not to be unduly deprived of liberty, privacy and so on provide *prima facie* objective reasons for not criminalizing certain activities. Therefore, such rights should not be trumped by trivial considerations. Both decisions to criminalize and decisions to override human rights are fair only when objective justifications can be produced. If this were not the case, it would hardly be worth recognizing the wrongful harm criteria as a constitutional constraint. The wrongful harm criteria should be constitutionalized as *necessary conditions* for using imprisonment as a form of punishment. If the state wants to send a person to jail, then it should demonstrate that her conduct resulted in objective harm. If this condition cannot be met, then some other form of punishment should be used.

A just reading of the Constitution requires judges to decide cases by choosing the interpretation that accords with the underlying principles of morality that are the Bill of Rights' *raison d'être*. Human rights are justice guarantees and as far as they have been constitutionalized, judges have to interpret them with reference to evolving societal standards of justice, precedent, and past practice. The judge will be constrained not only by the text of the Constitution, but also by the moral aim of the right being interpreted. If a judge's interpretation of a given right is too far removed from the purpose the right was designed to serve, then it will lack validity. Justice and fairness will be achieved when the interpretation of the right's scope can be reconciled with its intrinsic moral aim. For example, if the general moral rationale for the Eighth Amendment is to ensure fair punishment, then there is no reason why that right should not be interpreted expansively to protect people from all kinds of unjust and oppressive state punishment. It makes no sense to rely on semantics to interpret the right narrowly in order to circumvent the general moral aim that the right was designed to achieve. The United States Supreme Court has taken such an approach when considering the privacy right.

In the United States the due process right has been interpreted so as to require that substantive criminal laws be impartial and reasonable in content.[189] The right of

---

O'Neill, *Towards Justice and Virtue: A Constructive Account of Practical Reasoning* (Cambridge: Cambridge University Press, 1996); and Graham Walker, *Moral Foundations of Constitutional Thought* (Princeton: Princeton University Press, 1990).

188 As for the specific act of panhandling and free speech, see Helen Hershkoff and Adam S. Cohen, 'Begging to Differ: The First Amendment and the Right to Beg,' (1991) 104 *Harvard Law Review* 896.

189 *Lawrence v. Texas*, 539 U.S. 558 (2003).

personal autonomy delineated in *Griswold v. Connecticut*[190] was not an enumerated right; rather, it was interpreted from the privacy interests that are implicit in the First, Third, Fourth, Fifth and Ninth Amendments. In *Roe v. Wade*[191] the court said that the 'right of privacy, whether it be founded in the Fourteenth Amendment's concept of personal liberty and restrictions upon state action, as we feel it is, or, as the District Court determined, in the Ninth Amendment's reservation of rights to the people, is broad enough to encompass a woman's decision whether or not to terminate her pregnancy.' The personal autonomy constraint has been used to protect personal decisions relating to marriage,[192] child rearing and education,[193] contraception,[194] and so forth. Articles 5 and 8 of the European Convention for the Protection of Human Rights and Fundamental Freedoms and sections 7 and 8 of the Canadian Charter also protect similar personal interests. The unifying theme for the general presumption of liberty found in these provisions is based on Mill's idea that individuals should have a private sphere in which they are free to make decisions about their personal affairs without state intervention and where they can be free from unwarranted, unsolicited intervention by other uninvited individuals. The privacy/personal autonomy cases,[195] inter alia, demonstrate that the courts[196] have repeatedly drawn on not only precedent and the text of the Constitution, but also on conventional notions of justice when interpreting the scope of fundamental rights.

---

190 381 U.S. 479, 484 (1965).
191 410 U.S. 113, 153 (1973).
192 *Loving v. Virginia*, 388 U.S. 1 (1967).
193 Prince v. Massachusetts, 321 U.S. 158 (1944); Pierce v. Society of Sisters, 268 U.S. 510 (1925).
194 Griswold v. Connecticut, 381 U.S. 479 (1965); Eisenstadt v. Baird, 405 U.S. 438 (1972).
195 On evolution of autonomy as an important value, see J.B. Schneewind, *The Invention of Autonomy* (Cambridge, Cambridge University Press, 1998).
196 See *Armstrong v. State* 989 P. 2d 364, 372–374 (1999), in which it was noted that: 'John Stuart Mill recognized this fundamental right of self-determination and personal autonomy as both a limitation on the power of the government and as a principle of preeminent deference to the individual. He stated: "[T]he only purpose for which power can be rightfully exercised over any member of a civilized community, against his will, is to prevent harm to others."' See also *Moran v. MGH Institute of Health Professionals*, 15 Mass. L. Rptr. 417; *The Matter of Conservatorship of Groves*, 109 S.W. 3d 317, 328 (2003); and *Richards v. State*, 743 S.W. 2d 747, 751 (1987), in which Levy, J. dissenting, quoted Mill before concluding that: 'if we uphold the authority of the State to punish one's failure to use a seat-belt, we are one more step on our way to an Orwellian society in which the State can punish merely for smoking cigarettes, for not brushing one's teeth, or for being foolish.'

Harm as a Constitutional Requirement

I argued, in the last chapter, that the fundamental liberty interest protected by the U.S. Due Process Clause protects from criminalization activities that might not necessarily be punished with jail terms, because it outlaws criminalization that is a legislative response that is disproportionate to the societal problems at issue. For example, illegal parking could be criminalized because it causes coordination problems, and thus, the state could show that regulatory criminalization is a legislative response that is proportionate to the societal problems at issue. However, if the state imposed jail terms for illegal parking, the Eighth Amendment protection could be invoked to ensure that the *prima facie* justifiable criminalization is punished proportionately. Thus, the general proportionate legislative response protection can be supplemented with the proportionate punishment constraint. The latter right aims to protect people from being subjected to unjust state punishment, rather than to unfair conviction and labeling per se. The rights read together can be used to enforce the right not to be unfairly criminalized.

I will now examine a leading Canadian case, as the Canadian Supreme Court has made some very useful observations about using the harm criterion as a constitutional constraint. In Malmo-Levine[197] the appellant challenged a marijuana prohibition under section 7 of the Canadian Charter of Rights and Freedom, which holds that: '[e]veryone has the right to life, liberty and security of the person and the right not to be deprived of those rights except in accordance with the principles of fundamental justice.'[198] Despite slight differences of wording and past juridical interpretations, this right's scope would have a similar reach in the U.S. and Europe. In *Malmo-Levine* the appellants were convicted under the *Narcotic Control Act, R.S.C. 1985* (Can.) for possessing marijuana for personal use.[199] A conviction under the legislation did not carry a mandatory prison term, but the possibility of imprisonment is enough to satisfy the deprivation of liberty requirements found in section 7 of the *Canadian Charter*. The question focused on whether such a deprivation of liberty contravened a principle of fundamental justice.[200] The question before the court was whether the inclusion of cannabis in the *Narcotic Control Act, R.S.C. 1985* (Can.), as far as it related to the personal possession and use contrary to sections 3(1) and (2) of the *Act,* violated the defendant's constitutional right 'to life, liberty and the security of the person' and the right not to be deprived thereof 'except in accordance with the principles of fundamental justice' as set out in section 7 of the *Canadian Charter*.[201] The Court held that the risk of imprisonment was enough to activate the 'liberty' interest

---

197 [2003] S.C.C. 74.
198 Part 1, section 2(b), *Constitution Act 1982* (Can.).
199 *R. v. Malmo-Levine* [2000] B.C.C.A. 335.
200 *R. v. Malmo-Levine* [2000] B.C.C.A. 335.
201 *R. v. Malmo-Levine* [2000] B.C.C.A. 335.

under section 7. The analysis then proceeded to consider whether the deprivation of liberty was contrary to a 'principle of fundamental justice.'

The appellants argued that the Harm Principle constituted a principle of fundamental justice. It was argued that the deprivation of liberty contravened the harm justification for criminalization because possessing small amounts of marijuana for personal use poses no risk of harm to others.[202] Basically, the appellants were arguing that the state should not deprive people of their liberty via imprisonment without good reason and that harm to others would be the only sufficient reason for sending someone to jail. In *Malmo-Levine*[203] Braidwood J.A. set down the test for determining whether a principle constitutes a principle of fundamental justice within the meaning of section 7 of the *Canadian Charter*. His Honor summed the test up as involving at least three qualities: (1) it is a legal principle; (2) it is precise; and (3) there is a consensus among reasonable people that it is vital to our system of justice.[204] Arguably, Braidwood's approach is broadly reconcilable with Dworkin's *law as integrity* method.[205] In moral terms, the harm criterion is a constitutional measure of justice because it is an objective[206] standard for ensuring that penal detention is proportionate with the harmfulness of the detainee's wrongdoing. Speaking for the court, Braidwood J.A. held:

> I conclude that on the basis of all of these sources—common law, Law Reform Commissions, the federalism cases, Charter litigation—that the 'Harm Principle' is indeed a principle of fundamental justice within the meaning of s.7. It is a legal principle and it is concise. Moreover, there is a consensus among reasonable people that it is vital to our system of justice. Indeed, I think that it is common sense that you don't go to jail unless there is a potential that your activities will cause harm to others.[207]

Braidwood's interpretation of the Canadian *deprivation of liberty* right draws on deeply held conventional understandings of harm and wrong as criteria for criminalization. Unfortunately, the Supreme Court of Canada overruled the lower court's finding that the Harm Principle is a principle of fundamental justice within

---

202   *R. v. Malmo-Levine* [2000] B.C.C.A. 335.

203   *R. v. Malmo-Levine* [2000] B.C.C.A. 335, at para. 49 *et passim*.

204   *Id.* citing *Rodriguez v. British Columbia (Attorney-General)* [1993] 3 S.C.R. 519 at 590–591, 607 (per Sopinka J).

205   Braidwood draws on morality, precedent, the structure of constitutional argument in this area, and on a putative public inter-subjective deliberation about the public acceptability of the Harm Principle as a principle of fundamental justice. For Dworkin, objectivity hinges on personal conviction. However, this book adopts an inter-subjective deliberative approach. Cf. Dworkin, *op. cit. supra*, fn. 187 at pp. 33 *et seq*.

206   A public deliberation process would demonstrate the objectivity of the claim that the Harm Principle is a fundamental principle of justice for the purpose of depriving people of their liberty via imprisonment. See Postema, *op. cit. supra*, fn. 101.

207   *R. v. Malmo-Levine* [2000] B.C.C.A. 335 per totam curiam.

the meaning of section 7. The majority in the Supreme Court of Canada was of the view that harm was 'not the constitutional standard for what conduct may or may not be the subject of the criminal law for the purposes of s. 7.'[208] It was of the view that conduct would not necessarily have to pose a risk of harm to others to be criminalized. The majority held that the *harm* was not a criterion for determining justice[209] of criminalization decisions because: '[t]he justification for State intervention cannot be reduced to a single factor—harm—but is a much more complex matter.'[210] The court cited H.L.A. Hart who said: '[e]ven where there is harm to others in the most literal sense, there may well be other principles limiting the extent to which harmful activities should be repressed by law. So there are multiple criteria, not a single criterion, determining when human liberty may be restricted.'[211] The majority only paid lip service to the *legislative response that is proportionate to the societal problems* standard and the proportionate punishment standard.

The majority referred to a narrow range of problematic counterexamples in an attempt to demonstrate that criminalization and penal detention have not been limited to harmful conduct. But it did not analyze these crimes to ascertain whether they might now be inconsistent with section 7 of the *Charter*. The majority stated that:

> Cannibalism is an offense (s. 182) that does not harm another sentient being, but that is nevertheless prohibited on the basis of fundamental social and ethical considerations. Bestiality (s. 160) and cruelty to animals (s. 446) are examples of crimes that rest on their offensiveness to deeply held social values rather than on Mill's 'Harm Principle' ... A duel fought by consenting adults is an example of a crime where the victim is no less culpable than the perpetrator, and there is no harm that is not consented to, but the prohibition (s. 71 of the *Code*) is nevertheless integral to our ideas of civilized society ... Similarly, in *R. v. F. (R.P.)* (1996), 105 C.C.C. (3d) 435, the Nova Scotia Court of Appeal upheld the prohibition of incest under s. 155 of the *Criminal Code* despite a Charter challenge by five consenting adults.[212]

These counterexamples are not as convincing as the majority suggest. I have argued elsewhere that consent has its limits and that a person cannot consent to gross

---

208   *R. v. Malmo-Levine* [2003] S.C.C. 74, at para. 111.

209   *R. v. Malmo-Levine* [2003] S.C.C. 74 at para. 114. Likewise, it was held that there is no 'sufficient consensus that the Harm Principle is vital or fundamental to our societal notion of criminal justice.'

210   *R. v. Malmo-Levine* [2003] S.C.C. 74, at para. 109.

211   *Id.* citing H.L.A. Hart, 'Immorality and Treason,' originally appearing in *The Listener*, July 30, 1959, 162–163, reprinted in *Morality and the Law* (1971), at pp. 49–51.

212   *R. v. Malmo-Levine* [2003] S.C.C. 74, at para. 117.

harm.[213] Therefore, dueling would come within the purview of the Harm Principle. Bestiality would not set back the interests of others and therefore psychiatric and therapeutic treatment should be made available to assist those who engage in this type of abnormal conduct. Similar treatment programs should be available for consenting adults who engage in incest.[214] Incest would normally only involve self-harm, and paternalism does not provide a sound basis for criminalization let alone a justification for sending people to prison.[215] Jail is a form of *serious harm* so it makes sense not to inflict further harm on self-harmers. The majority in *Malmo* focused not only on the fact that harmless activities such as incest, bestiality, and blasphemous libel had been criminalized, but also noted that offenses such as bestiality and incest carry penalties of up to 14 years' imprisonment.[216] Instead of using these unjust pre-Charter laws to justify maintaining other unjust laws, the majority should have scrutinized the justice and fairness of imposing long jail terms in such cases.

As for cannibalism, it would come within the purview of the wrongful harm justification for criminalization as it causes harm in the great majority of cases[217] by interfering with the living relatives' interests.[218] Certainly, if the corpse basher or cannibal kills to gain access to a corpse, then the normal law of murder would be relevant. Although corpse bashing and cannibalism evoke powerful emotional reactions, the actual objective consequences are not too different from cremating a person after death or allowing a person to donate her body organs to science after death. In some cases it would be necessary to detain the cannibal if there is evidence that she poses a danger to the community, but in other cases a compulsory

---

213   Dennis J. Baker, 'The Moral Limits of Consent as a Defense in the Criminal Law,' (2009) 12(1) *New Criminal Law Review* 93.

214   Cf. Joseph Raz, *The Practice of Value* (Oxford: Clarendon Press, 2003) at p. 66. Raz suggests that if a woman gets pregnant in circumstances in which she knows that the person to be conceived will be deformed or damaged, she wrongs that person. This type of conduct would come within the purview of the Harm Principle, but the countervailing circumstances are likely to outweigh the case for criminalization.

215   Feinberg, Vol. III, *op. cit. supra*, fn. 124. See also Richard J. Arneson, 'Joel Feinberg and the Justifications of Hard Paternalism,' (2005) 11(3) *Legal Theory* 259; and Russ Shafer-Landau, 'Liberalism and Paternalism,' (2005) 11(3) *Legal Theory* 169.

216   Sections 155(2) and 160 of the *Canadian Criminal Code 1985* (Can.). Blasphemous libel carries a penalty of up to two years' imprisonment.

217   I have argued elsewhere that we do not need actual harm in every case. As long as the conduct normally results in harm then it will come within the purview of the Harm Principle. Dennis J. Baker, 'The Harm Principle vs. Kantian Criteria for Ensuring Fair, Principled and Just Criminalization,' (2008) 33 *Australian Journal of Philosophy* 66 at pp. 80 *et seq*. See also the discussion in the next section of this chapter.

218   For an alternative view of the wrongness of harming the dead, see Joan C. Callahan, 'On Harming the Dead,' (1989) 97(2) *Ethics* 342; Dorothy Grover, 'Posthumous Harm,' *The Philosophical Quarterly* (1989) 39(156) 334; and Barbara Baum Levenbook, 'Harming Someone After His Death,' (1084) 94(3) *Ethics* 407.

psychiatric confinement order might be sufficient. Sometimes the wrongdoer who interferes with a corpse might not be suffering from any mental ailment. For example, in England a group of animal activists removed the remains of an elderly lady from her grave in order to intimidate and harass her living relatives, because the relatives were breeding guinea pigs for scientific research.[219] This type of interference would come within the purview of the harm criterion because it harms the living family members.

Feinberg argues that when people are subjected to forms of psychological distress that are 'severe, prolonged, or constantly repeated, the mental suffering they cause may become obsessive and incapacitating, and therefore harmful.'[220] Even in those cases in which no one has been harmed, because, say, the dead person died from natural causes and had no relatives or friends to suffer the consequences of learning that their loved one's corpse had been bashed or eaten, the defendant could be convicted because the criminal law criminalizes in the standard case. As I argue in Chapter 4, conduct does not have to cause actual harm to come within the purview of the harm justification. It will come within the purview of the harm justification if it is conduct that causes harm in the standard case. Arguably, the great majority of people would have friends and relatives who would care if someone were to interfere with their relative's corpse.

Justice Arbour, dissenting in *Malmo-Levine*, held that the wrongful harm is not the only good justification for criminalizing conduct, but it is the only good justification for *jailing people*. Her Honor was of the view that the lawmaker had the power to criminalize marijuana possession, but that it was an overreach of that power to impose a jail term for mere possession. Under her line of reasoning the lawmaker could have imposed a proportionate fine for possession of marijuana, but not a jail term. This approach is correct because harm is the only bad consequence that can counterbalance the harmful consequences involved for those who are jailed. There might be other objective justifications for criminalizing conduct, but in the case of imprisonment the justification needs to demonstrate not only that the bad consequences of the wrongdoer's actions make her deserving of criminalization, but also that those consequences were of a kind that would justify a jail term. My interpretation is not jurisdiction specific; proportionate punishment would be a requirement in any advanced civilization.

LeBel and Deschamps JJ, also in dissent in *Malmo*, held that the marijuana prohibition was a disproportionate response to the societal problems at issue and, thus, arbitrary.[221] The *Canadian Charter* incorporates a general proportionality

---

219 Nick Britten, 'Pensioner's Body Stolen by Animal Rights Group is Found,' *The Daily Telegraph* (London), May 4, 2005.

220 Feinberg, *op. cit. supra*, fn. 8 at p. 46.

221 Their Honors expounded: '[T]he harm that marihuana consumption may cause seems rather mild on the evidence we have. In contrast, the harm and the problems connected with the form of criminalization chosen by Parliament seem plain and important. … Jailing people for the offense of simple possession seems consistent with the perception

standard as opposed to the rational and strict scrutiny standards that are used in the United States. Jailing a person for merely possessing marijuana for personal use contravenes the objective harm constraint, the objective wrongfulness constraint, and the proportionality constraint. As far as imprisonment (a physical deprivation of liberty) is concerned in the United States, it is better to refer to the Eighth Amendment of the *Constitution of the United States* 1787 than to the Due Process Clause. The Eighth Amendment, if read according to evolving standards of justice, could be invoked to strike down laws that carry prison sentences for wrongs that do not result in harm to others, because harming a person by subjecting her to the hard treatment that is involved in serving a jail term would be a disproportionate response unless the wrongdoer inflicted equivalent harm on others.[222]

The Eighth Amendment should be interpreted in a way that accords with its overall moral aim or purpose. The right's overall moral aim is to ensure that the state does not inflict unjust, oppressive or disproportional punishments on its citizens. In *Solem v. Helm*,[223] the right was interpreted with reference to its underlying moral rationale in order to achieve the type of just result that the right was intended to achieve. In that case, the respondent was convicted for uttering a 'no account' check for $100. The usual maximum punishment for that crime would have been five years' imprisonment and a $5,000 fine. The respondent, however, was sentenced to life imprisonment without the option of parole under South Dakota's recidivist statute because he had a number of prior convictions. The Supreme Court held that the 'Eighth Amendment's proscription of cruel and unusual punishments prohibits not only barbaric punishments, but also sentences that are disproportionate to the crime committed.'[224]

In *Solem v. Helm* the Court did not pluck the right not to be punished disproportionately out of thin air, but rather it referred to the pre-constitutional history of the right,[225] the Framers' original intention, the text of the Constitution,

---

that the law, as it stands, amounts to some sort of legislative overreach to the apprehended problems associated with marihuana consumption ... The fundamental liberty interest has been infringed by the adoption and implementation of a legislative response which is disproportionate to the societal problems at issue.' *R. v. Malmo-Levine* [2003] S.C.C. 74, at para. 280. The same would apply in Europe. See generally, Evelyn Ellis, *The Principle of Proportionality in the Laws of Europe* (Oxford: Hart Publishing, 2000).

222 See *Solem v. Helm*, 463 U.S. 277 (1983); *Robinson v. California*, 360 U.S. 660 (1962).

223 463 U.S. 277 (1983).

224 *Solem v. Helm*, 463 U.S. 277, 284–290 (1983).

225 In *Solem v. Helm*, 463 U.S. 277, 286 (1983) the Court convincingly and logically demonstrated that historically the *proportionality* requirement applied to all forms of state punishment. It noted that: 'The English Bill of Rights repeated the principle of proportionality in language that was later adopted in the Eighth Amendment: "excessive Baile ought not to be required nor excessive Fines imposed nor cruell and unusuall Punishments inflicted." 1 *W. & M.*, sess. 2, ch. 2 (1689). Although the precise scope of this provision is uncertain, it at least incorporated "the longstanding principle of English law

a number of precedents spanning over a century,[226] and the underlying moral rationale for the right before holding that: 'The principle of proportionality is deeply rooted in common-law jurisprudence. It was expressed in Magna Carta, applied by the English courts for centuries, and repeated in the English Bill of Rights in language that was adopted in the Eighth Amendment. When the Framers of the Eighth Amendment adopted this language, they adopted the principle of proportionality that was implicit in it.'[227]

The Court's historical analysis in *Solem v. Helm* is every bit as convincing as the historical analysis that was used by Justice Scalia in *District of Columbia v. Heller*[228] to justify reading the Second Amendment as providing individuals with a right to possess guns. However, more recently the Supreme Court[229] failed to follow *Solem*. In *Harmelin v. Michigan*,[230] the Supreme Court held that the Eighth Amendment allowed a state to impose a life sentence without the possibility of parole for the possession of 672 grams of cocaine. In that case, Justice Scalia failed to follow precedent and engaged in a game of semantics to argue that there was no historical foundation for reading the right as requiring jail sentences to be proportionate and just. In particular, Justice Scalia argued that the text of the Constitution did not expressly mention prison sentences and therefore they were not covered by the proportionality requirement.

Justice Scalia's reasoning cannot be reconciled with the moral purpose of the right or with the rationale for having a Bill of Rights. Coupled with this, Justice Scalia's historical analysis is not as convincing as that expounded in *Solem v.*

---

that the punishment ... should not be, by reason of its excessive length or severity, greatly disproportionate to the offense charged." R. Perry, *Sources of Our Liberties* 236 (1959); see 4 W. Blackstone, *Commentaries*, 16–19 (1769); ... (in condemning "punishments of unreasonable severity," uses "cruel" to mean severe or excessive). Indeed, barely three months after the Bill of Rights was adopted, the House of Lords declared that a "fine of thirty thousand pounds, imposed by the court of King's Bench upon the earl of Devon, was excessive and exorbitant, against magna charta, the common right of the subject, and against the law of the land." *Earl of Devon's Case*, 11 State Trials 133, 136 (1689).'

226   *Weems v. United States*, 217 U.S. 349 (1910); *Robinson v. California*, 360 U.S. 660 (1962); *Hutto v. Davis*, 454 U.S. 370, 374, (1982); *Woodson v. North Carolina*, 428 U.S. 280 (1976); *Coker v. Georgia*, 433 U.S. 584, 592 (1977); *Enmund v. Florida*, 458 U.S. 782 (1982); *Hutto v. Finney*, 437 U.S. 678, 685 (1978); *Ingraham v. Wright*, 430 U.S. 651, 667 (1977); and *Gregg v. Georgia*, 428 U.S. 153, 171–172 (1976).

227   *Solem v. Helm*, 463 U.S. 277, 284–286 (1983).

228   554 U.S. 570 (2008). A detailed comparative analysis is beyond the scope of this paper. See further, Dennis J. Baker, 'Collective Criminalization and the Constitutional Right to Endanger Others,' (2009) 28(2) *Criminal Justice Ethics* 3.

229   *Harmelin v. Michigan*, 501 U.S. 957 (1991); *Lockyer v. Andrade*, 538 U.S. 63 (2003).

230   501 U.S. 957 (1991).

Helm.²³¹ In that case, the Court noted that: 'It would be anomalous indeed if the lesser punishment of a fine and the greater punishment of death were both subject to proportionality analysis, but the intermediate punishment of imprisonment were not. There is also no historical support for such an exception. The common-law principle incorporated into the Eighth Amendment clearly applied to prison terms.' There is clearly no foundation for the contention that the principle of proportionality does not apply to prison sentences. Neither the text of the Eighth Amendment, nor its purpose or the history behind it supports such an exception. The death penalty, fines and imprisonment were all common forms of punishment when the Eighth Amendment was drafted. What made these common forms of punishment unusual or cruel? Fines and prison sentences were considered to be unusual and cruel when the severity of the penalty was greater than the gravity of the crime.²³² 'Even one day in prison would be a cruel and unusual punishment for the "crime" of having a common cold.'²³³ Likewise, the death penalty is unusual when it is used for offenses that do not involve killing.

Interestingly, Justice Scalia does not always stick to his narrow form of originalism.²³⁴ In *District of Columbia v. Heller*,²³⁵ Justice Scalia writing for the majority struck down a law prohibiting gun possession, but held that a person would not be allowed to possess guns in sensitive places such as government buildings, schools, universities and so on. His Honor came to this conclusion even though there is nothing in the text of the 27 words in the Second Amendment to justify this limitation. In earlier times, the older boys in rural areas would have taken a rifle to school without question. Justice Scalia relied on scant precedent to dress up this exception, but the reality is that Justice Scalia interpreted the Second Amendment as providing such an exception by considering conventional understandings about the need to keep guns out of such places. While Justice Scalia does not explicitly adopt the 'evolving standards of decency' standard, he does, in effect, when he makes an evaluative judgment about the need to keep guns out of sensitive places in contemporary society.

It is unfeasible to interpret rights by referring to a purely originalist historical analysis. Justice White explicitly recognizes this in his dissenting opinion in *Harmelin v. Michigan* when he notes that: '[t]he scope of the prohibition against cruel and unusual punishments has long understood the limitations of a purely historical analysis ... When it comes to the Eighth Amendment, the Court must employ a flexible and dynamic interpretation.'²³⁶ His Honor rightly opines that

---

231   463 U.S. 277, 289–290 (1983) citing *Hodges v. Humkin*, 80 Eng. Rep. 1015 (K. B. 1615).
232   *Earl of Devon's Case*, 11 State Trials 133, 136 (1689).
233   *Robinson v. California*, 360 U.S. 660, 667 (1962).
234   See for example, the discussion in Jack M. Balkin and Sanford Levinson, 'Understanding the Constitutional Revolution,' (2001) 87(6) *Virginia Law Review* 1045.
235   554 U.S. 570 (2008).
236   *Harmelin v. Michigan*, 501 U.S. 957, 1014–1015 (1991).

the court has recognized that a punishment may violate the Eighth Amendment if it is contrary to the 'evolving standards of decency that mark the progress of a maturing society ... In evaluating a punishment under this test, we have looked not to our own conceptions of decency, but to those of modern American society as a whole in determining what standards have "evolved."' It is not clear how future cases will be decided, but it is worth noting that in *Kennedy v. Louisiana*[237] the majority also adopted the 'evolving standards of decency' standard to produce a reasonable result. *Solem v. Helm* shows that it is possible to use moral standards to interpret the scope of the Eighth Amendment without engaging in judicial activism or inventing new rights that have no connection with the Amendment.

Can Courts Determine Objective Accounts of Harm?

Where do we draw the line? I will focus on the criterion of harm rather on the criterion of culpability,[238] because the courts only have to generalize about one of the three core grades of culpability (intention, recklessness and gross negligence) to determine whether a particular harm warrants a jail sentence. A deeper analysis will be required when it comes to determining the harmfulness of the wrong. The courts will determine proportionality with reference to the harmfulness of the potentially bad consequences involved, to determine whether putative offenders would deserve a jail sentence for the type wrongful harm involved. I noted above, moral culpability is putative at the *ex ante* criminalization and punishment stage. The lawmaker makes a generalization about the wrongness of actions that are intended to bring about bad consequences for others. If the United States Supreme Court were considering the justice of criminalizing and jailing people for rape, all it would need to do to satisfy the moral culpability requirement is rely on the general presumption that intentionally raping others is wrongful. It would then turn to the harm element to examine the empirical evidence and deeply held conventional understandings of harm to ascertain whether rape does in fact harm others and to what extent.

Harm is the objective element that will be more important in these cases, as the court would use it as a criterion to decide the constitutionality of laws imposing jail terms, as culpability is an element of criminalization regardless of whether the bad consequences are harmful (*e.g.*, culpably engaging in harmless exhibitionism on a public bus is *prima facie* criminalizable, even though a prison sentence would not

---

237   *Kennedy v. Louisiana*, 554 U.S. 407 (2008).
238   Of course, recklessness and gross negligence as a condition of criminal liability will only be reconcilable with an objective account of justice and morality, if the *subjectivist* approach is adopted. This approach achieves justice by excluding mere negligence as opposed to gross negligence as a basis for criminal liability. Negligent dangerous driving would be caught, so long as it involved the higher level of negligence rather than mere accidental negligence.

be a proportionate form of punishment because of its harm*less*ness). Furthermore, even gross negligence is sufficient *mens rea* to justify a jail sentence so long as the bad consequences are sufficiently harmful.[239] In many cases in which there is no harm there will also be no culpability. Were a petitioner trying to get a law struck down that jailed those who merely possessed marijuana for personal use, he or she would point to the fact that it does not culpably aim to harm others and therefore does not wrong anyone but the user. In other cases, the conduct will be harmful but only in a trivial sense. How grave does the harm have to be to justify a jail term? In other words, what is the threshold of harm for sending someone to jail? At this stage we are considering the threshold for using a prison sentence, rather than the length of that prison sentence.

To determine the length of a sentence, the lawmaker would consider the harmfulness of the conduct and the degree of culpability that the offender manifested in bringing the harm about. A crude formula might be: *culpability × bad consequence*, that is, $C \times BC$ (or in the case of jail sentences $C \times$ harm $(H) =$ sentence length.[240] Culpability would have three values: (1) gross negligence; (2) subjective recklessness (those who choose to take a risk); and (3) full intention (purpose). In this reverse order, full intention would have the higher wrongfulness value of 3, with mere reckless having the lower value of 1. I am of the view that (culpable ignorance) gross negligence is sufficient to satisfy the culpability requirement, but that mere negligence is not. I do not go into detail here, but by mere negligence I mean pure accidents rather than the type of accidents that occur in circumstances where the wrongdoer should have been aware that she was endangering others.

Unlike culpability, harm cannot be divided into three broad categories because it varies significantly in degree and character. For instance, is physical assault worse than causing a person economic harm? What if the physical harm is minor and the economic harm is great? Harm affects different people in different ways. Some people might prefer a black eye to having their new uninsured Bentley motorcar destroyed by vandals. The best we can do is to make some basic generalizations about standard cases. Harm could be divided into crude categories with murder having a value of 10 and littering at the other end of the scale having a value of 1.[241] Deciding which of the 10 categories to slot a given harm into would not be easy, but it certainly would not be impossible. I use categories rather than fixed rungs on a ladder because, like culpability, the harmfulness of a given bad consequence will be a matter of degree. It may very well fall between two rungs on the ladder. But there are many variables that need to be considered to determine how to categorize a particular harm. Economic harm could be measured

---

239   *R. v. Adomako* [1995] 1 A.C. 171.

240   See generally, Robert Nozick, *Philosophical Explanations* (Oxford: Clarendon Press, 1981) at pp. 363–397.

241   See, for example, the Minnesota Sentencing Grid; also Richard S. Frase, 'State Sentencing Guidelines Still Going Strong,' (1994–1995) 78 *Judicature* 173.

to some extent by the value of the loss suffered by the victim in monetary terms, but we would also have to factor in other variables such as physical violence and intimidation if the economic harm was brought about in violent circumstances, as is the case with armed robbery. Furthermore, physical violence against others can be measured to some degree by the extent of the physical injuries involved, though again we would have to consider other variables such as the psychological consequences that flow from certain physical attacks such as those that normally flow from rape.[242]

Another important variable is inchoateness, as is the case with attempts where the core moral justification for punishment and criminalization is moral culpability and bad action as opposed to actual consequences. Actual harm is not needed for the purpose of justifying penal detention in this context. Inchoate offenses are designed to criminalize and punish conduct 'in so far as it has an appropriate causal relationship to a primary harm, as making the occurrence of harm more likely; and the culpability of someone committing an inchoate offense, in so far as it involves more than the willful performance of conduct defined by law as criminal, will consist essentially in her awareness of that relationship—in the fact that she knowingly, and avoidably, does what makes the occurrence of a primary harm more likely.'[243] The subjectivist argument for criminalizing attempts is that those who attempt to commit a criminal harm are morally no less culpable than those who succeed in doing so. For instance, if x shoots at n with the intention of killing n, but misses, she is no less culpable than if she had succeeded in killing n. There is no doubt that deliberately creating this type of *danger* should be criminalized and punished with a jail term. Coupled with this, the moral culpability element is sufficient to warrant a jail sentence when the harm aimed for is very serious. The wrongfulness element is present, but the bad consequence element is not satisfied. The bad acts/actions are sufficient to justify criminalization regardless of whether the consequences transpire. The controversy is in deciding if and to what extent any sentence should be discounted in cases in which the culpable offender has not caused any harm. Should moral luck play a role in grading and labeling offenses? Clearly, in those cases in which the attempted harm was of a trivial nature, moral culpability alone would not be sufficient to justify jail sentences.

In many cases the harm aimed for is sufficiently serious to justify a jail sentence.[244] Nevertheless, the absence of harm-doing cannot be completely ignored when determining the gravity of attempts, *etc*. Retribution is about inflicting hard treatment on those who have wronged others. Proportionality means that both harm and culpability need to be considered when grading offenses and setting sentences.

---

242 There are many kinds of violence which impact different needs and interests. See for example, the discussion in Johan Galtung, 'Cultural Violence,' (1990) 27(3) *Journal of Peace Research* 291 at p. 292.

243 R.A. Duff, *Criminal Attempts* (Oxford: Clarendon Press, 1996) at pp. 132–133.

244 It is not too controversial to suggest that crimes such as attempted rape, murder, arson, car theft and so forth justify jail sentences.

The objective element of harm should be considered along with moral culpability when grading attempts. The type of harm that was aimed for by the attempter is important for determining the gravity of the attempt and also for determining the amount of retribution that is due. There is a difference between attempted shoplifting and attempted murder. The potential harm gives the legislature guidance about where the sentence tariff should be set. Furthermore, the *overall impact* of the wrongdoing has to be considered if we are to ensure that the wrongdoer gets her just deserts and nothing more. A proportionate and fair sentence should reflect the gravity of the harm-doing and wrongdoing as experienced by the putative victim.

Attempted murder is gravely wrong, but the gravity of the harm is reduced to endangerment. The attempter risked the life of his victim, but due to a futile attempt no harm has eventuated. As I noted above, many variables need to be considered when grading offenses/sentences. In case of attempted murder, robbery, rape, and so forth, the victim would be left distressed if nothing else.[245] But the fact remains that the overall negative impact of an attempted murder or robbery is significantly less than that of a completed murder or robbery and therefore attempts should be graded as less serious to reflect this. The *gravity* of the harm is less in the case of endangerment. Failing to consider the overall impact of the wrongdoing for the victim would allow the victim to benefit from moral luck (escape harm) and receive full retribution as if she had been harmed. This type of distortion would not only prevent the offender from benefiting from moral luck, but also force her to suffer retribution for consequences that did not eventuate. Fairness and justice mean that it makes sense to consider the overall impact of the wrongdoing (its consequences for the victim) and make appropriate discounts for inchoate offenses.

A harmfulness grid or ladder would provide the lawmaker with general guidance, but in the end many decisions will be determined as a matter of degree within a particular category of harm. Using a grid or ladder would mean considering all the variables and theorizing about where to slot a particular harm in each case to make sure that it is fairly labeled. Each decision would need to be supported with sound reasons and empirical evidence. A further variable that affects the harmfulness inquiry is the cumulative impact of certain harms. For instance, a single instance of littering does not pose a serious threat to the ecological balance that we benefit from collectively, but it would if everyone were to litter. If we consider the scale above with harms ranging from 1 to 10 with littering and similar harms at the bottom of the ladder, it is arguable that when x intentionally litters by dropping a coke can on the sidewalk she causes insignificant harm—harm that would fall between rungs 1 and 2 on the *harm ladder*[246] (C3 × H1 = 3). Although x has full intention, the harmfulness of her

---

245 The victim, having avoided harm, would no doubt also feel relieved.

246 That is, between rungs 1 and 2 on the harmfulness ladder because this is harmful enough in aggregate to warrant a criminal law response, but too trivial when individualized to warrant a jail sentence. I would expect shoplifting to fall between rungs 2 and 3 on the harm scale, with common assault possibly falling between rungs 3 and 4 and going upwards

conduct is too trivial to justify sending her to jail. But if the harmfulness of her littering is so trivial, why criminalize littering at all?

Harm does not have to be serious in an *individualized sense* to warrant a criminal law response rather than a private law response. Beyond the most obvious crimes that set back our individual interests, there are legions of others that set back our collective interests. It is plausible to argue that we have a collective interest in avoiding serious pollution. When many individuals litter our collective interests are set back. Gross[247] points out: '[s]ocial life, particularly in the complex form of civilized societies, creates many dependencies among members of a community.' The welfare of members of a community is dependent on each member of that community exercising a certain amount of restraint and precaution when pursuing his or her legitimate aims. It is also dependent on the members of the community cooperating to achieve certain common objectives.[248] Collective interests normally fall into one of two categories of interests: community or governmental. Community interests include those interests that are vital to individual welfare such as preserving health systems, national security, and the environment.[249] Meanwhile, preventing violations of governmental interests includes preventing tax evasion, maintaining the court system, preventing customs violations, and preventing the corruption of government officials.[250] We all have an individual stake in both community and governmental interests.

Feinberg notes that: '[t]he maintenance or advancement of a specific government interest may be highly dilute in any given citizen's personal hierarchy. I am not seriously harmed by a single act of contempt of court or tax evasion, though if such acts become general, various government operations that are as essential to my welfare as public health and economic prosperity would no longer be possible.'[251] The single act of environmental vandalism, littering, tax evasion, bribery and so on, not only invades a community interest in a cumulative sense, but also has harmful implications for individuals. 'Bribing of a public official harms me only indirectly or remotely, but it threatens direct harm insofar as it endangers

---

depending on the extent of any injuries or aggravating factors. Robbery might sit between rungs 6 and 7 with rape sitting between rungs 7 and 8. Clearly, conduct such as murder, terrorism and genocide would sit right at the top of the harmfulness ladder. Although this idea needs to be developed further, and supplemented with many more examples, and a deeper analysis, I tentatively suggest that a jail term would be appropriate only for conduct that has a bad consequence that falls between rungs 3 and 4 on the harm scale. Any harm below this would be too borderline to warrant imposing a jail sentence. Many variables will determine which category a particular harm belongs to. The variables of intention and recklessness will play a significant role in serious crimes.

247 Hyman Gross, *A Theory of Criminal Justice* (New York: Oxford University Press, 1979) at pp. 119–121.
248 *Id.*
249 *Id.*
250 *Id.*
251 Feinberg, *op. cit. supra*, fn. 8 at pp. 63–64.

the operation of government systems in whose efficient normal functioning we all have a stake.'[252]

Littering is criminalizable because the aggregate harm that would be caused by mass littering would be serious. In the modern world, there is ample evidence about global warming and the dangers posed by environmental vandalism. Were everyone in New York permitted to litter, this would have a greater impact on the collective interests of New Yorkers than 20 extra homicides per year. The offense of littering should not carry a jail sentence, however, because an individual should be held responsible only for her contribution to the overall harm. Although the aggregate harm of littering would be rather high on the harm scale, only a negligible share of that harm can be imputed to the individual who litters.[253] There is no doubt that tax evasion also results in harm in that it sets back our collective and individual interests. It sets back our collective interests in that there will be less money for public amenities such as hospitals and schools and it sets back our individual interests in that those who are honest suffer an economic loss by having to pay more to cover the eventual shortfall.[254]

Unlike littering, tax evasion could justify a jail sentence. By examining the tax evader's individual economic gain it would be possible to impute a measurable share of the aggregate social harm to that individual contributor. As it is not possible to measure her real contribution to the overall harm, the value of the tax evader's economic *gain* should be used to set a proportionate sentence. The courts should treat like cases alike. The jail sentence for tax evasion should be similar to those for normal theft cases, even though the theft involved in tax evasion does not directly impact any individual interests. Furthermore, if the tax evasion were for 20 dollars, then there should be no jail sentence as a person would not normally be sent to jail for stealing 20 dollars from an individual as opposed to the state. In the end it is a matter of degree and the lawmaker would have to demonstrate, at least in crude terms, though not with mathematical precision, that the wrongdoer's gain was a sufficient contribution to the aggregate harm to make it fair to impose a jail sentence.[255] The length of the jail term should be proportionate to the extent of the economic value of the theft in individualized terms, as even the evasion of 10

---

252 *Id.*

253 Baker, *op. cit. supra*, fn. 21.

254 Von Hirsch notes that punishing individual wrongdoing cannot be explained in terms of obtaining an unfair advantage, but suggests that some offenses 'might plausibly be explained in terms of unjustified advantage. Tax evasion is an example: it seems to involve taking more than one's share.' Von Hirsch, *op. cit. supra*, fn. 150 at p. 8; also von Wright, *op. cit. supra*, fn. 76 at p. 216. However, von Hirsch notes that the unfair advantage test does not offer much guidance on whether to jail a tax evader. Here I suggest that any jail time should be proportionate to the wrongdoer's individual gain, rather than her contribution to the loss caused by aggregate harm of many people evading tax because her contribution to the aggregate harm would be too trivial to measure.

255 This type of theft does not involve violence and does not impact directly on the interests of others, so these variables would have to be considered when considering

million dollars' tax would not set back our collective interests in any measurable way.

It is not possible to determine the fairness of the length of a sentence with any exactitude, nor is it possible to determine with precision when a wrong is serious enough to justify a jail sentence. If a sentence is justified in accordance with the potential offender's culpability and the harmfulness of her actions, what degree of each is required to warrant a short jail term? The shortest jail sentence might be between one and three days. Even three days in prison would be seriously harmful for those who are locked up. Therefore, the culpable harm-doing would have to be reasonably serious to warrant even a short jail term. I doubt that shoplifting goods worth less than $500 would justify a short jail term for a first time offender, but if we add the variable of repeat offending then it might be fair to resort to the use of a jail sentence. From the *ex ante* perspective the lawmaker could state that this is a trivial harm, but if a person chooses to recidivate, she can expect jail time eventually. Again we face the problem of where to draw the line. After all, retribution in a just society is not as simple as an eye for an eye.

I have argued that a person should not be jailed unless her wrongdoing has harmful (or potentially harmful) consequences. If we accept this proposition, then we are able to provide the courts with a realistic and manageable standard for reviewing criminalization that involves jail terms. Most constitutional judges could distinguish objective harm from a non-objective harm by drawing on deeply held conventional understandings of harm. Determining whether conduct is sufficiently harmless for the purposes of striking down a criminal statute that carries a jail term is not too different from determining whether panhandling involves an exercise of one's right to freedom of expression. The harm analysis carried out by the learned trial judge in *Malmo-Levine*[256] and followed by Justice Arbour in dissent in the Supreme Court of Canada[257] is particularly impressive in this respect. On the basis of the evidence put before the court, the trial judge found that moderate long-term use of marijuana by a healthy adult was not harmful, that there is no conclusive evidence to show that it causes irreversible organic or mental damage to the user, except in relation to the lungs, and that marijuana is not a highly reinforcing type of drug like heroin or cocaine.

The trial judge also found that there was no evidence of a causal relationship between marijuana use and other criminality. Her Honor noted that the health costs related to marijuana use are small in comparison to those associated with tobacco and alcohol consumption.[258] Coupled with this, these types of costs are remote harms. I argue in the next chapter that harm has to be fairly imputable to the person

---

whether jail is warranted. In this respect, Feinberg's Standard Harms Analysis could also be instructive. Feinberg, *op. cit. supra*, fn. 8 at pp. 215–216.

256 *R. v. Malmo-Levine* [2000] B.C.C.A. 335. See also *R. v. Parker* (1997), 12 C.R. (5th) 251 (Ont. Ct. Justice) and *R. v. Clay* (1997), 9 C.R. (5th) 349 (Ont. Gen. Div.).

257 *R. v. Malmo-Levine* [2003] S.C.C. 74.

258 *R. v. Malmo-Levine* [2000] B.C.C.A. 335.

being criminalized (for present purposes the person being deprived of her liberty via imprisonment) if the harm constraint is to be satisfied.[259] The learned trial judge reviewed an Australian government report completed in 1994[260] and noted that marijuana use harmed the health of only a minority of users, including persons with pre-existing diseases such as cardiovascular disease, respiratory disease, and schizophrenia or other drug dependencies, as well as pregnant women.[261] To the extent that the objective harm is only *self-harm*, it is not criminalizable.

The United States Supreme Court has also demonstrated some skill in drawing the line in these types of cases. In *Solem v. Helm* it was held that a court's proportionality analysis under the Eighth Amendment should be guided by objective criteria including the gravity of the offense and the severity of the sentence; the sentences imposed in similar cases; and whether more serious crimes have been treated more leniently.[262] This case demonstrates that judges are competent to determine the gravity of an offense and could do so by considering the harm caused or threatened and the culpability of the putative offender.[263] The Court noted that: 'There are generally accepted criteria for comparing the severity of different crimes, despite the difficulties courts face in attempting to draw distinctions between similar crimes.'[264] The problem of knowing where to draw the line, although troubling, does not arise merely in the area of deciding the justice of penal punishment.[265] The Court also referred to other objective variables such as violence, the gravity and inchoateness of the harm and also whether the offender was an accessory or principal. The Court summed up by noting: 'This list is by no means exhaustive. It simply illustrates that there are generally accepted criteria for comparing the severity of different crimes on a broad scale, despite the difficulties courts face in attempting to draw distinctions between similar crimes.'[266] The proportionality constraint has two limbs, ordinal and cardinal proportionality. Ordinal proportionality ensures equality by mandating that persons convicted of comparable crimes with similar criminal records receive comparable sentences. Meanwhile, cardinal proportionality considers the fairness of a given sentence from the *ex ante* criminalization perspective by setting sentences in accordance with the harmfulness and culpableness of the

---

259 Baker, op. cit. supra, fn. 21.
260 Wayne Hall, Nadia Solowij and Jim Lemon, National Drug Strategy: The Health and Psychological Consequences of Cannabis Use (Canberra: Australian Government Publishing Service, 1994).
261 *R. v. Malmo-Levine* [2000] BC.C.A. 335, at paras. 20–21.
262 *Solem v. Helm*, 463 U.S. 277, 290–294 (1983).
263 *Solem v. Helm*, 463 U.S. 277, 292 (1983).
264 *Solem v. Helm*, 463 U.S. 277, 292 (1983).
265 *Solem v. Helm*, 463 U.S. 277, 292 (1983) citing a number of examples where the Court has been called on to make similar evaluative assessments.
266 *Solem v. Helm*, 463 U.S. 277, 292 (1983).

potential wrongdoing. In *Solem v. Helm* the Court considered both cardinal and ordinal proportionality.

Drawing the Line

The French recognized harm as a general constitutional constraint around the same time as the United States Constitution was drafted. Articles IV and V of the French Declaration of the Rights of Man and of the Citizen 1789 expressly mention harm as a justice constraint. Article IV of the French Declaration states: 'Liberty consists in the freedom to do everything which *injures* no one else; hence the existence of the natural rights of each man has no limits except those which assure to the other members of the society the enjoyment of the same rights. These limits can only be determined by law.' Meanwhile Article V states: 'Law can only prohibit such actions as are hurtful to society. Nothing may be prevented which is not forbidden by law, and no one may be forced to do anything not provided by law.' There is little doubt that thinkers such as Rousseau, Kant[267] and Locke[268] influenced the Framers of the American Constitution. It is also evident that the Framers had similar views about harm, liberty, fair punishment and justice more generally. It was these ideals that led to the enactment of the Constitution. There is no reason to suggest that these types of general moral aims were beyond the Framer's grasp.

In this book, I have argued that the harm criterion should be considered as a standard for considering the proportionality of criminalization and punishment. It can be used to measure the proportionality of the crime label (that is, mere conviction without punishment) pursuant to the *legislative response* that is *proportionate to the societal problems at issue standard* or to measure the proportionality of punishment more generally pursuant to constitutional provisions such as the Eighth Amendment. The lawmaker could criminalize exhibitionism if it could show that criminalization was a proportionate response to the societal problems that arise from exhibitionism, but it could not jail the exhibitionist, nor could it impose an excessive fine such as $50,000, because the Eighth Amendment also requires fines to be proportionate with the wrongdoing involved. Given that the bad consequence flowing from exhibitionism is harmless, the Court could not refer to harm to determine the proportionality of fines. Instead, it would consider like cases and the gravity of the societal problems arising from exhibitionism. Harm works well as a measuring stick for offenses carrying jail terms, because jail time *per se* involves harm. But when there is no harm involved, the state bears the

---

267 David A.J. Richards, 'Human Rights and the Moral Foundations of the Substantive Criminal Law,' 12 *Georgia Law Review* 1395 (1979).

268 See also Jeffrey S. Koehlinger, 'Substantive Due Process Analysis and the Lockean Liberal Tradition: Rethinking the Modern Privacy Cases,' (1990) 65 *Indiana Law Journal* 723.

burden of justifying the case for criminalization. This will not be an easy burden to satisfy, as trivial claims of offense and disgust will not do.

The general constitutional right not be unfairly criminalized is found not only in provisions such as the personal autonomy and proportionate punishment protections, but in all the other specific rights read in sum. Clearly, one of the most fundamental rights that has been enshrined in a number of constitutional documents is the right not to be unfairly punished. Even an originalist reading of the Constitution cannot deny that this right exists. It exists, and it requires a dynamic normative interpretation if the moral aim of the right is to be achieved. The Supreme Court has recognized that punishment may have violated the proportionality requirement in the Eighth Amendment in the past by considering whether the offending punishment was contrary to the *evolving standards of decency that mark the progress of a maturing society.* 'In evaluating a punishment under this test, "we have looked not to our own conceptions of decency, but to those of modern American society as a whole" in determining what standards have "evolved,"[269] ... and thus have focused not on "the subjective views of individual Justices," but on "objective factors to the maximum possible extent,"... It is this type of objective factor which forms the basis for the tripartite proportionality analysis set forth in *Solem*.'[270]

The objective criteria used in *Solem* included: (1) the harmfulness of the crime in comparison to the punishment; (2) the sentences imposed in the jurisdiction for similarly grave offenses; and (3) whether other jurisdictions imposed a lesser sentence for the same crime. The 'evolutive interpretation'[271] doctrine would also allow the Strasbourg Court of Human Rights in Europe to consider similar factors when determining the proportionate punishment provision in the *European Convention*,[272] and while the 'margin of appreciation' doctrine allows that Court to take into account that the E.C.H.R. will be interpreted differently in different countries, the ordinal and cardinal proportionality requirements would mean that gross differences would be contrary to justice and thus arbitrary. Thus, if most countries do not jail shoplifters and a member state imposed a lengthy jail term for shoplifting, regardless of the margin of appreciation doctrine the Court would be compelled to uphold the shoplifter's right not to be unfairly punished.

---

269 This type of test can be read as a normative standard. See Postema, *op. cit. supra*, fn. 101.

270 *Harmelin v. Michigan*, 501 U.S. 957, 1014–1015 (1991).

271 See Eva Brems, *Human Rights: Universality and Diversity* (The Hague: Martinus Nijhoff Publishers, 2001) at p. 396. Cf. Howard Charles Yourow, *The Margin of Appreciation Doctrine in the Dynamics of European Human Rights Jurisprudence* (The Hague: Martinus Nijhoff Publishers, 1995) Cf. Lawrence v. Texas, 539 U.S. 558 (2003).

272 European Convention for the Protection of Human Rights and Fundamental Freedoms, 4 November 1950, 213 U.N.T.S. 222, (entered into force generally on 3 September 1953).

I have argued that the core objective measuring stick is harm when jail is involved. Harm is objective because sentences imposed within the jurisdiction or in other jurisdictions might be equally unfair. As I noted above, the majority in *Malmo-Levine* in the Supreme Court of Canada relied on disproportionate sentences as expressed in older laws such as those outlawing incest to justify upholding a disproportionate sentence for marijuana possession for personal use. Using objective harm to draw a line will not be easy in borderline cases. For instance, it would not be easy to determine whether the trivial harm involved in shoplifting warrants a very short jail term, so the court will have to be left some room for a margin for error. Nonetheless, the courts would have no difficulty in identifying sentences that are unjust in more than a trivial sense. If a person was given five years for stealing a pair of shoes, then clearly the U.S. Supreme Court could identify the disproportionality between the harmfulness of the wrong and the sentence imposed. The Court could also determine the proportionality of criminalization in cases where harmless conduct is subject to jail sentences—*i.e.*, the Court would not have to engage in judicial activism or stretch the meaning of the Eighth Amendment (dispense with an analysis of the prudential and historical factors that typically inform judicial determinations of the rights individuals have) in order to strike down laws jailing people for possessing sex toys, feeding homeless people, attending strip clubs, *etc*. Likewise, it would not have to invent any new rights or stretch the meaning of the Eighth Amendment to be able to determine the injustice of the 'three strikes and you are out' type sentences, *etc*.

In *Rammel v. Estelle*,[273] the U.S. Supreme Court upheld a life sentence for fraud crimes involving a sum of $230. Meanwhile, in *Harmelin v. Michigan*, the Court upheld a life sentence without the possibility of parole for possession of 672 grams of cocaine, while in *Lockyer v. Andrade*,[274] it upheld two consecutive 25 year sentences imposed under California's three-strikes law for shoplifting offenses involving the theft of $150 worth of videotapes. If the House of Lords could determine that that a 'fine of thirty thousand pounds, imposed by the court of King's Bench upon the Earl of Devon, was excessive and exorbitant [given the harm involved], against magna charta, the common right of the subject, and against the law of the land'[275] in 1689, it is difficult to believe that the United States Supreme Court in the twenty-first century does not have the expertise to interpret the Eighth Amendment in a way that is reconcilable with its *raison d'être*. Using harm as a criterion for determining the proportionality of grossly unfair sentences would not be controversial. These types of evaluative judgments are no different from those adopted to determine the scope of the free speech and privacy rights. The staunchest originalist could not deny that determining whether a person has a right to free speech and whether that right is overridden for a compelling state reason, involves some kind of moral assessment. The right to fair punishment

---

273　445 U.S. 263 (1980).
274　538 U.S. 63 (2003).
275　*Earl of Devon's Case*, 11 State Trials 133, 136 (1689).

is patently evident in the Constitution and should be recognized as providing a general right not to be unfairly punished. To continue to read down this right to circumvent its moral aim is wrong, when such a reading is so utterly out of keeping with our deeply held conventional understandings of justice. To impose such an interpretation is inconsistent with our constitutional sense of personal liberty and our respect for the rule of law.

Chapter 3
The Limits of Remote Harm and Endangerment Criminalization

Criminal Responsibility for the Acts of Another

In what follows, I use Justice Scalia's individual rights interpretation of the Second Amendment to outline the limits of remote harm and endangerment criminalization. I argue that what is really at issue with this type of criminalization is individual justice and whether it should be overridden for the collective good. I do not just dismiss the anti-gun lobby's claim that individual justice in such cases does more harm than good, because the empirical evidence demonstrates that the cost of firearm fatalities and injuries is enormous. I examine the empirical evidence and attempt to demarcate the limitations of using criminalization to override individual rights for the greater good. The general issue is about the conflict that arises when individual justice seems to do more harm than good. I outline the fundamental right not be criminalized for another's wrongdoing with reference to the gun possession exemplar and ask whether there are grounds for trumping this right for the collective good. I also examine culpable endangerment as an alternative moral justification for creating independent possession offenses. However, given that the general dangerousness of mere possession is not significant, the case for endangerment criminalization is weak.

The U.S. Supreme Court[1] recently held that the Second Amendment of the Constitution of the United States protects an individual's right to bear and keep arms (at least in the home). The Court's opinion will stimulate further debate for decades to come, as gun related injuries and fatalities are as prevalent as ever in the United States.[2] The question for present purposes is whether Justice Scalia's interpretation (although a seemingly reasonable interpretation in legal terms) can be reconciled with justice. I do not intend to add to the vast hermeneutic literature that debates whether or not the constitutionalized legal right to bear arms should have been interpreted as an individual right. Instead, I will examine the wider implications of criminalizing remote harms in order to achieve utilitarian goals. Blanket prohibitions against firearm possession seemingly interfere with a firearm possessor's fundamental rights in more ways than one. It is one thing to be denied

---

1   *District of Columbia v. Heller*, 554 U.S. 570 (2008).
2   For earlier discussion of this right, see *United States v. Emerson*, 46 F. Supp. 2d 598 (N.D. Tex. 1999).

a right to possess firearms for recreational and self-defense[3] purposes, but it is something entirely different to be criminalized for the harmful choices of others. The fundamental issue of justice that I focus on is not about the constitutional right to have a firearm for recreational or self-defense purposes, but about the right not to be criminalized and subjected to penal censure for engaging in blameless and harmless conduct (mere possession) simply because others choose to commit criminal wrongs (*i.e.*, misuse firearms).

The general justice question that persists is: should a person be bound to forfeit her right to engage in harmless/blameless activities so that others are not led to cause harm? It would not be just to hold a person criminally responsible for harm that is directly caused by others over whom she has no control. Individual justice means that a person should be held criminally liable only for her own bad choices. Criminalizing mere possession is a form of remote harm criminalization.[4] Remote harm criminalization occurs when the lawmaker criminalizes a particular activity that is innocuous *in itself* to prevent some other type of aggregate harm or risk of harm from transpiring. Would it be fair and just to introduce laws to prohibit people from owning automobiles simply because many people die in car accidents every year? Clearly, it would not be just to prohibit people from owning a car simply because this would prevent the grave aggregate harm that occurs each year when many drivers choose to drive dangerously (under the influence of alcohol, as a result of speeding and so on). The act of driving while under the influence of alcohol is a separate activity from merely owning and driving a car for legitimate purposes. Dangerous driving is already an offense, and rightly so, because the dangerous driver risks *causing direct harm* to others. Blanket prohibitions against firearm possession are a form of collective criminalization. These laws aim to protect society by punishing all possessors of firearms even though many will never misuse their firearms. The overall aim of such laws is to reduce the aggregate harm that flows from firearm fatalities and injuries. The laws do not aim to impose retribution for any direct harm-doing, because this can be achieved by criminalizing the minority of firearm possessors who independently cause direct harm by misusing their weapons.

This type of consequentialist criminalization and punishment contravenes the fundamental principle of justice that a person should not be held responsible for the criminal choices of others. Unqualified consequentialism fails to recognize

---

3   Lott argues that high rates of gun ownership protect society, because many are deterred by the possibility of a victim being armed. John R. Lott, *More Guns, Less Crime: Understanding Crime and Gun Control Laws* (Chicago: University of Chicago Press, 1998).

4   See Dennis J. Baker, 'The Moral Limits of Criminalizing Remote Harms,' 10(3) *New Criminal Law Review* 370 (2007); Andrew von Hirsch, 'Extending the Harm Principle: "Remote" Harms and Fair Imputation,' in *Harm and Culpability*, ed. Andrew P. Simester and A.T.H. Smith (Oxford: Clarendon Press, 1996) at pp. 259 *et seq*.

the separateness of persons.⁵ However, the consequentialist aims of the criminal law are permissible when appropriate constraints or qualifications are recognized. The germane justice constraint is the retribution constraint⁶—which is comprised of a number of sub-constraints such as the culpability, proximate causation and bad consequence constraints.⁷ Just deserts criminalization involves showing that the defendant intentionally/recklessly aimed or attempted to bring about a direct harm (or other sufficiently serious bad consequences).⁸ It is arguable that merely owning/possessing a firearm for recreational/self-defense purposes does not involve moral wrongdoing or *direct* harm-doing. Therefore, there appears to be no discernible moral basis for invoking the criminal law. Criminalization is a mechanism for censuring and punishing a person's culpable act when it directly results in bad consequences for others. Firearm possessor x should not be censured and condemned for firearm possessor y's independent choice to misuse a firearm. The lawmaker needs to be in a position to justify and explain the decision to criminalize to those individuals who would be affected by some act. If x intentionally rapes y, criminalization should communicate to x in terms that both he and everyone else in society could understand,⁹ that x deserves to be censured and punished for his harmful choice. The critical moral reasons we can offer to x to explain why it is just and fair to criminalize his activities are: that he deserves censure for choosing to rape y because he knew that his actions would directly bring about a serious and avoidable bad consequence for his victim. In this chapter, I examine whether it is possible to explain to x that if she chooses to merely possess a gun that it will be fair to punish her for doing so, even though mere possession does not result in direct harm.

Desert-constrained criminalization and punishment is reconcilable with fairness and justice, because it only allows a person to be punished when she has made

---

5   See generally H.L.A. Hart, 'Liberty, Utility, and Rights,' in *Essays in Jurisprudence and Philosophy*, ed., H.L.A. Hart, (Oxford: Clarendon Press, 1983) at p. 199. Also, Denis J. Galligan, 'The Return to Retribution in Penal Theory,' in Colin F. H. Tapper, *Crime, Proof and Punishment: Essays in Memory of Sir Rupert Cross* (London: Butterworths, 1981) at p. 149.

6   See generally, H.L.A. Hart, *Punishment and Responsibility: Essays in the Philosophy of Law* (Oxford: Clarendon Press, 1968) at pp. 1–27; Andrew von Hirsch, *Censure and Sanctions* (Oxford: Oxford University Press, 1993); Michael Moore, *Placing Blame: A General Theory of the Criminal Law* (Oxford: Clarendon Press, 1997) at pp. 83–188.

7   Dennis J. Baker, 'Constitutionalizing the Harm Principle,' (2008) 27(2) *Criminal Justice Ethics* 3 at pp. 4–16.

8   Criminalizable bad consequences will not always involve harm. See Dennis J. Baker, 'The Sense and Nonsense of Criminalizing Transfers of Obscene Material,' (2008) 26 *Singapore Law Review* 126; Andrew von Hirsch and Andrew P. Simester, *Incivilities: Regulating Offensive Behavior* (Oxford: Hart Publishing, 2006); Joel Feinberg, *The Moral Limits of the Criminal Law: Offense to Others* (New York: Oxford University Press, Vol. II, 1985).

9   J.R. Lucas, *Responsibility* (Oxford: Clarendon Press, 1993) at p. 284.

a choice to wrong others.[10] The core prerequisites for retributively constrained criminalization are: (i) that the agent brought about bad consequences for others; and (ii) that the agent culpably chose to bring about those bad consequences (or risked bringing them about) even though she knew those consequences would adversely affect the interests of others.[11] It is this type of culpable wrongdoing that makes a person deserving of individualized and proportionate criminalization when consequentialist harm prevention is the legislature's general aim. Similarly, in the context of inchoate liability, Douglas Husak[12] rightly notes that the retributive constraints include a harm constraint,[13] a culpability constraint,[14] and a proximate causation constraint.[15] Professor Husak does not explicitly deal with the distinction between direct and indirect harm-doing. However, given the emphasis that Husak puts on causation and *proximity*, it is clear that he supports the view that inchoate liability should be limited to those situations where a person *directly* aims to endanger or harm others. For example, when x fires a bullet at y's head with the intention of killing y and misses her head by one inch, no harm transpires. Nonetheless, this type of attempted harm is a form of direct endangerment—the victim's life was endangered by the bullet flying within one inch of her head.

The rationale for inchoate liability is harm prevention and when the above constraints are satisfied this rationale is reconcilable with justice. However, remote harm criminalization creates a more complex problem. Unlike inchoate criminalization, the culpability, direct harm, and proximate causation constraints cannot be satisfied. In what follows, I show that the harm caused by a person independently misusing a gun cannot be imputed to those who merely possess a gun. In addition, in the final sections of this chapter, I argue that a way round this problem would be to point to the general dangerousness of mere possession (endangerment) to satisfy the harm constraint, and make it an offense to culpably possess a gun (*i.e.*, proportionately criminalize the choice to subject others to the low level of endangerment posed by mere possession). But it is difficult to reconcile the latter argument with mere ownership of a motorcar, which is also a dangerous thing to keep as it poses a higher level of endangerment than a gun.

---

10   See Dennis J. Baker, 'The Harm Principle vs. Kantian Criteria for Ensuring Fair, Principled and Just Criminalization,' (2008) 33 *Australian Journal of Legal Philosophy* 66.
11   The consequences have to be sufficiently serious to warrant a criminal law response. See Baker, *op. cit. supra*, fn. 7.
12   Douglas N. Husak, 'The Nature and Justifiability of Nonconsummate Offenses,' (1995) 37 *Arizona Law Review* 151.
13   *Id.*, at p. 170.
14   *Id.*, at p. 171.
15   *Id.*, at pp. 172–173.

Empirical Evidence of Remote Harmfulness

Let us start by considering the direct harm and proximate[16] causation constraints. Does easy access to firearms result in tangible harm of an objective kind? Firearm deaths occur all year round, year after year. The literature on the firearm control debate is vast.[17] I do not intend to provide a detailed survey of that literature here, as a brief overview is sufficient for the purposes of demonstrating that there is an empirical link between widespread firearm ownership and increased firearm deaths and injuries. The United States arguably has the most liberal firearm ownership laws in the Western world. There is no doubt that easy access to firearms in this country is a source of great aggregative harm of an objective kind. In the United States firearm violence causes a large number of injuries each year, many of them fatal. Cook and Ludwig[18] note that: 'The magnitudes, trends, and distribution of these injuries form the statistical backdrop to the public debate over gun policy.' The sheer extent of the long-term carnage is shocking. In 1997 the statistics showed that 32,000 Americans died of gunshot wounds, while a further 81,000 people were seriously wounded.[19] This is more than double the number who died from AIDS or liver disease in that year.[20] The statistics show that more than one million Americans have been killed from firearm violence since 1965.[21] More Americans have been killed from domestic firearm use than have been killed in all foreign wars in which America participated during the twentieth century.[22] Arguably, the aggregate harm caused by high rates of firearm ownership in the U.S. is of an extraordinarily grave kind.[23] Furthermore, it is

---

16 Proximate causation is about demonstrating that a person directly and culpably caused and aimed for a specific harm. As Dressler puts it: 'The closest thing to a bright-line rule in the realm of proximate cause is this: *An act that is a direct cause of social harm is also a proximate cause of it.*' Joshua Dressler, *Understanding Criminal Law* (Newark NJ: LexisNexis, 2006) at p. 202.

17 See for example the works cited in Earl R. Kruschke, *Gun Control: A Reference Book* (Santa Barbara, CA: ABC-CLIO, 1995); Robert J. Spitzer, *The Politics of Gun Control* (Chatham, NJ: Chatham House, 1995) and Kristin A. Goss, *Disarmed: The Missing Movement for Gun Control in America* (Princeton, NJ: Princeton University Press, 2006) at p. 41.

18 Philip J. Cook and Jens Ludwig, *Gun Violence: The Real Costs* (New York: Oxford University Press, 2002) at p. 15.

19 *Ibid.*

20 *Ibid.*

21 *Ibid.*

22 'Gunshot fatalities impose a disproportionate public-health impact because so many of the victims are young. Homicide and suicide each rank among the top four causes of death for youths aged 10–34.' *Id.*, at pp. 15–17.

23 'Killing by all means other than guns occur in the United States at a rate per million population that is 3.7 times the non-gun homicide rate in England and Wales. But homicides by handguns occur in the United States at a rate per million population that is 175 times

not only the aggregate harm that flows from increased fatalities that is grave. Firearm injuries are also harmful in both the individual and aggregate sense in that many people are left with traumatic brain injuries, spinal cord injuries, and other permanent disabilities. The second greatest cause of spinal cord injuries in the United States is non-fatal firearm injuries.[24]

Is the situation worse in the U.S. because of liberal firearm laws? Hemenway has argued that the U.S. is distinguishable from a number of other Western countries because of its high rate of lethal violence.[25] He compares the U.S. statistics with statistics from Australia, Canada and New Zealand and concludes that the firearm murder rate is 10 times higher than the average of those three countries.[26] The difference is to a large extent explained by the fact that Australia, Canada and New Zealand have very tight firearm controls. Australia introduced strict firearm controls after the Port Arthur massacre, which involved a deranged gunman killing 35 people in a tourist town.[27] The Australian government of the day ordered a massive gun buyback, and introduced blanket prohibitions against owning many types of firearms and introduced a strict licensing scheme for other types. These measures have produced very positive results.[28] Arguably the Australian approach has been very successful because it focused on the general *dangerousness* of widespread firearm ownership, as opposed to the more narrow issue of the so-called dangerous people, that is, on keeping firearms out of the wrong hands.[29] The

---

as great ... While the magnitude of the difference that can be attributed solely to gun use cannot be determined with precision, as much as half of the difference between American and European homicide rates may be explained by differential resort in the United States to the most lethal of the commonly used instruments of violence.' Franklin E. Zimring and Gordon Hawkins, *Crime is Not the Problem: Lethal Violence in America* (New York: Oxford University Press, 1997) at pp. 109–110. See also Peter Squires, *Gun Culture or Gun Control* (London: Routledge, 2000) at pp. 51–55; 174–201; Ian Taylor, *Crime in Context, A Critical Criminology of Market Societies* (Boulder, Colo: Westview Press, 1999) at ch. 6.

24 David Hemenway, 'The Public Approach to Reducing Firearm Injury and Violence,' (2006) 17 *Stanford Law & Policy Review* 635 at p. 636.

25 *Id.*, at p. 635.

26 *Id.*, at pp. 635–637.

27 This remains the world's worst mass shooting, even surpassing the Virginia Tech shooting where a crazed gunman managed to discharge 170 rounds in nine minutes, killing 32 people and wounding a further 25.

28 It is noted in the *British Medical Journal* that after the massive gun buyback in Australia firearm fatalities were halved. Coupled with this, in the 18 years before the buyback there were 13 mass shootings, but in the 10 years following the gun buyback there has not been a single mass shooting in Australia. See 'Success in Gun Law Reform in Australia,' (2007) 334 *British Medical Journal* 284.

29 Leonardatos *et al.* rightly note that safe storage and licensing mechanisms are of no help when the owner is determined to kill a family member in a domestic dispute or to commit suicide. See Cynthia Leonardatos, Paul H. Blackman and David B. Kopel, 'Smart Guns/Foolish Legislators: Finding the Right Public Safety Laws, and Avoiding the Wrong Ones,' (2001) 34 *Connecticut Law Review* 157 at pp. 169–171, 177–180.

case for imposing blanket prohibitions against firearm possession is based on the idea that anyone could be a potential murderer if a firearm is easy to access.

Hemenway notes that: 'There is strong evidence, from more than a dozen case-control studies, that a firearm in the home in the United States is a risk factor for homicide and suicide, as well as unintentional firearm death. The evidence also shows that in states and regions with more firearms there are more violent deaths, because there are more gun deaths.'[30] The empirical evidence also shows that children are substantially more likely to be killed unintentionally with a firearm.[31] Furthermore, a person could be properly licensed as someone who is mentally stable and not dangerous, but might misuse a gun in a heated domestic situation,[32] even though that person does not display the characteristics of the typical wrong person to be licensed. When a person misuses a gun to kill another there is no doubt that the individualized harm (a dead person) is objective in nature. It is possible to demonstrate empirically that a gun wound is in fact harmful. The lawmaker might safely conclude that when x intentionally shoots his wife y in a domestic dispute that he has caused direct harm. The lawmaker might also conclude that when many people shoot others the aggregate harm is an objective fact[33] and that widespread gun possession enables some people to be in a position to misuse firearms and thus is a form of endangerment in that it makes all our lives statistically less secure. However, what the lawmaker is not able to do is link gun possessor n who lives in Washington (or anywhere else in the United States) to gun possessor s's independent choice to commit a direct harm by misusing a gun to kill someone in New York. Merely possessing a gun is not sufficient to link a possessor to the criminal choices of others whom she has never met or does not even know exist, because she has no control over the isolated choices of others. Mere possession is not a proximate cause of any direct individualized harm—thus, it is not possible to satisfy the proximate causation constraint.

The harm that transpires from widespread firearm possession is indirect or remote, because it is contingent on a firearm possessor or someone else (who might access a firearm) making an independent choice to misuse a firearm. There are a number of ways in which firearm possession could be indirectly connected to the grave aggregate harm that is caused when firearms are readily available, but I will

---

30   Hemenway, *op. cit. supra*, fn. 24 at p. 639.

31   See National Center for Health Statistics, *Trend C Table 292: Deaths for 282 Selected Causes*, 1888. Online: <http://www.cdc.gov/nchs/data/statab/gm292_3.pdf>. However, 15,000 adults are accidentally shot each year. See Karen D. Gotsch *et al.*, 'Surveillance for Fatal and Nonfatal Firearm Related Injuries – United States 1993–1998,' in *CDC Surveillance Summaries*, April 13, 2001, No. SS-2 (2001). <http://www.cdc.gov./mmwr/pdf/ss/ss5002.pdf>.

32   Violence Policy Center, *When Men Murder Women: An Analysis of 2004 Homicide Data*, 3. Online <http://.vpc.org/studies/wmmw2006.pdf>.

33   The aggregate medical cost of treating gunshot wounds was six million dollars per day in the 1990s. Hemenway, *op. cit. supra*, fn. 24 at p. 637.

limit my discussion to the situation in which the owner of a firearm (or someone else who is able to access it easily, for example, a friend or family member, *etc.*) goes on to misuse it at some future time. Merely possessing firearms in itself does not harm anyone, as the aggregate harm transpires only when many possessors of guns or others who access the possessors' guns, make independent choices to misuse firearms.[34] The majority of gun possessors will never misuse their firearms and may keep their firearms secure so that no one else does either. Nevertheless, the probabilistic statistical argument is that easy access to firearms (either because they are possessed in a home or can easily be obtained from the corner store) leads to increased firearm deaths and therefore enables the indirect aggregate harm that results from many acts of firearm misuse.

The objective harm constraint requires that the unwanted conduct be of a kind that does in fact cause harm or poses a real risk of harm to others. The objective harm or bad consequence constraint is not satisfied when a person aims for a good or neutral consequence. For example, drug taking does not produce objectively bad consequences for others. The harm involved in drug taking is self-harm and therefore it only has neutral consequences for others. Its criminalization cannot be justified on the grounds that it would prevent harm to others.[35] The inchoate criminalization of drug possession is unjust as it aims to use harmful criminalization to prevent self-harming drug use.[36] Notwithstanding that mere possession might facilitate self-harm, self-harm does not satisfy the *direct harm to others* retributive constraint.[37] Other crimes that are collateral to the criminalization of drug use such as money laundering are remote harms and would disappear if the primary offense of drug taking were decriminalized. Consequently, the inchoate crime of drug possession which aims to prevent self-harm, creates two types of crimes (that is, 'drug use [the problem we started with] and a criminal subculture doing business in drugs).'[38] The collateral crimes such as money laundering that flow

---

34 Von Hirsch, *op. cit. supra*, fn. 4 at p. 271.

35 The case for decriminalizing drugs has been made very effectively elsewhere, so I do not intend to address that issue here. See D.A.J. Richards, 'Drug Use and the Rights of the Person: A Moral Argument for Decriminalization of Certain Forms of Drug Use,' (1980–1981) 33 *Rutgers Law Review* 607; Douglas N. Husak and Peter de Marneffe, *The Legalization of Drugs: For and Against* (Cambridge: Cambridge University Press, 2005).

36 See generally, Baker, *op. cit. supra*, fn. 7.

37 Joel Feinberg, *The Moral Limits of the Criminal Law: Harm to Self* (New York: Oxford University Press, Vol. III 1986). See also Richard J. Arneson, 'Joel Feinberg and the Justifications of Hard Paternalism,' (2005) 11(3) *Legal Theory* 259; and Russ Shafer-Landau, 'Liberalism and Paternalism,' (2005) 11(3) *Legal Theory* 169.

38 Murphy and Coleman note that: 'From a utilitarian ... perspective we must think of the indirect costs of criminalization—costs that can sometimes make criminalization undesirable ... Ironically, among such costs can also be the protection of criminal interests—a so-called "crime tariff". Criminalizing drug use, for example, might well have the function of encouraging the growth of the underworld subculture to deal in narcotics—something that would not arise if people could get narcotics legally.' Jeffrie G. Murphy and Jules L.

from the criminalization of drugs are independently criminalizable as culpable direct harms. Unlike drug possession, legitimate gun possession does not come within the purview of inchoate liability, because inchoate liability is limited to dealing with proximate direct harm-doing—in the case of drug use, proximate self-harming. In general, if people merely possess a gun for recreational purposes, then it is not possible to claim that they possess it with the intent to commit self-harm or to harm others.

Proving that the remote conduct does in fact enable the aggregate harm that flows from the criminality of others is important; if there is no empirical connection then conduct will not constitute a remote harm. The British government recently used unfounded remote harms arguments to justify, among other things, the criminalization of begging and prostitution. It claims that curb crawling ought to be criminalized because it 'fuels exploitation and problematic drug use, and that going to prostitutes contributes to the spread of HIV/AIDS and STIs.'[39] However, the report does not present any empirical evidence to demonstrate that casual unprotected sex with a non-prostitute is any less risky than it is with a prostitute. Or that casual protected sex with a prostitute poses a greater risk of harm than casual protected sex with a non-prostitute. All kinds of casual and unprotected sex could cause the spread of H.I.V., but that does not mean the state has grounds to criminalize all those who are foolish enough to have unprotected sex with others, whether those others be prostitutes or not.[40]

The broken windows thesis is a further remote harm argument that was invoked to justify a crackdown on begging in England and America.[41] It, too, is not supported with firm empirical evidence. The British government has cited the broken windows thesis to defend its crackdown on begging and has argued for zero tolerance for minor incivilities.[42] According to the broken windows thesis, neighborhoods that neglect minor signs of decay and incivilities such as begging

---

Coleman, *Philosophy of Law: An Introduction to Jurisprudence* (Boulder CO: Westview Press, revised ed. 1990) at p. 138.

39   *Paying the Price: A Consultation Paper on Prostitution* (London: Home Office, Consultation Paper, 2004) at paragraphs 7:22 and 7:23.

40   This is to be distinguished from those cases where the defendant deliberately inflicts harm on others by infecting them with H.I.V. In England prosecutions have been brought using section 20 of the Offences Against the Person Act 1861 (U.K.), with the individuals convicted of grievous bodily harm after 'recklessly' transmitting H.I.V. during unprotected sex: *R. v. Dica* [2004] EWCA Crim. 1103; *R. v. Konzani* [2005] EWCA Crim. 706. See also Matthew Weait, 'Criminal Law and the Sexual Transmission of HIV: *R v Dica*,' (2005) 68(1) *Modern Law Review* 121; John R. Spencer, 'Liability for Reckless Infection,' (2004) *New Law Journal* 448. The Iowa Code makes it a felony to deliberately transmit H.I.V., Section 709C.1 of the Code of Iowa 2002: Part XVI Criminal Law and Procedure.

41   See *Young v. New York Transit Authority* 903 F. 2d 146 (2nd Cir. 1990).

42   *Respect and Responsibility—Taking a Stand Against Anti-Social Behaviour* (London: Home Office, White Paper Cm 5778, 2003) at paragraphs 1.8; 3.40–3.44.

open the door for more serious crime to take place.[43] This thesis asserts that 'disorder and crime are usually inextricably linked in a kind of developmental sequence.'[44] The authors of the broken windows thesis argue that neighborhoods with abandoned overgrown properties, with broken windows, undisciplined children walking the streets, gangs of teenagers hanging around storefronts refusing to move when asked to do so, unmarried people moving in, people drinking in the streets, street fights, accumulated litter, inebriates, beggars and prostitutes on the sidewalks and so forth attract more serious crime.[45]

Wilson and Kelling argue that many residents in the broken windows neighborhood will think that 'crime, especially violent crime, is on the rise, and they will modify their behavior accordingly ... Such an area is vulnerable to criminal invasion.'[46] Essentially, the broken windows theory postulates that neighborhood disorder, physical decay—such as graffiti, litter, and general shabbiness; and minor incivilities, such as public drinking, begging and vagrancy—will, if left unchecked, send a message to potential malefactors that the area is a defenseless target for criminal activities because no one cares.[47] In a recent article Kelling stated that: 'disorder not only creates fear but ... it is a precursor to serious crime.'[48] William Bratton, the former police commissioner of New York, transformed the broken windows thesis into order maintenance, which has been labeled as the 'quality of life initiative.'[49] Order-maintenance policing aims to create public order by aggressively enforcing laws against nuisance offenses like public drunkenness, begging, vandalism, public urination, loitering, prostitution and other minor misdemeanors.[50] This approach requires the police to focus on public order maintenance rather than mere law enforcement.[51] Wilson

---

43   *Ibid.*
44   James Q. Wilson, and George Kelling, 'Broken Windows: The Police and Neighborhood Safety,' (1982) Atlantic Monthly 29 at p. 31. Cf. Dennis J. Baker, 'A Critical Evaluation of the Historical and Contemporary Justifications for Criminalising Begging,' (2009) 73(3) Journal of Criminal Law 212.
45   *Id.* at pp. 31–32.
46   *Id.* at pp. 31–32.
47   *Ibid.*
48   George Kelling, 'Broken Windows, Zero Tolerance and Crime Control,' in Peter Francis and Penny Fraser, *Building Safer Communities* (London: Centre for Crime and Justice Studies, 1998).
49   Bernard E. Harcourt, 'Reflecting on the Subject: A Critique of the Social Influence Conception of Deterrence, the Broken Windows Theory, and Order Maintenance Policing New York Style,' (1998) 97 *Michigan Law Review* 291 at pp. 301–302. The author notes that: 'It is a policy of zero tolerance toward minor misdemeanor offenses, or what are called quality of life crimes.' Cf. William J. Bratton, 'The New York City Police Department's Civil Enforcement of Quality-of-Life Crimes,' (1995) 3 *Journal of Law & Policy* 447.
50   *Ibid.*
51   *Ibid.*

and Kelling[52] argue that the maintenance of order by the police allows other community control mechanisms to thrive, thereby encouraging orderliness and ultimately law-abiding behavior. They contend that the police should aim to create an environment in which criminality is thwarted. To achieve this, it is postulated that the police have to be less concerned with violations of criminal law and more interested in monitoring street life from a broader perspective.[53]

Additionally, they assert that behavior that may not appear to be seriously criminal, such as begging, drunkenness, vandalism, littering and soliciting have to be prevented, because these acts decrease 'respect' in neighborhoods and reduce the desire of the locals to enforce controls. They postulate that even non-criminal acts such as rowdy children and noise are antecedents to more serious crime.[54] Criminalization and police action are justified on the basis that inaction will create the types of conditions that could lead to higher crime rates.[55] The broken windows thesis does not claim that a particular person is harmed by broken windows, rather it claims that the indirect acts of incivility are a precursor to the more serious aggregative harm that allegedly transpires when independent others target the broken windows area. Hitherto, little empirical evidence has emerged to support the idea that disorder, left unchecked, causes crime.[56] The proponents of the broken windows thesis usually start by citing Skogan's research from the 1980s.[57] Skogan analyzed previous surveys of residents in 40 neighborhoods throughout a number of sizeable cities.[58] He did find that measures of social and physical decay correlated with some types of serious crime, but prefaced his work with a noteworthy caveat:[59]

---

52 Wilson and Kelling, *loc. cit. supra*, fn. 44.
53 Ibid.
54 Ibid.
55 Ibid.
56 Harcourt, *op. cit. supra*, fn. 49. Bernard E. Harcourt and Jens Ludwig, 'Broken Windows: New Evidence from New York City and a Five City Social Experiment,' (2006) 73(1) *University of Chicago Law Review* 271. See generally R. Matthews and J. Young, *Issues in Realist Criminology* (London: Sage Publications, 1992); Robert J. Sampson, Stephen W. Raudenbush and Felton Earls, 'Neighborhoods and Violent Crime: A Multilateral Study of Collective Efficacy,' (1997) 277 *Science, New Series* 918; Dan Hurley, 'On Crime as Science (A Neighbour at a Time),' (New York: *New York Times*, 6 January 2004); Robert J. Sampson and Stephen W. Raudenbush, 'Systematic Social Observation of Public Spaces: A New Look at Disorder in Urban Neighborhoods,' (1999) 105(3) *American Journal of Sociology* 603; and Jock Young, *The Exclusive Society* (London: Sage Publications, 1999).
57 Wesley G. Skogan, *Disorder and Decline* (New York: Free Press, 1990); and Wesley G. Skogan, 'Disorder, Crime and Community Decline,' in Tim Hope and Margaret Shaw, *Communities and Crime Reduction* (London: H.M.S.O., 1988).
58 Ibid.
59 Harcourt, *op. cit. supra*, fn. 49 at pp. 311–312.

Ironically, the data from the 40 neighborhoods cannot shed a great deal of light on the details of the relationship between disorder and crime, for the measures all go together very strongly. With only 40 cases to untangle this web, the high correlation between measures of victimization, ratings of crime problems, and disorder make it difficult to tell whether they have either separate causes or separate effects at the street level.

Notwithstanding this, Kelling and Coles have claimed that Skogan established a causal link between disorder and serious crime.[60] After reanalyzing Skogan's study, Harcourt[61] found that there were 'no statistically significant relationships between disorder and purse-snatching, physical assault, burglary, or rape when other explanatory variables are held constant, and that the relationship between robbery and disorder also disappears when the five Newark neighborhoods are set aside.'[62] Harcourt found that out of the 40 included neighborhoods in Skogan's sample, the strongest link occurred in five contiguous neighborhoods in Newark. When those neighborhoods were excluded the link disappeared totally.[63] Furthermore, he notes that only a few of the calculations included data from all the neighborhoods, because the various surveys failed to ask exactly the same questions.[64] He asserts that overall the data did not support the broken windows hypothesis.

The quality-of-life initiative that was initiated by New York Mayor Rudolph Guiliani in 1994 has also been cited repeatedly in support of the broken windows thesis. As noted above, this initiative adopted the zero tolerance approach stressed by the broken windows thesis. Guiliani ordered his police to enforce even the most minor offenses such as begging, disorderly behavior, public drinking, street prostitution and so on.[65] After the introduction of this initiative there was a remarkable reduction in the overall crime rate, especially for serious crime. A number of conservative commentators have claimed that New York's declining crime rates support the broken windows thesis.[66] Harcourt[67] argues that a number of factors contributed to the declining crime rates in New York including increased police numbers, shifting drug use, new computerized tracking facilities and demographics. He rightly notes that the current assessment of what caused the remarkable decline in New York's crime rates is too uncertain and too contested to

---

60   George Kelling and Catherine M. Coles, *Fixing Broken Windows: Restoring Order and Reducing Crime in our Communities* (New York: Simon & Schuster, 1996) at p. 24. See also Dan M. Kahan, 'Social Influence, Social Meaning, and Deterrence,' (1997) 83 *Virginia Law Review* 349 at p. 369

61   Harcourt, *op. cit. supra*, fn. 49 at pp. 309–329.

62   *Ibid.*

63   *Ibid.*

64   *Ibid.*

65   *Id.* at p. 331.

66   See Kelling and Coles, *op. cit. supra*, fn. 60. See also Eli B. Silverman, *NYPD Battles Crime: Innovative Strategies in Policing* (Boston: Northeastern University Press, 1999).

67   Harcourt, *op. cit. supra*, fn. 49 at pp. 331–339.

conclusively support the broken windows hypothesis.[68] Harcourt acknowledges[69] that the quality-of-life initiative perhaps did have an indirect effect on the decline in crime. But he asserts that it had very little to do with policing trivial incivility/ public disorder. Instead he believes that the decline may have been attributable to the zero policing approach adopted in New York, which arguably enhanced the scope of the power of surveillance offered, and this permitted better enforcement against actual misdemeanors.[70]

There is empirical evidence to suggest that the quality-of-life initiative allows police to collect 'more identifying information; that the policing strategy increases opportunity for checking records, fingerprints, DNA, and other identifying characteristics; and that it facilitates information gathering from informants.'[71] This measure does not hinge on sending a 'message to criminals that they cannot commit crime, [but rather on] the old-fashioned idea that more police contact, more background checks, and more fingerprinting will produce better crime detection.'[72] Furthermore, a number of other cities achieved equal or greater reductions in crime during this period without invoking the zero tolerance policing approach.[73] At the same time San Francisco adopted a less strident law enforcement approach, which also reduced arrests, prosecutions and imprisonment rates.[74] Although San Francisco is frequently derided by conservatives for its alternative crime policies, it registered reductions in crime during this same period that were in excess or equal to comparable cities and jurisdictions—including New York.[75]

Coupled with this, a landmark study undertaken by Sampson *et al.*[76] suggests that most major crimes are linked not to broken windows, but to two other neighborhood variables: concentrated poverty and 'collective efficacy.' The Chicago study carried out by Sampson, Raudenbush and Earls puts forth the concept of collective efficacy (collective efficacy is defined as social cohesion among neighbors and their willingness to intervene on behalf of the common

---

68 *Id.* at p. 339.
69 *Id.* at p. 342.
70 *Ibid.*
71 He notes that: 'To be sure, this alternative hypothesis is also based, in large part, on anecdotal evidence, and it is essential that it too be operationalized and empirically verified. Like the broken windows theory, it is at present an untested hypothesis.' *Ibid.*
72 Bernard E. Harcourt, 'Policing Disorder: Can We Reduce Serious Crime by Punishing Petty Offenses?' (2002) *Boston Review*, April/May.
73 *Ibid.*
74 Khaled Eddin-Taqi and Daniel Macallair, 'Shattering "Broken Windows": An Analysis of San Francisco's Alternative Crime Policies,' Centre on Juvenile and Criminal Justice, San Francisco, 2002: available online at <http://www.prisonpolicy.org/scans/windows.pdf>.
75 *Ibid.*
76 Sampson, Raudenbush and Earls, *op. cit. supra*, fn. 56; Hurley, *op. cit. supra*, fn. 56.

good),⁷⁷ which suggests that the greatest predictor of neighborhood crime is not broken windows or disorder. Instead, they suggest that crime is deterred by community presence.⁷⁸ The preliminary results from their study imply that the broken windows thesis lacks credibility. Sampson and Raudenbush⁷⁹ noted in their earlier study that: '[c]ontrary to the "broken windows" theory, however, the relationship between public disorder and crime is spurious except perhaps for robbery.'⁸⁰ Once the researchers factored other neighborhood characteristics thought to be associated with crime into their study, such as poverty and instability, the correlation with disorder disappeared for every type of crime tested apart from robbery. In the end they suggested that serious crime and disorder was more likely to be related to deeper social and economic disadvantages.⁸¹ Sampson *et al.*⁸² found that neighborhoods high in disorder did not have higher crime rates in general than those that had low levels of disorder once collective efficacy and structural antecedents were held constant.

They found that there was no high correlation between crime and disorder to start with. 'Even for robbery, the aggregate-level correlation does not exceed 0.5. In this sense, and bearing in mind the example of some European and American cities (*e.g.*, Amsterdam, San Francisco) where visible street level activity linked to prostitution, drug use, and panhandling [begging] does not necessarily translate into high rates of violence, public disorder may not be so "criminogenic" after all in certain neighborhood and social contexts.'⁸³ In other words, they found that structural disadvantage and attenuated collective efficacy was more likely to affect crime rates than the policing of disorder. They held that attacking public disorder through strong-handed policing may be a politically popular approach to reducing criminality, but is an analytically weak strategy as 'it leaves the common origins of both, but especially the last, untouched.'⁸⁴ Bottoms asserts that '[t]he "collective efficacy" approach is clearly empirically stronger than the "broken windows" thesis, but it would appear to need some development before it could directly provide such guidance.'⁸⁵

---

77   National Center for Policy Analysis, 'Involved Neighbors Reduce Crime,' (Washington, D.C.: January 9, 2004), <http://www.n c p a.org/iss/cri/>.
78   *Ibid.*
79   Sampson and Raudenbush, *op. cit. supra*, fn. 56.
80   *Ibid.*
81   *Ibid.*
82   *Id.* at p. 638.
83   *Ibid.*
84   *Ibid.*
85   '[I]t would seem that positive control signals should encourage, as an effect, residents' willingness to engage in the interventions that are a key element in collective efficacy. If this proposition is correct, then the "control signals" approach should be able to help to provide some of the more short-term policy options that appear to be largely missing in Sampson and Raudenbush's account,' Sir Anthony Bottoms, 'Incivilities, Offense, and

The co-author of the broken windows thesis, James Wilson, recently stated: 'I still to this day do not know if improving order will or will not reduce crime ... People have not understood that this was a speculation.'[86] If the government is going to criminalize incivilities such as begging, on the basis of broken windows, it should prove that there is a credible nexus between disorder and crime. My analysis of the available literature suggests that there is clearly no empirical evidence to support the broken windows thesis. Therefore, it does not provide a sound factual basis for criminalizing begging. We are able to distinguish gun possession, because the empirical evidence demonstrates it is in fact an enabling factor of the aggregate harm that transpires from many people misusing guns. The broken windows type indirect harm argument is baseless because, unlike gun possession, there is no empirical evidence to demonstrate that the remote acts of begging enable others to engage in criminality. Thus, my focus herein will be primarily on the remote harm that is enabled by gun ownership, because unlike the broken windows thesis, there is empirical evidence to support the contention that widespread gun possession is a *but for* cause of widespread gun misuse.

Firearm possession is a case of remote harm criminalization rather than inchoate criminalization. I have argued elsewhere,[87] that a remote harm is a harm that occurs when *x*'s innocuous conduct is an *enabling factor*—that is, a phenomenon that in fact creates the background conditions that enable the primary-harmer to be in a position to commit a culpable direct harm. For instance, if no one was allowed to own a car, then the phenomenon of car ownership would not exist and dangerous drivers would be disenabled from making the culpable choice to drive dangerously. Similarly, if no one was allowed to own a gun, then gun-harmers would be disenabled from making the culpable choice to use a gun to commit murder, *etc.* In the latter case, the remote-harmers (gun possessors collectively) enable gun misuse by demanding the right to bear arms and by utilizing the right by possessing guns. The remote-harmer (gun possessor) is only indirectly (remotely) connected to the direct harm-doer (the primary party who misuses a gun), because the harm is contingent on the primary-harmer making the independent criminal choice to commit a criminal harm. These types of indirect harm arguments are problematical, because '[a] difficult problem for imputation arises when *prima facie* innocent conduct is a *but for* cause of seriously harmful crime by independent parties.'[88] We need to know why it is just to blame an apparently *disconnected* and *blameless* party for the harmful choices of others. The culpability and direct harm constraints mean that criminalization should be limited to penalizing direct harm-doing (*i.e.*, the primary harm-doers). If the remote-harmer is also to be held

---

Social Order in Residential Communities,' in von Hirsch and Simester, *op. cit. supra*, fn. 8 at pp. 268–269.
    86   Hurley, *op. cit. supra*, fn. 56.
    87   Baker, *op. cit. supra*, fn. 4 at pp. 380–390.
    88   Joel Feinberg, *The Moral Limits of the Criminal Law: Harm to Others* (New York: Oxford University Press, Vol. I 1984) at p. 232.

responsible, then the primary harm has to be fairly imputable to both the remote harm-doer and those who subsequently carry out the primary harm.

Generally, the courts have refused to allow people to be held liable for being a mere *but for* cause (an enabling factor) of someone else's criminal harm-doing. Let us take the example of x, the owner of a corner store. X sells an ice cream to customer y, and y subsequently walks out of x's shop and throws the ice cream packaging on the ground. Should x be held responsible for y's littering? The harm is contingent on y making an intervening choice to throw the packet on the ground, but it would not have come about but for x selling the ice cream to y. Nevertheless, it is not clear why x is morally blameworthy (criminally condemnable) for this kind of remote harm. What about if x gives y a flyer advertising a political cause and y takes the flyer and then walks down the street a little further and throws it on the ground—would it be fair to blame x for the harm (the environmental harm caused to our collective interests from the accumulation of litter)? Ought x be held responsible for y's independent and voluntary choice to litter?

The above facts are similar to those of *Schneider v. New Jersey*.[89] In that case the U.S. Supreme Court held that people should not be criminalized for the criminal choices of independent parties who voluntarily choose to break the law in some way. The petitioner in that case had been convicted of violating an ordinance that prohibited anyone from circulating or distributing circulars and handbills in public streets.[90] The petitioner challenged the validity of the ordinance under the First Amendment, because it interfered with his free speech right. Under the ordinance, the distributor of the handbills was arrested only when the receivers of the handbills threw them in the streets.[91] The petitioner was arrested for handing out handbills to passers-by because some of those who had received them threw them away leaving the street and gutter covered with litter. The police arrested the petitioner and charged him with a violation of the ordinance, but did not arrest any of the people who actually engaged in the littering. The lower court upheld the validity of the ordinance on the ground that experience showed that littering of the streets results, *inter alia*, from the indiscriminate distribution of handbills. It held that the right of free expression is not absolute but subject to 'reasonable regulation and that the ordinance did not transgress the bounds of reasonableness.'[92] It was contended that the arrest was in keeping with the policy underlying the ordinance when the distribution resulted in the streets being littered with handbills, because

---

89   308 U.S. 147 (1939). One of the ordinances being dealt with in that case stated that: 'It is hereby made unlawful for any person ... to ... throw ... paper ... or to circulate or distribute any circular, hand-bills, cards, posters, dodgers, or other printed or advertising matter ... in or upon any sidewalk, street, alley, wharf, boat landing, dock or public place, park or ground within the City of Milwaukee.'

90   *Schneider v. New Jersey*, 308 U.S. 147, 158 (1939).

91   *Schneider v. New Jersey*, 308 U.S. 147, 156 (1939).

92   *Schneider v. New Jersey*, 308 U.S. 147, 155 (1939).

the distribution of the handbills was a but for cause of the primary harm: littering.[93] The lower court said the purpose of the ordinance was to prevent the sidewalk becoming unsightly and untidy.

In striking down the ordinance, Justice Owen J. Roberts, for the majority of the Supreme Court of the United States, observed that the rationale for the law was to prevent the streets being inundated with litter.[94] The offenders (those who handed out the handbills) were not charged themselves with littering the streets; instead, they were convicted upon the theory that the distribution of handbills would encourage others to engage in littering. Justice Roberts held that the purpose of keeping the streets clean and tidy was insufficient to justify a law that prohibited a person from distributing literature to those who are willing to receive it. Furthermore, he held that the burden imposed upon the city authorities in cleaning and caring for the streets, as an *indirect consequence* of the distribution of the handbills was not sufficient to override the offender's free speech rights. Justice Roberts stated that the constitutional protection did not deprive the city of all its power to prevent street littering, because there were other permissible methods for preventing littering. 'Amongst these is the punishment of those who actually throw papers on the street.'[95]

How then do we impute a share of the aggregate harm, and blame for it, to individual gun possessors who have never misused a firearm? The harm constraint is satisfied in an individual sense when we hold an individual responsible for his culpable choice to misuse a firearm to directly harm another. The individual who misuses the firearm causes direct harm to her victim, whereas those persons who merely possess or sell firearms in their corner store are a collective, non-proximate enabler of the aggregate harm that transpires from the ready availability of firearms. I argue below that, to the extent that the enablers are not blamed for directly causing a firearm death or injury (which is the case with possession offenses) and are merely blamed at a lower level for the lesser crime of possession, blame could hinge on the culpable choice to engage in this type of independent dangerous conduct. The *actus reus* of these types of crimes would be possession of a firearm. But to the extent that these offenses are justified merely as preventing aggregate harm, the question is: what is the culpable link between the remote-harmers and the aggregate harm? The aggregate harm that flows from gun possessors being enablers of the many acts of gun misuse cannot satisfy, unless we can find a way of fairly imputing a share of that blame to the individual possessor. The rationale for gun possession offenses is to criminalize conduct that increases the risk of direct harm. But unlike inchoate liability the relevant culpability and proximate direct harm constraints are not satisfied. Merely aiming to possess a firearm should not make the possessor complicit in the gun crimes of the world at

---

93   *Schneider v. New Jersey*, 308 U.S. 147, 156 (1939).
94   *Schneider v. New Jersey*, 308 U.S. 147, 156 (1939). See also *Martin v. Struthers*, 319 U.S. 141, 148 (1943).
95   *Schneider v. New Jersey*, 308 U.S. 147, 156 (1939).

large, as seems to be the case when we hold all firearm possessors responsible for the aggregate harm that flows from the criminal choices of a minority of firearm owners who go on to make the choice to misuse their weapons.

Nonetheless, a person in an emotional domestic situation could resort to using a firearm in the heat of the moment and regret it later. Likewise, many young mentally disordered offenders[96] have been able to commit mass murder in schools and other public places in the United States because of the ready availability of firearms. In the domestic situation, it is arguable that if easy access to firearms were not possible, then those in domestic disputes would have a chance to calm down. The firearm is particularly deadly and sudden. The competing interests here are the majority's interest in public safety and in avoiding the high aggregate costs that flow from the harm caused by widespread firearm ownership as opposed to the right of the individual to be held criminally responsible only for her own wrongful harm-doing. In the next two sections, I examine whether blanket prohibitions criminalizing all those who merely possess a firearm can be reconciled with justice.

Fairly Imputing Aggregate Harm to Individuals

Blanket prohibitions against firearm ownership have consequentialist aims. These laws aim to override individual justice for the greater good of reducing our chances of becoming a victim of a firearm wound or worse. In the last section, I briefly outlined the conceptual distinction between inchoate offenses and remote harm criminalization. I noted that remote harms are not the same as inchoate offenses, because inchoate offenses such as attempts, conspiracy and incitement are reconcilable with the culpability and direct causation of harm constraints. Inchoate liability is just because it is possible to impute an individualized direct harm (or direct endangerment) to the wrongdoer. For instance, if x attempts to kill y by shooting at y's head but misses by pure chance, the justice constraint is satisfied because of x's moral culpability. X directly sought a bad consequence and this justifies criminalization. The moral culpability, proximate causation and objective harm constraints are satisfied. It is not necessary for the conduct to result in actual harm so long as the wrongdoer intentionally aimed to harm another.[97]

---

96 The Virginia Tech massacre being a recent tragic example. Unfortunately, those who are struck down with mental illnesses such as schizophrenia are usually at an age where they are likely to be attending university or college. But there have also been shootings in schools, which is probably attributable in part to other factors such as violent video games and movies. However, such postulations need to be tested with sound empirical evidence. These are areas where more empirical research is needed. However, making it nearly impossible for such people to access firearms does seem to be a logical solution.

97 'A person who tries to cause a prohibited harm and fails is, in terms of moral culpability, not materially different from the person who tries and succeeds: the difference in outcome is determined by chance rather than by choice, and a censuring institution such

These types of inchoate offenses aim at harm prevention and are legitimate in terms of justice. The same can be said for the inchoate offenses of solicitation[98] and conspiracy.[99] The problem with firearm possession is that the possessor does not directly aim to bring about a bad consequence (harm) for others. In fact, the firearm possessor may aim for the good consequence of enjoying a firearm for recreational or security purposes.[100] A person may possess a stockpile of firearms without a harmful incident ever transpiring.

In this section, I examine the constraints set out in the law of complicity to ascertain whether it might be fair to hold all gun possessors collectively responsible for the collective harm-doing of the minority that misuse guns. I have demonstrated above that there is a strong empirical link between mass possession and the aggregate harm that possession laws aim to reduce. Nonetheless, justice can be served only if it is possible to culpably link the remote-harmer to the aggregate harm. A sufficient culpability link is required to justify enacting independent possession offenses. It is not only necessary to be able to impute some blame for the aggregate harm to the individual remote-harmers, but also to distribute that blame proportionately in accordance with their minor and individually remote contributions.[101] There are two alternative possibilities for satisfying the culpability and fair imputation of harm constraints. First, the constraints might be satisfied when it can be shown that the remote-harmer (firearm possessor) is culpably linked to the primary harm (increased firearm injuries and fatalities). Second, these requirements might be satisfied by demonstrating that the gun possessor commits an act of endangerment and thus should be punished at this level, because of her willingness (culpable choice) to possess a gun with the knowledge that it endangers others. Independent possession offenses would allow for proportionate labeling and punishment. But as we will see, such offenses are very difficult to justify when the probability of harm transpiring is very low.

---

as the criminal law should not subordinate itself to the vagaries of fortune by focusing on results rather than culpability.' Andrew Ashworth, *Principles of Criminal Law* (Oxford: Oxford University Press, 5th ed. 2006) at p. 445.

98   The inciter aims for direct harm by using the hands of another to bring that harm about. Therefore, both the moral culpability and objective harm constraints are satisfied.

99   The justification for conspiracy is largely harm prevention. 'Whereas in attempts the doing of a "more than merely preparatory" act is required as evidence of the firmness of the intent, in conspiracy it is that the parties are committed to carrying out the crime. Another part of the justification for an offense of conspiracy is that persons who go so far as to reach an agreement to commit a crime, and are caught before the agreement is carried out, may not be significantly less blameworthy or less dangerous than persons who conspire and succeed in bringing about the substantive offence.' Ashworth, *op. cit. supra*, fn. 97 at p. 455.

100   See generally, Georg Henrik von Wright, *The Varieties of Goodness* (London: Routledge & Kegan Paul, 1963) at pp. 114–135.

101   See Baker, *op. cit. supra*, fn. 7 at pp. 18–19.

Let us consider the first option. According to the first proposal, a culpability link would be sufficient to reconcile remote harm liability with the requirements of fairness and justice. Deciding whether blame should be imputed to the remote-harmer for contributing to the aggregate harm is a moral question: should the law impute blame for what will happen if x does n and this causes y to do s to both x and y at different levels? That is, should the law punish y at the primary harm level—misusing a gun—and x at the remote harm level for enabling y's gun misuse by possessing a gun (*i.e.*, for intentionally possessing a gun knowing that it presents a general low risk of endangerment? I draw on the ideas of moral culpability and individual responsibility to ascertain whether it might be just to impute a share of the blame for the aggregate harm caused by mere possession to all possessors regardless of whether their weapons are ever misused. The question is whether the remote-harmer is somehow culpably[102] associated with the primary-harmer's wrongful actions. If she is, then there might be a *prima facie* case for criminalization, as it will be just to impute proportionate blame to her for her remote contribution to the primary harm.

What is meant by culpable involvement? Andrew von Hirsch argues that: 'We are speaking of situations where the original actor, through his conduct, in some sense affirms or underwrites the subsequent [criminal] choice'[103] of the primary-harmer. Affirm or underwrite means that the remote-harmer's conduct would have to underwrite the final harm that is likely to transpire. An exemplification of the concept of culpable association is evident in accomplice liability. Joshua Dressler explains that: 'Accomplice liability is derivative in nature. That is, an accomplice is not guilty of an independent offense of "aiding and abetting"; instead, as the secondary party, he derives his liability from the primary party with whom he has *associated* himself.'[104] Culpable involvement in the accessory situation hinges on the secondary party's culpability. If the secondary party's contribution to the principal's harm-doing is unintentional then there will be no justification for imputing blame to her. *Per contra*, if x gives y a gun intending that y use it to murder another, then x clearly underwrites y's act of murder.[105] It is fair to impute blame to her y's more serious wrong (murder) as she has participated in a culpable way by intentionally supplying the murder weapon with the intention that it be used to commit murder. She associates herself culpably by intentionally assisting and can be held responsible for the primary harm, that is, the murder, as

---

102 Normative (I prefer the concept of culpability—as normative is somewhat assuming) involvement involves underwriting the primary-harmer's criminal choice. Andrew von Hirsch, 'Varieties of Remote Harms and Rationales for their Criminalization,' Cambridge University, Unpublished Mimeo (2006).

103 *Id.*

104 See Dressler, *op. cit. supra*, fn. 16 at p. 498. See also Joshua Dressler, 'Reassessing the Theoretical Understandings of Accomplice Liability: New Solutions to an Old Problem,' (1985) 37 *Hastings Law Journal* 91.

105 Cf. *Backun v. United States*, 112 F. 2d 635, 637 (4th Cir. 1940).

she indirectly helps the principal to achieve the direct harm. Professor Dressler[106] notes that most courts:

> hold that a person is not an accomplice in the commission of an offense unless he 'share[s] the criminal intent of the principal; there must be a community of purpose in the unlawful undertaking'. In the words of Judge Learned Hand, the complicity doctrine requires that the secondary party 'in some sort associate himself with the venture, that he participate in it as in something that he wishes to bring about, that he seek by his action to make it succeed.'

However, should a person not be held liable when she *knows* that her intentional assistance could assist the principal to engage in criminality? Arguably, it would be fair to impute equal blame to a secondary party when she intentionally assists a principal and is extremely reckless as to the side-effects of her intentional assistance. The English courts use the doctrine of oblique intention to impute intention to those who have acted with extreme subjective recklessness in causing the death of another. In England the jury may find that the result was intended even when it was not the wrongdoer's purpose to cause it, so long as the result was a virtually certain consequence of the wrong committed, and the wrongdoer knew that it was a virtually certain consequence. For present purposes, I will refer to oblique intention as a form of *extreme subjective recklessness*.[107] In the United States oblique intention or extreme subjective recklessness is used to impute intention to those who '[c]onsciously disregard a substantial and unjustifiable risk to human life.'[108] This type of imputation of intention for extreme recklessness is normally applied only in murder cases.[109] However, Sanford Kadish argues that blame could be imputed to a secondary party who consciously disregarded '"a substantial and unjustifiable risk" that the other person would commit the crime, the risk being "of such a nature and degree that, considering the nature and purpose of his conduct and the circumstances known to him, its disregard involves a gross deviation from the standard of conduct that law-abiding persons would observe."'[110]

In many cases mere knowledge (subjective recklessness as opposed to extreme subjective recklessness) has been sufficient for satisfying the intention requirement.

---

106 Dressler, *op. cit. supra*, fn. 16 at p. 514. See also Sanford Kadish *et al.*, *Criminal Law and its Processes: Cases and Materials* (New York: Aspen Publishers, 2007) at pp. 589 *et seq*.

107 *R. v. Woolin* [1999] A.C. 82. One either intends or one does not. Extreme subjective recklessness is recklessness, not intention. See John Finnis, 'Intention and Side-Effects,' in *Liability and Responsibility*, R.G. Frey and C.W. Morris (Cambridge: University Press, Cambridge, 1991) at pp. 32–64.

108 This standard is used to impute intention for second-degree murder. See Dressler, *op. cit. supra*, fn. 16 at p. 556.

109 *Id.* Cf. *R. v. Woolin* [1999] A.C. 82.

110 See Sanford Kadish, 'Criminal Law: Reckless Complicity,' (1997) 87 *Journal of Criminal Law & Criminology* 369 at p. 385.

I refer to subjective recklessness as involving those situations where the secondary party foresaw that there was a real possibility or substantial risk that an offense would be committed by the person whom she had intentionally assisted.[111] If *x*, a gun seller, is in the process of selling a gun to customer *y* and overhears *y* on his cell phone jokingly telling his mate that he is in the process of purchasing a gun so that he can kill his wife and her lover, but sells the gun anyway, *x* would do so with knowledge of *y*'s intentions and would realize that there is a real possibility of *y* carrying out the murders. Ought this level of subjective recklessness be sufficient for the purposes of imputing full intention to *x* for double murder?

Arguably, when a person sells a gun without sharing the purchaser's criminal intent, she should not be held liable for the principal's criminality unless she acted with extreme subjective recklessness. The oblique intention[112] culpability requirement would relieve the reckless gun seller of criminal liability, because even if the seller intends to sell the gun with mere knowledge of a purchaser's planned double murder, it would be pushing it to hold that the seller knew that the virtually certain side-effect of her intentional sale would be double murder. Merely overhearing someone rambling nonsense about a planned murder might put a gun seller on her guard, but it would not be sufficient information for the seller to conclude with certainty that the purchaser would go on to commit double murder after leaving the store. The jury is not likely to infer that the gun seller foresaw double murder as a virtually certain consequence of her intentional sale. Oblique intention would require that the foreseen side-effects of the wrongdoer's intentional assistance be: 'so immediately and invariably connected with the action done that the suggestion that the action might not have that outcome would by ordinary standards be regarded as absurd.'[113]

The problem with the English oblique intention standard is that it would also relieve defendant in *R. v. Bryce*[114] of liability, because it would be stretching it to

---

111   The English courts seem to be of the view that intentional assistance with *subjective-reckless* as opposed to *extreme-subjective-reckless* foresight of the principal's proposed criminality is sufficient for holding a secondary party liable: *R. v. Bryce* [2004] EWCA Crim. 1231. Ormerod erroneously interprets the *real or substantial possibility* test laid down in *R. v. Bryce* as oblique intention: David Ormerod, *Smith and Hogan, Criminal Law* (Oxford: Oxford University Press, 12th ed. 2008) at p. 195. However, oblique intention is about imputing intention for murder where the risk-taking was of such a high and serious degree that 'it might be fairly said that the actor "as good as" intended to kill his victim and displayed ... unwillingness to prefer the life of another person to his own objectives.' Dressler, *op. cit. supra*, fn. 16 at p. 555.

112   For a deeper discussion of oblique intention, see Itzhak Kugler, *Direct and Oblique Intention in the Criminal Law: An Inquiry into Degrees of Blameworthiness* (Aldershot: Ashgate, 2002) at pp. 1–7.

113   Hart, *op. cit. supra*, fn. 6 at pp. 113–120. See also Glanville Williams, 'Oblique Intention,' (1987) 46 *Cambridge Law Journal* 417.

114   [2004] EWCA Crim. 1231. In that case, the defendant arranged accommodation for the principal in a caravan near where the victim resided and also drove the principal to

argue that the defendant in that case foresaw that the virtually certain consequence of his assistance would be murder, since, at the time he assisted him, the principal was still of two minds as to whether to go through with the killing. The Kadish-type extreme recklessness test is preferred because it would not catch the subjective reckless gun seller, but would catch the extreme subjective recklessness involved in *R. v. Bryce*[115] where the defendant consciously disregarded a *substantial and unjustifiable* risk that the principal would commit murder; and his assistance was a gross deviation from the standard of conduct that law-abiding persons would observe. In *R. v. Bryce*[116] the court seemed to moved towards the *substantial and unjustifiable* risk standard, but substantial in that case was interpreted as meaning a *real possibility*, whereas substantial in the U.S. case law refers to taking a *great* risk where there is little or no justification for taking that risk.[117]

Arguably, the U.S. extreme recklessness approach would also catch those who intentionally assist crimes of recklessness, that is, those who either have it as their purpose to encourage another to engage in particular reckless acts (*e.g.*, a passenger demanding that the driver speed through a school zone intending that the driver do so)[118] or intentionally assist the principal to engage in reckless criminal acts (*e.g.*, where a hostess allows a totally intoxicated guest to borrow her car[119] so that the guest can drive home via the middle of New York). Assisting crimes of negligence

---

the crime scene the day before the murder was committed, with knowledge of the principal's intention to kill the victim.

115   [2004] EWCA Crim. 1231.
116   [2004] EWCA Crim. 1231.
117   See Dressler, *op. cit. supra*, fn. 16 at p. 556 and the cases cited therein.
118   Here the passenger encourages a dangerous act that could lead to further unintentional harm—it is her intention to encourage the acts (the substantial and unjustifiable risk-taking involved in dangerous driving) that would make her an accomplice to the dangerous driving and any unintentional harm that results. See Sanford Kadish, 'Complicity, Cause and Blame: A Study in the Interpretation of Doctrine,' (1985) 73 *California Law Review* 323 at pp. 347–349. Also, *State v. McVay* 132 A. 436 (R.I. 1926).
119   There is an important conceptual distinction between recklessly aiding the reckless criminality of another and intentionally aiding the reckless criminality of another. Williams provides an example of each: *n* would *recklessly* aid his son to drive recklessly if *n* knows that his son has a habit of driving in a reckless manner, if *n* realized after leaving the house for a long walk that he had forgotten to secure his car keys so that his son would not be able to use the car in his absence—and if *n*, instead of returning to secure the keys takes the chance that his son will not find the keys. *N* would *intentionally* assist his son's reckless driving if he allowed his son to use the car knowing that his son has a tendency to drive recklessly. However, for the latter to fall within the *substantial and unjustifiable* risk category, the father would have to know that his son almost always drives dangerously—has record for doing so, and has been barred from driving, *etc*. See Glanville L. Williams, *Complicity, Purpose and the Draft Code – 2* (1990) *Criminal Law Review* 98 at p. 99. Kadish reworks Williams' intentional assistance of recklessness criminality example, to demonstrate its criminalizableness under the *substantial and unjustifiable* risk standard. See Kadish, *op. cit. supra*, fn. 110 at pp. 380 *et seq*.

cannot incur accomplice liability, because it would be logically impossible for a person to aid a principal to engage in criminality that the principal was not even aware she was committing.

Extreme recklessness would be sufficient for the purposes of imputing equal blame to both the principal and secondary party. However, a less stringent standard of subjective recklessness could bring the subjective reckless gun seller within the purview of the criminal law. It would not be fair to impute equal blame to those who act only with mere recklessness as to the likely consequences of their acts of assistance (that is, those who recklessly assist and are indifferent as to the primary-harmer's criminal intentions). These persons do not share the primary-harmer's intent to bring about the ultimate harm and only foresee the primary-harmer's criminality as a real possibility. In such situations accessories, who know about the principal's bad intentions and recklessly assist, ought to have some blame imputed to them for their reckless contribution. It is not, after all, too much to ask the seller to forfeit a single gun sale in such exceptional circumstances.

Nevertheless, in such cases, criminalization should reflect the secondary party's lower level of culpable contribution. Therefore, the appropriate form of criminalization would be to enact a separate facilitation offense that would allow the offender to be punished in proportion to the harmfulness and culpableness of her contribution.[120] This approach also deals with the problem that arises when a lawful supplier of routine goods or services foresees that there is a real possibility that a particular customer is likely to use such goods and services to engage in criminality,[121] because the facilitation offense would have to be proportionate with the seriousness of the principal's criminality. If x sells a gun foreseeing that there is a real possibility that it would be used in a murder, then proportionate punishment for facilitating this type of serious wrongdoing would be fair. In trivial cases, proportionality would rule out having a facilitation offense at all. Reckless contributions to trivial crimes such as assisting a prostitute by dry cleaning a dress that she intends to use to attract curb crawlers[122] should not be criminalized, because the contribution to the principal's trivial harm-doing is not sufficient to satisfy the harm constraint for the purposes of criminalizing secondary assistance. Direct criminalization of the principal's trivial wrongdoing would be sufficient

---

120 Facilitation offenses should be used to deal with those forms of assistance in which the secondary party does not deserve to be blamed equally with the principal because she did not share the same intent as the principal with respect to the substantive offense. For a discussion of this alternative, see Robert Weisberg, 'Reappraising Complicity,' (2000–2001) 4 *Buffalo Criminal Law Review* 217 at pp. 261 *et seq*. Kadish *et al.*, *op. cit. supra*, fn. 106 at pp. 601 *et seq*.

121 See George P. Fletcher, *Rethinking the Criminal Law* (Boston: Little Brown, 1978) at p. 676. See also J. Finn, 'Culpable Non-Intervention: Reconsidering the Basis for Party Liability by Omission,' (1994) 18 *Criminal Law Journal* 90.

122 For this and further examples, see Rollin M. Perkins and Ronald N. Boyce, *Criminal Law* (New York: The Foundation Press Inc., 3rd ed. 1982) at pp. 746–747.

for dealing with the harm involved. Enacting independent gun possession offenses could not be justified by referring to this type of culpable involvement, as the possessor does not recklessly assist the acts of gun misuse carried out by independent others.

Professor Williams points out a further important distinction, which brings us closer to the remote harm exemplar. He outlines the important conceptual distinction between assisting/helping and influencing/encouraging a principal to commit a crime. Glanville Williams rightly argues that though subjective recklessness would be sufficient for imputing some blame to those who assist a primary-harmer, it would not be sufficient for imputing blame to those who merely encourage or influence a principal's independent criminal choices.[123] Mere recklessness is not enough to establish a culpability link when a person merely influences or encourages the commissioning of a crime, because the association is too remote. When a person recklessly *encourages* rather than *assists* another to commit a crime, something more than mere knowledge that she is running a risk of influencing another to commit a crime is needed to demonstrate culpable involvement. In such cases the remoteness of the accessory's influence means that she has no real control over the principal's actions. The secondary party's actions merely influence and she is not in a position to withdraw that influence if it is inadvertent.

Williams[124] discusses those situations in which a primary-harmer is merely influenced or encouraged by the actions of another. For instance, media coverage of violent street protests could influence some quasi-political groups to organize such protests so as to attract publicity for their grievances. Likewise, media coverage of prison riots could encourage further rioting. When a television station broadcasts prisoners on the rampage on a prison roof, destroying property and displaying banners conveying their message to the public and so forth, it could encourage the prisoners to continue rioting so as to attract additional publicity for their grievances. There is, for instance, little doubt that the media coverage of the nude protests in London in 2005 influenced the protestors' decision to go nude. Nonetheless, the television station should not be held criminally responsible for

---

123 Here liability is based on the normative concept of intention. As Williams notes: '[T]he normal doctrine of causation does not apply to accessories, so that it need not be proved that the act or encouragement or influence was a but-for cause of the crime. However, the act intended to influence the perpetrator must reach his mind, and must be of a kind that may be expected to influence him.' Glanville L. Williams, 'Complicity, Purpose and the Draft Code – 1,' (1990) *Criminal Law Review* 4 at p. 9.

124 *Id.* at p. 10.

merely foreseeing[125] that its actions could encourage nude protests.[126] Williams[127] asserts in the influencing situation it would also be necessary to also show that it was the accessory's purpose to influence or encourage the primary harm. Merely anticipating that you might encourage a riot or nude protest by giving it media coverage would not be sufficient. It is not the television station's purpose to encourage the criminal activities of the rioters and protestors.

The idea of purpose is important for establishing a culpability link in the influencing context, because the secondary party is not in a strong position of control or closely linked to a given primary-harmer. *Per contra*, an assister/helper is in a strong position to control whether or not she assists/helps another to commit a crime—unless her assistance is completely accidental or results from mere negligence—and she would not be held criminally liable for negligently assisting. It would be morally objectionable to hold the remote influencer/encourager blameworthy for merely foreseeing a primary harm as a definite side-effect of her lawful (remote) conduct.[128] The firearm possession situation is analogous in that it would not be fair to criminalize mere possession on the basis that the possessors foresee the aggregate harm that may be caused by others misusing firearms. Similarly, if *x* produces a movie depicting some kind of horrific crime, and only because of that film a member of the public voluntarily imitates the crime, then the remote harm will be imputable to the imitator as well as to the movie producer only if the

---

125 I stress the importance of not allowing people's rights to be curtailed by the fear that others will engage in criminal conduct. As expounded in *Beatty v. Gillbanks* [1882] 9 Q.B.D. 308, it is 'the unlawful that must yield to the lawful, and not vice versa': *Howard E. Perry & Co Ltd v. British Railways Board* [1980] 1 W.L.R. 1375. See also *Church of the Lukumi Babalu Aye Inc. et al. v. City of Hialeah*, 508 U.S. 520 (1993) at p. 539; *Turner Broadcasting System, Inc. v. F.C.C.*, 512 U.S. 622 (1994) at p. 10; *Schaumburg v. Citizens for a Better Environment*, 444 U.S. 620 (1980); *Superior Court Trial Laws Association v. Federal Trade Commission*, 493 U.S. 411 (1990) at p. 447; *Ward v. Rock Against Racism*, 491 U.S. 781(1989) at p. 805; *United States v. Moses* Nos. 17778-72 and 21346-72 (D.C. Super. Ct., Nov. 3, 1972). See also Madeline S. Caughey, 'Note: Criminal Law—The Principle of Harm and its Application to Laws Criminalizing Prostitution,' (1974) 51 *Denver Law Journal* 235 at p. 252.

126 'Bicyclists Ride in Protest, and in Little Else,' (New York: *New York Times*, June 12, 2005).

127 Williams, *loc. cit. supra*, fn. 123.

128 For instance, in *Beatty v. Gillbanks* (1892) 9 Q.B.D. 308, 'the Salvation Army foresaw that when they assembled they would be set upon, because they knew that this was the policy of their opponents; but that did not make them responsible for being set upon. The reason for the limitation is partly the result of our notion of responsibility, which we attribute to the immediate wrongdoer, not to the innocent party who merely foresees the wrongdoing. It would be an intolerable extension of criminal responsibility if people who were exercising their lawful rights and liberties were to be responsible for the acts of deliberate mischief-makers.' Glanville L. Williams, *Textbook of Criminal Law* (London: Stevens & Sons, 2nd ed., 1983) at p. 86.

film did in fact incite others to commit the harm and it was the producer's purpose to cause that harm.[129] This would be criminalizable as a solicitation offense.[130]

In *Beatty v. Gillbanks*[131] it was held that the Salvation Army had acted lawfully in congregating in Weston-super-Mare even though its officers knew from past experience that this would cause an opposing organization, the Skeleton Army, to attack them. The Salvation Army anticipated and knew that it was likely that the Skeleton Army would behave unlawfully, but it was not its purpose to encourage this unlawful behavior. Its purpose was merely to congregate.[132] The aforementioned scenarios concerning the media coverage of the prison riot and the Skeleton Army attack are good examples of remote harms, rather than examples of secondary criminal participation. The limits that apply in the accessory liability situation also apply to remote harms. When the remote-harmer's purpose is to encourage another to commit a crime, it can be fairly stated that she becomes culpably involved in that crime. However, negligently or even recklessly encouraging or influencing the criminal choices of others is not sufficient to establish a culpability connection in either the accessorial or remote harm liability context.[133] In the firearm possession context, the remote-harmers do not have a close connection with the primary harm-doers. Nor is it the gun possessor's aim to encourage others to misuse firearms. Remote possession factually enables increased gun crime, but merely owning a gun does not influence the criminal choices of those who decide to misuse a gun.

A careful analysis of the doctrines for imputing blame and harm in the inchoate and complicity criminalization contexts brings us in a full circle back to where we started, as we are still no closer to justifying blanket gun prohibitions. The limitations have been twofold. Firstly, mere possession is not a proximate cause of the individual acts of direct harm that form the aggregate harm caused by the widespread misuse of guns. Widespread gun possession merely enables those who decide to misuse a gun to gain easy access to a gun. Second, the only persons with any culpable link to the direct harm that is caused are those gun users who choose to misuse their guns. Coupled with this, their culpable misuse is already criminalized in crimes such as murder, manslaughter, and so forth.

---

129 Feinberg, *op. cit. supra*, fn. 88 at p. 244.
130 If a terrorist makes a film inciting terrorism, then this is a solicitation offense. See Kadish *et al.*, *op. cit. supra*, fn. 106 at pp. 572 *et seq.*; Dressler, *op. cit. supra*, fn. 16 at pp. 449 *et seq.*
131 (1892) 9 Q.B.D. 308.
132 Williams, *op. cit. supra*, fn. 123 at p. 12.
133 Williams, *op. cit. supra*, fn. 119 at p. 103.

Endangerment as a Justification for Criminalizing Gun Possession

The empirical evidence outlined above demonstrates that mere possession endangers not only the possessor but also innocent others—it increases the risk of both possessors and non-possessors becoming a victim of death or serious injury. Nonetheless, one does not have to dig very deep to see that overriding the right not to be unfairly criminalized in order to prevent endangerment or aggregate harm more generally for the greater good is a slippery slope. Would it be fair to introduce blanket prohibitions against city dwellers owning automobiles? Such a law would not impose any significant burden, but it would mean that the automobile owner would have to make some major adjustments to her lifestyle. Arguably, the automobile owner's change of lifestyle would be no more burdensome than that of the smoker who as been denied the right to smoke in public places on the basis that passive smoking is directly harmful to non-consenting others. An automobile is similar to a firearm in some respects, because it is a luxury that many people could do without.[134] Four million Londoners use the Underground everyday and in places such as Hong Kong 90 percent of the population use public transportation.[135] The aggregate harm involved in mass automobile use is twofold, in that the harm is comprised of both mass road fatalities/injuries[136] and global warming.[137] People who are addicted to automobiles are not likely to give them up without some coercion, but in the current climate criminalizing excessive automobile use is not likely to be taken seriously despite its overall aggregate harmfulness.

---

134 This postulation is based on the exemplar cities of Hong Kong and London, as these cities are densely populated and compact and have ample and sufficient public transportation. Clearly, in regional centers and smaller towns and cities the automobile is still a necessity.

135 'Car ownership in Hong Kong is very low at only 48 cars/1000 population compared to, for instance, 377 in the U.K., 325 in Japan and 485 in the U.S. ... Hong Kong is placed 15th in the 30 wealthiest countries in the world, yet in terms of car ownership per head, it has only a sixth of the average of these 30 countries.' See Sharon Cullinane, 'Hong Kong's Low Car Dependence: Lessons and Prospects,' (2003) 11(1) *Journal of Transport Geography* 25 at p. 26.

136 Many more people die in America each year from road accidents than from firearm fatalities. 'Road traffic injuries and fatalities accounted for 1.2 million deaths worldwide (2.2 percent of global mortality in the year 2002) and 2.6 percent of the total global burden of disease, measured in terms of lost years of healthy life.' See Kavi Bhalla *et al.*, 'A Risk-Based Method for Modeling Traffic Fatalities,' (2007) 27(1) *Risk Analysis* 125. There are five times as many automobile fatalities each year in the United States as there are firearm fatalities. See Juha Luoma and Michael Sivak, 'Characteristics and Availability of Fatal Road-Crash Databases in 20 Countries Worldwide,' (2007) 38(3) *Journal of Safety Research* 323. See also Hemenway, *op. cit. supra*, fn. 24 at pp. 646–650.

137 Lucas W. Davis, 'The Effect of Driving Restrictions on Air Quality in Mexico City,' 116(1) *The Journal of Political Economy* 38.

Trumping rights on the utilitarian calculus is even less convincing when we consider other examples. What about the aggregate long-term economic harm that flows from having liberal abortion laws? It is arguable that abortions are a great source of aggregate harm because of current negative birth rates.[138] Today's negative birth rates are tomorrow's economic woes. In the United States in 2005 there were 1.31 million abortions performed; and, according to official figures, there were 45 million abortions performed from 1973 through to 2005.[139] I noted above that more than one million Americans have been killed from firearm violence since 1965.[140] If the aggregate harm of gun misuse is merely to be counted in terms of lost lives, then aborting 45 million potential productive lives makes the aggregate harm caused by firearm fatalities pale into insignificance. Likewise, deliberate car misuse (intentional speeding and so forth) results in many more lost lives than deliberate gun misuse. During the same period there were only around one million firearm fatalities. Some will argue that fetuses are not actual lives so the harm is of a different nature, but that would be to overlook the fact that we are talking about aggregate harm not individual harm. Firearm possession prohibitions are justified by referring to the overall good that such laws are likely to achieve. The individual harm that is caused to a particular gunshot victim is punished separately as murder, and so forth. The harm is different in the individual sense because fetuses are unborn, but the long-term aggregate harm is of similar nature to the economic impact of high rates of firearm injuries and deaths. Nonetheless, those who advocate zero population growth on the grounds that it would reduce human consumption of non-renewable resources, preserve the natural environment and reduce global warming, might argue that abortions reduce population growth and thus prevent aggregate harm of a different kind.[141] But gun deaths would also have the effect of reducing population growth. Outlawing cars in cities would not reduce population growth because lives would be saved, but cars consume resources and contribute significantly to global warming. Most liberal commentators would not suggest that abortion should be criminalized for the greater good of America, that is, to prevent the grave economic harm that is almost certain to transpire from allowing negative birth rates to go unchecked. Nor would they accept the opposite argument and introduce a one or no child policy into the U.S. Arguably, criminalization would

---

138   See Maxime Fougère and Marcel Mérette, 'Population Ageing and Economic Growth in Seven OECD Countries,' (1999) 16(3) *Economic Modeling* 411; David M. Cutler, *et al.*, 'An Ageing Society: Opportunity or Challenge?,' (1990) 1 *Brook Papers Economic Activity* 1–73; David Miles, 'Modeling the Impact of Demographic Change Upon the Economy,' (1999) 109(452) *The Economic Journal* 1–36.

139   Rachel K. Jones, 'Abortion in the United States: Incidence and Access to Services, 2005,' (2008) 40 *Perspectives on Sexual and Reproduction Health* 6.

140   Cook and Ludwig, *op. cit. supra*, fn. 18, at p. 15.

141   See generally, Lester R. Brown, *Outgrowing the Earth: The Food Security Challenge in an Age of Falling Water Tables and Rising Temperatures* (New York: W.W. Norton & Company, 2005); John J. Ray, *Conservatism as Heresy* (Sydney: A.N.Z. Book Co., 1974).

mean that many accidental births would result in more productive members of society—these people would be able to replenish the workforce as older people retire. Alternatively, it could lead to population growth, which could lead to further environmental degradation.

A case that sits in the middle is China's one child policy, which is enforced with non-criminal[142] measures. It is a policy that is aimed at reducing population growth and does not impose any significant long-term burdens such as forcing people to have and raise a child they do not want, as the criminalization of abortion might do. Nonetheless, being denied the right to have more than one child is far more significant than being denied the right to own a firearm. Arguably the one child policy is the lesser of two evils. The alternative is to allow the population to spiral out of control thereby causing mass starvation.[143] There is no doubt that in certain contexts we do need to override individual rights for the greater good.[144] Science is helping us to produce more and more food and we are getting better at distributing aid and technology to third world countries, but in the long term a part of the solution for reducing global warming obviously seems to lie in sensible population growth. These postulations are presented merely to provoke critical thought on the issue at hand—the criminalization of gun possession for the greater good. What these examples show is that a mere body count does not tell us much. Blanket abortion and gun prohibitions, like the one child policy, indiscriminately burden some but not others. Some do not want children, some people want more than one child; some people do not want guns; other people do want guns, and so on.

The above examples are presented to highlight that at best the statistics on gun fatalities/injuries merely demonstrate that widespread possession is a form of dangerousness—that is, guns endanger their owners and others. However, it is crucial to understand that this type of evidence in itself fails to demonstrate the wrongness of mere possession. A crude balancing of the benefits and burdens of a given activity does not provide a critical moral justification for criminalizing it, because utilitarianism, proportionalist, or consequential-type justifications are usually little more than the rationalization of positions taken on other grounds.[145]

---

142   Notably, it is not a crime to have more than one child in China. Instead, penalties are limited to fines and no conviction or trial is involved.

143   See C.J. Smith, *China in the Post-Utopian Age* (Boulder, CO: Westview Press, 2000); Frank W. Elwell, *A Commentary on Malthus's 1798 Essay on Population as Social Theory* (Lewiston, NY: Edwin Mellen Press, 2001); L.T. Evans, *Feeding the Ten Billion—Plants and Population Growth* (Cambridge: Cambridge University Press, 1998); and Antony Trewavas, 'Malthus Foiled Again and Again,' (2002) 418 *Nature* 668.

144   See Ronald Dworkin, *Taking Rights Seriously* (King's Lynn: Duckworth, 1977), at p. 200.

145   John Finnis, *Fundamentals of Ethics* (Oxford: Clarendon Press, 1983), at p. 94. Cf. Finnis's argument: 'Any moral theory which admits into its method even purportedly restricted proportionalist principle is going to overlook the wrong in certain serious wrongs. If those practices are admitted by such theories to be wrongful, the wrongfulness will be misidentified and mislocated. It will be alleged to consist in considerations not

The decision to criminalize must be justified in accordance with the retributive constraints that are guided by practical reasonableness. I noted above that the core constraints are the culpability, harm (bad consequence), and proximate causation constraints. Can endangerment,[146] as opposed to actual harm, satisfy the harm constraint? Feinberg uses the Standard Harms Analysis to consider whether those harms that are 'neither perfectly harmless nor directly and necessarily harmful' should be criminalized. The elements of this standard are:

a. the greater the gravity of a possible harm, the less probable its occurrence need be to justify prohibition of the conduct that threatens to produce it;
b. the greater the probability of harm, the less grave the harm need be to justify coercion;
c. the greater the magnitude of the risk of harm, itself compounded out of gravity and probability, the less reasonable it is to accept the risk;
d. the more valuable (useful) the dangerous conduct, both to the actor and to others, the more reasonable it is to take the risk of harmful consequences, and for extremely valuable conduct it is reasonable to run risks up to the point of clear and present danger;
e. the more reasonable the risk of the harm (the danger), the weaker is the case for prohibiting the conduct that creates it.[147]

Endangerment is criminalizable under the above standard because it risks harming others. Gardner and Shute point out that:[148] 'One could sideline [the harm requirement] by saying that the Harm Principle is a rule of thumb, and tolerates some departures from its standard. One could also sideline [it] by observing that the Harm Principle's standard is met if the class of criminalized acts is a class of which *tend* to cause harm.' My view is simply that endangering others falls within the purview of the wrongful harm justification for invoking the criminal

---

only unconvincing in their causal hypotheses but also intrinsically beside-the-point in their identification of the person harmed and of the nature of that harm, and thus of the person wronged,' *id.*, at p. 105. See also John Finnis, *Natural Law and Natural Rights* (Oxford: Clarendon Press, 1979) at pp. 161–197.

146   I take the view that there is a conceptual distinction between harm and endangerment. Robinson notes that: 'Creation of risk of harm is not necessarily a harm in itself. But acts which create only a risk of harm may in fact cause harm. Swinging a fist at a person may not injure him as intended, but it may cause apprehension of injury that is itself a harm.' Paul H. Robinson, 'A Theory of Justification: Societal Harm as a Prerequisite for Criminal Liability,' (1975) 23 *UCLA Law Review* 266 at p. 268. *Per contra*, Finkelstein asserts that risk is harm. See Claire Finkelstein, 'Is Risk Harm?,' (2002–2003) 151 *University of Pennsylvania Law Review* 963.

147   Feinberg, *op. cit. supra*, fn. 88 at pp. 215–216.

148   John Gardner and Stephen Shute, 'The Wrongness of Rape,' in *Oxford Essays in Jurisprudence*, ed. Jeremy Horder, fourth series (Oxford: Oxford University Press, 2000) at pp. 215–216.

law—endangerment is about harm prevention—and preventing wrongful harm to others is a legitimate justification for invoking the criminal law.[149] The harm constraint will be satisfied if the lawmaker can demonstrate that the proscribed activities risk harming others. Feinberg's gravity and probability constraints are important for determining whether a particular activity is sufficiently dangerous for the purposes of invoking the criminal law. 'The greater the magnitude of the risk of harm, itself compounded out of gravity and probability, the less reasonable it is to accept the risk.'[150]

The culpability constraint raises more complex issues, because the endangerment might be brought about either directly or indirectly. Direct endangerment would occur if a person drove dangerously (that is, drove through a school zone at 140 miles per hour), fired a gun indiscriminately into a crowd or pulled the trigger of an unloaded gun at a person who is asleep,[151] poured petrol through the front door of another's home and ignited it,[152] flew an airliner full of passengers while intoxicated, had reckless sex,[153] failed to maintain basic safety standards in a factory,[154] and so forth. In such cases, the agent's recklessness and proximity to the direct risk taking would be sufficient to satisfy the culpability constraint. Indirect endangerment might result from a person possessing dangerous equipment that might be misused at some stage in the future—or possessing equipment that is dangerous to store, as would be the case with storing explosives in a residential suburb. The dangerousness of storing nuclear and biological weapons, explosives, grenades, and missiles is indirect in that any harm is contingent on the material accidentally exploding; or on an intervening actor making a choice to misuse these materials to harm others. Guns are only indirectly harmful because their possession requires an intervening actor to make the choice to use the gun to harm others. Guns, unlike explosives, are not innately dangerous, because they cannot accidentally explode.

---

149   Baker, *op. cit. supra*, fn. 10 at pp. 80–84. See also Dennis J. Baker and Lucy Xia Zhao, 'Responsibility Links, Fair Labeling and Proportionality in China: A Comparative Analysis,' (2009) 13 *UCLA Journal of International Law & Foreign Affairs* 1.

150   Feinberg, *op. cit. supra*, fn. 88 at pp. 215–216.

151   Dressler, *op. cit. supra*, fn. 16 at p. 121.

152   *R. v. Hyam* [1975] A.C. 55. See the discussion of specific and general offenses of endangerment in K.J.M. Smith, 'Liability for Endangerment: English Ad Hoc Pragmatism and American Innovation,' (1983) *Criminal Law Review* 127.

153   See the cases discussed in Dennis J. Baker, 'The Moral Limits of Consent as a Defense in the Criminal Law,' (2009) 12(1) *New Criminal Law Review* 93.

154   See Lynn K. Rhinehart, 'Would Workers be Better Protected if They Were Declared Endangered Species? A Comparison of Criminal Enforcement Under the Federal Workplace Safety and Environmental Protection Laws,' (1994) 31 *American Criminal Law Review* 351; Robert G. Schwartz, 'Criminalizing Occupational Safety Violations: The Use of "Knowing Endangerment" Statutes to Punish Employers Who Maintain Toxic Working Conditions,' (1990) 14 *Harvard Environmental Law Review* 487.

The possessor of explosives or radioactive materials might claim that these types of dangerous materials are not intended to be used to harm others, but it would be permissible for the government to criminalize possession of such materials, because explosives, grenades, biological and nuclear weapons, and so forth, are by their very nature exceedingly dangerous. A more remote form of endangerment would be one in which private citizen x possesses classified scientific information outlining how to build weapons of mass destruction, because, like a gun, its dangerousness is contingent on a human agent making a choice to misuse it. In *Stanley v. Georgia* the Supreme Court expounded that: 'the State may no more prohibit mere possession of obscene matter on the ground that it may lead to antisocial conduct than it may prohibit possession of chemistry books on the ground that they may lead to the manufacture of homemade spirits.' Free speech is important, and some information that might be misused does belong in the public domain. However, clearly the dangerousness of some technical information would make it permissible to limit its accessibility so that it cannot be misused to cause catastrophic results.[155] A further aspect of indirect harm is the time factor. Some activities threaten immediate and continuing endangerment or aggregate harm, whereas others merely threaten some remote future interest. For example, x's possession of a dangerous weapon such as a gun would pose immediate danger to x and others—in that it could be misused at any time. As previously stated, a gun is not inherently dangerous in the way that explosives and radioactive materials are, because its dangerousness is contingent on a human agent making a choice to misuse it. But the threat of misuse is a continuing and immediate source of dangerousness. *Per contra,* x having an abortion would not endanger[156] the interests of others in an immediate sense, but might contribute to the future aggregate economic harm that is likely to transpire from today's negative birth rates. Likewise, to the extent that automobile use contributes to global warming, the harm is not immediate but something that is likely to accumulate over a period of time.

Determining the risk factor of gun possession with any exactitude is beyond the scope of this chapter. However, a rough estimate does provide some insight into the dangerousness of mere possession. I have already given the statistics from a sample year, 1997, to show the extent of gun violence: 32,000 Americans died of gunshot wounds that year, and a further 81,000 people were seriously wounded.[157] If we take the 1997 figures and apply them to a population of 290 million, the chance of being killed by a firearm is one in 9,062 and the chance of being seriously injured by a firearm is one in 3,580. Thus, widespread gun possession enables a form of

---

155 See generally, Seumas Miller and Michael J. Selgelid, 'Ethical and Philosophical Consideration of the Dual-Use Dilemma in the Biological Sciences,' (2007) 13(4) *Science and Engineering Ethics* 523.

156 Here, I use endanger in a very loose sense—to incorporate setbacks to economic interests.

157 Cook and Ludwig, *op. cit. supra*, fn. 18 at p. 15.

endangerment that makes our lives statistically less secure by a one in 9,062 chance, and our physical safety less secure by a one in 3,580 chance. The dangerousness issue has arisen in a number of cases in which a defendant has knowingly risked infecting others with H.I.V. by having unprotected intercourse. The Australian courts have held that the appropriate level of risk for direct endangerment is that 'of appreciable danger' and have ruled that a one in 2,000 chance of harming others was not sufficient.[158] However, it is arguable that if x drives his car through a school zone at 140 miles per hour, the risk of one in 2,000 would be sufficient for imposing a reasonably severe sentence for this type of *direct* endangerment, as the risk is high and the gravity of the likely harm is great.

A risk factor as low as 1 in 9,062 might be sufficient to justify the enactment of an endangerment offense if the likely harm is very great (as is the case with gun misuse), so long as the possession offense is labeled in the non-serious category and is punished proportionately in accordance with the low level of dangerousness involved—that is, in accordance with the extent of a given possessor's contribution to the general endangerment. Mere firearm possession might enable grave harm to transpire, but the probability of the harm transpiring is reasonably low, and so any prison sentence should be of no more than six to 12 months. In most cases, a fine would probably be a sufficient penalty, but given the gravity of the individualized harm that is likely to transpire, repeat offenders could be imprisoned where appropriate. The culpability constraint would be satisfied for the possession offense as opposed to the remote direct harm that might transpire from others misusing their guns, so long as the act of possession was intentional. If x intentionally possesses a gun, criminalization would communicate to x in terms that she and everyone else in society could understand; that x deserves to be censured and punished for choosing to endanger others. The critical moral reasons we can offer to x to explain why it is just and fair to criminalize her activities are: that she deserves proportionate criminal punishment for choosing to possess a gun because she knew that her actions would pose a low risk of danger for others. The low risk would have to be considered when labeling such an offense.

There is nothing wrong with prohibiting people from possessing materials that unreasonably endanger others. In some cases the remote-harmer endangers others by creating the 'demand' for the conduct that causes the primary harm. It is worth noting that possessing child pornography is a remote harm, because those who merely purchase child pornography do not come into contact with the children. Nor do they necessarily have any close association with the child pornographer. The purchaser of these ghastly materials might not care who produced them or where they came from. Dempsey argues, however, that:[159] 'Users of child pornography not only create the market for such material, but they also create the

---

158 See the cases discussed in David Lanham, 'Danger Down Under,' (1999) *Criminal Law Review* 961 at pp. 963–964.

159 Michelle M. Dempsey, 'Rethinking Wolfenden: Prostitute Use, Criminal Law, and Remote Harm,' (2005) *Criminal Law Review* 444, 453–454. Cf. Suzanne Ost, *Child*

incentive for pedophiles and profiteers to satisfy that market through the abuse of children.' Likewise, the purchasers of ivory collectively form the lucrative ivory market that is poaching's *raison d'être*. This market indirectly increases the risk of harm to the endangered elephant population. Even though *x* does not kill the elephants or even come into contact with them, her ivory purchases would create a demand for ivory. But this alone is not sufficient to establish a culpability link. As I noted above, merely influencing another's criminal choice is not sufficient for establishing a culpability link. Should the television crew be held criminally liable for creating the demand for nude and violent street protests? Would it not be an intolerable extension of criminal responsibility if television crews and others were held criminally liable for exercising their lawful rights and liberties, simply because it might encourage others to engage in criminal harm-doing?

This brings us to the next requirement set by Feinberg. That is, we need to evaluate the social value of the conduct involved. 'The more valuable (useful) the dangerous conduct, ... the more reasonable it is to take the risk ... and for extremely valuable conduct it is reasonable to run risks up to the point of clear and present danger.'[160] By creating the demand for child pornography and ivory, the remote-harmers increase the risk that a child or elephant will be harmed and, unlike televising protests, possessing child pornography and ivory is not valuable or useful—such conduct serves no social purpose whatsoever. *Per contra*, media coverage of protests involves free speech and serves a highly valuable purpose— informing the public about what is going on in the world.[161] I have argued elsewhere that dimension is added to the case for criminalizing child pornography by the fact that the possessor/purchaser deliberately and knowingly receives the fruits of a grave criminal harm.[162] By receiving a good that can only be produced through wrongful harm, the possessor underwrites the wrongful harm. Here, derivative

---

Pornography and Sexual Grooming: Legal and Societal Responses (Cambridge: Cambridge University Press, 2009) at pp. 115–119.

    160   Feinberg, *op. cit. supra*, fn. 88 at pp. 215–216.

    161   Baker notes that the free expression right is based on four values: '(1) individual self-fulfilment, (2) advancement of knowledge and discovery of truth, (3) participation in decision making by all members of the society (which is "particularly significant for political decisions" but "embraces the right to participate in the building of the whole culture") and (4) achievement of a "more adaptable and hence stable community."' C. Edwin Baker, *Human Liberty and Freedom of Speech* (New York: Oxford University Press, 1989), 47. Dworkin outlines two justifications for free speech: '[T]he first treats free speech as important instrumentally, that is, not because people have any intrinsic moral right to say what they wish, but because allowing them to do so will produce good effects for the rest of us. The second kind of justification of free speech supposes [that it] is valuable, not just in virtue of the consequences it has, but because it is an essential "constitutive" feature of a just political society that government treat all its adult members ... as responsible moral agents.' Ronald Dworkin, *Freedom's Law: The Moral Reading of the American Constitution* (Oxford: Oxford University Press, 1996) at pp. 199–200.

    162   Baker, *op. cit. supra*, fn. 4 at pp. 386–388.

liability works from the premise that the remote-harmer culpably chooses to associate himself with the primary-harmer's wrongdoing. When a pedophile chooses to possess images of real children he chooses to associate himself with the primary-harmer's wrongdoing because he chooses to support and underwrite the criminal harm-doing by purchasing the end product. He knows as a matter of virtual certainty that a child has been harmed in the production process, as he has the images as proof. His knowledge of the harm-doing is certain, and he chooses to take the fruits of the harm *ex post facto*.

When *x* sells a gun to a potential killer she might not know for sure whether he will use it to kill, but when *x* purchases ivory or child pornography she knows as a matter of fact that a harm has been committed to produce such products. Similarly, the gravamen of the offense of receiving stolen goods is the receiving of the goods with knowledge that they were stolen. It is wrong for a person to possess or receive goods that she knows are stolen, because she knows the goods have become available only because someone has committed a wrongful harm. These cases are distinguishable from the television crew cases, as the social and moral implications are different. The aim of possessing child pornography or stolen goods is to intentionally benefit from a known criminal harm, whereas the *telos* of giving media attention to a nude protest is not intentionally to benefit from the protestors' criminal activities. Any benefit in the latter situation is inadvertently acquired and is socially valuable and useful. The overall aim is to inform the public about events that are taking place in the real world. Furthermore, there is no empirical evidence to suggest that media coverage of such events makes them more violent and dangerous.

However, drawing the line in the firearm case is not so clear-cut. I have outlined a weak case for possession offenses based on the gun possessor's culpable possession and knowledge of the possession's dangerousness. But does this mean that intentionally purchasing a car with the knowledge that it will damage the environment and endanger others should be criminalized? Private cars are not a necessity in cities, nor are guns. *Per contra*, delivery trucks, ambulances, police cars, fire engines and so forth are socially valuable. Thus, limiting motor vehicle use to these types of socially valuable vehicles might be permissible in the right context. The gun possessor might argue that unlike child pornography and ivory, guns have a reasonably important social purpose. Joyce Malcolm[163] outlines the case for interpreting the right to bear arms as found in the Second Amendment as

---

163   Joyce Lee Malcolm, *To Keep and Bear Arms: The Origins of an Anglo-American Right* (Cambridge MA: Harvard University Press, 1994) at p. 164. 'The argument that today's National Guardsmen, members of a select militia, would constitute the only persons entitled to keep and bear arms has no historical foundation. Indeed, it would seem redundant to specify that members of a militia had the right to be armed. A militia could scarcely function otherwise. But the argument that this constitutional right to have weapons was exclusively for members of a militia falters on another ground. The House committee eliminated the stipulation that the militia be "well-armed," and the Senate, in what became

an individual right. Malcolm traces the right back to its English roots and produces a wealth of evidence to support her conclusion that '[t]he Second Amendment brought the American Constitution into closer conformity with its English predecessor. In both cases, the intention was to guarantee citizens the means of self-defense and to ensure that when, in the course of time, it was necessary to raise standing armies, they would never pose a danger to the liberties of the people.' The question is whether the latter arguments are sufficient to demonstrate the social value of firearms in the twenty-first century. I cannot see why not.

However, it might also be argued that in a time when people lived in remote and isolated parts of the wilderness without access to emergency services or in cities without organized police forces, having a firearm would have been a necessary form of protection. Likewise, in a time following British oppression and in a time when standing armies would pose a threat to the new fledgling democracy, having a right and a means to revolution would have been much more compelling. The contemporary situation is, of course, much different. The United States is now an old and secure democracy—it is a military superpower—it has one of the most sophisticated and best resourced police forces in the world (including the FBI and CIA) and it has emergency services that are second to none. The reality might be that in modern America guns are not needed for self-defense[164] or to defend oneself from standing armies, or as a means of revolution. In fact, it is arguable that in America today a person would have a greater liberty interest in being able to access the Internet than she would in keeping arms. Of course, these are controversial claims, but they do highlight the difficulty of determining social value.

The social value of firearms might also be distinguished from that of abortion, because denying a couple the right to abort a child not only denies them the right to choose whether or not to have a child, but also results in their being forced to maintain a child that they do not want. It is very expensive to raise a child to adulthood and it involves a major long-term commitment both financially and socially. However, the child-bearer (who has paid the price both economically and socially of raising children for 18 years) could ask why retiree x who has remained childless should be able to rely on the benefits that will flow from the child-bearer's earlier financial and social sacrifice? However, the long-term financial burden and social responsibility involved in having a child should not be forced on anyone.[165] Such laws would be no different than a draconian law stating that all people born in 1980 should have a child by the end of the year.

---

the final version of the amendment, eliminated the description of the militia as composed of the "body of people."' *Id.*, p. 163.

164 Garry Kleck, *Targeting Guns: Firearms and their Control* (Piscataway, NJ: Aldine Transaction, 1997) at p. 154. It is worth noting that modern police forces manage to do a reasonable job of keeping people safe in other Western countries. Notably, in Britain, the police do not even carry arms.

165 The criminal law is not the way to achieve justice in this context. Increasingly, justice is being achieved in many OECD countries by using various tax mechanisms to

Per contra, criminalizing firearm possession would not impose any burdens. Notwithstanding this, the case for criminalizing gun possession on the basis of general dangerousness is extremely weak. It is not possible to determine wrongness by comparing the aggregate harmfulness of abortion, motorcars and guns, but it is evident that the aggregate harm posed by gun possession pales into insignificance in comparison to that posed by motorcars. It is arguable that punishing those who misuse guns provides a sufficient remedy.

In this chapter, I started from the premise that there is an important issue of justice involved when a person is criminalized for exercising her lawful right merely because it might enable another to engage in criminality. It is one thing to be denied the right to enjoy recreational shooting, but it is something entirely different to be criminalized for exercising your lawful right to do so. Glanville Williams encapsulates the wrongness of remote harm criminalization in the following passage:

> An extreme view of criminal responsibility might be that a man is under a duty to act in such a way that others are not led to cause harm, so that in some circumstances he would be responsible for harm that is directly caused by others, even though without his authorization or encouragement. This does not represent the criminal law. The legal attitude is that a man is primarily responsible only for what he himself does or incites.[166]

By conceptualizing harm as endangerment, I have been able to demonstrate that mere possession is harmful in itself and therefore the retributive constraints against collective criminalization can be satisfied. My analysis, however, shows that the dangerousness involved is trivial because of the low likelihood of it transpiring in an individualized sense. Furthermore, unlike many dangerous items such as nuclear materials, grenades, bombs, explosives, and so on, guns have some social value. For many, recreational shooting is a valuable sport and for others the Second Amendment guarantees their right to have access to this means of self-defense. Furthermore, it allowed the people to be in a position where they could raise standing armies to protect their liberties.

Overall the aggregate harm that flows from firearm possession seems to sit right on the line. It appears that the case for overriding the justice constraint in the firearm context is weak. But merely criminalizing gun misuse *per se* has proven to be insufficient for preventing gun deaths. Similarly, merely criminalizing dangerous driving has not prevented dangerous driving from transpiring. However, the evidence of dangerousness would be sufficient to justify outlawing certain types of firearms, or possession in sensitive places. Thus, Justice Scalia's opinion

---

distribute some of the financial burden to childless people. This is a much fairer solution than resorting to the criminal law.

166 Williams, *op. cit. supra*, fn. 128 at pp. 390–391.

for the majority in *District of Columbia v. Heller*[167] can be reconciled with justice. The case for criminalization is much stronger in those cases in which further justifications can be produced. As Justice Scalia rightly suggests, regulation would be permissible where the firearm possessor is a dangerous person, a former felon, has a mental illness, wants to possess a gun in sensitive areas such as schools, and so forth. Likewise, military firearms are exceptionally dangerous and possessing such guns has no recreational value and would be somewhat akin to possessing bombs, missiles, and grenades. The potential dangerousness of such weapons means that the right to possess them could be overridden. Coupled with this, the case for overriding the right to possess guns would be much stronger in those situations in which it could be demonstrated that the criminal law is the only effective means for preventing aggregate harm that is likely to transpire. A stringent licensing and storage scheme would also be reasonable. The utilitarian aim of reducing the aggregate harm caused by firearms is perfectly legitimate, but the requirements of justice mean that the blanket criminal prohibitions against gun ownership should not be used to achieve such a goal.

---

167   554 U.S. 570 (2008).

Chapter 4
The Harm Principle vs. Kantian Criteria for Ensuring Fair Criminalization

Kantian Criteria for Ensuring Fair Criminalization

Dan-Cohen and Ripstein have argued that the harm criterion should be jettisoned as a criterion for guiding criminalization decisions. *Per contra*, I take the view that wrongful harm is effective for ensuring that criminalization decisions meet the requirements of fairness and justice in most cases. Fairness is achieved when those being criminalized are only held responsible for harms that can be fairly imputed to them. Dan-Cohen[1] asserts that the wrongful harm should be replaced with what he calls the *dignity principle*, that is, 'the main goal of the criminal law ought to be to defend the unique moral worth of every human being.' According to this theory it is fair to criminalize an agent's actions when they use another person as mere means to an end. Ripstein draws on Kant's philosophy more generally and proposes a 'sovereignty principle,' which holds that all violations of 'equal freedom' are criminalizable.[2] They claim that the harm criterion is under-inclusive in that it fails to provide a rationale for criminalizing certain harmless wrongs. Both Dan-Cohen and Ripstein erroneously argue that there are certain wrongs that cannot be criminalized under the harm criterion, because they are harmless wrongs. In this chapter, I argue that the harm constraint can meet the challenges outlined by Ripstein and Dan-Cohen. The harm justification/constraint provides a superior criterion for ensuring that criminalization decisions accord with the requirements of fairness and justice.

Dan-Cohen and Ripstein seem to overlook the fact that the harm constraint is not merely about minimizing criminalization, but rather it is about ensuring that criminalization decisions meet the requirements of fairness and justice. The issue involves more than reducing the volume of criminal laws. It is about providing legislature with clear guidance about what it should or should not criminalize. Kant's philosophy emphasizing *moral autonomy* and *respect for persons* does not give the legislature guidance about which wrongs can be fairly criminalized. As I note below, it would not be fair to criminalize all violations of dignity and moral freedom (*e.g.*, false promising, mere trespass to goods, *etc.*).

---

1 Meir Dan-Cohen, 'Defending Dignity,' *Boalt Working Papers in Public Law*, University of California, Berkeley, Paper 99, (2002) at p. 1.
2 Arthur Ripstein, 'Beyond the Harm Principle,' (2006) 34(3) *Philosophy & Public Affairs* 215 at p. 216.

The harm criterion could be invoked to increase the scope of our current body of criminal law, but its growth would reach an ultimate limit and meet the requirements of fairness, since it would only allow wrongdoing of a harmful kind to be brought within the purview of the criminal law. There are some wrongful torts that involve intentional harm-doing such as some forms of defamation, but it would not be unjust or unfair to criminalize intentional defamation that results in *harm*.[3] It is worth bearing in mind that there are not many torts that could be brought within the purview of the criminal law just because they result in wrongful harm. The harm justification is supplemented with an elaborate set of mediating principles that would speak against criminalizing most civil wrongs.[4] Furthermore, the requirement of *mens rea* (full intention or recklessness/culpable ignorance) removes a vast range of harms from the scope of the criminal law. The requirements of the *mens rea* doctrine prevent harms that result from accidents or mere negligence from being criminalized. Nevertheless, some *intentional* wrongs that are currently dealt with pursuant to the civil law could be brought within the purview of the criminal law without violating the requirements of fairness. The problem with Dan-Cohen and Ripstein's use of mere moral wrongdoing criteria for criminalization is that it would allow a range of trivial wrongs to be brought within the purview of the criminal law regardless of the requirements of fairness. The wrongful harm constraint only allows wrongful harms to be criminalized. If conduct is harmless then why bother criminalizing it? Coupled with this, a proper application of the harm constraint on balance would lead to more decriminalization than it would criminalization.

According to Dan-Cohen's[5] dignity principle, only those criminal laws that are not necessary for protecting human dignity are morally objectionable. Meanwhile, Ripstein[6] draws on Kant's philosophy more generally and proposes a *sovereignty principle*, which holds that violations of *equal freedom* are criminalizable regardless of the consequences that are brought about (or aimed for) by the intentional violation of freedom. Ripstein draws on the idea of equal

---

3   To some extent this is attributable to the way in which the criminal and civil law evolved out of one body of law: Carleton Kemp Allen, *Legal Duties* (Oxford: Clarendon Press, 1931) at pp. 221–252 and John A. Jolowicz, *Lectures on Jurisprudence* (London: Athlone Press, 1963) at pp. 344–358.

4   According to Feinberg, harm is only a sufficient condition. Joel Feinberg, *The Moral Limits of the Criminal Law: Harm to Others* (New York: Oxford University Press, Vol. I, 1984) at p. 10. But as I noted in Chapters 1 and 2, the lawmaker could be morally compelled to criminalize serious harms such as marital rape to protect society. The unreasonableness of expecting an individual to take proceedings on her own responsibility to protect her interests also distinguishes crimes from private wrongs and would be a factor that would weigh heavily when applying Feinberg's mediating maxims. Similarly, a pragmatic application of the mediating principles would speak against criminalizing intentional wrongful harms (*i.e.*, some forms of defamation) that have historically been dealt with under the civil law.

5   Dan-Cohen, *op. cit. supra*, fn. 1 at p. 1.

6   Ripstein, *op. cit. supra*, fn. 2 at p. 216.

freedom that is derived from Kant's *Universal Principle of Right*[7] in an attempt to develop his theory of freedom (sovereignty). Dan-Cohen adopts the narrower criterion offered by Kant's second formulation of the Categorical Imperative. Both authors argue that the Harm Principle should be jettisoned, because it allegedly would allow certain so-called harmless wrongs, such as rape by deception and secret trespasses into private homes to go unchecked. As I point out below, rape by deception and trespasses into private homes are generally harmful or pose a risk of harm and therefore come within the purview of the wrongful harm justification for criminalization.

Dan-Cohen also argues that the harm criterion is fallible, because it would allow a person to consent to the harm involved in slavery,[8] gladiatorial battles and so forth. In the next chapter, I argue that gladiatorial battles and slavery are criminalizable harms that can be brought within the purview of the wrongful harm justification for criminalization. The issue in these cases concerns the moral limits of consent in the criminal law. Dan-Cohen is right to question the scope that Feinberg[9] gave the *volenti non fit injuria* maxim. Consent has an important role to play in criminalization decisions, but consent is defeasible in certain circumstances. In this chapter, I argue that Kant's second formulation of the Categorical Imperative cannot provide general criteria for guiding criminalization decisions. It can be invoked in special paradigm cases to explain the moral limits of consent and also explains the wrongness of many activities, but it does not give legislatures guidance about when it is appropriate to criminalize those wrongs.[10]

Mere wrongdoing does not give the state sufficient guidance about what can be fairly criminalized. Nor can this type of deontological wrongdoing explain what is special about the punitive response. As Murphy notes: 'The purpose of law is to maintain a system of peace wherein each citizen will enjoy the most extensive liberty compatible with like liberty for others. This is the only reason why rational autonomous persons would contract to give up liberty; and only in terms of this end is state coercion justified. The role of criminal punishment in such a system is instrumental—it is justified solely by reference to the end of maintaining a peaceful system of ordered liberty.'[11] Generally, I defend the harm

---

7 Ripstein calls his principle the 'sovereignty principle.' He asserts that the most forceful expression of it is found in 'Kant's political philosophy, particularly in the *Doctrine of Right*, Part One of the Metaphysics of Morals.' *Id.* at p. 215.

8 Dan-Cohen, *op. cit. supra*, fn. 1 at pp. 156–157.

9 Joel Feinberg, *The Moral Limits of the Criminal Law: Harm to Self* (New York: Oxford University Press, Vol. III, 1986) at pp. 98–142.

10 Cf. John Gardner and Stephen Shute, 'The Wrongness of Rape,' in Jeremy Horder, *Oxford Essays in Jurisprudence* (Oxford: Oxford University Press, 4th Series, 2000) at pp. 193 *et seq*.

11 '[T]he criminal law is not to be understood as that branch of law that deals with a special kind of immorality (or rights violations), but rather as that branch of law which uses a certain technique (punishment) to control any kind of immorality that cannot be kept at an optimal level by purely private means.' See Jeffrie G. Murphy, 'Does Kant Have a Theory

justification/constraint in light of the claims made by Dan-Cohen and Ripstein and argue that Kant's philosophy does not provide us with general criteria for ensuring that criminalization decisions meet the requirements of fairness. I also argue that Kant's deontology, emphasizing moral autonomy and respect for persons, does not provide us with adequate criteria for ensuring fair and just criminalization.

Before I outline Dan-Cohen and Ripstein's arguments for jettisoning the harm constraint, I will briefly outline the core elements of Kant's idea of human dignity and freedom as laid down in the *Groundwork* and in the *Principle of Universal Right*. I do this to demonstrate that neither Dan-Cohen's nor Ripstein's normative arguments tell us why mere deontological wrongdoing is worthy of criminal censure and condemnation. Lawmakers have to be able to rationally defend criminalization decisions to those who are being criminalized, the victims and everyone else in society. To do this the lawmaker needs not only to focus on deontological wrongness (disrespect for humanity and so forth) but also on the badness of the wrongful act/action/consequence involved, as the latter is a core element of criminalizable wrongness. If x intentionally steals y's car, the decision to criminalize x's wrongdoing can be communicated to x in terms that both she and everyone else in society can understand. It can be explained to x that she deserves censure and criminal condemnation for deliberately bringing about a bad consequence of a serious nature for another person. The objective reasons we can offer to x to explain why it is just and fair to prohibit her from stealing property from others include that this has bad consequences for the victim in that it harms the victim's interests. The consequences flowing from the wrongdoing are that y no longer has a car. The fact and the extent of x's censure can be dialectically defended in rational discussions with her, the victim, and third parties. The harmful act/actions/consequences also give the lawmaker guidance about whether it is appropriate to use the criminal law to deal with the wrongdoing involved or whether some other form of regulation would be more appropriate. Merely telling x that she is being criminalized for violating y's freedom would not be sufficient for this purpose. Dan-Cohen and Ripstein apply Kant's philosophy to a social problem (that is determining when it is fair to criminalize conduct) that it is not equipped to deal with. Dan-Cohen and Ripstein refer to distinct aspects of Kant's philosophy, so I will deal with their arguments separately. I will start by outlining what is meant by respect for persons. I will then consider this in the context of the arguments presented by Dan-Cohen. Subsequently, I outline and critique Ripstein's sovereignty principle and defend the harm constraint in light of it. In this chapter, I also consider a further objection against Dan-Cohen's principle of respect for persons—that is, dignity's failure to protect non-human animals from harm.

---

of Punishment,' (1987) 87 *Columbia Law Review* 509 at p. 516. In our scheme, the criminal law should only be used to prevent bad consequences (harm and certain privacy violations) that cannot be kept at an optimal level by other means.

Kant's Second Formulation of the Categorical Imperative

Kant holds that the moral status of actions is not determined according to the best overall outcome that those actions might produce (utility), but rather in accordance with our moral duty. Duty requires that we treat others, and ourselves, in a manner that is consistent with human dignity.[12] The aim of Kant's theory is to provide a precise criterion for making moral judgments, not for determining criminality. The core question is: how can we determine what actions are consistent with moral respect for ourselves, and others? Kant argued that our capacity for rational thought provides a sound basis for making such determinations. The basic idea behind Kant's moral law is that whenever a moral agent acts in an intentional manner, the agent's action implicitly warrants (or wills) the same action for everyone, and if a moral agent's act complies with his or her moral duties (*e.g.*, the duty to respect humanity as an end in itself), then the action is one that he or she could *rationally* (that is, consistently) recommend (or will) for all other moral agents.[13]

In the first section of the *Groundwork*,[14] Kant attempts to derive his core principle of morality from ordinary moral thought. Specifically, he attempts to derive this principle from considerations concerning what is unconditionally good.[15] Kant claims that the only thing that is unconditionally good is a good will. Kant asserts that the consequences of an action done with a good will and the aims and inclinations of the agent with the good will are morally insignificant. What, then, is it to act with a good will? It is, Kant argues, a matter of doing one's duty for duty's sake, regardless of one's feelings and the *consequences* of doing so. One acts for duty's sake (rightfully) when she acts from principles that accord with the fundamental principle of morality.[16] This is expressed in the first formulation of the fundamental principle of morality: *The Formula of Universal Law*: 'Act only on that maxim[17] through which you can at the same time will that it should become

---

12   Carl Joachim Friedrich, *The Philosophy of Kant: Immanuel Kant's Moral and Political Writings* (New York: The Modern Library, 1949) at pp. 140 *et seq*.

13   Immanuel Kant, *Groundwork of the Metaphysics of Morals*, 1785, translated from the German by Herbert James Paton, *The Moral Law* (London: Hutchinson University Library, 1972) at pp. 57 *et seq*.

14   *Ibid*.

15   *Id*. at Chapter 1.

16   *Ibid*.

17   According to Kant, 'A maxim is a subjective principle of action and must be distinguished from an objective principle—namely, a practical law. The former contains a practical rule determined by reason in accordance with the conditions of the subject (often his ignorance or agains his inclinations): it is thus a principle on which the subject acts. A law, on the other hand, is an objective principle valid for every rational being; and it is a principle on which he ought to act—that is, an imperative.' *Id*. at p. 84.

a universal law.'[18] If a person is unable to will that an action become a universal law, then the action is morally impermissible.

The general thrust of this command is that those maxims that are universalizable are in accord with duty; to act out of them would be morally creditable.[19] Universalizable maxims are those that we can act on.[20] For example, making false promises is wrong and is not universalizable, because every rational being would not adopt such a law as a principle of action.[21] Likewise, it would not be morally acceptable for x to rape y, because the victim could not act on x's maxim of rape.[22] A person can will her maxim as a universal law if she can do so without contradiction.[23] The maxim that, 'One should rape others when it is expedient to do so' could not become universal law, because the victim is being asked to serve an end in which she cannot be given adequate reasons for sharing or sanctioning. She is being asked to allow herself to be treated as a mere means, which degrades her humanity.

In the second section of the *Groundwork*, Kant begins by emphasizing that our knowledge of our duty is *a priori* and based on the exercise of reason. He then argues that facts about our duties are necessary facts, and that this shows that they must be based on a categorical imperative: that is, that our duties apply to us insofar as we are rational beings, regardless of the contingent aspects of their nature.[24] Furthermore, for Kant the Categorical Imperative can only exist if we are able to base it on something that has an absolute worth.[25] That something is the existence of rational beings, which, he says, is an end in itself. This leads to Kant's preferred formula for applying the moral law, that is, *The Formula of Humanity as an End in Itself*.[26] Kant premises the Categorical Imperative on humans because they have

---

18   Onora O'Neill, *Constructions of Reason: Explorations of Kant's Practical Philosophy* (Cambridge: Cambridge University Press, 1989) at pp. 126–127.

19   Likewise, it would be contrary to duty to act on those maxims that are not universalizable. *Id.* at p. 134.

20   'A maxim is thus always some sort of general principle under which we *will* a particular action. Thus if someone decides to commit suicide in order to avoid unhappiness, she may be said to act on the principle or maxim "I will kill myself whenever life offers more pain than pleasure."' Paton, *op. cit. supra*, fn. 13 at p. 20.

21   *Id.* at pp. 67–68.

22   O'Neill, *op. cit. supra*, fn. 18 at p. 139.

23   Christine M. Korsgaard, *Creating the Kingdom of Ends* (Cambridge: Cambridge University Press, 1996) at p. 14.

24   Paton, *op. cit. supra*, fn. 13 at pp. 71 *et seq*.

25   *Id.* at pp. 90–91.

26   'Although this formulation is "at bottom one and the same thing" as the first one, it is, in another sense, already an application of the supreme moral principle; for it indicates to us what kind of maxims could be willed as universal laws. We thus learn what right actions are, whether in morality or politics; for they involve our not using ourselves as means to our subjective ends. Man should not merely be subject to another will, but he should be his

an absolute worth as persons.²⁷ Kant ascribes to human nature three key inclusive capacities or original predispositions, that is, animality (animality in man, taken as a living being), humanity (humanity in man, taken as a living and at the same time as a rational being) and personality (personality in man taken as a rational and at the same time a responsible being).²⁸ Animality belongs to everyone as a living being, and it is the stimulus for our instinctual desires, *i.e.*, our desire to acquire food (preserving our physical health, *etc.*), to propagate the species (the sexual instinct), and to engage with others (the social instinct).²⁹ These survival instincts are pre-rational. Humanity takes the 'intermediate position between animality and a rational, free and accountable personality.'³⁰

The basic feature of humanity is simply the capacity to take a rational interest in something: to make decisions according to reason, to desire and value objects as worthy of pursuit or to realize them as ends.³¹ 'Put most generally, humanity is the capacity to set ends through reason.'³² Personality differs from humanity in that the predisposition to personality is the rational capacity to respect the moral law and to act having moral law as a motive of the will. Kant 'identifies personality with [the *Formula of Autonomy*], in the sense of the ability to give oneself the moral law through reason, which is the ground of dignity.'³³ Rational nature incorporates an absolute worth in the sense of *dignity*, and this intrinsic value admits of no equivalent and thus cannot be compromised or replaced.³⁴ Our rational nature gives us dignity and worth as persons, which means we have a value beyond price.³⁵ If a substitute or equivalent can be found for a thing, then it has a price.³⁶ It has dignity (an intrinsic value) if there is no substitute or equivalent for it.³⁷ It is the priceless and non-substitutable dignity and worth of persons that makes them objects of respect.

---

own law-giver.' Hans Reiss and Hugh Barr Nisbet, *Kant's Political Writing* (Cambridge: Cambridge University Press, 1970) at pp. 18–19.

27   Paton, *op. cit. supra*, fn. 13 at p. 91.

28   See also Howard Caygill, *A Kant Dictionary* (Oxford: Blackwell Publishers, 1999) at p. 230.

29   Allen W. Wood, *Kant's Ethical Thought* (Cambridge: Cambridge University Press, 1999) at p. 118.

30   Caygill, *loc. cit. supra*, fn. 28.

31   Korsgaard, *op. cit. supra*, fn. 23 at p. 114.

32   Wood, *op. cit. supra*, fn. 29 at p. 118.

33   *Id.* at p. 118. 'The idea of every rational will as universally legislative is not directly a formula of any moral principle but only a way of representing the ground or authority of other moral principles [such as the *Universal Law* and the *Humanity as an End in Itself* formulae].' *Id.* at p. 163.

34   Paton, *op. cit. supra*, fn. 13 at p. 96.

35   *Id.* at p. 35.

36   *Ibid.*

37   *Ibid.*

Only by following the unconditional dictates of reason (which is the source of will) do we arrive at the moral law; since will is a type of reason, following the dictates of reason means following the dictates of will itself.[38] We are subject only to the laws of our reason and this makes us autonomous. For a rational agent to be a true end in herself she also has to be the author of those laws that she is compelled to abide by; it is this that gives her absolute value.[39] It is the capacity for autonomy that makes moral agents ends in themselves.[40] Hence, the *Formula of Autonomy* formulation encapsulates Kant's claim that we can realize our autonomy only by acting in conformity with the moral law. Compliance with the moral law does not restrain our freedom since we legislate the moral law for ourselves.[41] The moral law is not forced on us from without; its source is to be found in our own rational nature. Indeed, it is only by acting morally that we are able to achieve genuine freedom by transcending the contingent desires and inclinations that are beyond our control.[42] 'Strictly speaking ... Kant ascribes dignity not to humanity, but to personality, that is, not rational nature in general but to rational nature in its capacity to be morally *self-legislative*.'[43] Respecting others is about treating them as self-governing beings.

Kant uses humanity to demonstrate how a Categorical Imperative or practical law is 'connected (wholly *a priori*) with the concept of the will of a rational being as such.'[44] 'The ground for this moral principle is: *Rational nature exists as an end in itself*. This is the way in which a man necessarily conceives his own existence: it is therefore so far a *subjective* principle of human actions. But it is also the way in which every other rational being conceives his existence on the same rational ground which is valid also for me; hence it is at the same time an *objective* principle, from which, as a supreme practical ground, it must be possible to derive all laws for the will. The practical imperative will therefore be as follows: *Act in such a way that you always treat humanity whether in your own person or in the person of any other, never simply as a means, but always at the same time as an*

---

38 *Id.* at p. 93.

39 *Id.* at p. 34.

40 'The Formula of Autonomy—though the argument is obscurely stated—is derived from combining the Formula of Universal Law and the Formula of the End in Itself. We have not only seen that we are bound to obey the law in virtue of its universality (its objective validity for all rational agents); we have also seen that rational agents as subjects are the ground of this Categorical Imperative. If this is so, the law which we are bound to obey must be the product of our own will (so far as we are rational agents)—that is to say, it rests on "the Idea of the will of every rational being as a will makes universal law". ... "it is precisely the fitness of the [rational agent's] maxims to make universal law that marks him out as an end in himself."' *Id.* at pp. 33–34.

41 *Id.* at pp. 93–95.

42 *Ibid.*

43 Wood, *op. cit. supra*, fn. 29 at p. 115.

44 *Id.* at p. 111.

end.'[45] There are two separate aspects to fulfilling the requirements of the second formulation of the Categorical Imperative. Firstly, one must not act on maxims that (negatively) use persons as mere means, because this would be to act on maxims that no other could possibly sanction.[46] Secondly, we are required to avoid the pursuit of ends that others cannot share. We do this by treating them (positively) as ends in themselves.[47] It is this formulation of the Categorical Imperative that is the foundation of the principle of respect for persons. Persons are ends in themselves and can be a source of definite laws, because they have an absolute worth. Rational agents differ from inanimate things in that they are self-legislating, because they give themselves the laws by which they act. Conversely, inanimate objects (non-agents: including animals, *etc.*) such as rocks act according to the laws of nature. A rock cannot give itself the moral law.

The moral significance of the distinction between things and persons is that the will of the rational moral agent is inherently good (a person who has a good ethical disposition is to be valued because of their goodness), and it is the rationality of this will that is the foundation for this inherent goodness.[48] Therefore, it is immoral to frustrate the *autonomy* of the rational will by using the moral person as a mere means. In other words, one can permissibly use things, such as rocks, in any manner they deem fit (except for when they have an instrumental value to an agent), but one cannot permissibly use a person in any way he or she deems fit, because the self-legislating autonomy of the rational will has an inherent goodness (worth). Timmons notes that:[49] 'Our natures as autonomous agents provide the objective basis for right and wrong action. Actions that destroy or degrade humanity are *prima facie* wrong; actions that promote humanity are *prima facie* right. Thus, for example, maintenance of one's own autonomy requires that we omit actions that destroy or degrade autonomy.'

When x recognizes that y is entitled to respect as a person, x refrains from treating y as an inanimate object or as a mere thing.[50] Treating other agents (persons) as *mere* means has the effect of overpowering and damaging their

---

45 Paton, *op. cit. supra*, fn. 13 at p. 91.

46 O'Neill, *op. cit. supra*, fn. 18 p. 113.

47 'The failure is dual: The victim of deceit cannot agree to the initiator's maxim, so is used, and *a fortiori* cannot share the initiator's end, so is not treated as a person. Similarly with a maxim of coercion: Victims cannot agree with a coercer's fundamental principle or maxim, which denies them the choice between consent and dissent, and further cannot share a coercer's ends.' *Ibid.*

48 Cf. Richard Dean, 'What Should We Treat as an End in Itself,' (1996) 77(4) *Pacific Philosophical Quarterly* 268.

49 Mark Timmons, 'Motive and Rightness in Kant's Ethical System,' in Mark Timmons, *Kant's Metaphysics of Morals: Interpretative Essays* (Oxford: Oxford University Press, 2002) at p. 286.

50 Thomas E. Hill, 'Humanity as an End in Itself,' (1980–1981) 91 *Ethics* 84 at pp. 85–90.

agency. It destroys or undercuts their agency and willing.[51] When we act on maxims or pursue ends in ways that pre-empt the willing of others and 'deny them the possibility of collaboration or consent—or dissent'[52] we use them as tools or instruments in order to implement our own project. For this reason, we have a perfect duty to refrain from making false promises to others, because they cannot consent to our acting on such a maxim. Kant uses the false promising exemplar to demonstrate that it would be irrational to agree to certain maxims.[53] According to the second formulation of the Categorical Imperative it would be wrong to make false promises, because it treats the recipients of the promises *merely* as means to an end, rather than as ends in themselves with an absolute worth. The promissor uses the promisee's *capacity* to set and act on ends as a tool, a capacity she enjoys as a rational human being.[54] But would we want to criminalize all false promising? I would think not. Unfortunately, the Categorical Imperative does not make distinctions between non-criminalizable morally wrongful promising (*i.e.*, we would not criminalize *x* who comes home totally inebriated after falsely promising his estranged wife that he would give up alcohol, if she has let him move back into to the matrimonial home on that condition) and criminally wrongful promising (*i.e.*, the fraudulent director who breaks a promise or makes misrepresentations to her shareholders, which may have very harmful consequences, *etc.*). The Harm Principle would distinguish these cases of moral wrongdoing by identifying the extra consequential element of harm. It would also allow a number of countervailing considerations to be considered.

Kant's second formulation of the Categorical Imperative can be plausibly adapted to provide an account of the moral wrongness (moral impermissibility) of certain acts that disrespect humanity, but not the criminalizableness of those acts.[55] For instance, a rapist treats his victim as a mere means when he acts on his subjective maxim in the pursuit of his end to rape.[56] The rapist uses the non-consenting victim as a mere means; he treats her as a non-existent or impersonal thing. The rapist fails to treat the humanity of his victim as an end in itself, because he uses her dignity as a means to something that has a mere price. By raping the non-consenting victim he treats her with a lack of respect, because he treats her *capacity* to set ends as tools, and so as something that has a price.

---

51   O'Neill, *op. cit. supra*, fn. 18 at p. 138.
52   *Ibid*.
53   The false promising example relates to the strict duty to others: 'the man who has a mind to make a false promise to others will see at once that he is intending to make use of another man merely as a means to an end he does not share. For the man whom I seek to use for my own purposes by such a promise cannot possibly agree with my way of behaving to him, and cannot himself share the end of the action.' Paton, *op. cit. supra*, fn. 13 at p. 92.
54   Dennis Klimchuk, 'Three Accounts of Respect for Persons in Kant's Ethics,' (2003) 7 *Kantian Review* 38 at p. 53.
55   See Gardner and Shute, *op. cit. supra*, fn. 10 at p. 210.
56   *Ibid*.

He acts as though her humanity is substitutable for a mere price, the price being his project to have sex. As Benn[57] puts it, by failing to consider how his project affects others, its bearing on their ends and projects, the rapist fails to consider what differentiates persons from tools or mere things, namely their awareness of themselves as natural persons. A person is 'a subject with a consciousness of [him or herself] as agent, one who is capable of having projects, and assessing [his or her] achievements in relation to them. To conceive someone as a person is to see [him or her] as actually or potentially a chooser, as one attempting to steer [his or her] own course through the world.' This assessment also accords with our deep conventional understanding of the harmfulness and wrongfulness of rape.

The Categorical Imperative distinguishes between treating someone as a *mere* means to an end and as a means to an end. It is possible to treat others as means to our ends without disrespecting them as persons, so long as we treat them as means and as ends at the same time.[58] For example, it is not disrespectful to use the services of those who have an end in serving us such as restaurant waiters, toilet cleaners, trash collectors, lawyers, professors, doctors and so on. They are not only able to consent to our maxim, but also *share* our end as it fulfils their ends of earning a living and so on. There is nothing wrong, for Kant, with such usage of other people since this use is cooperative, it is not the use of a person as a mere means. The absolute worth of rational nature as an *end* in itself is distinguishable from ends that only have a relative worth, or price, as relative ends can be rationally sacrificed to obtain something else of equivalent or greater worth.[59] It would not be disrespectful for researchers to use consenting human subjects as tools for gaining empirical results or to earn a Ph.D.

Per contra, if the experimenter were to use human subjects as a part of a scientific experiment without their knowledge or consent (or by misleading them about the true nature of the experiment) this would treat them as a mere means to an end (the end of acquiring scientific results or a Ph.D. *etc.*).[60] The researcher would pursue an end that the human subjects are unable to sanction or share. The experimenter disrespects her human subjects by failing to distinguish their intrinsic value as persons from their immediate use as a part of her experiment. It is morally indefensible to treat others in a way which they are not able to sanction. Doing so treats them as an 'instrument or tool, which cannot, does not, consent to the ways in which it is used; such action fails to treat others as persons, who can choose, and may withhold consent from actions that affect them.'[61] Respect is about recognizing in others the subject of 'morally significant enterprise,' which provides a reason

---

57 Stanley I. Benn, *A Theory of Freedom* (Cambridge: Cambridge University Press, 1988) at p. 103.
58 Wood, *op. cit. supra*, fn. 29 at p. 143.
59 *Id.* at p. 115.
60 Ruth Macklin and Susan Sherwin, 'Experimenting on Human Subjects: Philosophical Perspectives,' (1975) 25 *Case Western Reserve Law Review* 434.
61 O'Neill, *op. cit. supra*, fn. 18 at p. 106.

for not treating them as instruments or as obstacles to one's own inclinations, as if they had no view of their own that was worthy of consideration.[62]

It is not clear as to how such a criterion could offer the legislature clear guidance about what it may fairly criminalize. Lying to your friends might use them as a mere means, but that does not necessarily mean that this type of wrongdoing should be criminalized. The harm criterion is superior here, not only because it allows the lawmaker to consider the badness and seriousness of the wrongness involved, but since this gives the legislature guidance about why any particular act might be *prima facie* criminalizable rather than merely morally impermissible. The legislature does not only look at the wrongness of rape, but also the gravity of the actual bad consequence. It is the gravity of the bad consequence that allows the legislature to fairly label the offense as serious or non-serious and to determine the appropriate sentence. The bad consequence gives lawmakers clear guidance about when it should invoke the criminal law to protect legitimate interests. The lawmaker can consider the consequences of the wrongdoing both at the individual and aggregate level and ask whether it is conduct that warrants a criminal law response because it would not be reasonable to expect one person to take private action to put a stop to it. The harm criterion allows the legislature to evaluate the criminalizableness of bad consequences that are brought about deliberately by moral agents in a way that deontological wrongness does not. It is the gravity of the consequences (acts/actions in the case of attempts and reckless endangerment—which are measured against the gravity of the potential consequences) that allows the lawmaker to make a firm conclusion about whether the unwanted conduct is of a kind that warrants a criminal law response.

Dan-Cohen and Ripstein's Criticisms of the Harm Principle

Under the Harm Principle conduct only involves harm when it *wrongfully* sets back a human interest.[63] I have argued that it is fair to criminalize wrongful harm, as harm provides us with a further objective condition for criminalizing evil intentions.[64] The fairness constraint is satisfied, because it is fair to punish those who intentionally harm others. However, it would not be fair or just to criminalize all forms of deontological wrongdoing merely because evil thoughts are combined with bad/actions consequences. For instance, an estranged husband wrongs his ex-wife when he falsely promises that he will not cheat on her again, if she lets him move back into the matrimonial home. If the estranged husband moved back into the matrimonial home on this condition and thereafter slept with the babysitter, the

---

62 Stanley I. Benn, 'Individuality, Autonomy, and Community: An Essay in Mediation,' (1978) *Bulletin Australasian Society of Legal Philosophy* 1 at p. 5.

63 See generally Feinberg, Vol. I, *op. cit. supra*, fn. 4.

64 Cf. Joseph Raz, *The Morality of Freedom* (Oxford: Clarendon Press, 1986) at p. 414.

wife would be able to claim she was wronged by the false promise. But it would not be fair to criminalize this type of trivial false promising despite its deontological wrongness. The criminal law involves censure, punishment and stigma. Therefore, it should be used as a last resort. In this situation Dan-Cohen could plausibly argue that the husband has wronged his wife by making a false promise. Dan-Cohen could not claim that it is *fair* to criminalize this type of wrongdoing. His justification for criminalization does not explain why it would not be fair to invoke a criminal law response. Criminalizing this type of false promising would be unfair as it does not result in harm or any other bad consequences of sufficient gravity to make it deserving of criminal condemnation. Criminalizing this type of wrongdoing would be contrary to our deeply held conventional standards of justice.

Dan-Cohen's[65] approach is over-inclusive in that it would allow conduct to be criminalized regardless of the fairness requirement. On the other hand, Dan-Cohen argues that the harm criterion falls short of the fairness requirement, because it cannot be used to justify the criminalization of certain gross acts (*e.g.*, rape by deception). There is no doubt that rape by deception is wrong. Gardner and Shute[66] use Kant's second formulation of the Categorical Imperative to identify the wrongness of rape by deception. Gardner and Shute argue that rape is harmless in certain circumstances even though this sounds oxymoronic. They postulate that in some cases the rape victim will not know that she has been raped nor will she ever find out. This is assuming that she was totally inebriated (to the point of oblivion) during the rape and that the wrongdoer used a prophylactic. According to Gardner and Shute this is not physiologically impossible, because not all rapes involve damaging or painful force, 'which will inevitably bring it to light later.'[67] They observe that: 'those who have drawn attention to the phenomena [*sic*] of "date rape" have highlighted, one may be raped while sexually aroused, even while sexually aroused by the attentions of the rapist, and one may be aroused, of course, while drunk or drugged.'[68] Gardner and Shute postulate that the victim's life does not change for the worse in such circumstances. They argue that the victim would have no feelings about the rape, since she would not remember the actual physical attack.

Similarly Dan-Cohen,[69] referring to *State v. Minkowski*,[70] claims that rape can be harmless when the victim is oblivious of the rape. In that case a number of female patients were oblivious to the fact that they had been used for sex by a medical practitioner who was meant to have been treating them for a medical condition. Dan-Cohen[71] makes the point that the harm in this type of case would

---

65 Dan-Cohen, *op. cit. supra*, fn. 1 at p. 153.
66 Gardner and Shute, *op. cit. supra*, fn. 10 at p. 197.
67 *Ibid.*
68 *Id.* at p. 196.
69 Dan-Cohen, *op. cit. supra*, fn. 1 at p. 153.
70 204 Cal. App. 2d. 832 (1962).
71 Dan-Cohen, *loc. cit. supra*, fn. 69.

normally be psychological.[72] But if the victims never learn of the violation they will not be harmed. He also argues that these types of violations *wrong* the victims despite their awareness of the rape, as they have been used as a mere means. On the theory presented in Chapter 2 of this book, criminalization would be justified by pointing to what the wrongdoer knew, not what the victim knew. Since the doctor knows that rape is a wrongful harm it would be fair to punish him for his culpable choice.

Gardner and Shute argue that the rape is harmless when it does not cause any physical damage and when it is not brought home to the victim. Dan-Cohen states that it is harmless when it is brought home to the victims so long as they do not remember being raped, because any distress would be psychological. The Gardner and Shute example is a much more convincing example of harmless wrongdoing. Arguably, this kind of rape is harmless if it is never *brought home to the victim*. But this is not a general proposition. The harm is hidden from the victim but the wrongdoer is well aware of what he had done. Generally, harm does not have to be brought home to the individual victim involved for it to come within the purview of the wrongful harm justification for criminalization. There is no need for a victim to discover the hidden harm for it to constitute a criminalizable harm. But it will have to be discovered by someone if it is to be labeled as criminal conduct from an *ex post* perspective in a court of law, regardless of whether the harm criterion or Dan-Cohen's theory is used to justify its criminalization. In the real world conduct can be criminalized from an *ex ante* perspective so long as it is conduct that normally poses a risk of harm to others, but an individual's specific harmful acting can only be brought within the purview of the criminal law from an *ex post* perspective according to the facts of the particular case.

Hidden harms do not really constitute harmless wrongs. For example, if an administrator of a deceased estate discovered that a private nurse had embezzled millions of dollars from her elderly employer's bank account leaving just enough so that the elderly employer would have been able to maintain her then comfortable lifestyle for another week if she had lived, without her elderly employer discovering the theft because she was suffering from Alzheimer's disease (the nurse knows and is fully culpable for choosing to engage in harmful conduct), or without having her then lifestyle affected because she had enough to maintain her status at the time, we could hardly say that the elderly victim was not harmed just because the embezzlement was not brought home to her. Clearly, her interests were set

---

72 This type of psychological distress could potentially constitute harm pursuant to the Harm Principle. As Feinberg points out, 'an affront or an insult normally causes a momentary sting; we wince, suffer a pang or two, then get on with our work, unharmed and whole. But if the experience is *severe*, prolonged, or constantly repeated, the mental suffering it causes may become obsessive and incapacitating, and therefore harmful.' Feinberg, Vol. I, *op. cit. supra*, fn. 4 at p. 46. If this type of rape was detected it would result in harm (the physical violation of the woman's person) and harm in the form of the incapacitating effects of the psychological trauma.

back even though she was not aware of the setback.[73] Her accumulative economic interests were set back at the time of the theft despite her being in a state of oblivion. The conduct would not have been criminalizable from an *ex post* trial perspective at the time of the theft, because the courts cannot convict a person (that is, by finding her guilty according to the rules of evidence in a court of law) until the crime is discovered and prosecuted.

Criminalization decisions are decided from an *ex ante* perspective. Because embezzlements result in wrongful harm we are able to say from an *ex ante* perspective that intentional embezzlements ought to be criminalized. In the case above, the nurse could only be labeled as a criminal at the individual level from an *ex post* perspective if her crime were discovered. The individual offender who commits an undetected harm would only be labeled as a criminal if her harm-doing came to light, because at an individual level it is not possible to prosecute undetected crimes. Nevertheless, the conduct is generally criminalizable from an *ex ante* perspective even though some victims will never discover that they were harmed or subjected to conduct that normally results in harm.

Gardner and Shute point out that undetected rapes are harmless when the victims do not discover that they were raped, but,

> [i]n no jurisdictions known to us is it true that rape is a crime only when harmful [when it is detected by the victim at an individual level]. Even the pure [so-called harmless: rape that is not brought home to the particular victim involved] case is classified as rape, and criminally so. One could sideline it by saying that the Harm Principle is a rule of thumb, and tolerates some departures from its standard. One could also sideline the [so-called harmless] case by observing that the Harm Principle's standard is met if the class of criminalized acts is a class of which tend to cause harm, and that is true of rape in spite of the possibility of the case [that is harmless because it was not discovered by the particular victim involved] ... The test is passed by the [harmless] case of rape with flying colors. If the act in this case were not criminalized then, assuming at least partial efficiency on the part of the law, people's rights to sexual autonomy would more often be violated.[74]

---

73   This cannot be distinguished from rape by deception, as the rape victim's resources have been set back in the same tangible way as the victim of embezzlement. The harm has occurred in a tangible way in the embezzlement case and merely awaits discovery by someone. The victim's accumulative financial resources have been diminished and set back from the moment the embezzlement takes place. Rape by deception does not need to be detected to amount to harm against the individual victim, but once detected it would be caught by the Harm Principle regardless of whether the individual victim learned of it in any individual case.

74   Gardner and Shute, *op. cit. supra*, fn. 10 at pp. 215–216.

The nucleus of Gardner's and Shute's argument is that conduct can be criminalized as a harmful wrong even if the individual victim was not harmed due to a lack of awareness (*i.e.*, the deceased employer who was oblivious to an embezzlement or the rape victim who was unaware of the fact she was raped), because these types of wrongs normally result in harm.

Gardner and Shute's argument is markedly different to that put forward by Dan-Cohen. To start with, Gardner and Shute support the harm criterion as a yardstick for measuring the justice of criminalization. Furthermore, they merely invoke the second formulation of the Categorical Imperative to explain the wrongness of rape. They do not suggest that the *wrongness* of rape by deception *per se* is the basis for criminalizing it. An individual can only be criminalized from the *ex post* perspective if her wrongdoing is discovered. Criminalizing conduct from an *ex ante* perspective is possible so long as the conduct normally results in wrongful harm or poses a real risk of harm, regardless of whether the given victim discovered the harm. *Per contra*, Dan-Cohen argues that the hidden rape is criminalizable merely because of its deontological wrongness.

From a general *ex ante* perspective Dan-Cohen could say all rapes should be criminalized, but the rape would have to be detected for the rapist to be labeled as a criminal from an *ex post* perspective in a given case. X might be raped without realizing it but if the rape is caught on CCTV, it would not matter if x never discovered it. Even though the individual victim in this case may not have been harmed physically or psychologically because the rape was never brought home to her, rape is conduct that normally results in harm (gravely bad consequences) and it would be fair to hold the perpetrator criminally responsible. The decision as to whether the rapist (who raped knowing there was no consent and that doing so is a wrongful harm) should be held responsible at the individual level is decided from an *ex post* perspective in a court of law according to the rules of evidence. Undetected rape is *prima facie* criminalizable from an *ex ante* perspective because it is conduct that normally involves wrongful harm and the wrongdoer chooses to risk this type of harm and should not be able to rely on the luck of its not being detected. *Ex ante* criminalization decisions are not guided by those cases that go undetected.

Dan-Cohen's theory is unable to criminalize hidden wrongs, because undetected crime is only brought within the purview of the criminal law when it is discovered. Dan-Cohen could argue that it is criminalizable so long as it is discovered, because it involves moral wrongdoing as the victim is treated as a mere means. But he would be unable to defeat the harm criterion with his harmless wrongdoing argument. Dan-Cohen not only fails to show that the harm criterion is unable to fairly criminalize rape by deception, but also fails to provide a feasible alternative for ensuring that criminalization decisions meet the requirement of fairness. The second formulation of the Categorical Imperative would allow all forms of wrongdoing to be criminalized regardless of the fairness requirements. The husband who falsely promises his wife that he will clean her car would be caught by Kant's Categorical Imperative. The Categorical Imperative is not able to effectively constrain unfair and unprincipled criminalization.

It gives the legislature no guidance, as many trivial wrongs could be criminalized under the Categorical Imperative. Line jumping is wrong as it uses the other customers as a mere means. But we would not necessarily want to give the legislator a free hand to criminalize any act that merely involves moral wrongdoing. This would lead to unfair and unprincipled criminalization. Wrongs that do not result in sufficiently grave bad consequences do not warrant a criminal law response. It would be inefficient, excessive and unnecessary to criminalize queue jumping. It is essential that the conduct involve something other than wrongdoing and the harm criterion provides an additional objective element in that it requires the wrongdoing to result in bad consequences. There are cases that cannot be dealt with under the wrongful harm or wrongful criteria, but in those cases alternative explanations of the badness of the unwanted consequences have to be produced to justify invoking the criminal law.

Under Kant's theory[75] morally rightful actions are those that treat human beings as ends in themselves, whereas morally wrongful actions are those that treat them as a *mere* means to an end. It is a general deontological theory that is useful for identifying rightful and wrongful conduct. It does not tell us which of those wrongs *deserves* a criminal law response. The harmful consequences of wronging others by raping them or making false promises are not factors that can be used for making distinctions between the various wrongful actions as determined by Kant's deontological theory. The Categorical Imperative can be invoked to explain moral wrongdoing in certain cases, but as a scheme it does not work in tandem with other moral theories (for example, it cannot be supplemented with consequentialist theories). It is about acting out of duty or moral obligation. A significant implication of deontology is that a person's behavior can be wrong even if it redounds by fluke to the wronged person's advantage. *Per contra*, the Harm Principle allows the lawmaker to examine the negative outcome—the harmfulness of the defendant's actions. The gravity of the harm gives the legislature further guidance as to why it might be fair to criminalize a particular wrong. This is where the Categorical Imperative fails as a guide for what can be fairly criminalized. According to the Categorical Imperative, rape and false promising are equally wrong. Consequently, Dan-Cohen's theory suggests that rape and false promising are equally criminalizable. The harmful consequences of false promising and rape have no role to play in determining their wrongness or criminalizableness in Dan-Cohen's Kantian scheme.

---

75 '[A] normative moral theory—a theory that purports to reveal what features of an action at bottom make the action right or wrong—is just a theory of moral relevance ... The Humanity formulation of the Categorical Imperative serves this role in Kant's ethics. ... [I]t is facts about the bearings of one's actions on the maintenance and flourishing of humanity (as Kant understands this notion) that are the morally relevant facts determining the (objective) deontic status of an action.' Timmons, *op. cit. supra*, fn. 49 at pp. 285–286.

Harm and Wrongdoing to Non-Humans

A further problem with using Kant's Categorical Imperative as a criteria for guiding legislatures with criminalization decisions is simply that it is a part of a strict deontological scheme that attempts to provide a mechanism for identifying the rightness and wrongness of activities that affect humans. Actions are morally wrong only when they are inconsistent with the status of a person as a free rational being. Kant's categorical duties are based on *a priori* reasoning about the general nature of things, and thus apply no matter what the circumstances are. Legal academics like to pull the second formulation of the Categorical Imperative from the inclusive system in which it works and in doing so try to get it to answer problems that it is not equipped to deal with. It works as a part of a particular philosophical method. It is not even an inclusive criterion for determining the criminalizableness of wronging humans, but it does at least explain the wrongness of certain actions that affect humans. But it cannot explain the wrongness of harming animals, let alone why harming animals should be criminalized. The second formulation of the Categorical Imperative cannot tell the legislature why it might or might not be fair and just to invoke the criminal law to protect foxes from foxhunters. I have argued above that the wrongful harm justification can deal with harm to animals. Harm forms a part of the rationale for criminalizing those who wantonly harm animals. The harm criterion can be combined with a non-dignity account of wrongdoing. Those who harm animals deserve criminal censure, because they know that it is wrong and harmful to wantonly harm animals.

The Categorical Imperative only provides person centered reasons[76] for explaining moral wrongdoing. It is over-inclusive as a criterion for guiding criminalization decisions because it would catch certain harmless wrongs (*i.e.*, false promising: husbands who make false promises that do not result in harm to their wives); and is under-inclusive in that it cannot explain why it is fair to criminalize wanton harm to animals. It is designed to determine the rightness and wrongness of all actions (or according to Dan-Cohen, the criminalizability of all actions). Those who hunt foxes are entitled to know why it is fair for them to face the wrath of the criminal law for enjoying their sport. Feinberg's formulation of the Harm Principle is also under-inclusive in that it does not explain why it is fair to criminalize foxhunting or bullfighting, but this can be overcome by referring to our deeply held conventional understandings about the wrongness such conduct. It is clearly wrong for people to wantonly destroy animals and this conduct is properly criminalized as a wrongful harm, as set out in Chapter 2 of this book.

Why does Kant's second Categorical Imperative fail to provide a standard for demonstrating that it is fair to criminalize harm to animals? On its face, Kant's logocentric morality seems to support the idea that non-persons can be used in an abominable fashion to serve the ends of persons. Kant's theory is notoriously anthropocentric (or rather it is logocentric), that is, it is based on the idea that

---

76   Benn, *op. cit. supra*, fn. 57 at Chapter 1.

'rational nature, and it alone, has an absolute value.'[77] For instance, Kant states: 'The first time [the human being] said to the sheep, Nature gave the skin you wear not for you but for me, and then took it off the sheep ... he became aware of the prerogative he had by nature over all animals, which he no longer saw as fellow creatures, but as a means and tools at the disposal of his will for the attainment of the aims at his discretion.'[78]

Two leading Kantian scholars have argued that Kant's moral law does offer limited (indirect) protection to non-human animals. Professors Wood and O'Neill[79] argue that the Categorical Imperative imposes indirect duties on human agents, which direct them to use animals prudently. They argue that Kant's *Formula of Humanity as an End in Itself* is able to deal with ethical questions about how we should treat irrational non-humans.[80] The logocentric feature of Kantian ethics is simply that it recognizes no value that is independent of the dignity of rational nature. This aspect of Kant's theory seems to provide a barrier[81] to protecting irrational nature. Notwithstanding this, Wood and O'Neill postulate that protecting irrational nature is reconcilable with Kant's logocentrism. According to Wood and O'Neill, Kant goes wrong by using a personification principle. 'This principle says that rational nature is respected only by respecting humanity in someone's person, hence that every duty must be understood as a duty to a person or persons.'[82] The gist of their argument is simply that logocentric ethics, which grounds all duties on humanity or rational nature, should not be guided by a personification principle. They assert that rational nature should be respected not only by respecting human dignity but also by respecting things that bear certain *relations* to it, by being fragments of it or necessary conditions of it.[83]

O'Neill[84] argues that the most persuasive rationale for enlarging the extent of moral concern for rational natures is that some are considered to be irrational or incipiently rational (almost rational), that is, they exhibit 'fragments of rationality, but are not presently persons according to Kant's narrow use of the term.' Such a rationale has been used persuasively to cover human beings whose 'rational agency is either potential (infants) or temporarily reduced (in illness) or fading

---

77 Allen W. Wood and Onora O'Neill, 'Kant on Duties Regarding Nonrational Nature,' (1998) *Proceedings of the Aristotelian Society* 189. Wood and O'Neill write independent papers on this topic, but come to a similar overall conclusion. The papers are located together in accordance with Aristotelian Society practice. For the sake of clarity I refer to their overall argument, but distinguish points by referring to the authors individually and to exact page numbers where appropriate.
78 *Ibid.*
79 *Id.* at p. 190.
80 *Ibid.*
81 *Id.* at p. 195.
82 *Id.* at p. 196.
83 *Id.* at pp. 197–198.
84 *Id.* at p. 221.

(the senile), or borderline (the severely retarded).'[85] O'Neill asserts that the same line of reasoning can be applied to non-human animals. But this is not correct, animals do not have fragments of humanity in a genetic or biological sense, nor do they have fragments of human intelligence (they are not rational or intellectual in same supreme way as humans); therefore I doubt they could be brought within the protection offered by the second formulation of the Categorical Imperative. A person's humanity cannot be reduced by the fact that her rationality is reduced or is in a retarded or underdeveloped state; infants and the senile always maintain the status of humanness, not only genetically, but also because they always have *de facto* rationality and intellectuality.

A person cannot become a fragment of a human merely by being very young or senile and consequently is entitled to equal respect as a human regardless of age, mental capacity and so forth. The protection accorded to animals is less than that accorded to persons. Wood and O'Neill seem to acknowledge as much when they assert that Kant did not intend non-human animals to be available for unrestricted human use, but he did not regard them as *ends in themselves*. O'Neill states: 'It is true that he denies that non-human animals have rights, or that they can bind us to any duties, and that he never regards them as ends in themselves. Nevertheless, in allowing that harming non-human animals is an indirect violation of duties to humanity Kant endorses more or less the range of ethical concern for non-human animals that more traditional utilitarians allowed: welfare but not rights.'[86] Non-human animals ought not be used wantonly, that is, 'destroyed or cruelly misused, although they may be sold, used for labor (but not excessive labor) and killed (painlessly) for food.'[87] This kind of concession would not apply to humans, because humans ought never be killed or sold, *etc*.

The respect for humanity principle cannot be invoked to justify criminalizing those who harm animals. Simply applying the second formulation of the Categorical Imperative to the treatment of animals would have absurd results. The bullock that is slaughtered to provide meat and leather is used as a mere means, because it is only the butcher and his customers who benefit from the bullock's death. Yet we would not want to criminalize those who run a slaughterhouse, unless it resulted in a wanton use of animals. How do we distinguish this from elephant poaching? The simple explanation is that elephants are an endangered species; if they were not they could probably be farmed as farming might not be a wanton use. Likewise, the monkey that is used as a part of animal testing in a Cambridge University laboratory is used as a mere means. It is only the experimenter that benefits from the monkey's suffering, so the monkey could not share the experimenter's end. Yet, we would not want to criminalize these kinds of legitimate uses, as the experimenter does not act wantonly if her research is geared towards saving that species or towards developing medicines and so forth.

---

85 *Ibid*.
86 *Id*. at p. 223.
87 *Id*. at p. 221.

Therefore, independent moral arguments need to be produced to deal with those situations where animals are used wantonly (*e.g.*, dog fighting, poaching, *etc.*). Human agents do not have a direct duty to respect non-human animals under the Categorical Imperative, because irrational creatures are not rational choosers. Raz's[88] interest theory holds that non-human animals may not have rights as such, but that humans have certain duties *vis-à-vis* non-human animals. Animals are clearly harmed in an objective sense when they are killed and tortured and they are wrongfully harmed because humans have a moral duty not to *wantonly* torture or destroy them. Conventional morality does more to explain the wrongness of harming animals, because we have deep conventional understandings about the wrongness of wantonly destroying animals. Kant's critical morality is rigid and cannot be reworked to explain the wrongness of harming animals.

My analysis differs from O'Neill's and Wood's, because I am of the view that animals do not have fragments of human rationality or humanity more generally (a fox might plan and think whereas a fetus cannot, but this type of rationality is not human intelligence). Nonetheless, animals might be protected from *wanton* harm on the basis of sentience. A strong argument could be based on the fact that humans are highly intelligent, well-socialized *knowers* who are able to comprehend that cutting a leg or ear off a dog is going to cause that dog immense physical pain and that this pain is going to be identical to what a human would feel if her leg or ear were cut off. A human being can understand that pain is a bad consequence, because it is empirically provable with science. We might not share humanity with animals but we do share basic animality with them and feel pain and suffer injury in the same way. A human can also understand that inflicting pain on an animal is going to result in a bad consequence for the animal (for example, throwing boiling oil on a puppy dog is going to result in the same misery, in raw terms of pain and injury, as throwing it on a person). It can also be explained to a human that if you intentionally (without justification or excuse) throw boiling water on a puppy you will be acting wrongly as you have a non-correlative duty not to wantonly harm animals and will be censurable for violating that duty. Of course, the great difficulty for future work in this area will be determining when a use of an animal is wanton. To satisfy the *non-wanton use* restraint the human harmer would (at a bare minimum) have to demonstrate that his or her use of the animal serves some important social value and involved the least cruel means available. This will not be easy to satisfy and recreation is not likely to be sufficient.

The core difference between animals and humans is that animals lack human intelligence and personhood and are only protected from wanton use. Humans are protected from all use. Unlike Wood and O'Neill, I am of the view that a fetus would have 'fragments of *humanity*' rather than fragments of *rationality* (*i.e.*,

---

88 See Joseph Raz, *The Morality of Freedom* (Oxford: Clarendon Press, 1986) at Chapter 7. Matthew H. Kramer, *Rights, Wrongs and Responsibilities* (Chippenham, Wiltshire: Palgrave, 2001) at pp. 28 *et seq.*

fetuses are *potential* humans and are distinguishable from the senile and infants as the latter have already acquired the status of being a full human). Infants and the senile not only have fragments of rationality, but are also full human beings in a biological and genetic sense and their *de facto* human rationality does not affect their human status. A fetus has not acquired the status of full personhood, but it certainly has fragments of humanity and is entitled to some respect on that basis. The amount of respect owed would depend on its stage of development. If we are talking about a woman taking the morning-after pill, then not too much respect is owned as the potentiality of her unprotected sexual relations developing into a person might be very remote. Here we are merely talking about the seeds of humanity. If we are talking about an abortion six weeks into the pregnancy we are talking about destroying something that clearly has fragments of humanity. This is seen in the many enactments that specifically aim to protect fetuses. If a man were to punch a woman in the womb thereby causing her a miscarriage, his liability is likely to be for more than assault. The rationale for such laws is the protection of something that is regarded as being more than a mere thing, because it has fragments of humanity.[89]

The basic sentience argument raised above with respect to animals would also apply to fetuses to the extent that their nervous systems are sufficiently developed to feel real pain. The wanton use restraint might be satisfied if it is just a mere matter of causing pain to a sentient creature, because the mother might assert that she is not wantonly using the creature but protecting herself from the burden of raising a child to adulthood. She might argue that the burden of raising and paying for an unwanted child for 18 years is significant and given that the fetus is not yet a rational feeling human and is merely the seeds of humanity (or more controversially in advanced pregnancies: fragments of humanity), her right not to be forced to have an 18-year sentence of raising a child makes the abortion non-wanton use. Coupled with this, the mother has full personhood and should be able to decide how to live her life. But if we accept that, unlike animals, a fetus has fragments of humanity if not rationality, then at some point during gestation that humanity must be of a sufficient degree to make abortion intolerable regardless of the mother's

---

89 In the U.S. in 2004 Congress enacted the *Unborn Victims of Violence Act of 2004* (Public Law 108–212), which recognizes a fetus as a legal victim if it is injured or killed during the commission of any of the 68 existing Federal crimes of violence. The law recognizes the fetus as a member of the species *Homo sapiens* from the moment it is conceived. See also section 1(1) *Infant Life (Preservation) Act 1929* (U.K.). This section makes it an offense to 'destroy the life of a child capable of being born alive, by any wilful act that causes a child to die before it has an existence independent of its mother.' Section 5(1) of the *Abortion Act 1967* (U.K.) exempts surgeons from liability under the 1929 Act. See also *Attorney-General's Reference (No. 3 of 1992)* [1994] 2 All E.R. 121 where a woman's partner stabbed her thereby causing her baby to be born with injuries, the injuries eventually led to the baby's death, and the father (who was also the stabber) was able to avoid a murder charge as transferred malice could not be transferred from the mother to the fetus and then to the born baby.

right not to be forced to raise a child she does not want. If the pregnancy has been let go too far then the mother should have the child and consider adoption.

All abortions are wrong as they destroy fragments of humanity and once the fetus starts to develop a nervous system the abortion would involve inflicting gross pain (wrongful harm) on a sentient creature. A human knower who can understand the damage involved inflicts the pain and destruction on (fragments of) *humanity*. If it is accepted that a fetus has fragments of humanity, then abortion is not only wrong but also *prima facie* criminalizable. It is only *prima facie* criminalizable since destroying fragments of humanity is not the same has destroying or damaging a human. We have non-correlative duties to fetuses, but a fetus does not have a right to life because it is a fragment of life not life per se (it is a potential life or the seeds of human life). Once a baby is born alive,she has full personhood and has an equal right to life to that held by the mother. There is a fine and controversial balance here, but the non-correlative duty to respect fragments of humanity has to compete with the mother's right not to be burdened with having a child she does not want. It is not easy to draw a line, but it is plausible to suggest that if the fetus is terminated early then the mother's right prevails. After all, the fragments of humanity are almost non-existent in the very early stages of the pregnancy and at that stage would be better described as the seeds of humanity.

Likewise, the pain to a sentient creature justification for criminalization is much weaker at the early stage as its nervous system is probably insufficiently developed for the pain to be described as abominable.[90] Abortion is *prima facie* wrong and thus *prima facie* criminalizable, but the case for criminalization is overridden by the mother's competing interest in having a right not to be forced raise a child. As I noted in the last chapter, a stronger override argument might be raised in the overpopulation context because abortion might be necessary to preserve humanity, which is the rationale for China's one child policy. One cannot respect humanity by forcing it to materialize merely to starve to death.

---

90 Arguably, the majority of the U.S. Supreme Court drew the line in the right place in *Gonzales v. Carhart*, 550 U.S. 124 (2007). In that case, the majority upheld a prohibition against 'partial-birth abortion' as it involves removing the fetus in an intact condition, because after 12 weeks' gestation it is normally too big to be removed by the suction method commonly used. This seems sensible, as it is pointless to value fetuses in one enactment (see the preceding footnote) and then allow abortion to be used as a mere convenience for those who are too irresponsible to use prophylactics or to seek a timely abortion. Having said that, a blanket prohibition against 'partial-birth abortion' would not be appropriate as there may be genuine medical cases where it is necessary to save the mother's life.

Ripstein's Sovereignty Principle

Ripstein proposes a sovereignty principle, which holds that violations of *equal freedom*[91] provide the legitimate basis for criminalization.[92] Ripstein uses Kant's concept of external freedom that is specific to the *Doctrine of Right* in an attempt to prevent the growth of unfair and unprincipled criminalization. He does not concern himself with the Categorical Imperative, but rather concentrates on the notion of external freedom.[93] 'The foundational assumption in Kantian morality is that human freedom has unconditional value, and both the *Categorical Imperative* and the *Universal Principle of Right* flow directly from this fundamental normative claim: the Categorical Imperative tells us what form our actions must take if they are to be compatible with the universal value of freedom, and the universal principle of right tells us what form our actions must take if they are to be compatible with the universal value of freedom, regardless of our maxims and motivations.' The *Universal Principle of Right* holds: 'Freedom (independence from being constrained by another's choice), insofar as it can coexist with the freedom of every other in accordance with a universal law, is the only original right belonging to every other man by virtue of his humanity.'[94] Our innate right to freedom is derived from the concept of human dignity: 'Do not make thyself a mere Means for the use of others, but be to them likewise an End.'[95] From this, Kant derives the universal principle of justice which requires that we: 'Act externally in such a manner that the free exercise of thy Will may be able to co-exist with the Freedom of all others, according to a universal Law.'[96]

Kant asserts that coercion is legitimate if is used to prevent a hindrance to freedom, because a hindrance to a hindrance to freedom is itself a means to freedom.[97] Using the juridical law is not itself a hindrance to freedom, because the threat of sanction does not deprive a would-be criminal of freedom in the way that her crime would deprive its victim of freedom.[98] Kant's *Principle of Right* aims to give each person the right to pursue his or her freely chosen ends as he or she sees fit. External freedom is action that proceeds unimpaired by others. Ripstein's

---

91 The first objection is that the notion of freedom is not measurable and so cannot be equal or unequal. For an irrelevant sense in which freedom is measurable, see Ian Carter, *A Measure of Freedom* (Oxford: Oxford University Press, 1999).

92 Ripstein, *op. cit. supra*, fn. 2 at p. 216.

93 See Ripstein's opening footnote. *Ibid.*

94 Immanuel Kant, *Metaphysics of Morals* (1797), translated from the German by Mary J. Gregor, *Practical Philosophy: The Cambridge Edition of the Works of Immanuel Kant* (Cambridge: Cambridge University Press, 1999) at p. 393.

95 Immanuel Kant, The Philosophy of Law: An Exposition of the Fundamental Principles of Jurisprudence as the Science of Right, translated from the German by William Hastie, *The Philosophy of Law* (Edinburgh: T. & T. Clark, 1887) at p. 54.

96 Gregor, *op. cit. supra*, fn. 94 at p. 386.

97 *Id.* at pp. 287–288.

98 Hastie, *op cit. supra*, fn. 95 at p. 46.

sovereignty principle (drawing on Kant) requires a person to act externally (use her free choices) so that they can co-exist with the freedom of all others in accordance with a universal law. He postulates that those actions that are able to co-exist are not criminalizable and that those actions that cannot co-exist are criminalizable. A person can only determine the rightfulness of her actions by locating them in a system of external actions to assess their harmony with that system as a whole.[99]

The moral basis for juridical laws of freedom lies in our capacity to set and pursue our own ends.[100] Ripstein argues that a person's external actions will impinge on the external freedom of others when they prevent those others from being free to pursue their ends as rational beings or subject those others to her choices. If x requires y's permission to use the means that x has to pursue her ends then she will not be free.[101] Ripstein also asserts that, if y uses x or uses x's means without her consent, then y will hinder x's freedom. According to Ripstein, it would be fair to criminalize actions when they interfere with the capacity of others to set ends for themselves. Our freedom is impinged when our decisions as to which ends we will pursue depend on the choices of others.[102] Ripstein asserts that people can wrongfully interfere with your freedom in three core ways: 'by depriving you of the means you use in pursuit of those ends, or making you pursue ends you do not share, or using your means to pursue those ends.'[103] External freedom is about being independent from being compelled by the choices of others. In summation, Ripstein's sovereignty principle clearly mirrors Kant's fundamental principle of right. He asserts that freedom in the sovereignty principle is,

> understood as each person's ability to set and pursue his own purposes, consistent with the freedom of others to do the same. You are independent if you are the one who decides what ends you will use your powers to pursue, as opposed to having someone else decide for you ... This interest in independence is not a special case of a more general interest in being able to set and pursue your purposes. Instead, it is a distinctive aspect of your status as a person, that entitles you to set

---

99   Philip M. Kretschmann, 'An Exposition of Kant's Philosophy of Law,' in George T. Whitney and David F. Bowers, *The Heritage of Kant* (Princeton: Princeton University Press, 1939) at pp. 252–253. Immanuel Kant, *Metaphysics of Morals* (1797), translated from the German by Mary J. Gregor, *Practical Philosophy: The Cambridge Edition of the Works of Immanuel Kant* (Cambridge: Cambridge University Press, 1999) at p. 393. Immanuel Kant, The Philosophy of Law: An Exposition of the Fundamental Principles of Jurisprudence as the Science of Right, translated from the German by William Hastie, The Philosophy of Law (Edinburgh: T. & T. Clark, 1887) at p. 54. Gregor, *op. cit. supra*, fn. 94 at p. 386. *Id.* at pp. 287–288. Hastie, op. cit. supra, fn. 95 at p. 46.

100   Katrin Flikschuh, 'Kantian Desires,' in Timmons, *op. cit. supra*, fn. 49 at p. 194.

101   Arthur Ripstein, 'Authority and Coercion,' (2004) 32(1) *Philosophy & Public Affairs* 1 at pp. 7–8.

102   *Ibid.*

103   *Ibid.*

your own purposes, and means that you are not required to act as an instrument for the pursuit of anyone else's purposes.[104]

Ripstein asserts that the wrongful harm criteria should be discarded and replaced with his sovereignty principle. He puts forward similar arguments as Dan-Cohen for jettisoning the harm criterion. Ripstein refers to a number of highly abstract harmless wrongs, which he claims cannot be fairly criminalized in accordance with the Harm Principle. He postulates that certain wrongs do not result in harm, so the harm criterion does not explain why the conduct ought to be criminalized. He starts off with the example of a harmless trespass.[105] In Ripstein's example the trespasser uses burglar's tools to enter into someone's home to take a nap on her bed. The trespasser does not cause any damage to the locks and uses hygienic covers so she does not leave any germs on the homeowner's bed. The hypothetical trespasser does not weigh much so she does not cause any wear and tear to the mattress. The trespasser naps for some hours whilst the homeowner is at work and then leaves without the homeowner ever finding out about the trespass. Ripstein asserts that it would be fair to criminalize this type of undetected trespass, but that its criminalization could not be justified in terms of constituting wrongful harm.

It is true the wrongful harm rationale for criminalization does exclude certain harmless trespasses from the scope of the criminal law. But Ripstein's trespass is not harmless. If *detected*, this kind of trespass would not only involve a violation of the owner's freedom, but would also harm the owner. It sets back one's interest in security. It sets back the interest we have in maintaining those proprietary resources that provide us with a secure habitat. These kinds of invasions threaten the general security of property and those security interests that cushion our welfare interests that are protectable under Feinberg's formulation of the Harm Principle.[106] Trespasses into private homes could be criminalized to protect our elementary sense of security. If people were allowed to freely trespass into the private homes of others, then people would generally feel less secure and our

---

104 Ripstein, *op. cit. supra*, fn. 2 at p. 231.
105 *Ibid.*
106 Feinberg, Vol. I, *op. cit. supra*, fn. 4 at pp. 63, 207. Duff notes that: 'There are substantive offenses related to secondary harms: thus although one reason for criminalizing "assault" might be that it is likely to lead to the primary harm of actual violence and injury (by the assaulter of the victim), the law defines it as a substantive offense, of bringing about the secondary harm of fear and violence.' R.A. Duff, *Criminal Attempts* (Oxford: Clarendon Press, 1996) at p. 130.

entire property law system would be jeopardized.[107] Coupled with this, invading the homes of others results in the further bad consequence of privacy loss.[108]

Even if the privacy invasion does not constitute harm, it certainly has bad consequences of a criminalizable kind. This type of privacy invasion also wrongs the homeowner. These types of trespasses can be distinguished from those that are dealt with as a tort, because they involve the private home. It is true that wrongful harm could not be used to exclude certain harmless trespasses from the scope of the criminal law (*e.g.*, mere trespasses to goods). It is possible to commit a trespass to goods without setting back the owner's long-term interests. While a person has a proprietary interest in maintaining exclusivity over her goods, a mere trespass does not set back her long-term interest in such a resource. The case is different in the case of larceny as her right to exclusive possession (exclusivity) has been violated and her interest in that resource has been set back by the permanent deprivation. *Per contra*, if x takes possession of y's hat (without any intention of permanently depriving y of it) and hides it for a few hours for a joke, she violates x's exclusivity right in that good, but she does not set back x's long-term interests. No harm results from this type of wrongdoing. Similarly, a person may be wronged without being harmed, *e.g.*, where someone wrongly breaks a 'promise that redounds, by fluke, to the promisee's advantage.'[109] In some cases the trespass may incidentally improve the resource that has been trespassed upon. These types of trespasses are rightly dealt with through the use of tort law. Ripstein's approach would criminalize both trespasses into the private home and trivial trespasses to goods.

Ripstein postulates that even if trespasses into the private home are harmful in the standard case, they cannot cause harm when they go undetected. I noted above, that the criminalization question from an *ex ante* perspective concerns the standard case, not those individual cases that go undetected. The homeowner many never discover the trespass, but if she does the criminal law needs to be able to protect her interests. He does not, however, explain how a person could claim her freedom had been violated if the trespass never came to light. The Harm Principle merely requires the conduct to be of a kind that normally results in wrongful harm. It is

---

107 A number of empirical studies suggest that the victims of burglary find the trespass and invasion of privacy leaving them feeling less secure. Mike Maguire and Trevor Bennett, *Burglary in a Dwelling* (London: Heinemann, 1982); Roger Tarling and Tonia Davison, *Victims of Domestic Burglary: A Review of the Literature* (London: H.M.S.O., 2000); and Mike Maguire and Jocelyn Kynch, *Public Perceptions and Victims' Experiences of Victim Support* (London: H.M.S.O., 2000).

108 Trespassing into a private home could leave the owner feeling violated and insecure. It would amount to a significant interference with his or her proprietary resource and would also constitute a wrongful privacy intrusion. See Andrew von Hirsch and Nils Jareborg, 'Gauging Crime Seriousness: A "Living Standard" Conception of Criminal Harm,' in Andrew von Hirsch and Andrew Ashworth, *Proportionate Sentencing: Exploring the Principles* (Oxford: Oxford University Press, 2005) at p. 212. See also Gardner and Shute, *op. cit. supra*, fn. 10 at pp. 202–203.

109 Feinberg, Vol. I, *op. cit. supra*, fn. 4 at p. 35.

also fair to invoke the criminal law to stop people from engaging in conduct that poses a real risk of harm to others. Actual harm is not needed for the purposes of invoking the criminal law. This is also the rationale for criminalizing attempts and other forms of non-consummated criminality. If a would-be burglar enters someone's house through an open window and reaches for a silver teapot that is sitting on the homeowner's sideboard with the intention of stealing it, but quickly withdraws upon noticing a large Doberman approaching and thereafter makes an escape without taking or damaging anything, the owners might not be harmed. The owners might never discover that someone had entered their house for such a purpose. Even if we suppose that this kind of attempt is harmless in that it is not sufficient to interfere with the owner's privacy and elementary security interests, it would be criminalizable from an *ex ante* perspective, since the completed crime would normally set back their property interests. The standard burglary exposes its potential victims to a real risk of harm.

In the example above, the burglar's acts are more than preparatory. He came close to removing the silver teapot. This kind of harmless attempt is criminalizable under the Harm Principle, because it poses a real risk of harm to others.[110] Even if trespassing into private homes is totally harmless in certain circumstances, it is conduct that normally causes actual harm to others.[111] Harmless wrongs can be dealt with pursuant to the wrongful harm justification for criminalization 'if their criminalization diminishes the occurrence of them, and the wider occurrence of them would detract from people's prospects—for example, by diminishing some public good, such as people's sense of ease with their living environment.'[112]

Some offenses are inchoate versions of offenses that are inchoate themselves.[113] Attempted burglary provides such an example. A person commits burglary by 'entering a building as a trespasser with an intent to commit one of the following: (a) theft or attempted theft; (b) criminal damage or attempted criminal damage; or (b) infliction of grievous bodily harm or attempted grievous bodily harm.' Trespassing *per se* is not normally regarded as a criminal offense, but it is when a person trespasses with the intent to commit a substantive offense.[114] Inchoate offenses are designed to criminalize conduct 'in so far as it has an appropriate causal relationship to a primary harm, as making the occurrence of harm more likely' and where the wrongdoer is aware of the causal relationship but chooses to

---

110 Feinberg, Vol. I, *op. cit. supra*, fn. 4 at p. 10.
111 Gardner and Shute, *op. cit. supra*, fn. 10 at p. 216.
112 *Ibid.*
113 Duff, *op. cit. supra*, fn. 106 at p. 130.
114 Section 9 *Theft Act 1968* (U.K.). See also sections 68–70 of the *Criminal Justice and Public Order Act 1994* (U.K.); and section 63 of the *Sexual Offenses Act 2003* (U.K.). Section 4 of the *Vagrancy Act 1824* (U.K.) makes it an offense to be found on private premises for an unlawful purpose.

increase the chances of the primary harm being brought about.[115] The great majority of burglaries result in harm and involve culpable offenders. Such acts belong to a class of acts that either cause harm or pose a risk of harm to others.[116] Since the Harm Principle only 'requires that criminalization of an action will prevent harm, not that the action itself be harmful,' the risk of harm can be considered.[117] Ripstein understates the reach of the wrongful harm criteria.

In the alternative, Ripstein argues that trespasses into a person's home (even when undetected[118]) are criminalizable because they interfere with the homeowner's freedom. The trespasser wrongs the homeowner 'by using the powers that are external to [her] person—[her] property—without [her] permission.'[119] In a separate paper he asserts that, for Kant, rummaging through someone's home or goods for purposes that she does not share violates her ability to be 'the one who determines the purposes to which they will be put.'[120] The trespasser wrongs the homeowner by depriving her of the ability to be the one who determines how her property will be used. This is an intuitively plausible alternative explanation of the moral wrongdoing involved in trespasses into homes. But if Ripstein's account of mere wrongdoing were the sole criterion for limiting criminalization, then this could lead to further unfair and unprincipled criminalization decisions.

Ripstein relies heavily on Kant's narrow concept of autonomy. He states: 'You remain free to use your other powers to pursue other purposes. But a part of being free to use your powers to set and pursue your own purpose is having a veto on the purposes you will pursue. You need more than the ability to pursue purposes you have set; you also need to be able to decline to pursue purposes unless you have set them. When I usurp your powers, I violate your sovereignty precisely

---

115 'However, whilst not denying that this may be the appropriate way to understand many inchoate offenses, the latter view will give a different account of others, particularly those involving an intention directed towards a primary harm. For in such cases, on the latter view, the wrongness of the conduct consists in its intentional, not merely causal, relationship to some primary harm; and the culpability depends also on the way in which she directs her action towards that harm.' Duff, *op. cit. supra*, fn. 106 at pp. 132–133.

116 'The "subjective principle" would also be accepted by the consequentialist as a justification for criminalizing complete attempts: the defendant was trying to break the law, and therefore constitutes a source of social danger no less (or little less) than that presented by "successful" harm-doers.' Andrew Ashworth, *Principles of Criminal Law* (Oxford: Oxford University Press, 2003) at p. 447.

117 *Ibid.*

118 According to Ripstein, 'I can nap in your bed while you are away, but any wrongs against your person will be committed in your presence, although not necessarily with your awareness of them.' Ripstein, *op. cit. supra*, fn. 2 at p. 241.

119 *Ibid.* See Gregor, *op. cit. supra*, fn. 94 at pp. 402–405.

120 Ripstein, *op. cit. supra*, fn. 101 at p. 10. 'For Kant, property in an external thing—something other than my own powers—is simply the right to have that thing at my disposal with which to set and pursue my own ends.' *Id.* at pp. 11–12.

because I deprive you of that veto.'[121] The Harm Principle protects autonomy in a much wider sense than Kant envisaged.[122] Autonomy is reduced to vanishing point in Kant's formulation as it only allows 'one set of principles which people can rationally legislate and they are the same for all. Nobody can escape [his or her] rule simply by being irrational and refusing to accept them. Personal autonomy, by contrast, is essentially about the freedom of persons to choose their own lives.'[123] The boarder concept of personal autonomy, as expounded by Raz, can also explain the harmfulness of interfering with the property of others by referring to the eventual *bad consequences* it has for those affected:

> Respect for the autonomy of others largely consists in securing for them adequate options, *i.e.*, opportunities or the ability to use them. Depriving a person of opportunities or of the ability to use them is a way of causing him harm. Both the use-value and the exchange-value of property represent opportunities for their owner. Any harm to a person by denying him the use or the value of his property is a harm to him precisely because it diminishes his opportunities. Similarly, injury to the person reduces his ability to act in ways which he may desire. Needless to say a harm to a person may consist not in depriving him of options but in frustrating his pursuit of the projects and relationships he has set upon.[124]

Hence, there is no question that the violations that Ripstein refers to can amount to harm when detected. As for those violations that go undetected by the individual victims, the above analysis explains why the Harm Principle would reach these types of harmless wrongs from an *ex ante* perspective. Ripstein's sovereignty principle does not provide the legislature with sufficient guidance about what it may fairly criminalize. It could allow conduct to be criminalized in situations where it would not be fair to invoke the criminal law. For example, it could be used to criminalize harmless trespasses to goods. We are not even able to distinguish a

---

121 'The other way I can subject you to my choice is by injuring you or in the limiting case, killing you, putting your powers to an end.' See Ripstein, *op. cit. supra*, fn. 2 at pp. 234–235.

122 'Such a rationale explains why a minimum of political liberty is a welfare interest. It is not that one cannot subsist without liberty. It is instead, that one cannot formulate, select, and pursue one's own purposes where there is excessive outside interference with one's choices, associations, and expressions.' See Andrew von Hirsch, 'Injury and Exasperation: An Examination of Harm to Others and Offense to Others,' (1985–1986) 84 *Michigan Law Review* 700 at p. 705.

123 Raz, *op. cit. supra*, fn. 64 at p. 371. See also Jeremy Waldron, 'Moral Autonomy and Personal Autonomy,' in John Christman and Joel Anderson, *Autonomy and the Challenges to Liberalism* (Cambridge: Cambridge University Press, 2005) at pp. 309–310; O'Neill, *op. cit. supra*, fn. 18 at pp. 53–54; 66; and Feinberg, Vol. III, *op. cit. supra*, fn. 9 at pp. 94 *et seq.*

124 *Id.* at p. 413. See also Andrew P. Simester and Andrew von Hirsch, 'Rethinking the Offense Principle,' (2002) 8(3) *Legal Theory* 269 at p. 281.

harmless trespass from a harmful trespass; both would be criminalized under the sovereignty principle.

Coupled with this, the sovereignty principle does not factor in those other mediating or countervailing considerations that can be used to override a *prima facie* case of criminalization. The sovereignty principle is not sophisticated enough to provide the sole criterion for ensuring that criminalization decisions meet the requirements of fairness and justice. It could not show when *prima facie* criminalization should be tolerated for other countervailing reasons. The sovereignty principles does not allow for the type of sophisticated analysis that is required for ensuring that criminalization decisions meet the requirements of fairness. I have aimed to highlight some of the obvious weaknesses in using Kantian criteria exclusively to determine the criminality status of various actions and in doing so I have demonstrated that the Harm Principle provides a superior alternative. The wrongful harm justification for criminalization as formulated in this book (that is, to cover animals and remote harms) can meet the challenges raised by Ripstein and Dan-Cohen. Ripstein and Dan-Cohen do not provide feasible alternatives. The core problem with the sovereignty principle and the second formulation of the Categorical Imperative is that they do not limit criminalization to situations where it is fair to invoke the criminal law. These principles are not apt for distinguishing mere moral misdemeanors from civil wrongs or civil wrongs from criminal wrongs. Furthermore, I point out in Chapter 6 that these types of critical moral principles are too narrow to offer guidance in conventional contexts.

Chapter 5
The Moral Limits of Consent as a Defense to Criminal Harm-Doing

Objectivity and Consent

In this chapter, I examine the objective limitations of consent as a defense to criminal harm-doing. Throughout this book I have argued that we should produce objective arguments to justify criminalization decisions. In the next chapter, I make it clear that by objective I do not mean critical morality. Feinberg claimed that his wrongful harm provided a critical moral justification for criminalization (*i.e.*, a transcultural justification), but as we will see, harm itself depends on conventional understandings and socialization and thus cannot be objective as a matter of truth or in a transcultural sense. Therefore, by objective I have something much more modest in mind. In the next chapter, I argue that the objectivity that is attainable by subjecting harm claims to the inter-subjective scrutiny of communally situated moral agents is probably the best we can do, and that this is sufficient for identifying objectively bad consequences.

In this chapter, I make reference to the Kantian concept of human dignity to outline the moral limits of consent as a defense. But my account of human dignity is not grounded in the type of critical morality that Kant had in mind. I accept that there may be not critical or moral realist foundations for such a concept, but argue that because we have deep conventional understandings about the cardinal value of humanity and the inalienable right to life, conventional morality supports a concept of dignity similar to that envisaged by Kant. Consent is itself an objective reason for excusing wrongful harm-doing to others, but it can be overridden by other objective considerations of greater importance. A person can, as an exercise of her personal autonomy, consent to certain harms. But as we will see, there is a crucial difference between waiving rights that are grounded in an exercise of personal autonomy and waiving rights that violate a person's human dignity. I conclude that, regardless of consent, certain grave harms violate a person's dignity as a human being to a serious degree and therefore are wrongful and criminalizable. I ask whether *R. v. Brown*[1] (where the majority rejected consent as a defense to intentionally causing actual bodily harm) and *R. v. Konzani*[2] (where the majority asserted that fully informed consent could have provided the *reckless* H.I.V. transmitter with a defense) are reconcilable with our deep conventional

---

1   [1994] 1 A.C. 212.
2   [2005] EWCA Crim. 706.

understanding of the value of human life and dignity. Once there is a proper *prima facie* case for criminalization, then consent could be sufficient to provide a defense in certain circumstances.

Harm to others is not the only objective justification for invoking the criminal law[3] but it is the relevant justification for present purposes, because it is the criminalization of serious physical harm to others that is being considered. In his two later volumes, Feinberg argues that 'legal moralism' and 'legal paternalism' are insufficient grounds for criminalizing conduct.[4] Feinberg's views on paternalism are entirely correct. The cases discussed in this chapter do not concern paternalism, because the defendants were criminalized for harming others. In the defense context, the harm-doer raises consent as a defense when she is being prosecuted for criminally harming the consenter. I accept that consent annuls wrongdoing when the conduct causes trivial harm or where it changes the nature of the conduct. For example, when a person consents to sexual intercourse she converts what otherwise would be a criminal harm into a harmless and desirable activity.[5] But if a person consents to having her hands amputated with a chainsaw, her consent would not convert what otherwise would be a serious harm into a harmless or justifiable activity. I am concerned with consent in the context of serious harm-doing to others (*e.g.*, breaking the bones of the consenter, blinding the consenter, killing and eating the consenter, seriously wounding the consenter, *etc.*).

Consent provides an objective justification for allowing a person to make choices that may involve consenting to harm, but consent is not absolute. Consent protects personal autonomy, but it does not allow a person to degrade or destroy the human dignity of the consenting party. Rational autonomy in the Kantian sense (which accords with our deep conventional understandings of humanity) differs from personal autonomy, because it is an absolute. 'Personal autonomy, by contrast, is essentially about the freedom of persons to choose their own lives.'[6] Respecting personal autonomy is fundamentally different from respecting the humanity in our fellow humans. One cannot alienate her right to be treated with a *minimum* degree of respect as a human being merely by being irrational.[7] A person

---

3   See the proposed Privacy Principle in Chapter 6.

4   Joel Feinberg, *The Morals Limits of the Criminal Law: Harmless Wrongdoing* (New York: Oxford University Press, Vol. IV, 1988) and Joel Feinberg, *The Moral Limits of the Criminal Law: Harm to Self* (New York: Oxford University Press, Vol. III, 1986).

5   George P. Fletcher, *Basic Concepts of Legal Thought* (New York: Oxford University Press, 1996) at p. 109.

6   Joseph Raz, *The Morality of Freedom* (Oxford: Clarendon Press, 1986) p. at 371. See also Deryck Beyleveld and Roger Brownsword, *Human Dignity in Bioethics and Biolaw* (Oxford: Oxford University Press. 2001); Deryck Beyleveld and Roger Brownsword, 'Human Dignity, Human Rights, and Human Genetics,' (1998) 61(5) *Modern Law Review* 661; and Neil C. Manson and Onora O'Neill, *Rethinking Informed Consent in Bioethics* (Cambridge: Cambridge University Press, 2007) at pp. 20–21.

7   Onora O'Neill, *Constructions of Reason: Explorations of Kant's Practical Philosophy* (Cambridge: Cambridge University Press, 1989) at pp. 53–54, 66. See also

can alienate her personal autonomy, but she cannot alienate her human dignity. For example, a prisoner waives her personal autonomy by wronging others, but should still be treated as a human being. As Dworkin notes:

> [W]hen we jail someone convicted of a crime in order to deter others, we do not treat him with beneficence; on the contrary, we act against his interests for the general benefit. But we insist that he be treated with dignity in accordance with our understanding of what that requires—that he not be tortured or humiliated, for example—because we continue to regard him as a full human being, as someone whose fate we continue to treat as a matter of concern ... We understand we are jailing a human being whose life matters, that our reasons for doing so are reasons we believe both require and justify this imprisonment, that we are not entitled to treat him as a mere object at the full disposal of our convenience, as if all that mattered was the usefulness, of the rest of us, of locking him up.[8]

The prisoner may waive certain personal autonomy rights. Likewise, sadomasochists and H.I.V. consenters may exercise their personal autonomy to waive certain rights, but waiving rights that merely involve an exercise of personal autonomy is not the same as alienating one's human dignity.[9] A person may exercise her personal autonomy and thus waive many rights without being subject to state interference, but another person cannot rely on that waiver to diminish her humanity. I argue below that the importance of personal autonomy means that consent is a valid defense unless the harm crosses the threshold of degrading the human dignity of the consenter to a serious degree. The threshold has to be very high if we are to protect personal autonomy. When a harm-doer treats a consenter as a mere means to her end rather than as end in itself, she violates the consenter's dignity. Only serious physical harm or death would be a sufficient violation of human dignity for the purposes of rejecting consent as a defense in the criminal law. Anything less would unduly restrict a person's personal autonomy. It is the gravity of the harm in cases such as *R.v. Konzani* and arguably *R. v. Brown* that results in a criminalizable violation of dignity. It is not the gravity of the harm alone that overrides consent as a defense, but rather

---

Onora O'Neill, 'Public Health or Clinical Ethics: Thinking Beyond Borders,' (2002) 16(2) *Ethics & International Affairs* 35 at pp. 36–37.

8   Ronald Dworkin, *Life's Dominion: An Argument About Abortion, Euthanasia, and Individual Freedom* (New York: Knopf, 1993) at p. 236. Dworkin draws on Kant's second formulation of the Categorical Imperative where consent in the personal autonomy context does not alter the rightfulness or wrongness of disrespecting human dignity. In Kant's scheme, '[I]t is facts about the bearings of one's actions on the maintenance and flourishing of humanity (as Kant understands this notion) that are the morally relevant facts determining the (objective) deontic status of an action.' Mark Timmons, *Kant's Metaphysics of Morals: Interpretative Essays* (Oxford: Oxford University Press, 2002) at pp. 285–286.

9   See generally Thomas E. Hill, *Autonomy and Self-Respect* (Cambridge: Cambridge University Press, 1991) at pp. 14–17.

it is the fact that the harm is directly aimed at diminishing the human status of the victim. The victim may very well welcome the harmful treatment, but we have deep conventional understandings about humanity and the importance of respecting it for our collective benefit. We respect the personal autonomy of self-harmers, because we do not criminalize self-harm. But we do not exempt those who harm others and rely on their consent as a defense, because they harm others in a grave way.

A person could consent to being harmed in a grave way by having all her property destroyed (*i.e.*, a person could consent to having her livelihood destroyed, her Caravaggio and Rembrandt paintings destroyed, her Rolls-Royce crushed and so forth), as this does not degrade her dignity. Antithetically, grave harms, such as transmitting fatal diseases, throwing acid in a person's eyes so as to blind her, or amputating her legs, treat the consenter as something less than a human being. Kant's account is useful for illustrating the importance of humanity and the need to respect the humanity in others, but we do not have to resort to critical morality or moral realism to justify criminalizing those who disrespect the humanity of others, because we have deep conventional understandings about the value of humanity. It would be objectively fair to reject consent as a defense, when the consenter is treated as less than a human being. When *x* leaves *y* permanently disabled *x* degrades *y*'s dignity in an intolerable way. Dworkin[10] draws on Kant's respect for human dignity principle to develop a wider normative concept of humanity on which these types of arguments can be grounded.[11]

Feinberg does not recognize that consent is a defeasible concept. According to Feinberg the type of wrongful harm inflicted in *R. v. Brown* and *R. v. Konzani* would be morally acceptable, because for him genuine consent nullifies the wrongness of such activities. Most of the academic criticism of *R. v. Brown* has focused on the non-objective harm arguments that permeated the majority judgments. Some have argued *Brown* was unjust because there were no objective justifications for invoking the criminal law.[12] Ashworth asserts that criminalizing the activities in

---

10   Dworkin, *op. cit. supra*, fn. 8 at pp. 33–37. See generally Stanley I. Benn, *A Theory of Freedom* (Cambridge: Cambridge University Press, 1988).

11   In a narrower sense, it is Hill's interpretation of Kant's principle that is the core basis of my argument for rejecting consent as a defense. Hill, *loc. cit. supra*, fn. 9.

12   In *R. v. Brown* [1994] 1 A.C. 212, Lord Mustill and Lord Slynn of Hadley in dissent attempt to provide an objective justification for permitting consent as a defense. However, their arguments are less than convincing, as they refer to 'private morality' rather than to objective morality more generally. The idea of private morality as stated in the Wolfenden Committee Report (see *Report of the Committee on Homosexual Offenses and Prostitution* (London: Home Office, Cmnd 247, 1957) at paragraphs 13 and 61) does not provide an objective basis for allowing consent to act as a defense against serious harm-doing to others, so long as the conduct is of an intimate nature or takes place in a private home. Surely their Lordships are not suggesting that it would be permissible to kill and eat another human being for sexual gratification, so long as the victim consents and the conduct is of an intimate nature or takes place in a private home. Privacy would only protect

Brown invades 'the realm of personal autonomy where each competent, responsible adult should reign supreme.'[13] Simester and Sullivan[14] assert that: '[i]n *Brown* the House of Lords held that, in the context of sadomasochistic sexual activity, the infliction of actual bodily harm upon a consenting adult "victim" was an offence. From the perspective of the Harm Principle, there is no wrong to V since the activity occurs with V's consent. But from the perspective of *legal moralism*, D's conduct may be regarded as inherently wrong—and therefore legitimately criminalizable. Indeed, V's consent simply makes V, too, a participant in the offence.'

In *R. v. Brown* the majority makes reference to the need to protect society from sadomasochism, but does not demonstrate that this type of conduct is harmful to anyone other than the actors involved. Furthermore, Lord Jauncey of Tullichettle makes reference to the potential remote harms that may flow from allowing a person to consent to direct harm, as a further basis for rejecting consent as a defense. His Lordship stated: 'the possibility of proselytization and corruption of [other] young men is a real danger.'[15] I have argued above that a person can only be held responsible for influencing the harmful criminal choices of others when the eventual harm can be fairly imputed to the influencer.[16] Nevertheless, the majority was persuaded just as much by the gravity of the objective harm involved. Even though the majority made reference to non-objective considerations, its decision is principled. I argue that the criminalization of the actions in *R. v. Brown* was *prima facie* fair, because the actions were objectively harmful and the harm-doer deliberately disregarded the humanity of the consenter for his own personal gain. I argue that consent is not sufficient to override this type of wrongful harm-doing, because it degrades the dignity of the consenters to a degree that is intolerable in Western societies, which recognize the cardinal importance of respecting humanity. The H.I.V. cases[17] are distinguishable in that the harm was inflicted recklessly rather than intentionally, but the harm-doing in those cases was irreparable and of a permanent nature. I argue below that consent should not be a defense to this type of harm-doing, because it also treats the consenter as less than a human being.

---

innocent conduct or trivial harm-doing of an intimate or private nature. See *Lawrence v. Texas*, 539 U.S. 558 (2003). Cf. Matthew Weait, 'Harm, Consent and the Limits of Privacy,' (2005) 13 *Feminist Legal Studies* 97 at p. 109.

13   Andrew Ashworth, *Principles of Criminal Law* (Oxford: Oxford University Press, 5th ed., 2006) at p. 41.

14   Andrew P. Simester and Graham R. Sullivan, *Criminal Law: Theory and Doctrine* (Oxford: Hart Publishing, 2nd ed., 2004) at p. 16.

15   *R. v. Brown* [1994] 1 A.C. 212 at 246.

16   See also Dennis J. Baker, 'The Moral Limits of Criminalizing Remote Harms,' (2007) 10(3) *New Criminal Law Review* 370; Dennis J. Baker, 'Collective Criminalization and the Constitutional Right to Endanger Others,' 28(2) *Criminal Justice Ethics* (2009).

17   *R. v. Konzani* [2005] EWCA Crim. 706. See also *R. v. Dica* [2004] 3 All E.R. 593.

Harm and Consent: Stubborn Counterexamples

It is important to recognize that it is wrongful harm-doing that is criminalizable, not harm-doing *per se*. The focus has to be on nullifying the wrongness of infecting another with a fatal disease, blinding her, amputating her legs and so forth, as the harmfulness of such conduct cannot be nullified by consent. Harm to others is only criminalizable if it involves wrongdoing. I noted above that Feinberg[18] expounds harm in three senses: (i) harm as damage, (ii) harm as a setback to interests, and (iii) harm as wrongdoing. The harm as used in the Harm Principle is an amalgamation of senses (ii) and (iii). Harm must be caused by *wrongful* conduct to be a candidate for criminalization. Harm occurs under the harm criterion when x's interests are set back by the wrongful conduct of y.[19] The concept of harm as used by Feinberg represents 'the overlap of senses two and three: only setbacks of interests that are wrongs, and wrongs that are setbacks to interests, are to count as harms in the appropriate sense.'[20] A person has the right not be harmed by the intentional (inexcusable/unjustifiable) actions of others.[21]

Feinberg does not deny that those who consent to serious harm-doing are harmed, but asserts that the harm is not wrongful because consent nullifies the wrongdoing involved.[22] The issue is not whether the sadomasochists, H.I.V. consenters, gladiators, and so on are harmed, but whether they are wrongfully harmed. Feinberg asserts that consent is absolute in that it nullifies the wrongness of harming others[23] regardless of the gravity of the harm involved.[24] According to the *volenti non fit injuria* doctrine, we cannot complain that we have been wronged

---

18 Joel Feinberg, Vol. I, *The Moral Limits of the Criminal Law: Harm to Others* (New York: Oxford University Press, 1984) at p. 215.

19 *Id.* at pp. 33–34.

20 *Id.* at p. 36.

21 Inculpating factors (wrongfulness) such as intention and exculpatory considerations such as excuse and justification are important aspects of the wrongness of harm-doing to others and are relevant in a putative sense from the *ex ante* criminalization perspective. Feinberg uses these factors to make a putative claim about culpability as an aspect of wrongness for the purposes of justifying *ex ante* criminalization decisions. Feinberg makes an *ex ante* generalization that culpable harm-doing ought to be the business of the criminal law, because this type of harm-doing is wrongful in a way that negligent and/or unintentional harm-doing is not. Of course, whether a particular individual acted with intention (or unjustifiably/inexcusably) is a question of fact for a court to decide in individual cases at the *ex post* trial stage. Clearly, in many cases where the harm-doing is trivial (common assault *etc.*) a defense of consent will be available to *justify* the wrongdoing. See J.L. Austin, 'A Plea for Excuses,' (1956–1957) *Proceedings of the Aristotelian Society* 1 at pp. 2–3; and for a more recent discussion, see Heidi Hurd, 'Justification and Excuse, Wrongdoing and Culpability,' (1999) 74 *Notre Dame Law Review* 1551.

22 Feinberg, Vol. IV, *op. cit. supra*, fn. 4 at p. 20.

23 *Id.* at p. 329.

24 *Id.* at pp. 68–173, 328.

if we have authorized the harm-doing.[25] Consent will provide a valid defense in certain circumstances, but the defense will be denied when there are objective justifications for doing so.

It is worth noting that Feinberg also postulates that although the wrongness of killing another and eating her for sexual gratification would be nullified by consent, it could be criminalized because of the difficulty in determining the genuineness of the consent involved, as the consenter is dead. Feinberg asserts that: 'To the extent that *B*'s consent is not fully voluntary, the law is justified in intervening "for his sake."'[26] However, I focus on the limits of genuine consent rather than on issues concerning the authenticity of consent. Authenticity is about consent that is considered to be defective, because the consenting parties did not give their consent autonomously, were not sufficiently rational, well informed, free from duress and so on.[27] McConnell argues that if certain rights such as the right to life and so forth became alienable the rights of others would be jeopardized.[28] He asserts that allowing consent to justify killing would make all our lives statistically less secure, because it would be difficult to determine the genuineness of consent in those cases where the victim has been killed.[29] This is an independent argument for limiting consent as a defense, but it does not deal with the sadomasochist/ H.I.V. transmitter where the genuineness of the consent can be ascertained. When we see someone consenting to harmful treatment or to a violation of his or her core rights we tend to focus on the authenticity of the consent. But as O'Neill observes, 'this is a desperate line of argument: there is all too much evidence that people sometimes genuinely consent to action which may seem deeply unacceptable, even to action that profoundly injures, oppresses or degrades them. Across the board insistence that any consent to such action must be flawed merely suggests an underlying refusal to consider the possibility that justification requires more than actual consent.'[30]

---

25   *Id.* at pp. 11, 100.

26   Feinberg asserts: 'Given the uncertain quality of evidence on these matters, and (in the case of slavery) the strong general presumption of non-voluntariness, the state might be justified in presuming non-voluntariness conclusively in every case as the least risky course.' In the case of euthanasia Feinberg notes that: 'the only possible reason for maintaining the present absolute prohibition is that it is necessary to prevent mistakes and abuse': Feinberg, Vol. III, *op. cit. supra*, fn. 4 at pp. xviii–xix.

27   *Id.* at pp. 125–126, 269–343.

28   See generally Terrance McConnell, *Inalienable Rights: The Limits of Consent in Medicine and Law* (Oxford: Oxford University Press, 2000).

29   *Ibid.*

30   Onora O'Neill, 'Kant and the Social Contract Tradition,' in François Duchesneau, Guy Lafrance, and Claude Piché, *Kant Actuel: Hommage à Pierre Laberge* (Montréal: Bellarmin, 2000) at pp. 185–200.

Objectivity and the Limits of Consent in *R. v. Konzani*

Feinberg's Harm Principle allows a person to consent to all kinds of gross harms. A person might consent to death, permanent disablement of a severe kind such as blinding and so forth. Is it morally right to let people consent to *irreparable* injury of an extraordinarily grave kind such as being permanently blinded? Clearly, if a person allows another to infect her with a fatal disease, or to kill and eat her for sexual gratification[31] and so forth, she would be irreparably harmed. But is she wrongfully harmed? How much harm can a person inflict on others before the criminal law can be invoked to protect the human dignity of the consenter? In this section, I consider whether it is permissible for a person to consent to being infected with a deadly disease. Duff[32] has argued that Kant's idea of respect for humanity could be invoked to limit consent in such cases, but does not develop this type of argument. Nor does he consider the distinction between degrading humanity (that is, consenting to grave harm that does not end the life of the consenter) and alienating humanity (that is, consenting to death: alienating a person's whole freedom—powers of rational choice). It is one thing to demonstrate a loss of dignity when a person alienates her right to life,[33] but determining when harm degrades a person's human dignity for the purposes of criminalization in other cases is not so straightforward. It is not easy to establish a serious loss of dignity when the consenter has merely been harmed—especially, when the harm is reparable.

There are two ways in which a person could degrade her humanity. Firstly, a person might alienate her right to life, which she cannot do without also forfeiting her humanity. Secondly, a person could alienate her right to maintain a minimum degree of dignity as a human being. The deontological force of this argument comes from the principle that a person's rational nature incorporates an absolute worth in the sense of *dignity*, and this intrinsic value admits of no equivalent and thus cannot be compromised or replaced.[34] A human's rational nature gives her dignity and worth as a person, which means she has a value beyond price.[35] If a substitute or equivalent can be found for a thing, then it has a price.[36] It has dignity (an intrinsic value) if there is no substitute or equivalent for it.[37] It is the priceless

---

31 Ray Furlong, 'Frenzy builds for German "cannibal" trial,' Article from BBC News: <http://news.bbc.co.uk/go/pr/fr/-/2/hi/europe/3258226> (published: December 2, 2003).

32 Anthony R. Duff, 'Harms and Wrongs,' 5 *Buffalo Criminal Law Review* 13 (2001–2002).

33 See Dworkin, *loc. cit. supra*, fn. 8. Cf. Lance K. Stell, 'Dueling and the Right to Life,' (1979) 90(1) *Ethics* 7.

34 Immanuel Kant, *Groundwork of the Metaphysics of Morals*, 1785, translated from the German by Herbert J. Paton, *The Moral Law* (London: Hutchinson University Library, 1972) at p. 96.

35 *Id*. at p. 35.

36 *Id*.

37 *Id*.

and non-substitutable dignity and worth of persons that makes them objects of respect. As note above, Kant uses humanity to demonstrate how a Categorical Imperative or practical law is 'connected (wholly *a priori*) with the concept of the will of a rational being as such.'[38]

> The ground for this moral principle is: *Rational nature exists as an end in itself.* This is the way in which a man necessarily conceives his own existence: it is therefore so far a *subjective* principle of human actions. But it is also the way in which every other rational being conceives his existence on the same rational ground which is valid also for me; hence it is at the same time an *objective* principle, from which, as a supreme practical ground, it must be possible to derive all laws for the will. The practical imperative will therefore be as follows: *Act in such a way that you always treat humanity whether in your own person or in the person of any other, never simply as a means, but always at the same time as an end.*[39]

I noted in the last chapter that there are two separate aspects to fulfilling the requirements of the second formulation of the Categorical Imperative. Firstly, one must not act on maxims that (negatively) use persons as mere means, because this would be to act on maxims that no other *rational* being could possibly sanction.[40] Secondly, we are required to avoid the pursuit of ends that others cannot share. We do this by treating them (positively) as ends in themselves.[41] It is this formulation of the Categorical Imperative that is the foundation of the principle of respect for persons. Persons are ends in themselves and can be a source of definite laws, because they have an absolute worth. Rational agents differ from inanimate things in that they are self-legislating, because they give themselves the laws by which they act. This very abstract Kantian conceptualization of the value of humanity accords with our deeply held conventional understandings of humanity. Communally situated moral agents in Western societies have inter-subjectively endorsed the Kantian conceptualization of the value of humanity.[42]

---

38   *Id.* at p. 111.
39   *Id.* At p. 91.
40   O'Neill, *op. cit. supra*, fn. 7, at p. 113.
41   'The failure is dual: The victim of deceit cannot agree to the initiator's maxim, so is used, and a fortiori cannot share the initiator's end, so is not treated as a person. Similarly with a maxim of coercion: Victims cannot agree with a coercer's fundamental principle or maxim, which denies them the choice between consent and dissent, and further cannot share a coercer's ends': *id.*
42   It would also be inter-subjectively accepted by all rational agents; see Christine M. Korsgaard, 'The Reasons We Can Share: An Attack on the Distinction Between Agent-Relative and Agent-Neutral Values,' (1993) 10(1) *Social Philosophy and Policy* 24. Also, Gerald Postema, 'Objectivity Fit for Law,' in *Objectivity in Law and Morals*, ed. Brian Leiter (Cambridge: Cambridge University Press, 2001) at pp. 99–143.

Arguably, the principle of respect for persons provides a stronger case for limiting consent in the *R. v. Konzani* context than it does in the *R. v. Brown* context. There are two alternative bases for this claim. Firstly, it is arguable that the H.I.V. consenter in *R. v. Konzani* alienates her inalienable right to life. However, this is a controversial claim, because there is no guarantee that the consenter will die in the immediate future. With modern treatments the H.I.V. consenter could live for decades.[43] Even if the consenter lives for some years, it cannot be denied that any shortening of a person's life, regardless of the length of time, is irreparable (treatable but not reparable) harm of an extraordinarily grave kind. Since the harm is of an extraordinarily grave kind and is irreparable, *R. v. Konzani* provides a stronger case for claiming that the consenter's dignity has been degraded in a serious way. *R. v. Konzani* is distinguishable from *R. v. Brown* not only because the harm is serious and of an irreparable kind, but also because it is inflicted recklessly rather than intentionally.

In *R. v. Konzani*[44] the appellant learnt in 2000 that he was H.I.V. positive and was informed on that occasion, and on subsequent occasions, of the risks of transmitting the infection, and of the potential harmful consequences of doing so. Nevertheless, the appellant had sexual relationships with three young women without informing any of them of his condition. He repeatedly had unprotected sexual intercourse with the young women knowing that by doing so that he was exposing them to a *real* risk of serious harm. As a result, all three of his sexual partners contracted H.I.V. He withheld vital information about his condition from them and it was found that none of the complainants had consented to the risk of contracting H.I.V. The defendant argued that infection with H.I.V. is something the victims risked by having unprotected sexual intercourse and therefore they had impliedly consented to the risk of contracting H.I.V.

The Court held that 'before the consent of the complainant could provide the appellant with a defense, it was required to be an informed and willing consent to the risk of contracting H.I.V.'[45] In particular, the Court noted that there is a crucial difference between taking a risk of the potentially adverse consequences of unprotected sexual intercourse, 'and giving informed consent to the risk of infection of a fatal disease.'[46] For the purposes of section 20 of the *Offences Against the Person Act* 1861 (U.K.), the required mental ingredient of the offense is established if the defendant was reckless.[47] Thus, so long as the defendant knew or foresaw that his non-consenting partner might suffer bodily harm and chose to expose her to that risk, recklessness would be established.

---

43 See the discussion *infra*.
44 [2005] EWCA Crim 706, at paras. 10–22.
45 *R. v. Konzani* [2005] EWCA Crim. 706, at para. 18.
46 *R. v. Konzani* [2005] EWCA Crim. 706, at para. 22.
47 *R. v. Cunningham* [1957] 2 Q.B. 396, as approved in *R. v. Savage* [1992] 1 A.C. 699.

The Court was wrong to hold that informed consent would have been sufficient to provide the defendant in *Konzani* with a defense. A person should not be able to rely on consent as a defense when she *knows* that there is a very real risk that the consenter will suffer grave harm. Of course, it is important that there be a real risk of harm. If a person has full knowledge that her partner has H.I.V. but freely chooses to have unprotected sexual intercourse, then she is consenting to more than a remote risk of grave harm. It is not easy to draw a clear line, as those who engage in unprotected *casual sex* are also risking their human dignity. The critical issue is whether or not there was a real risk (as opposed to a remote risk) of harm transpiring and whether the person risking the consenter's safety was fully aware of that real risk. A person should be able to take remote chances with her own safety as this preserves her personal autonomy. Promiscuous people (swingers) who risk infection by having unprotected sexual relations with strangers could not be criminalized for infecting others for merely knowing their sexual practices make it likely that they are carriers of the virus. This would be too great an extension of criminal responsibility. The harm-doer would have to have actual knowledge that she posed a real risk to the consenter because she knew she was a carrier.

A further problem with the H.I.V. cases is that it is not possible to predict the eventual harm with any exactitude. The current treatment for H.I.V. infection is a highly active antiretroviral therapy. This treatment is reasonably effective and offers increased life expectancy for many H.I.V. sufferers. Research in the United States suggests that current treatment methods could give many sufferers a life expectancy of 32.1 years from the time of infection, if treatment were started soon after the patient became infected.[48] The highly active antiretroviral therapy does not always achieve optimal results and in some situations it has had a success rate of below 50 percent, because some patients are intolerant to the medication and there are drug-resistant strains of H.I.V.[49] It is not possible to predict with any certainty the eventual outcome of being infected with H.I.V. But is it safe to say that the infected party's life will probably be shortened and that, barring medical advances, she will have to undergo regular treatment for the rest of her life.

The H.I.V. cases pose some problems as the consenter is only consenting to a risk of harm and it is not certain what that harm might be. Nonetheless, we are able to turn to other straightforward examples to strengthen the case for limiting consent as a defense. For instance, if a person intentionally amputates a consenter's arms and legs with a chainsaw, intentionally pokes the consenter's eyes out so as to blind her or intentionally kills and eats the consenter for the sake of achieving sexual gratification, then the consenter will suffer irreversible harm of an extraordinarily grave kind. The difference with these examples is that the violence is *intentional* and the harm easy to measure. There is no reason why *recklessness* cannot take

---

48 Bruce R. Schackman *et al.*, 'The Lifetime Cost of Current H.I.V. Care in the United States,' (2006) 44(11) *Medical Care* 990.

49 Stephen L. Becker *et al.*, 'Young H.I.V.-Infected Adults Are at Greater Risk for Medication Nonadherence,' (2002) 4(3) *Medscape General Medicine* 21.

the place of *intention* or why *real risk of harm* cannot take the place of *certain harm*, so long as we exercise due caution. For example, when x drives her Bentley at 160 miles per hour in a 30 mile per hour speed zone whilst intoxicated she does not aim to harm anyone, but her recklessness poses a real risk of harm to others. There is no need to be able to identify the exact *ex post facto* harm at the *ex ante* criminalization stage, so long as the reckless behavior generally poses a real risk of grave harm.

It is only the activities of the harm-doer that are subject to criminalization. A person can take risks with her own safety so long as it does not involve another party. There is a difference between a person risking her own life by taking an unseaworthy vessel into rough seas and someone else risking her life by transporting her in a vessel that is not seaworthy. The organizers of people-smuggling often take risks with the lives of those whom they smuggle. Should the operators of a vessel that is not seaworthy be able to escape liability for manslaughter by asserting that their drowned (or asphyxiated) passengers consented to dying at sea, because they knew the risks of traveling with such operators?[50]

Similarly, masochism is not a mere case of self-harm and we do *not* criminalize the consenter. Instead, it is the actions of the harm-doer that are criminalized. The issue is whether x can gravely harm y when y freely consents to the wrongdoing. It is not merely about y using herself as a mere means to an end, but about a second party using her as a mere means to an end. If x, a sadomasochist, consents to y (who is also a sadomasochist) poking her eyes out, she has not only used herself as a mere means, but has also allowed y to use (wrong and harm) her to a grave degree. Y has used x as a mere means and is criminally liable for wrongfully harming her without excuse or justification. In effect sadomasochists and gladiators wrong not only themselves, but also each other. Conversely, the apotemnophiliac[51] or suicidal maniac wrongfully harm themselves.

The lawmaker is entitled to prevent people from harming and wronging others when the harm is exceptionally grave, but it is not entitled to criminalize self-harm. The harm to *others* justification for criminalization provides an important restraint, because suicide and self-harm also involve disrespect for dignity. It may be morally wrong to attempt suicide, but self-harm falls outside the purview of the Harm Principle.[52] The Harm Principle limits criminalization to those situations where a person *harms others*. We are all morally bound to respect humanity in our own person as well as in the persons of others, but that does not mean that those who

---

50 The authorities suggest not. In *Wacker* [2003] Q.B. 1207, 58 illegal entrants into the U.K. suffocated in a shipping container because a lorry driver recklessly failed to open the air vents.

51 An apotemnophiliac is one who self-harms. A common case is where the apotemnophiliac keeps cutting his or her arms. See generally, Russ Shafer-Landau, 'Liberalism and Paternalism,' (2005) 11(3) *Legal Theory* 169 at p. 170.

52 Feinberg presents a powerful case against criminalizing harm to self. Feinberg, Vol. III, *op. cit. supra*, fn. 4.

consent to being harmed by others (*e.g.*, the victim of a failed euthanasia attempt or the H.I.V. consenter) or those who harm themselves should be criminalized. It means we ought to criminalize those who inflict the harm in those cases.

The degree of moral wrongdoing involved in serious self-harm and serious harm to others is equal, but self-wrongs are not criminalizable because they do not wrong or harm others. The smoker may damage her health, but this would be self-harm. It is morally wrongful to harm oneself in a grotesque way or to commit suicide and this might give the lawmaker reasons for providing healthcare programs to help those self-harmers who seek help, but the criminal law cannot be used to punish those who attempt suicide or are suffering from apotemnophilia, *etc.* The legislature's remedies in this context would be limited to providing appropriate healthcare. It is only those who recklessly subject others to a real risk of harm or intentionally inflict harm on others that should be subject to penal sanction. Once the victim reciprocates the harm, then she too would be criminally liable. But reciprocation and mutual participation differ from paternalism, because criminalization is only available when one party harms another.

Let us look at the detail of the aforementioned arguments. Clearly, if a person gives a cannibal permission to kill and eat her for the sake of sexual gratification she has been wronged regardless of consent, because the cannibal has violated her inalienable right to life.[53] According to Kant, one owes oneself the same respect as one owes others.[54] Kant states that:

[A] human being is regarded as a person, that is, as the subject of a morally practical reason, is exalted above any price; for as a person (*homo noumenon*) he is not to be valued merely as a means to the ends of others or even his own ends, but as an end itself, that is, he possesses a dignity (an absolute inner worth) by which he exacts respect for himself from all other rational beings in the world ... *Humanity in his person* is the object of the respect which he can demand from every other human being, but which *he must also not forfeit.*[55]

---

53 '[S]imilarly, a Kantian might argue that a person cannot release others from the obligation to refrain from killing him: consent is no defense against a charge of murder. To accept principles of this sort is to hold that rights to life and dignity are, as Kant believed, rather like a trustee's rights to preserve something valuable entrusted to him: he has not only a right but a duty to preserve it.' Hill, *loc. cit. supra*, fn. 9. See also Terrance McConnell, *op. cit. supra*, fn. 28 at pp. 31 *et seq.*; Arthur Kiflik, 'The Inalienability of Autonomy,' (1984) 13(4) *Philosophy & Public Affairs* 271 at p. 275; and Immanuel Kant, *The Philosophy of Law: An Exposition of the Fundamental Principles of Jurisprudence as the Science of Right*, translated from the German by William Hastie, *The Philosophy of Law* (Edinburgh: T. & T. Clark, 1887) at p. 119.

54 John Rawls, *Lectures on the History of Moral Philosophy* (Cambridge, MA: Harvard University Press, 2000) at pp. 191–192.

55 Immanuel Kant, *Metaphysics of Morals* (1797), translated from the German by Mary J. Gregor, *Practical Philosophy: The Cambridge Edition of the Works of Immanuel Kant* (Cambridge: Cambridge University Press, 1999) at p. 557.

This type of moral claim is widely accepted in Western society. When *x* allows *y* to kill and eat her, *x* not only allows *y* to use (wrong) her as a mere means—violate her dignity to a serious degree, but also alienate her humanity—she ceases to be a person. 'The foundational assumption in Kantian morality is that human freedom has unconditional value, and both the *Categorical Imperative* and the *Universal Principle of Right* flow directly from this fundamental normative claim: the Categorical Imperative tells us what form our actions must take if they are to be compatible with the universal value of freedom, and the universal principle of right tells us what form our actions must take if they are to be compatible with the universal value of freedom, regardless of our maxims and motivations.'[56] The *Universal Principle of Right* holds: 'Freedom (independence from being constrained by another's choice), insofar as it can co-exist with the freedom of every other in accordance with a universal law, is the only original right belonging to every other man by virtue of his humanity.'[57] Freedom is about having the power to choose. A person is free if she is independent from being compelled by the choices of others. A person alienates her humanity if she rids herself of the capacity of choice. Maintaining humanity is about retaining a sufficient degree of your freedom and powers to set and pursue your own purposes. 'You need more than the ability to pursue purposes you have set; you also need to be able to decline to pursue purposes unless you have set them. When I usurp your powers, I violate your sovereignty precisely because I deprive you of that veto.'[58] When a person consents to death she allows her powers of choice to be put to an end.[59]

Consent will not override the *prima facie* wrongdoing involved, as the moral duty to maintain your humanity is absolute. Hill[60] notes that there may be no specific range of inalienable rights, but that there is at least one cardinal right that cannot be waived. That is, the right to maintain a certain level of respect as a rational being. Hill holds that: '[N]o matter how willing a person is to submit to harm by others, they ought to show him some respect as a person ... This respect owed by others would consist of a willingness to acknowledge fully, in word as well as action, that person's basic equal moral status as defined by his other rights.'[61] Wellman[62] argues that, given the time delay between being infected with H.I.V. and when those infected might actually die, such consenters forfeit

---

56   Timmons, *op. cit. supra*, fn. 8 at p. 286.
57   Gregor, *op. cit. supra*, fn. 55 at pp. 393.
58   Arthur Ripstein, 'Beyond the Harm Principle,' (2006) 34(3) *Philosophy & Public Affairs* 215 at pp. 234–235.
59   *Ibid.*
60   Hill, *op. cit. supra*, fn. 9 at pp. 15–16.
61   'To the extent that a person gives even tacit consent to [harms] incompatible with this respect, he will be acting as if he waives a right which he cannot in fact give up.' *Id.* at p. 16.
62   Carl Wellman, 'The Inalienable Right to Life and the Durable Power of Attorney,' (1995) 14 *Law and Philosophy* 245 at p. 257.

their humanity rather than alienate it. But the consenter to H.I.V. has not really forfeited her humanity. Instead, she has postponed its alienation by consenting to H.I.V. infection, which can take a considerable period of time to end her life. The actual alienation of life only takes place at some unknown and unpredictable time in the future.

When a person kills another and eats her/him for sexual gratification, consent will not be sufficient to nullify the wrongdoing involved because the victim ceases[63] to be a person immediately—her/his powers are put to an end at once. In the H.I.V. cases the victim's whole freedom (humanity) is not alienated immediately, but rather alienation is certain to take place at sometime in the future—that is, when the victim eventually passes away. The long-term result is that the consenter to H.I.V. puts her powers to an end at some future stage. If the victim is only 16 and is able to live for the maximum of 32 years that current treatment might achieve, she would pass away at the age of 46, which is young in contemporary times. In the H.I.V. cases non-violent means are used to inflict grave harm, but this does not alter the wrongness of infecting others with deadly diseases. A person might use slow-acting poison, which would not involve any violence, to kill someone, but that does not alter the fact that the victim ceases to be a person at some stage in the future when the poison works.

The point to keep in mind regarding the H.I.V. cases is that the consenter does not cease to be a person straight away. She is still alive, fit, alert and able to make rational choices. Nonetheless, H.I.V. transmission results in irreparable harm of an extraordinary kind regardless of whether the consenter has alienated her right to life, because the grave harm involved more generally degrades the consenter's dignity as a human being who is communally situated in a society that cares for its members. The irreparable nature of the harm involved in infecting others with H.I.V. provides a sound objective justification for limiting consent. The consenter may change her mind after the moment of passion has passed. It is one thing to consent to reversible or curable harm; it is something entirely different to consent to irreparable harm of an extraordinarily grave kind.

Moral philosophers, such as Dworkin[64] and Hill,[65] argue that it is permissible to tolerate some violations of dignity in special circumstances. Weait[66] refers to the kinds of relationships and contexts in which consent might provide a permissible defense. In particular, he refers to the loving Roman Catholic couple who are conscientiously prevented from using prophylactics and wish to have a child. If the father is H.I.V. positive, is it permissible for the mother to consent to the real risk of infection for the purposes of having a child? The type of relationship and

---

63 *R. v. Konzani* [2005] EWCA Crim. 706; *R. v. Dica (Mohammed)* [2004] EWCA Crim. 1103 and *R. v. Barnes (Mark)* [2004] EWCA Crim. 3246.

64 See generally Dworkin, *op. cit. supra*, fn. 8.

65 See generally Hill, *op. cit. supra*, fn. 9 at p. 31.

66 Matthew Weait, 'Criminal Law and the Sexual Transmission of H.I.V: *R v Dica*,' (2005) 68(1) *Modern Law Review* 121 at p. 132.

religious backgrounds of the consenter do not provide an objective justification for tolerating consent as a defense. But the importance of having a child might provide an objective justification for tolerating disrespect for the mother's dignity. But there are too many variables to make a firm conclusion for present purposes (*e.g.*, the couple may already have children, the child might be born with H.I.V. and so on). Nevertheless, there may be a case for making exceptions in such circumstances. What is clear is that consenting to a real risk (real risk meaning that the harm-doer is aware that they are carrying H.I.V.) of grave harm for no purpose other than to have sexual intercourse is not permissible, because the couple can easily take the negligible precaution of using a prophylactic. If the disease is accidentally transmitted even though the couple took reasonable precautions, then there should be no criminal liability.

Objectivity and Wanton Use of Humans

I digress,to emphasize that the respect for persons principle is not equivalent to the so-called Golden Rule, *Quod tibi non vis fieri*.[67] Kant held that there is no equivalence between this precept and his Categorical Imperative, because the Golden Rule can only provide moral guidance if one presumes a prior moral judgment: the judgment of how others should treat oneself.[68] The convicted criminal could say to the judge: 'If you were me you would not want to be sentenced, therefore *etc.*' The Golden Rule does not provide a basic justification for moral judgments, but rather provides a means of converting self-regarding moral judgments (judgments about how others should treat the moral agent) into other-regarding judgments (judgments about how the agent should treat others).

The sadomasochist (who wishes to be harmed) could not derive the principle of non-maleficence from the Golden Rule. In fact the sadomasochist could draw the opposite conclusion, that is, that she ought to harm others. She could harm them as she is only doing what she is asking them to do to her. The Golden Rule would allow for such a conclusion. Deriving a principle of non-maleficence requires the moral condemnation of the masochist's self-regarding desire that others harm her. Kant argued that the universal law formulation of the Categorical Imperative requires no presumed moral judgments. Kant's Categorical Imperative can be invoked, as it does not require self-regarding moral judgments as the basis of other-regarding moral judgments. Furthermore, the Golden Rule cannot be used to derive judgments concerning one's moral duties to oneself. One such duty, Kant argued, was that of not committing suicide. Suicide contradicts the fundamental desire of self-preservation just as the act of intentionally killing another does.[69]

---

67   Do unto others as one would have others do unto you.
68   Rawls, *op. cit. supra*, fn. 54 at pp. 198–199.
69   'What is wrong with the Golden Rule (in both its positive and negative versions) is that as stated it allows natural inclinations and the special circumstances to play an improper

The respect for persons[70] principle can be invoked to explain the indefeasible wrongness of inflicting grave harms on others. The wrongness of such actions cannot be made good by consent regardless of whether the consent is fully informed and the harm is a source of great pleasure for the victim. Duff[71] rightly notes that harm-doers in *R. v. Brown* treated their victims with a lack of respect as persons. But it is more convincing to claim that a person's dignity has been violated in a serious way when the harm is of an irreparable and extraordinarily grave kind such as in those cases where the consenter is killed and eaten by a cannibal for sexual gratification, is blinded with acid, has her legs and arms cut off, or contracts a fatal disease. The case is not so clear in the *R. v Brown* situation where the harm is reparable and more borderline.

The Categorical Imperative is a deontological principle that does not provide the types of criteria that are needed to give legislatures proper guidance as to whether a particular violation of dignity is worthy of criminalization. For instance, mere false promising and common assault would treat those affected with a lack of respect as persons according to the Categorical Imperative. I have noted above that a core problem with using Kant's Categorical Imperative in criminalization ethics is that it alone cannot be used to distinguish moral wrongs that warrant a criminal law response from those that require a civil law response or no response at all. The wrongness of false promising and rape is equal according to a literal application of Kant's second formulation of the Categorical Imperative. Serious physical injury and trivial physical injury to humans is equally wrongful according to the Categorical Imperative. This need not concern us, because the idea of respect for humanity is something that is inter-subjectively endorsable by communally situated agents. Furthermore, such agents would appreciate that subjecting consenting others to gross physical harms is paradigmatically disrespectful. It is necessary to consider the objective harm involved and its impact on the communally situated consenter to determine whether the violation of dignity is worthy of criminalization. It is the gravity of harm that determines whether the violation of dignity is worthy of criminalization. If x throws acid in y's eyes, thereby blinding y, she violates y's dignity and because of the gravity of the irreversible harm, it is a violation that is not only wrongful. X understands the nature of humanity and the badness of wantonly harming others. X also understands that consent does not change the nature of her actions against a fellow human—she acts unilaterally in treating the humanity of the victim as though it is worthless.

R. v. Brown can be distinguished from the H.I.V. cases in a number of ways. Firstly, the harm was inflicted intentionally and was certain to transpire. Secondly, the harm was not of an irreparable kind. And thirdly, the harm was not

---

role in our deliberations. But in saying this Kant implies that the Categorical Imperative procedure specifies the proper role.' *Id.* at 191–192.

70 Gregor, *loc. cit. supra*, fn. 55.
71 See generally Duff, *op. cit. supra*, fn. 32.

of a kind that was likely to alienate the consenter's right to life at some time in the future. In *R. v. Brown*[72] a group of homosexual sadomasochists voluntarily and enthusiastically committed acts of violence against each other, because they achieved sexual gratification from being subjected to violence and pain. The appellants were arraigned on various counts under sections 20 and 47 of the *Offences Against the Person Act 1861* (U.K.), for inflicting wounds and actual bodily harm on the genital and other areas of the body of the consenting victims. A core issue in that case concerned consent and whether it could be used to nullify the *prima facie* wrongness of the sadomasochistic activities.

The trial judge stated that consent was not a viable defense to intentionally inflicting harm beyond a certain threshold (actual bodily harm or greater). The appellants appealed unsuccessfully to the House of Lords. The majority of the Law Lords held that: 'although a prosecutor had to prove absence of consent in order to secure a conviction for *mere assault* it was not in the public interest that a person should wound or cause actual bodily harm to another for no good reason and, in the absence of such a reason, the victim's consent afforded no defense to a charge under section 20 or 47 of the *Act of 1861*.'[73] The Court said that satisfying sadomasochistic desires did not provide the appellants with a good reason for inflicting gross harm on each other. Consent was not a permissible defense, because the appellants had admitted that they had committed the harmful acts and the acts clearly interfered with the health and comfort of the mutual participants.[74] The *gravity* of the harm influenced the decision, as this was not merely a case of common assault.[75] The appellants had committed violent acts against each other including nailing their prepuces and scrota to a board, inserting hot wax into their urethras, burning their penes with candles and incising their scrota with scalpels, which caused the exudation of blood and put them at risk of contracting septicemia and H.I.V.[76]

The harm in *Brown* was distinguished from the type of harm that flows from mere assault. In *Brown* the harm was not irreparable or permanent. It certainly violated the dignity of the consenters, but was the violation of dignity serious enough to justify criminalizing the harm-doers? The *volenti non fit injuria* doctrine does pull some weight and provides a defense for less serious harm-doing to others. But it has to be reconciled with the more fundamental concept of humanity as an end in itself. In the current context, I argue that criminalizable disrespect for dignity is disrespect that violates the consenter's dignity in a serious way. We can only know whether the violation is serious if we consider the actual or potential harmfulness of the violation.

---

72   [1994] 1 A.C. 212.
73   *R. v. Brown* [1994] 1 A.C. 212.
74   *R. v. Brown* [1994] 1 A.C. 212.
75   Cf. *Reg. v. Orton* (1878) 39 L.T. 293.
76   *R. v. Brown* [1994] 1 A.C. 212 at p. 246.

R. v. Brown involved a borderline dignity violation, as the harm was of a borderline kind. There is no doubt that the consenters were harmed. The harm was wrongful not because it violated the consenters' rights not to be harmed (as would be the case under the Harm Principle), but because it violated their dignity as human beings. A person can waive her right not be harmed, but she cannot waive her right to maintain a certain level of dignity as a human being. It is not the disrespect in itself that makes the conduct in *R. v. Brown* criminalizable, but the *degree* of the disrespect. We measure the degree of disrespect by evaluating the gravity of the harm-doing involved. Respect at this level means that when wrongful harm goes beyond a certain cut-off point, consent will not provide a defense. *Brown* seems to sit right on the line as personal autonomy is a powerful countervailing consideration and the harm was not of a permanent or irreparable nature.

Other Conventional Considerations

The threshold for overriding consent has to be very high. The physical wounds involved in unnecessary plastic surgery could be worse than those witnessed in *R. v. Brown*, but the overriding consideration is its impact on the humanity of the consenter. A person is able to consent to dangerous plastic surgery that is not necessary, such as a facelift. The benefits of this sort of unnecessary plastic surgery are not as valuable as life-saving surgery or surgery that is needed to correct disfigurement. At best one would argue that this kind of cosmetic surgery merely provides psychological benefits that are associated with vanity. What makes plastic surgery morally permissible? Surgery involves intentional violence that may cause serious bodily harm, but the purpose of the surgery is to advance the patient's long-term interests—dignity. Any long-term harm is a mere side-effect of the surgery, which is aimed at advancing the patient's interests and human dignity. In the case of tattooing, ear piercing, football *etc.* the purpose (*telos*) of participating is not to cause harm, but to allow the consenters to freely express themselves. These types of practices do not violate the dignity of the consenter and have long-term benefits. In the case of gridiron football there is a remote risk of serious harm transpiring, but the harm is a mere side-effect of playing a risky sport. The participants in a football match do not intentionally or recklessly aim to harm their fellow players. We do not criminalize accidents. If a surgeon is grossly negligent the criminal law could be invoked. Similarly, if a football player deliberately or recklessly harms another player the criminal law could be invoked.

A patient can consent to having unnecessary plastic surgery in order to advance her interests in the long term. She risks the side-effects for the long-term benefit of improving her health or appearance. The ephemeral setback (wounds and suffering) results in a long-term benefit: it advances the recipient both physically and psychologically in the long term and therefore does not degrade her dignity. It might also cause long-term physical and psychological harm, if it all goes horribly wrong. Nevertheless, unlike sadomasochism, plastic surgery is not conduct that aims (or is intended) to cause harm or violate the dignity of the consenter. The only harm that is likely to eventuate is attributable to the unintended risks of surgery. The harm is separable from the overall aim or purpose of this type of surgery, which maintains the dignity of the patient rather than degrades it. The surgeon does not *aim* or have it as her purpose to leave her patient permanently disfigured or disabled. If a surgeon amputates a patient's legs to prevent gangrene spreading, this maintains the patient's dignity, but if she amputates them merely because the patient does not want her legs anymore, she would violate the dignity of the patient.

The sadomasochists might object. They might argue that the *telos* of participants' activities in sadomasochism is merely to achieve sexual gratification. But this ulterior aim cannot be separated from the harm-doing—violation of dignity. The harm has to be repeated each time the recipient wants to receive sadomasochistic pleasure. The two are inseparable—the sexual gratification can only be achieved while the harm is being inflicted. It can only be achieved by violating the dignity of the participants and does not result in some kind of overall advancement of the victim's dignity. *Per contra*, a medical operation has a different *telos*. Surgery's *telos* involves a one-off wound for a long-term benefit and the long-term aim is separable from the short-term setback to the physical health of the patient. But this does not mean that a person could consent to all kinds of surgery. The surgery would have to be aimed at advancing the interests of the patient. For example, a person could not consent to a lobotomy, because it would violate her dignity in a morally unacceptable way.

The *telos* of sadomasochism is to achieve sexual gratification but this cannot be separated from the harm-doing—which involves a violation of dignity each time the participant wants to achieve sexual gratification. Likewise, that harm caused by grossly harmful and unnecessary plastic surgery is distinguishable from the benefits of reasonable plastic surgery that aims to advance a person's long-term interests. There are many forms of surgery that are *unnecessary* and *damaging* (where the risks are well known to the surgeons) that need closer regulation. In some cases it would be legitimate to limit consent as a defense and invoke the criminal law as some patients are addicted to unnecessary and damaging surgery. Surgeons who rely on consent to perform unnecessary and damaging plastic surgery on patients that are clearly addicted (we only need to think of many celebrities) could be brought within the purview of the criminal law in certain situations. The crucial difference is that surgery aims to advance the interests and dignity of patients whereas unreasonable surgery and sadomasochism are about advancing personal autonomy in a way that is not reconcilable with maintaining dignity.

Harm plays a crucial role, as the state cannot criminalize conduct without an objective justification. In Feinberg's scheme a person's right not to be wrongfully harmed derives from the idea of preserving personal autonomy. Feinberg allows a person to exercise her personal autonomy to waive the right not to be harmed, but does not explain the wrongness of gravely harming a consenter. What makes this kind of reliance on consent wrongful is the harm-doer's knowledge of its implications for the humanity of the victim. It is the union of this culpable knowledge and the gross harm that supplies the justification for criminalization. We have deep conventional understandings about wanton and gross harms and about the value of humanity, so those who choose to degrade the dignity of others have sufficient knowledge of its wrongness.

I have argued that in those cases where the consenter alienates her life there is a serious violation of dignity. Similarly, when a person consents to blinding, unnecessary amputation, a lobotomy, being poisoned or infected with a deadly substance, the harm is irreversible and of an extraordinarily grave kind and therefore there is a strong case for claiming that the consenter's dignity has been violated in a serious way. I noted that H.I.V. transmission poses some problems, because the harm is not instant and the long-term harm is not as remarkable as immediate death. In fact, the worst of the harm during the intervening years would be psychological distress and the trauma associated with receiving treatment. I have also concluded that *R. v. Brown* raises greater problems because it is a borderline case. The harm is reparable and the conduct involved an exercise of personal autonomy. The injuries were not life-threatening but they were not mild either. *Brown* is a case that sits on the line. It is arguable that we have a collective interest in preventing people becoming desensitized to inflicting such violence on their fellow humans. Arguably, we also have a collective interest in preventing the wanton spreading of deadly diseases.

Chapter 6
The Morality of Criminalizing Conventional Wrongs

The Hollowness of Feinberg's Offense Principle

Under the theory articulated by Joel Feinberg, in order for conduct to be criminalizable, it must not only be harmful or offensive, but must also be wrongful.[1] In the case of criminal harms, the case for wrongness is usually straightforward. But establishing wrongness in the case of offensive behavior is more difficult, and it will not do (as Feinberg himself seems to have done) simply to assert that it is always wrong to cause an offended state in another without justification or excuse. Furthermore, even if a feasible account of normatively wrongful offense can be developed, we need to know why the bad consequence of offense is serious enough to justify invoking the criminal law. Essentially, Feinberg was right to suggest that conduct is only criminalizable when it involves wrongdoing. In the case of harmful conduct, it is the wrongdoing (the culpable decision to harm) and the objective harmfulness of the acts/consequences that flow from that wrongdoing that provide the moral justification for invoking the criminal law. The harmful consequence also provides the lawmaker with guidance as to why the wrongdoing is of a kind that should be brought within the purview of the criminal law.[2] In the case of offense, Feinberg argues that it is *wrongful* offense that provides the basis for criminalizing offensive behavior. Hence, it is the consequence of disgust combined with the fact that a person intentionally caused another to be disgusted that forms the basis for criminalization under the Offense Principle. Anything more than disgust would probably bring the conduct within the purview of the harm criterion. I argue in this chapter that a better approach would have been to test the boundaries of privacy violations and other conventional incursions that interfere with a person's right to be let alone as bad consequences, because the

---

1 Joel Feinberg, *The Moral Limits of the Criminal Law: Offense to Others* (New York: Oxford University Press, Vol. II, 1985) and Joel Feinberg, *The Moral Limits of the Criminal Law: Harm to Others* (New York: Oxford University Press, Vol. I, 1984).

2 Obviously some forms of wrongdoing are best regulated by private law (false promising, breaching contracts, *etc.*). Other forms of wrongdoing are best regulated by social norms. For example, queue jumping obviously does not warrant any kind of legal response. It is worth noting that social norms and habit control the behavior of most people, not coercive state force.

union of these types of bad consequences and culpability might constitute the type of normative wrongness that is required for invoking the criminal law.

I will start by outlining the inadequacy of Feinberg's Offense Principle. Feinberg's Harm Principle differs to Mill's in that it is not an exclusive ground for justifying criminalization. In addition, he asserts that: 'It is always a good reason in support of a proposed criminal prohibition that it is probably necessary to prevent serious offense to persons other than the actor and would probably be an effective means to that end if enacted.'[3] Feinberg argues that a separate Offense Principle is needed because ephemeral annoyances, disappointments, disgusts, embarrassments, and detested conditions, such as fear, anxiety, and trifling ('harmless') aches and pains do not necessarily result in harm.[4] Some offensive encroachments (interferences) might set back our interests and thus come within the purview of the Harm Principle, but most forms of offense do not result in harm. Even gross offenses such as public displays of earrings made from human fetuses,[5] vomit eating in front of others in the confines of a public bus, copulating in public spaces, and so forth, do not amount to harm. Since, '[harm] even in the broad untechnical [conventional] sense rules out mere transitory disappointments, minor physical and mental "hurts", and a miscellany of disliked states of mind, including various forms of offendedness, anxiety, and boredom as harms, since harm in the broad sense is any setback of an interest, and there is (typically) *no interest* in the avoidance of such states.'[6] Feinberg uses the concept of offense to provide a normative justification for criminalizing those harmless but offensive acts, which include 'offenses proper (*e.g.*, revulsion and disgust) hurts (*e.g.*, "harmless" throbs and pangs), and "others" (*e.g.*, shame and embarrassment).'[7] Feinberg[8] uses the verb 'to offend' as a catch-all: it means to create in another an experience or psychological state of a universally disliked kind, *e.g.*, disgust, fear, shock, anger, humiliation, embarrassment, shame, hurt, anxiety, boredom and so on.[9] Offense might leave the victim feeling annoyed, disgusted, harassed, invaded, violated, disappointed, frightened, anxious, and so forth.[10]

Some commentators have suggested that the wrongful harm justification for criminalization could be expanded to cover the worst kinds of offense.[11] This would be plausible for those more serious violations of privacy, but Feinberg was right to the extent that he argues that harm cannot be stretched to cover all those

---

3   Feinberg, Vol. II, *op. cit. supra*, fn. 1 at p. 1.
4   *Id.* at pp. 1–2.
5   *R. v. Gibson* [1991] 1 All E.R. 649.
6   Feinberg, Vol. I, *op. cit. supra*, fn. 1 at p. at 48.
7   Ibid.
8   Feinberg, Vol. II, *op. cit. supra*, fn. 1 at pp. 1–3.
9   *Id.* at pp. 1–2.
10 Ibid.
11 Harlon L. Dalton, 'Disgust and Punishment,' (1986–1987) 96 *Yale Law Journal* 883.

harmless wrongs that we might want to regulate.[12] The Offense Principle allows the legislature to bring a wide range of harmless but unwanted activities within the purview of the criminal law. Nonetheless, Feinberg's formulation of the Offense Principle is vacuous; as it does not distinguish offense doing that is wrong (results in objectively bad consequences) from that which is right or tolerable because it has neutral or good consequences. Feinberg's Offense Principle has the potential to allow offensive conduct to be criminalized regardless of the requirements of fairness and justice. Feinberg states that only *wrongful* offense is criminalizable, but he fails to provide a theory of wrongful offense. His Offense Principle is modeled on his Harm Principle. Firstly, the word 'offense' like the word 'harm' has both a general and a particular normative meaning. In the general sense it refers to 'any or all of a miscellany of disliked mental states.'[13] In the normative sense it only refers to those disliked mental states that are caused by the wrongful (*right-violating*) conduct of others.[14]

Offense in the sense as used in the Offense Principle 'specifies an objective condition—the unpleasant mental state must be caused by conduct that really is wrongful.'[15] Whereas 'offense in the strict sense of ordinary language specifies a subjective condition—the offending act must be taken by the offended person to wrong him whether in fact it does or not.'[16] For instance, the strict sense requires resentment: *x* is offended subjectively when *y* causes *x* to suffer a disliked state; *x* is able to attribute that state to the *wrongful* conduct of *y*; and *x* subjectively resents *y* for his role in causing her disliked mental state.[17] Offense as laid down in Feinberg's Offense Principle is meant to be criminalizable when it causes wrongful resentment. 'The Offense Principle as we shall interpret it then applies to offended states in either the broad or general sense—that is either with or without resentment—when these states are in fact *wrongfully* produced in *violation* of the offended [person's] *rights*.'[18] It is essential that the victim be wronged, but there is no need for the victim to feel wronged in a subjective sense. Feinberg requires the offense to be wrongful, but he only provides an explanation of the wrongfulness (culpability) of causing offense rather than a theory of criminalizable offense doing (wrongfulness with certain objectively bad consequences: wrongness). He does not explain the wrongness of disgust or why the consequence of disgust that is brought about intentionally is worthy of penal censure. Feinberg ineffectually

---

12 I have already highlighted the dangers of stretching harm arguments to the limit. For an account of legal moralistic rather than objective harm arguments and their misuse in criminalization policy, see Bernard E. Harcourt, 'Collapse of the Harm Principle,' (1999–2000) 90 *Journal of Criminal Law and Criminology* 109.
13 Feinberg, Vol. II, *op. cit. supra*, fn. 1 at p. 2.
14 *Ibid.*
15 *Ibid.*
16 *Ibid.*
17 *Id.* at pp. 2–3.
18 *Id.* at p. 2.

asserts that 'there will always be a wrong whenever an *offended state* (in the generic sense) is produced in another without justification or excuse.'[19] Even if culpably causing disgust were worthy of normative reproach, this alone would not justify penal reproach in many cases.

According to Feinberg, offensive conduct is criminalizable when it violates rights.[20] However, as Feinberg tells us, interests cannot be set back from being offended, because we do not have a recognizable interest in avoiding offense. Offensive conduct cannot set back or violate our interests (*primitive* long-term or welfare-type interests), because offense is ephemeral and does not affect any tangible interests, unless it has an incapacitating psychological impact.[21] The problem with Feinberg's approach is that it appears to hold that the legislature can criminalize any intentional affront that is produced without justification or excuse.[22] Feinberg adopts the theory of moral wrongdoing that he developed in his Harm Principle. However, intentionally causing harm (violating another's right to a personal or propriety resource) 'entails by its very meaning that the action is *prima facie* wrong.'[23] The particular normative character of culpably causing harmful consequences means that the elements of moral culpability and harm-doing are sufficient to explain its wrongness. Harm is a wrongful consequence that can be normatively recognized. Under the Harm Principle, objective justifications can be produced for invoking the criminal law. It is feasible to argue that an intentional, unjustifiable/inexcusable violation of a person's right not to have her proprietary or personal resources (interests) set back is *prima facie* criminalizable. The setback to interests is an objective consequence (*i.e.*, its natural properties, pain, physical disfigurement, deprivation of economic resources) that provides the lawmaker with guidance as to why it is fair to criminalize that type of wrong.

Feinberg's Mediating Maxims and Critical Morality

Feinberg ineffectually replaces: 'unjustifiable invasions of interests' with 'unjustifiably causing offended states in the generic sense,' as the criterion for determining wrongdoing in the offense context. 'There will always be a wrong whenever an *offended state* (in the generic sense) is produced in another without

---

19 *Ibid.*

20 *Ibid.*

21 If the offense 'is severe, prolonged, or constantly repeated, the mental suffering it causes may become obsessive and incapacitating, and therefore harmful': Feinberg, Vol. I, *op. cit. supra*, fn. 1 at p. 46.

22 As I noted above, without justification or excuse in Feinberg's scheme is about *intentionally* causing harm or offense without an excuse or justification.

23 'Without such a connection to a moral theory the Harm Principle is a formal principle lacking specific concrete content and leading to no policy conclusions.' See Joseph Raz, *The Morality of Freedom* (Oxford: Clarendon Press, 1986) at p. 414.

justification or excuse.'[24] This merely shows that the offense was brought about culpably, it does not explain the wrongness and criminalizableness of such offense doing. What makes the consequence of disgust *per se* worthy of criminalization? To mediate the potential expansive reach of an Offense Principle that allows any intentional (without justification or excuse) offense doing to be criminalized, Feinberg's grounds his Offense Principle on nuisance law and argues that the legislator should weigh the seriousness of the offense 'caused to unwilling witnesses against the reasonableness of the offender's conduct.'[25] To determine the seriousness of the offensive conduct the legislator needs to consider four factors: the magnitude of the offense, the avoidability of the offense, whether the offended person voluntarily assumed the risk of offense, and, if any, the abnormal susceptibilities of the offended person. The first maxim concerning the magnitude of the offense has a number of sub-elements that are used to consider the seriousness of the offense. Those sub-elements consider the seriousness of the offense with reference to its intensity, durableness and extent.[26]

The legislature is required to evaluate '[t]he intensity and durability of the repugnance produced, and the extent to which repugnance could be anticipated to be the general reaction to the conduct that produced it.' If the offense is very intense it is regarded as more serious. Likewise, if the offensive experience is of greater durability it is regarded as being more serious. Being subjected to an exhibitionist's naked display would not be as intense (serious) on an open beach as it would be when the audience is held captive, such as in a train carriage. Similarly, the offense caused by inadvertently spotting a nudist from a distance in a German park would not be as intense (serious) as it would be to witness a similar sight in a confined public space, such as in a public bus. The captive spectator in the bus would find the offense intense and durable because it is up close, inescapable and more than transitory. Feinberg puts a particular emphasis on the *extent* requirement.[27] If the susceptibility to a given offense is widespread then the gravity of the offense is considered to be greater.[28] The more widespread the offense, the stronger the case becomes for criminalization and the countervailing considerations would have to be much weightier to override the case for criminalization.[29] Feinberg states: 'What we cannot say is that conduct is properly prohibited under the Offense Principle if and only if offense is the anticipated reaction of more than 50 percent of all potential observers, or 75 percent, or 99 percent, or 100 percent. Again, all we are warranted in saying is that the higher the projected percentage, the stronger

---

24 Feinberg, Vol. II, *op. cit. supra*, fn. 1 at p. 2.
25 *Id.* at p. 26.
26 *Id.* at pp. 34–35.
27 *Id.* at p. 27.
28 *Id.* at p. 35.
29 *Id.* at p. 27.

the case for prohibition.'[30] This majoritarian reasoning suggests that conduct could be criminalized so long as it is offensive enough to enough people.

Furthermore, Feinberg's Offense Principle does not require the offended witnesses to provide sound normative reasons for taking offense. He suggests that the extent standard replaces the need to provide any reasons (let alone sound normative reasons) for criminalizing offense. Feinberg[31] explicitly states that there is no need to determine whether the offense-taker has good reasons for taking offense. 'There are a number of reasons for not requiring that offense be taken reasonably ... and for not including the degree of reasonableness of an offense among the determinants of its seriousness.'[32] He asserts that the *extent* of the offense standard makes such an inquiry superfluous, because it is 'extremely unlikely, that virtually everyone would have an unreasonable disposition to be offended by a certain kind of experience.'[33] Thereafter, he argues that it would be dangerous to allow the legislature to second-guess the reasonableness of the offense-taker's emotional reactions to offensive conduct.[34] In effect, the extent of the offense standard is substituting the missing wrongness constraint, which requires that the conduct be wrong and have normative consequences (or potential consequences) of a kind that are worthy of criminal condemnation.

With the wrongness constraint missing, the *extent* and *intensity* of the culpable offense seem to be the sole determinants of criminalization. This approach more or less decides the criminality status of offensive conduct by counting the number of people who find it seriously offensive. The higher the number of people offended, the stronger the case would be for criminalization. The counterbalancing considerations concerning the reasonableness of the offensive conduct would have to be compelling to prevent widespread or very serious offense from being criminalized.[35] Measuring offense according to the dictates of the majority has the potential to lead to unjust results. A large number of people could claim that interracial hand-holding, homosexuals, lesbians, begging,[36] and so forth are criminalizably offensive. Feinberg argues that applying the mediating maxims to evaluate the reasonableness of the offensive conduct is enough to guard against criminalizing innocent conduct. He states: 'If I wanted a reason against ever criminalizing interracial hand-holding and the like, all I had to do was cite the reasonableness of such conduct it would forbid, its intimate personal importance, its independent social value ... its status as expression, the unavailability of reasonable alternatives ... and so on.'[37] The better

---

30 *Ibid.*
31 *Id.* at p. 35.
32 *Ibid.*
33 *Ibid.*
34 *Ibid.*
35 *Id.* at p. 27.
36 See generally, Hartley Dean, *Begging Questions: Street-Level Economic Activity and Social Policy Failure* (Bristol: The Policy Press, 1999).
37 Feinberg, Vol. II, *op. cit. supra*, fn. 1 at p. 29.

approach would be to ask what, if anything, makes conduct such as lesbian and interracial hand-holding *prima facie* morally wrong?[38] What are the criminalizable consequences of such conduct? Here, the disgust is caused by the offended party's ignorance. Do the offended parties have objective reasons for taking offense? The reasonableness of the conduct is only relevant once we have a *prima facie* case of criminalizable offense.

Feinberg's approach not only allows conduct that lacks any apparent moral wrongness to be criminalized, but it also has the potential to allow reprehensible offense to avoid criminalization. A simply quantitative weighing of interests could allow certain offensive insults to go unchecked. Would a harmless but highly offensive racial slur that only offends a very small number of people be considered serious enough to be protected under Feinberg's Offense Principle? If racial abuse was directed at an extremely small ethnic minority only a few people might be offended, so the case for criminalization would be weak. Feinberg suggests that this can be overcome by moving the emphasis from the widespreadedness of the offense to its intensity.

> [A] banner saying that 'All Americans are Pigs' would tend to offend most Americans to some extent, but few very intensely, whereas 'All American blacks are pigs' might offend fewer but those much more intensely. If John Smith, the only black on the bus, sees it, he will be shocked and outraged. If the sign says simply 'John Smith is a pig,' ... Smith may be more offended on balance than he would be by the insult to his race, but the sign will be even more ominously personal and threatening, and his evoked feelings appropriately more intense. Clearly, the pointed and personal character of the offense tends to make up in 'weight' for its lack of widespreadedness.[39]

This kind of departure from the extent standard highlights its irrelevance. It shows that the number of people offended does not alter the moral character of the individual acts of offense. Merely referring to the *intensity* of the offense is insufficient for grounding a case of criminalization. The sight of the interracial couple holding hands, or two lesbians kissing might cause profound offense to some, but this does not mean that it would be objectively fair to criminalize these activities. Feinberg uses intensity as a *prima facie* reason for criminalizing offense against minorities, that is, the profoundness of the offense is a determiner for criminality in his scheme. The appropriate way to build a *prima facie* case for criminalizing offense is to demonstrate that the unwanted conduct is wrong.

The question should be: Why is the racial insult against the small minority morally wrongful? Its wrongness stems from the fact that it treats those affected

---

38 See also Andrew P. Simester and Andrew von Hirsch, 'Rethinking the Offense Principle,' (2002) 8(3) *Legal Theory* 269 at pp. 271–273.

39 Feinberg, Vol. II, *op. cit. supra*, fn. 1 at p. 30.

as less than full members of the community.[40] It is wrong because it degrades the dignity of the minority and to ascertain the objectivity of this claim we must ultimately appeal to the underlying norms that inform the wrongness of failing to treat minorities with equal respect as human beings.[41] The underlying norms are simply that all humans are equal and are entitled to be treated as equal and full members of society. Treating others as less than full members of the community has the bad consequence of unequal treatment (discrimination). Evaluating the intensity and widespreadedness of the offense does not answer this question. The core normative reason for regulating this kind of offense is found by examining the bad consequences that flow from the discriminator's culpable choice, that is, the objective consequence of treating certain members of the community as less than full members of society.

An Offense Principle that evaluates offense by merely counting the number of people that have been affronted, without giving a full account of why the conduct is worthy of criminal censure, has the potential to allow the prejudices of the majority to dictate criminalization decisions. Feinberg's Offense Principle uses culpability and all forms of disgust as a basis for invoking the criminal law; such an approach could allow unreasonable reactions and prejudices to be used to criminalize offensive conduct that might not have objective consequences of a kind that are worthy of criminal condemnation.[42] Such an approach would lead to unfair and unprincipled criminalization decisions. In some communities the mere status or existence of homeless people, same-sex couples, *etc.*, has caused profound offense because such lifestyles are considered to be *contra bonus mores et decorum*.[43] Robert Ellickson, a Yale University law professor, has argued that idle vagrants offend the Anglo-American work ethic.[44] A normative theory of criminalization that focuses on moral wrongness rather than mere responsibility (based on intentionality) for bringing about a neutral or good consequence would not allow this type of innocuous conduct to be criminalized. As I noted in Chapter 2, wrongness is about showing that the agent aimed to bring about some bad consequence. Disgust is a bad consequence, but only when it is objectively taken. Thus, if a person aims to disgust her black colleague by saying, 'blacks are not as intelligent as whites,' then the lawmaker is able to point to the underlying norms which inform this kind of disrespect (the norms that tell us that the consequence of unequal treatment is bad, *etc.*), to demonstrate the wrongness of this type of offensive behavior. Once

---

40 Ronald Dworkin, *Taking Rights Seriously* (King's Lynn: Duckworth, 1977) at p. 198.
41 I discuss this idea at length in the final sections of this chapter.
42 Simester and von Hirsch, *op. cit. supra*, fn. 38 pp. at 272 *et passim*.
43 Angus Erskine and Ian McIntosh, 'Why Begging Offends: Historical Perspectives and Continuities,' in Dean, *op. cit. supra*, fn. 36 at pp. 41–49.
44 Robert C. Ellickson, 'Controlling Chronic Misconduct in City Spaces: Of Panhandlers, Skid Rows, and Public-Space Zoning,' (1995–1996) 105 *Yale Law Journal* 1165 at pp. 1181–1184.

we get to this stage, then we need to consider the gravity of those consequences to determine whether a criminal law response is a proportionate way of dealing with the wrongdoing.

Feinberg tries to counter the looseness of allowing any *disgust taking* and mere culpability to form a justification for invoking the criminal law by subjecting the offense doing to a reasonableness evaluation. Reasonableness in his scheme is determined by five factors:[45] (1) The personal importance of the offensive conduct to the actor; (2) its social utility; (3) its free expression value (Feinberg puts a particular emphasis on the value of free speech and suggests that the offensive conduct would hardly ever outweigh the value of free speech[46]); (4) the availability of alternative times and places where the conduct would cause less offense; and (5) the nature of the location where the offense takes place also has some bearing on its reasonableness[47] (*i.e.*, people would be expected to tolerate nudity at a designated nudist park or beach, because it is widely known that it is common in such places). Likewise, a person might be expected to tolerate the sight of a nude model if she attends a life drawing class, but would not be expected to sit next to a naked person in the confines of a public bus.

Feinberg argues: 'The more people can expect to be offended, *ceteris paribus*, the stronger the case for legal prohibition. "Other things," however, are rarely equal. It is important to remember that certain kinds of valuable, or at least innocent actions, can be expected to offend large numbers of people ... The interracial couple strolling hand in hand down the streets of a deep southern town might still cause shock, even shame and disgust, perhaps to the majority of white pedestrians who happen to observe them.'[48] As I noted above, Feinberg asserts that if the legislature wanted to produce a *reason* against criminalizing conduct, such as interracial hand-holding, all it would have to do is cite the reasonableness of the conduct: 'The behavior of the interracial couple has much to be said for it: it is reasonable, personally valuable, expressive and affectionate, spontaneous, natural, and irreplaceable, and the offense it causes is easily avoidable.'[49] Feinberg seems to be using the mediating maxims to override what is not yet a *prima facie* case of wrongness. *Prima facie* wrongness is a prerequisite for criminalization. Interracial relationships do not involve moral wrongdoing in a normative sense, so such displays are not criminalizable to start with. Generally speaking,

---

45   Feinberg, Vol. II, *op. cit. supra*, fn. 1 at p. 44.
46   Feinberg asserts that: 'No amount of offensiveness in an expressed opinion can counterbalance the vital social value of allowing unfettered personal expression.' *Id.* at pp. 38–39.
47   *Ibid.*
48   *Ibid.*
49   *Id.* at p. 29.

mediating factors are claims for overriding or tolerating conduct that is *prima facie* criminalizable.[50]

Constitutional override constraints have a dual function in that they can also be used to strike down laws that criminalize conduct that is not *prima facie* criminalizable.[51] A principled approach to criminalization should start by demonstrating that there is a *prima facie* objective justification for invoking the criminal law. Feinberg misses this point because he does not attempt to develop a theory of objectively criminalizable offense. Such a theory should start by asking: what are the criminalizable consequences of this type of wrongdoing? The moral wrongness constraint is established by demonstrating that the agent intentionally tried to bring about bad consequences of a criminalizable kind. Feinberg would also have benefited significantly by considering the objective badness of certain forms of offense doing, rather than merely assuming that culpableness and offense doing were the only preconditions for criminalization in the offense paradigm.

As noted at the outset of this book, the aim of Feinberg's work and that of this book is to find ways to make criminalization normative. In a provocative essay in 2000,[52] Andrew Ashworth asked whether the criminal law is a lost cause. Ashworth noted that many activities are criminalized without a principled justification being supplied and concluded that the criminal law is so misused that it has become a lost cause. The famous debate between H.L.A. Hart and Lord Devlin was basically about principled versus unprincipled criminalization. Hart argued that there was no principled (critical moral) justification for criminalizing many of the activities that Lord Devlin advocated criminalizing, such as homosexuality and prostitution. Hart argued for principled criminalization, which he suggested would be criminalization that could be justified by pointing to critical moral standards.[53] Hart took the view that the culpable harm provided a critical moral justification for criminalization. Hart views critical moral standards as those that are correct.[54] Feinberg refers to critical morality as true morality, which according to him is 'a collection of governing principles thought to be "part of the nature of things,"

---

50 Andrew von Hirsch, 'Toleranz als Mediating Principle,' in Andrew von Hirsch, Kurt Seelmann and Wohlers Wolfgang, *Mediating Principles* (Baden-Baden, Germany: Nomos Verlagsgesellschaft, 2006) at pp. 97 *et seq.*

51 See *Lawrence v. Texas*, 539 U.S. 558 (2003), where a law criminalizing homosexuals was struck down. The conduct was not *prima facie* criminalizable, because it did not involve moral wrongdoing in a normative sense. Hence, the constitutional constraint was not used to override a *prima facie* case of criminalization, but rather was used to thwart the enforcement of positive morality: conduct that is not criminalizable to start with.

52 Andrew Ashworth, 'Is the Criminal Law a Lost Cause,' (2000) 116 *Law Quarterly Review* 225.

53 H.L.A. Hart, *Law, Liberty and Morality* (London: Oxford University Press, 1963), at pp. 17–53.

54 H.L.A. Hart, *Essays in Jurisprudence and Philosophy* (Oxford: Clarendon Press, 1983), 248 *et passim.* Cf. Stanley Fish, *There's No Such Thing as Free Speech and It's a Good Thing Too* (New York: Oxford University Press, 1994) at pp. 200–229.

critical rational and correct.'[55] Like Hart, Feinberg argues positive morality (*i.e.*, community, cultural or conventional *conceptualizations of harms*) only provide a justification for criminalization to the extent that 'it is also a correct rule of morality, capable of satisfying a transcultural critical standard.'[56] Feinberg attempts to limit criminalization by arguing that normative or objective moral accounts of harm can be used to constrain positive or conventional accounts of harm being used to justify penal censure. Critical moralists seem to take the view that deep personal conviction or *practical reasoning* allows moral agents to identify objective or normative accounts of harm.[57] I take the view that the morality can be principled, but I have a much more modest conceptualization of the moral agent, as I take the moral agent to be nothing greater than a communally situated human being. If practical reasoners are merely communally situated humans trying to solve conventional conflicts, then it is fairly clear that it is impossible for such creatures to identify fully correct accounts of harm and badness.

Standards identified by human thinkers cannot be truly correct as not only is it impossible for us to know whether a standard is truly correct, in practice all *reasoning* (notwithstanding that some think these standards are mind-independent) is influenced by societal evolution, convention and human biases. The human mind is not a computer! In this chapter, I argue that it is not possible to claim that certain conventional wrongs are truly wrong, bad or harmful in a transcultural sense. Notwithstanding this, I take the view that *principled* justifications can be supplied for criminalizing many conventionally contingent wrongs. Principled, in this sense, means that it is possible to speak *objectively* about whether an action is right or wrong in a conventional sense. There is no doubt that inter-subjective deliberation will give us better results, but it cannot tell us whether a particular moral standard is correct.

Hart suggests that an objective account of harm can be discovered and therefore can provide a critical moral justification for or against criminalization. But the harm principle itself is a conventional construct and conceptualizations of harm depend on convention. It might be argued that deep (deep meaning *long* held and widely shared understandings in Western society) conventional agreement about the harmfulness of certain acts such as murder is sufficient for providing a principled harm argument for outlawing it. This provides a *strong* conventionally objective case for outlawing such wrongs. However, Feinberg supplements the harm principle[58] with an offense principle,[59] which holds that culpable offense doing also provides a critical moral justification for criminalization. The problem

---

55   Joel Feinberg, *The Moral Limits of the Criminal Law: Harmless Wrongdoing* (New York: Oxford University Press, Vol. IV, 1988) at p. 124.

56   *Ibid.*

57   Ronald Dworkin, 'Objectivity and Truth: You'd Better Believe It,' (1996) 25(2) *Philosophy & Public Affairs* 87.

58   Feinberg, Vol. I, *op. cit. supra*, fn. 1 at p. 1.

59   Feinberg, Vol. II, *op. cit. supra*, fn. 1 at p. 1.

with offensive conduct and trivial harms is that there is no deep or constant (*intersubjectively shared*) agreement about the badness or wrongness of such acts. I could provide many examples, but I think nudity in ancient art, modern movies and art, and in many tribal cultures might be sufficient for tentatively claiming that exhibitionism has not been constantly considered to be bad, harmful or wrong. Feinberg[60] is particularly critical of Lord Devlin's positive morality, but it is not clear that Feinberg's offense principle rests on anything more than positive morality. Feinberg does not explain why culpable *offense doing* is inherently wrong in a critical moral sense rather than a conventional sense—or why standards cannot be developed from *conventional morality* to provide principled justifications for criminalization.

I develop the idea of conventional objectivity more fully throughout the chapter. The basic theory is that we are able to draw on our deeply held conventional understandings of wrong and harm (including our scientific and biological accounts of harm and bad consequences—and also conventional understandings about privacy and autonomy in modern society) to formulate a case either for or against criminalization. We may change our minds about what is bad, harmful and wrong depending on the social context. Hence, our conceptualizations of harm and wrong depend on conventional understandings of harm and on socialization. Therefore, we may claim that something is objectively harmful within a certain conventional context but this is entirely different to claiming that something is bad or harmful in a transcultural critical objective sense. Obviously at the most basic level, all societies have similar conventional understandings about the badness, wrongness and harmfulness of conduct such as genocide, murder, starvation, torture and so on. Understandings have emerged because humans have drawn on basic biological information, human instincts and evolving social norms to solve conventional conflicts. Trans-culturally, there are shared understandings about the badness and harmfulness of fairly primitive harms such as the harmfulness of wantonly amputating another's hand. For instance, the justification for chopping a thief's hand off for shoplifting in some countries hinges on an understanding that it is bad and harmful to wantonly amputate a person's hand. It is because hand amputation is understood to be bad and harmful that it is used as a punishment rather than a reward. I do not know of any state where the conventional understanding is that hand amputation is good and thus should be used as a *reward* in its society. The same might be said for the *death* penalty. There is no transcultural disagreement about death (capital punishment) or hand amputation being bad and harmful; rather the disagreement is about whether such punishments are proportionate or necessary given our respect for humanity and life. But this does not mean those acts are truly harmful or bad. Wanton hand amputation might be objectively harmful when assessed against conventional understandings of harm, but this alone cannot be used to *prove* that it is objectively harmful in a critical moral sense. Empirical information (*i.e.*, biological, scientific and medical explanations of pain and

---

60 Feinberg, Vol. IV, *op. cit. supra*, fn. 55 at pp. 124–173.

damage) and our *conventional* understanding of pain, hurt and *culpability* is more than sufficient for providing an objective account of the harmfulness of *wanton* hand amputation.

Ashworth's[61] claim that the criminal law has been influenced by the political demands of the day is beyond dispute and unless we can identify appropriate constraints, it might be impossible to have a principled criminal law. If the harm and offense principles do not provide critical reasons for constraining criminalization, then it might not be possible to distinguish Feinberg's justifications (culpable harm and culpable offense) for criminalization from those of Devlin. I argue that both Hart and Feinberg were wrong merely to assume that there is a critical moral type of harm and a conventional moral type of harm. I take the view that culpable harm and culpable offense only provide conventional justifications for criminalization. I focus on Feinberg's offense principle, because the conventional nature of culpable offense doing provides the clearest case for challenging the claim that criminalization can be constrained by critical moral accounts of harm and offense. It is difficult to see the correctness (critical objectivity) of wrongness claims concerning many forms of offense doing such as that caused by public exhibitionism. The aim of this chapter is to show that offense to others does not provide a critical moral justification for invoking the criminal law.

J.L. Mackie[62] used 'retribution' as a test case for objectivity. He would have had a field day with Feinberg's offense principle. I am a supporter of Feinberg's criteria, but I think the meta-ethical foundations that he claims for his harm and offense criteria are open to question. Feinberg promises a normative conception of wrong distinct from a positive one of the sort Devlin relies on, but 'offense to others' delivers a conception that is indistinguishable from a merely positive one. If harm and offense are anything that a person *subjectively* perceives to be harmful or offensive then Feinberg's principles are vacuous. To counteract this possibility, Feinberg argues that the harm or offense must be objective or normative. Feinberg seeks to base his harm and offense principles on objective foundations but fails. When it comes to the offense principle, the weakness of Feinberg's critical objectivity claim is most evident. I argue that, even though there is no critical moral justification for criminalizing exhibitionism, it is possible to draw on conventional morality to provide a principled case for criminalizing it in certain contexts.

---

61   Ashworth, *op. cit. supra*, fn. 52.
62   J.L. Mackie, 'Retributivism: A Test Case for Ethical Objectivity,' in Joel Feinberg and Hyman Gross, *Philosophy of Law* (Belmont, CA: Wadsworth Publishing Company, 1991) 667 at p. 684. See also J. L. Mackie, 'Morality and the Retributive Emotions,' (1982) 1 *Criminal Justice Ethics* 3.

Criminalization, Convention and Legitimacy

The criminal law gives any government immense power over its people because disobeying a criminally codified command can result in stigmatization and severe punishment (conviction, imprisonment, fines, *etc.*). Why are citizens of a given state[63] bound or obliged to follow the guides of acceptable behavior as set out in the criminal law? Since the criminal law is a *punitive* response to unwanted behavior, its authority is contingent on its legitimacy.[64] In this chapter, I attempt to explain when a criminal law might be principled rather than critically correct or critically objective (*i.e.*, compatible with critical moral standards of fairness). I argue that certain human acts/actions are deserving of the crime label because they produce bad consequences (or risk producing bad consequences as is the case with attempts, endangerment, *etc.*) of an avoidable kind (avoidable in that the wrongdoer culpably aimed for the bad consequences and could have chosen otherwise) for others. The harm might be indirect and thus threaten the community (state) by damaging its institutions (*i.e.*, perjury, bribery, and environmental damage are collective harms); or the harm might be directly victimizing, as is the case with murder, theft, rape, and so forth. The issue of indirect or collective harm is controversial as it is difficult to individualize any wrongdoing.[65]

Many criminal laws are codified (deeply held) conventional commands, such as laws against rape, assault, murder, theft, fraud and so forth. A given criminal law will have authority[66] regardless of whether it serves a legitimate purpose, but the criminal law as a general social control *institution* will retain its legitimacy and authority only if the bulk of its commands are understood as being principled—that is, understood to be fair in accordance with our conventional understandings of justice and fairness. It is not possible to state the cut-off point in numerical terms, but if more than 50 percent of a given state's laws served no legitimate purpose (*i.e.*, some goal that is understood to be legitimate by communally situated moral agents), were unjust and draconian, then the result might be revolution.

---

63   Elsewhere, I have argued that many Western principles of justice, such as the proportionate punishment and fair labeling of criminality requirements, unfortunately do not set some magic universal standard that all others are morally bound to follow. These principles are difficult to apply in international contexts, not only because different countries have different views of *harmfulness*, but also because the United States and England do not follow the principles of justice they advocate for other countries. For example, a person can be jailed for life in the U.S. for stealing videotapes so long as she has two prior convictions. Dennis J. Baker and Lucy X. Zhao, 'Responsibility Links, Fair Labeling and Proportionality in China: Comparing China's Criminal Law Theory and Doctrine,' (2009) 14(2) *UCLA Journal of International Law & Foreign Affairs* 1–56.

64   David Beetham, *The Legitimation of Power* (Basingstoke: Macmillan, 1991).

65   Dennis J. Baker, 'Collective Criminalization and the Constitutional Right to Endanger Others,' (2009) 28(2) *Criminal Justice Ethics* 3.

66   See generally, Joseph Raz, *The Authority of Law* (Oxford: Oxford University Press, 2009).

For instance, most people in advanced Western societies would not tolerate jail terms of 50 years for shoplifting.[67] We have deep conventional understandings about the trivial nature of the harmfulness of shoplifting and therefore do not see lengthy jail terms as a necessary government response. When the bulk of a state's laws, whether they be private law or public laws, serve some legitimate purpose (purposes that are conventionally understood and accepted as legitimate), the law in that state will retain its posited authority. Although there are many unjust criminal laws that serve no legitimate purpose, the bulk of the jailable offenses in the United States do seem to be aimed at genuine wrongs.[68] Arguably, many unjust laws retain their authority because the general institution of criminal law and punishment retains its authority because the bulk of the individual laws that underwrite its existence are accepted as legitimate—these laws are just in that they serve a legitimate (conventionally accepted) purpose.

We implicitly agree to have law in order to maintain society for the good of humanity, but we also realize that the state might misuse the law or simply get it wrong. Thus, the law itself has to be subject to a number of fairness constraints. The state is merely members of society acting as a collective and we need to know why the commands of the majority as expressed in laws have authority over us as individuals. As we will see, many activities that are deemed bad and often as harmful by the state (the collective/community/society) often involve little more than someone flouting a seemingly innocuous social custom, as is the case with exhibitionism. Since this type of conduct is harmless, the harm criterion does little to answer the question: What makes exhibitionism criminalizable?

Criminalization is a process of labeling certain actions as punishable by the state in order to solve social conflicts (cooperation problems) that arise in competitive plural societies. I argue below that constraints such as the harm and culpability constraints are only objective to the extent that there is deep conventional agreement about what constitutes a punishable harm, but once we get into territory where there is disagreement about what ends are inter-subjectively sharable by all agents communally situated, a principled case for criminalization is difficult to identify. Furthermore, it is almost impossible to identify a critical moral account of criminalizable harm and offense. At the inter-jurisdictional level there is deep agreement about the badness and wrongness of acts that result in primitive harm,

---

67 But people can be socialized so as to tolerate the criminalization and punishment of harmless wrongs such as kissing in public. The majority in a given community might not see this as being draconian. It is a jailable offense to kiss (even a peck on the cheek) in public in Dubai: 'British Couple Appealing Dubai Kiss Conviction,' (New York: *New York Times*, March 14, 2010)

68 Even many apparent *malum prohibita* crimes such as prohibitions concerning parking cars (*i.e.*, such laws allow for fair use of public spaces) and rules about which side of the road to drive on (*i.e.*, these laws facilitate the free and safe movement of people) serve the well-being and advancement of humanity by allowing for the benefits of cooperative living to be realized.

such as gross physical harm (*e.g.*, biologically painful harms such as starvation, blinding, amputation, torture, *etc.*), but beyond those primitive harms agreement is totally contingent on jurisdictional and cultural conventions. Conventional harms and conventions are born and must die together.[69] Primitive harms do not rely on convention, as there are other biological and scientific explanations of the badness and harmfulness of such acts. We could adopt a grander scheme and argue that the normativity of harm hinges on critical agent-relative reasons.[70] As the Harvard philosopher Christine Korsgaard puts it: 'Values may be inter-subjective: not part of the fabric of the universe or external truth, but nevertheless shared or at least sharable by agents.'[71] Inter-subjectively, 'normative claims are not the claims of a metaphysical world of values upon us: they are claims we make on ourselves and each other.'[72]

But Korsgaard has a Kantian inter-subjectivity of all reasonable agents in mind. The word *sharable* reflects Kant's unwillingness to engage in anthropological reasoning when thinking about the content of morality. It is impossible to claim that criminal law is normative in this sense, because anthropological information has to be considered given the conventional nature of the problems criminal law addresses. Principled criminalization might be identified by examining what is

---

69   Bentham highlights the conventional nature of property in the following phrase: 'Property and the law are born and must die together.' Charles Milner Atkinson, *Bentham's Theory of Legislation* (London: Oxford University Press, Vol. I, 1914) at pp. 146–147.

70   Objectivity is derived through a deliberative process. '[A]greement of rational, reasonable, and competent deliberators, resulting from an ideally operated deliberative process, may be our best mark of correctness of the judgments in question; but that agreement does not make the judgment correct. ... In this point, objectivity as publicity fits Kant's view that ... if the judgment is valid for everyone who is in possession of reason, then its ground is objectively sufficient. This is sufficient for objectivity but not correctness ("truth" in Kant's discussion). Objectivity, understood as an inter-subjective validity demonstrated by the agreement of all those possessed of reason, does not constitute correctness ... but it provides the touchstone whereby we assure ourselves, from where we are, that the set of truth of judgments we accept is not idiosyncratic.' Gerald Postema, 'Objectivity Fit for Law,' in Brian Lieter (ed.), *Objectivity in Law and Morals* (Cambridge: Cambridge University Press, 2001) at p. 121.

71   Christine M. Korsgaard, 'The Reasons We Can Share: An Attack on the Distinction Between Agent-Relative and Agent-Neutral Values,' (1993) 10(1) *Social Philosophy & Policy* 24 at p. 32. Korsgaard states that: 'One reason I take this option to be important is this: I think that its lack of ontological or metaphysical commitments is a clear advantage of Inter-subjectivism; we should not be Objective Realists unless, so to speak, there is no other way. This is not just because of Ockham's razor. A conviction that there are metaphysical truths backing up our claims of value must rest on, and therefore cannot explain, our confidence in our claims of value. Metaphysical moral realism takes us the *long way around to end up where we started—at our own deep conviction that our values are not groundless*—without giving us what we wanted—some account of the source of that conviction.'

72   *Id.* at 51.

actually shared in specific communities, but this would not be normative in the Korsgaardian sense—as it is contingent on what is shared in specific context and at specific points in time. Even Kant would have changed some of his conventional views, if he were still alive.

Culturally situated inter-subjective agents might identify principled justifications for criminalization, but there would be nothing *critically objective* about the standards that they might develop. Furthermore, my conception of principled is neutral between different reasons why agents might inter-subjectively share their ends, and therefore neutral between what I describe as the critical moralist's reason for arguing that ends should be shared and other reasons for so arguing. I merely critique critical morality to highlight the impossibility of claiming that particular acts such as exhibitionism are objectively wrong in a critical moral sense and therefore are *prima facie* criminalizable. The exhibitionism/privacy exemplar is used in the final sections to highlight the vacuity of the claim that bad acts/consequences such as public nudity can be defined as universally wrong and bad.[73]

It is fairly easy to show that core instances of criminality (rape, theft, murder, *etc.*) are principled if we accept deeply held conventional conceptualizations of *harm*, autonomy and culpability. However, there is much less agreement when it comes to criminalizing *offensive* conduct and soft harms. A principled conventional account of the badness of offending others might be possible, but it is impossible to provide a critical moral account of its criminalizability. The best we might be able to do is accept that Devlin was right to argue that everyone (communally situated) inter-subjectively shares the end of social harmony, but that everyone might also share the end of social toleration when social harmony is merely disturbed by tolerating conventionally harmless conduct that involves the fundamental liberty and equality interests of those causing the offense. For instance, homosexuality and prostitution are consensual activities between adults behind closed doors and criminalizing them would violate the offenders' privacy, equality and autonomy rights.

I argue that unexplained claims of objectivity or critical morality are not sufficient to refute Devlin's theory. Per contra, an *inter-subjectively constrained*[74] conventional morality might explain the difference between good reasons for criminalization and those that purely cater to idiosyncratic prejudice. The critical moralist does not merely aim to constrain conventional morality by subjecting it to critical scrutiny, but also claims that the end product provides a correct,

---

73 See John Tasioulas, 'Crimes of Offense,' in Andrew von Hirsch and Andrew Simester, *Incivilities: Regulating Offensive Behavior* (Oxford: Hart Publishing, 2006) at pp. 149–171.

74 If conventional morality were not constrained by inter-subjective endorsement, it would be of no use as it would provide no guidance whatsoever. But this does not mean that our conventionally situated agents are able to claim their harm or offense arguments are correct or transcultural. The best they might do is try to constrain unbridled and unprincipled conventional criminalization.

transnational or universal account of the criminalizability of certain harmful and offensive acts. These claims overlook that fact that the wrongness and badness of the acts (and consequences that flow from certain social interactions) are circumstantially and conventionally contingent. In the following sections, I outline the challenges for critical moral claims of harm and offense. I cannot see why a strong conventional account of culpable harm and offense doing is not sufficient for providing a principled account of the criminalizability of certain acts. But the latter involves accepting that very often we will get it wrong. There is no reason why deeply held conventional understandings of wrong and harm cannot be used as constraints for ensuring that criminalization decisions are principled. The core problem for lawmakers is that once they move away from accounts of harm and wrong where there is almost omnipresent social agreement about the act's harmfulness, as is the case with gross physical harms (*i.e.*, primitive harms—such as, physical starvation, blinding, wounding, and so on), the harmfulness of the conduct becomes conventionally contingent—and if we move far enough away from the harm paradigm it becomes impossible to even describe the unwanted conduct as conventionally harmful.

If we can imagine a bad consequence (unwanted conduct) dartboard, primitive harm would be the bull's eye, and as we move concentrically away from the bull's eye the harms become more conventionally contingent and ultimately the unwanted consequence is not harmful at all, but a mere flouting of some custom or social norm. The basic elements of wrongness for the purpose of criminalization are: bad act/consequence and culpability. It is conventionally understood that the union of these make an agent's actions *wrong* and ultimately criminalizable. Culpability is about telling an agent in advance, 'if you aim (or disregard an obvious risk) for a particular bad consequence then you will punished for your choice.' The bad act/consequence constraint is not too controversial when it is actual harm (or risk of harm in the case of attempts and endangerment—except that people disagree about whether offense and soft harms constitute harm—such as some privacy violations, or defrauding the wealthy) that is being presented as the bad act/action/consequence. Conventionally, there is deep agreement about the legitimacy of criminalizing wrongful harm. There might also be agreement about the need to regulate conventionally contingent wrongs such as exhibitionism, but what is clear is that a critical moral or critically objective account of the wrongness of *offending others* is vacuous.

If Hart, Feinberg and countless others want to dismiss Lord Devlin's positive morality, then they had better show why their accounts are different. Furthermore, their claim that only critical moral conceptualizations of harm and offense provide principled justifications for criminalization is nonsensical, because they have not shown why their accounts of harm and offense are critical. It is not clear how Feinberg's account of offense, or harm for that matter, is correct in a transcultural sense. I argue that conventional harms and offense as identified (inter-subjectively) by communally situated deliberators is sufficient to scrutinize criminalization decisions and to identify a principled case for criminalization. There is deep conventional agreement about the harmfulness and offensiveness of wrongs such as privacy violations; and this may be sufficient to justify criminalization in certain communities but not others.

The Vacuity of Critical Moral Accounts of Harm and Offense

What are the moral aims of the criminal law? The object and function of law generally is not too different to that of conventional morality. Mackie provides a superlative *précis* of the function of morality and its relation with law.

> Protagoras, Hobbes, Hume, and Warnock are all at least broadly in agreement about the problem that morality [and ultimately law] is needed to solve: limited resources and limited sympathies together generate both competition leading to conflict and an absence of what would be mutually beneficial cooperation.[75]

> The essential device [for creating society—cooperation] is a form of agreement which provides for its own enforcement. Each of the parties has a motive for supporting the authority who will himself have the job of punishing [or awarding private law remedies such as damages, injunctions and so forth] breaches of the agreement (and will himself have a motive for doing so). Consequently each party will have double reason for fulfilling his side of the bargain: the fear of punishment [or having to pay damages *etc.*] for breaking it, and the expectation of benefits from keeping it, because the fulfillment by the [majority] of other parties of their sides of the bargain is fairly well assured by the same motives.[76]

Whether we are talking about morality by agreement[77] or the social contract[78] more generally, there is ample empirical evidence to support the claim that society is formed by some kind of agreement;[79] and also that some individuals are not going to keep their side of the bargain in such a big web of complex agreements and inter-agreements.[80] Consequently, informal moral commands are codified into

---

75 J.L. Mackie, *Ethics: Inventing Right and Wrong* (New York: Penguin Books, 1977) at p. 111.
76 *Id.* at 109. See also David Lewis, *Convention: A Philosophical Study* (Oxford: Blackwell Publishing, 2002).
77 David Gauthier, *Morals By Agreement* (New York: Oxford University Press, 1999).
78 Thomas M. Scanlon, *What We Owe To Each Other* (Cambridge MA: Harvard University Press, 2000).
79 See generally F.J.M. Feldbrugge, *The Law's Beginnings* (Leiden: Brill Academic Publishing, 2003); A.S. Diamond, *Primitive Law: Past and Present* (London: Methuen & Co. Ltd., 1971).
80 The hard empirical evidence is documented in the national crime statistics and in the tens of thousands of judgments flowing out of the courts each year concerning private disputes.

law so that violations will be deterred with punishment or private law remedies.[81] Mackie[82] cites *game theory* in his discussion of the evolution of morality, but is careful to note that even the most advanced theory could not explain the complexity of the way in which moral principles have evolved from the process of human socialization and civilization. We benefit from aviation, telecommunications, university education, travel; that is, from property and services and the laws that are designed to regulate the fair distribution of such goods and services. It is in these areas that the law is also needed to prevent harm to others: health and safety standards and regulations against fraud and deceptive practices are designed to reduce harmful practices. Each individual has an interest in maintaining the state and its institutions, because they advance cooperative living and ultimately human flourishing. Modern accounts of morality have deprived the inter-subjective thinker of a social milieu.[83]

Raz[84] notes that law serves a number of social functions including the prevention of undesirable behavior (this is mainly achieved by enacting criminal and tort laws); the provision of facilities and mechanisms to allow private arrangements to be regulated and protected between individuals; the provision of services and the redistribution of goods; and the provision of facilities for solving unregulated disputes. Society is necessary for the advancement and well-being of humanity and it is maintained and promoted directly and indirectly by law. Laws cover many areas because of the complexity of modern living. We have criminal law, contract law, family law, trusts law, consumer protection law, tort law, environmental laws, tax laws, *etc*. Tax laws have both an indirect and direct impact, as they force individuals to hand over a portion of their income, but that income is spent on communal infrastructure, *etc*. Tax law allows revenues to be collected in a transparent way so that the public might benefit indirectly from the provision of universities, schools, roads, courts, police, welfare for the poor and so on. Providing welfare for the poor and so on reduces conflicts that might arise from extreme distribution disparities that flow from inability.[85]

Principled criminal laws should be formulated by drawing on rationally constructed principles of justice, that is, principles that have evolved from deeply held conventional understandings of justice and fairness, as is the case

---

81 A communitarian theory of criminalization might explain why it is just to punish breaches of the agreed morality, because such violations attack society/community and the secondary institutions that advance society and ultimately human flourishing and well-being.

82 Mackie, *op. cit. supra*, fn. 75 at pp. 115 *et seq.*

83 Alasdair MacIntyre, *After Virtue: A Study in Moral Theory* (Notre Dame, IN: University of Notre Dame Press, 1984); S. Shapin, *A Social History of Truth: Civility and Science in Seventeenth-Century England* (Chicago, IL: University of Chicago Press, 1994).

84 Raz, *op. cit. supra*, fn. 66 at pp. 168–179.

85 Dennis J. Baker, 'A Critical Evaluation of the Historical and Contemporary Justifications for Criminalising Begging,' (2009) 73(3) *Journal of Criminal Law* 212.

with the harm principle. Of course, accounts of harm will vary given the limits of epistemological inquiry and of human rationality. Human agents invent crimes to manage conventional conflicts that arise from communal living. Criminal law is a system of social control[86] that allows a given community to manage itself. It is used to manage genuine conflicts, but unfortunately also to criminalize conventionally harmless wrongs and to control less powerful groups in society.[87] Criminal laws that are not limited to proscribing wrongs that are harmful, or otherwise violative of the autonomy, are unprincipled. For example, the acts referred by Lord Devlin[88] are not conventionally harmful or violative of the autonomy of others, because even conventional accounts of harm and wrong cannot explain how consenting adults engaging in homosexuality and prostitution harms or violates the autonomy of others. Devlin does not run into error by suggesting that without criminalization society would disintegrate, but rather he runs into error by postulating that certain *harmless* violations of conventional norms would cause social disintegration and thus should be criminalized. There is no empirical support for his claim that activities such as homosexuality and prostitution would cause the same type of social disintegration that would transpire if wrongful harms such as murder, rape, theft, robbery, *etc.* were not criminalized.[89]

Rational deliberators should draw on the best social information available including deep conventional understandings of justice, harm, privacy, autonomy and so on, when making criminalization determinations. Criminal law's evolution has often been shaped by unjust considerations, because lawmakers were not sufficiently enlightened and rational at various stages in our history to understand the injustice of some of their decisions.[90] In the sixteenth century the masses lacked the capacity to understand that humans could not really be witches and therefore many women were criminalized for allegedly engaging in witchcraft.[91]

---

86   Donald Black, *The Behavior of Law* (New York: Academic Press, 1968) at p. 2.

87   Richard Quinney, *The Critique of Legal Order* (Boston: Little Brown, 1974) at p. 16; William Chambliss and Robert Seidmann, *Law, Order, and Power* (Reading MA: Addison-Wesley, 1982); Reiman, *The Rich Get Richer and the Poor Get Prison* (Boston: Allyn & Bacon, 4th ed. 1995) at p. 7.

88   Patrick Devlin, *The Enforcement of Morals* (Oxford: Oxford University Press, 1965).

89   The only check we have against idiosyncratic prejudice is the inter-subjective endorsement procedure, which requires idiosyncratic justifications for criminalization to be tested against the reasoned views of others, and the best empirical and historical information available. It also has to be subjected to the prevailing standards of justice.

90   Sayre notes that: 'primitive English law started from a basis bordering on absolute liability.' Francis Bowes Sayre, 'Mens Rea,' (1932) 45(6) *Harvard Law Review* 974 at p. 977. See also the idiosyncratic prejudice that Stephen, like Devlin, tried to dress up as morality. James Fitzjames Stephen, *Liberty, Equality, Fraternity*, Stuart D. Warner (eds), (Indianapolis: Liberty Fund, 1993).

91   It has been noted that: '[e]ven if an illness was explicable by medical theory, it might still be seen as originating in the evil will of another person. A distinction was made between a cause in the mechanic sense—*how* a certain person was injured—and cause in the

We no longer criminalize witchcraft as we have sufficient empirical information to be able to rationally understand that humans cannot have supernatural powers. The issue of objectivity even in the limited conventional sense is fundamental, as it can explain the wrongness[92] of actions such as genocide, murder, rape and so forth. Reason allows inter-subjective thinkers to see that the gross physical harm-doing involved in culpable genocide is objectively bad and wrong regardless of the context or circumstances. Conventionally it is understood as a gross and wanton use of human life. The same deliberator would also understand that the wrongness of exhibitionism is conventionally contingent—to ascertain its badness and ultimately its wrongness the deliberator has to also consider the underlying social norms that inform it.

Wrongness grounded in critical morality is non-invented *inherent* wrongness—that is those wrongs that are truly wrong—objectivity here is about claiming that the proposition that *x is wrong* is an absolute truth. Wrongness that is supposedly discovered as a truth (ethical wrongness grounded in moral and epistemological realism) is distinguishable from wrongness that is derived from communally situated agents inter-subjectively reflecting on evolving standards of justice. The latter is about considering how your culpable actions will impact the interests of others in certain social contexts. The union of bad act/consequence and culpability (as conventionally understood) is sufficient for establishing wrongness and thus a conventionally objective case for criminalization. The case for criminalization may not be objective in a critical moral sense, but it is be the best we can do. A communally situated moral agent can act rationally and can be a detached observer who is appraised of the principles of justice that have evolved (such as the harm principle, culpability constraint, *etc.*), and the relevant social facts and conventions; and thus can be in a position to reason and understand that certain culpable actions are wrong and worthy of punishment.

The conventional account is more constructive in criminalization ethics, as it allows the theorist, philosopher, politician, citizen to draw not only on abstract concepts such as justice, autonomy, harm, fairness, equality, humanity, *etc.*, that

---

purposive sense—*why* this person not another was injured. When people blamed witches they did it not out of mere ignorance, but because it explained why a certain misfortune had happened to them, despite all their precautions; why for example, their butter did not "come".' A.A.D.J. MacFarlane, 'Witchcraft in Tudor and Stuart Essex,' in J.S. Cockburn (ed.), *Crime in England 1550–1800* (Cambridge: Methuen & Co., 1977) at p. 83.

92   The badness and wrongness of many acts is conventionally contingent, but other acts are accepted as wrong and bad in nearly all jurisdictions. However, universal agreement very rarely extends far beyond a core set of primitive harms—harms that are biological and scientifically identifiable as bad and which impact all humans more or less in the same way. If you amputate a person's legs, she will be crippled regardless of whether she lives in Brazil or New York. In some sub-contexts, such harms may be welcomed (*i.e.*, by sadomasochists)—but I can think of no modern state where such a harm would be generally welcomed by the masses.

have been thought about and developed by thinkers for generations,[93] but also empirical information, context, convention, social practice, *etc.*, to formulate practically useful *guiding principles* for constraining unjust criminalization in competitive societies. The reflective endorsement approach is about applying the criminalization label to violations that humans can reason are wrong because of their impact on genuine human interests in organized, cooperative, coordinated, civilized societies. The constraints against unprincipled criminal law might include criteria such as harm and culpability. Critical moral accounts of harm differ in that such harms are always harms regardless of the time and context.

The most extreme claims of objectivity or normativity come from the moral realists who claim that certain actions are wrong in a mind-independent[94] way— that is, wrong regardless of whether there are humans available (including socially conditioned humans) to conceptualize their wrongness. It is nonsensical to argue that the consequences of death, physical pain or harm are bad consequences in thought-independent terms, not only for humans but also for animals, trees and all life forms on the planet. The ontological idea that the consequence of death or physical harm to a life form would in fact be bad and really would exist in strong mind-independent terms is oxymoronic because it relies on human preconceptions of the 'what if.' The bad consequences that would allegedly exist independently of human thought, such as an earthquake wiping out a species, are only bad according to a human conceptualization of bad. The realist claim is that it is not that this would not be bad without humans, but that it would exist as something different. Maybe it would have a different label, but it would be the exact same physical set of events. Furthermore, wrongness is a human construct that rests on culpability (*mens rea*)—that is, human intentions. Animals instinctually avoid harm and death. Even if humans did not exist and could not conceptualize a snake biting and killing an elephant, merely because it erroneously feared that the elephant was going to stand on it, the death of the elephant would exist. However, the snake cannot be culpable. Thus, it can harm the elephant (harm as conceptualized by humans) but it cannot wrong it, because it cannot *know* any different. Putative self-defense might justify a human acting as the snake did, but a snake does not have the capacity to comprehend wrongness and thus does not need to defend its actions. Likewise, a

---

93 See for example, John Stuart Mill, *On Liberty and Other Essays* (Oxford: Oxford University Press, 1991); and more generally D.D. Raphael, *British Moralists 1650–1800* (Oxford: Oxford University Press, 1969).

94 As Rescher puts it: 'The issue of objectivity in the sense of mind-independent is pivotal for realism. A fact is objective in this mode if it obtains thought-independently—if any change merely in what is thought by the world's intelligences would leave it unaffected. With objective facts (unlike those which are merely a matter of inter-subjective agreement) what thinkers think just does not enter—what is at issue is thought-invariant or thought-indifferent.' Nicholas Rescher, *Objectivity: The Obligations of Impersonal Reason* (Notre Dame, IN: University of Notre Dame Press, 1997) at p. 104.

volcano might harm a species by wiping out the rainforest on which it depends for food, but the earthquake does not *wrong* those creatures.

Domestic cats have a tendency not only to kill birds and mice for food, but also to torture such creatures by playing with them for many hours before eating them. In some cases, the cat will not even eat the bird or mouse but will merely use it for the fun of playing with it. When a human sees a bird/mouse being tortured as a cat plays with it, she tries to rescue the bird/mouse—especially birds because of conventional norms about birds being good and mice being vermin. The human intervener sees the cat's wanton use of its prey as bad. However, no one would consider punishing the cat, as rational humans realize that a cat does not have the reflective and rational capacities of a human being and therefore realize that the cat does not bring about the bad consequences culpably.[95] *Per contra*, when a person intentionally aims to bring about avoidable bad consequences for others it is her moral culpability and the badness of the consequences (harm for a fellow human being) that provides the lawmaker with conventional justification for criminalization. It is fair to punish those who deliberately harm others because harm-doing produces bad consequences for those who are harmed and the harm-doer *knows* that she is committing a wrong by inflicting such harm. It violates the genuine rights of the victims.

Critical morality allows the lawmaker to claim that certain acts are truly wrong, but does allow the lawmaker to explain why. Conventional morality allows the lawmaker to claim that certain acts are wrong because they contravene our conventional understandings of wrong. The even more sophisticated realist argument is that certain acts are wrong in a mind-independent sense. Science based ontology might be useful for claiming that biological harm such as blinding a human, amputating her legs, subjecting her to a lobotomy, *etc.*, is truly damaging and painful in an ontological and scientific sense and thus *bad*. But how could intentional human action (blameworthy actions—*i.e.*, actions involving culpability) be mind-independent? Surely the intentional harm-doing has to be carried out by a creature of human intelligence with a mind that is in operation for it to be willed and intended. It is our conventional conceptualization of culpability

---

95 In both the East and West, it was once normal for animals and inanimate objects to be prosecuted. Professor Evans noted long ago that: '[T]he primitive man ... like the ignorant masses of civilized communities, do not take into consideration whether objects from which they suffer injury are intelligent agents or not, but wreak their vengeance on stocks and stones and brutes, obeying only the rude instinct of revenge. The power of restraining these aboriginal propensities, and of nicely analyzing actions and studying mental conditions in order to ascertain degrees of moral responsibility, presupposes a high degree of mental development and refinement and great acuteness of psychological perception, and is, in fact, only a recent acquisition of a small minority of the human race. The vast bulk of mankind will have to pass through a long process of intellectual evolution, and rise far above their present place in the ascending scale of culture before they attain it.' Edward Payson Evans, *The Criminal Prosecution and Capital Punishment of Animals* (London: Faber and Faber, 1987) at p. 184.

(and harm) that is doing all the work in these moral theories. When a human thinks, plans, deliberates and then harms others, the willed harm could hardly be mind-independent. It can only be understood as wrong, if there is a human *knower* to grasp its wrongness. It is wrong because a creature (a human being) that has enormous intelligence, that has evolved and socialized itself for millennia,[96] is able to draw on its intellect (rational capacity), on social convention, empirical and biological facts, and conventional understandings[97] to realize the wrongness of intentionally harming others.

When conflicts or clashes arise between human agents, the same inter-subjective agents reflect to determine which party is *intentionally* (recklessly) acting unjustly—that is, committing a wrong. For instance, the idea of queuing for customer service is a convention that evolved to solve the conflict that would arise if everyone tried to be served at the same time. Likewise, the culpability constraint evolved[98] from the reflective endorsement process as it became clear that intentionally/recklessly[99] aiming to bring about *avoidable* (culpable) bad consequences for others was different to accidentally doing so. The deliberator does not have to reflect too deeply to understand that those who fail to queue without excuse or justification act at the expense of all those who have.

A conventional approach[100] acknowledges that acts are only wrong for humans if humans conceptualize them as being wrong, bad and harmful—and that for humans to do this they have to draw on social information and consider contexts. Blame and fault are conventional concepts that have evolved from human rationality—human reasoning about fairness and justice and the related institutions and social practices that have evolved as humanity has become civilized and socialized. It is unproductive to attempt to demonstrate that criminal wrongs are objectively wrong in the critical sense.[101] Moral principles such as the culpability principle are instantiated in the

---

96 Many principles of justice have evolved slowly and what seems obvious now was not even thought of in even the most advanced ancient civilizations. *Ibid.*

97 Erving Goffman, *Relations in Public, Microstudies of Public Order* (New York: Basic Books, 1971).

98 It was once normal for people to be prosecuted for any harm caused by their 'slaves, animals, other members of their household, and even by inanimate things which belonged' to them. Albert Levitt, 'The Origin of the Doctrine of Mens Rea,' (1922–1923) 17 *Illinois Law Review* 117 at p. 120. See also Frederick Pollock and Frederick William Maitland, *The History of English Law Before the Time of Edward I* (Cambridge: Cambridge University Press, Vol. II, 1923) at pp. 470–480.

99 Thomas Nagel, *The View From Nowhere* (New York: Oxford University Press, 1986) at p. 186.

100 Some commentators tend to exaggerate the objectivity provided by reason and fail to acknowledge that it is susceptible to convention and the limitations of human rationality. David Wiggins, *Needs, Values, Truth* (Oxford: Oxford University Press, 1998) at pp. 195 *et seq*; Thomas Nagel, *The Last Word* (New York: Oxford University Press, 1997).

101 Incorporating the complex question of truth into criminalization decisions does not seem to achieve anything. See generally, Richard Rorty, *Objectivity, Relativism, and*

world, but are human constructs. The culpability condition requires a mind of some kind—mind-dependence and *rationally grounded social transactions*. A cat torturing a mouse is not a rationally grounded social transaction, because cats lack rationality and operate outside our social milieu. Soldiers are rational human agents who are able to draw on principles of justice, social norms, *etc.* to engage in rational social transactions. Consequently, if a group of soldiers were to torture prisoners of war, they would be acting irrationally and would also contravene deeply held social rules about not torturing others. The soldiers have sufficient rationality and empirical information to understand the conventional implications of their actions. The soldier is able to consider the relevant social information and conventional principles of justice to identify the wrongness of torture. Principles of justice such as the harm principle, autonomy principle,[102] the culpability principle,[103] the equality principle,[104] among others, have been developed and constructed by humans, and have improved as humans have gained better insights.

Even if it is possible to determine the absolute truth of certain moral propositions about the inherent wrongness of certain crimes or the metaphysical status of offending others, there are many crimes such as exhibitionism[105] that cannot be explained as having truly bad consequences for all people at all times. I have not seen a convincing account of the truth of the proposition: *being naked in public is truly wrong in an inherent universal sense*. It is not a mere case of whether offense and disgust are properties that are instantiated in the world,[106] but whether exhibitionism does in fact produce an inherently bad consequence. Socialization seems to provide the better explanation of the disgust causing properties of public nudity. There is nothing inherently wrong with the nudist using a public beach (100 years ago wearing a modern bikini in public would have been the equivalent of

---

Truth: Philosophical Papers (Cambridge: Cambridge University Press, Vol. I, 1991). See also Richard Joyce, *The Myth of Morality* (New York: Cambridge University Press, 2001).

102   J.B. Schneewind, *The Invention of Autonomy* (Cambridge: Cambridge University Press, 1998).

103   Rollin M. Perkins, 'A Rationale of Mens Rea,' (1939) 52(6) *Harvard Law Review* 905.

104   W.T. Blackstone, 'On the Meaning and Justification of the Equality Principle,' (1967) 77(4) *Ethics* 239.

105   Nagel, one of the staunchest defenders of moral realism, has argued that exhibitionism is only wrongful in a conventional sense. See Thomas Nagel, 'Concealment and Exposure,' (1998) 27(1) *Philosophy & Public Affairs* 3.

106   Husak recently attempted to ascertain the metaphysical status of offense—whether the property of offense really exists. Husak was unable to demonstrate that offense really exists and concluded that '[m]any theorists appear to believe that disgust realism is not needed to justify legal intervention; ... in the end it is necessary to examine empirical data about our disgust mechanisms.' Douglas Husak, 'Disgust: Metaphysical and Empirical Speculations,' in von Hirsch and Simester, *op. cit. supra*, fn. 73 at pp. 110–111. See also Aurel Kolnai, 'The Standard Modes of Aversion: Fear, Disgust and Hatred,' (1998) 107 *Mind* 581.

being nude today, and 100 years from now nudity might be the norm on beaches—this is ignoring the health issues related to skin cancer which might send the trend the other way). Nevertheless, as I point out below, we might regulate public nudity for the sake of solving cooperation problems concerning the ethical use of public spaces in complex plural societies. The conventional approach would allow the conventional implications to be considered, whereas critical moral standards do not. Critical moral accounts of badness of *offending others* (such as that provided by Feinberg) have failed to demonstrate the inherent wrongness of public nudity, because outside of human thought, socialization, context and convention it does not produce a bad consequence and is not absolutely wrong in a universal sense.[107]

It is not only the wrongness of offensive acts that is conventionally contingent, since genuine harms are also conventional. For instance, if x were to paint a yellow stripe across the Mona Lisa, his conduct would be classified as criminal (harm) damage,[108] but unless we consider the underlying social norms it is not possible to comprehend the wrongness, badness or harmfulness of intentionally painting an additional feature on an old painting. Let us assume that x is a private collector, so conventional property rights are not violated. If x owns the painting then surely x is entitled to destroy it. Some might argue that the additional paintwork is further art and adds dimension to the original artwork. It certainly does not diminish the owner's essential or *primitive-type* survival resources in the way that destroying a remote tribe's only source of water and food would.[109] The objective wrongness of conventional harms and offenses can only be ascertained by considering contextual, circumstantial, social and empirical factors. Therefore, the objectivity of this type of harm is conventional and thus is subject to all the inconsistencies and biases that affect the reasoning of inter-subjective agents communally situated. Remember my communally situated agents do not have the supernatural capacity envisaged by Nagel, Kant or Korsgaard. They are just socialized humans drawing on societal

---

107 '[D]isgust and nausea, we can plausibly suppose, are self-contained psychological items, conceptualizable without any need to appeal to any projected properties of disgustingness or nauseatingness … The question, now, is this: if, in connection with some range of concepts whose application engages distinctive aspects of our subjective make-up in the sort of way that seems characteristic of evaluative concepts, we reject the kind of realism that construes subjective responses as perceptions of associated features of reality and does no work towards earning truth, are we entitled to assume that the responses enjoy this kind of explanatory priority, as projectivism seems to require.' John McDowell, *Mind Value and Reality* (Cambridge MA: Harvard University Press, 1998) at p. 157.

108 This would be an offense under the *Criminal Damage Act 1971*.

109 Economic harm is shaped significantly by conventional ideas of ownership. Unlike pain, torture, death, amputation, rape and so forth, the harmfulness of theft, property damage, and embezzlement varies from culture to culture depending on whether the culture has a communal or individual conceptualization of property ownership, or whether it even recognizes property. In the most primitive sense, harm to essential resources such as shelter, food and water supplies could be described as harmful in a universal sense as it would impact all humans biologically in the same way.

practices to try and work out what conventional values should be protected through criminalization. In this sense, it is necessary to understand conduct in light of the social norms that inform it.[110]

Similarly, if a person takes a coin and scratches the paintwork on another person's new Rolls-Royce, the car owner has been harmed in a conventional sense. However, if it is a case of a minor scratch it seems that the car owner has only been offended (rather than harmed), because she has been socialized and trained to enjoy the aesthetics[111] of motorcars with perfect paintwork. The scratch, if shallow, would not need to be repaired as the car would not rust, nor would it affect the car's usability. The reality in modern complex societies is that many genuine harms and offensive wrongs can only be understood by considering the underlying social norms, as bad acts/consequences have a substantial man-made element—these bad consequences occur as a result of the complex way in which we have socialized ourselves and because we agree to have our freedom constrained in certain social contexts in order to achieve the levels of cooperation that are essential for society, community, and civilization to function and exist.

In what follows, I will outline the vacuity of Feinberg's claim that culpable 'offense doing' provides a critical moral justification for criminalization. The harm principle is less problematic, because there is deep conventional agreement not only about the most primitive harms, but also about many non-primitive harms such as destroying cultural artifacts like the Mona Lisa.[112] The core issue in the harm principle context will be to ensure the harm is genuine and that the criminal law is a proportionate legislative response. I think the offense principle is much more controversial, as it is not clear that preventing offense *per se* is needed to promote human flourishing or that it solves conflicts that need to be solved by the criminal law. I also examine whether Feinberg's offense justification for criminalization can be distinguished from Devlin's. I set the scene by briefly discussing the conventionally contingent nature of harm.

---

110 Gordon P. Baker and Peter M.S. Hacker, *Language, Sense and Nonsense: A Critical Investigation into Modern Theories of Language* (Oxford: Basil Blackwell, 1984) at pp. 257–258.

111 Here, objective agreement might be impossible. For instance, in *R. v. Gibson* [1991] 1 All E.R. 649, the defendant was convicted for outraging public decency by displaying earrings made out of human fetuses in an art gallery. Interestingly, I subjectively cannot see the art in such a display. Likewise, many Westerners would like to have a Caravaggio hanging in their drawing room, but might not want decorated skulls from New Guinea hanging in their drawing room. Social conditioning obviously affects tastes in a fundamental way. See generally, Frances Berenson, 'Understanding Art and Understanding Persons,' in S.C. Brown (ed.), *Objectivity and Cultural Divergence* (Cambridge: Cambridge University Press, 1984).

112 Mackie rightly notes that the aim of morality is to advance the human cause. See Mackie, *op. cit. supra*, fn. 75 at pp. 169–199.

Conventionally Contingent Harms

Wrongs emerged naturally as society became more complex and as more intricate cooperation problems arose. Experience taught people that it was necessary and good to avoid harms and other bad consequences, especially those of the *avoidable* (culpable) kind. Let us consider conventional harms in light of Feinberg's harm principle. Feinberg[113] expounds harm in three senses: (i) harm as damage, (ii) harm as a setback to interests, and (iii) harm as wrongdoing. Harm as used in Feinberg's formulation of the harm principle is an amalgamation of senses (ii) and (iii). Harm must be caused by *wrongful* (culpable) conduct to be a candidate for criminalization. Harm occurs under the harm principle when x's interests are set back by the wrongful conduct of y.[114] The concept of harm as used by Feinberg represents 'the overlap of senses two and three: only setbacks of interests that are wrongs, and wrongs that are setbacks to interests, are to count as harms in the appropriate sense.'[115] The term interest when used in this way refers to a stake that a person has in his or her well-being. According to Feinberg, one's interests taken as a whole consist of all those things that one has a stake in. In the singular, one's personal interest 'consists in the harmonious advancement of all one's interests in the plural.'[116] These interests, or as Feinberg puts it, 'the *things* these interests are in, are distinguishable components of a person's well-being: s/he flourishes or languishes as they flourish or languish.'[117]

Feinberg explains the badness of harm-doing by referring to a trichotomy of interests including welfare interests and those security and accumulative interests that cushion our welfare interests.[118] Welfare interests are at the core of Feinberg's scheme. They are interests of a kind shared by almost everyone 'in the necessary means to [their] more ultimate goals, whatever the latter may be, or later may come to be.'[119] Welfare interests include our interest in prolonging the continuance of our life for a foreseeable period of time, preserving our physical health and security, maintaining minimum intellectual acuity and emotional stability, being able to engage in social intercourse and to benefit from friendships, sustaining minimum financial security, sustaining reasonable living conditions, avoiding pain and grotesque disfigurement, preventing unjustified anxieties and resentments (intimidation), and to be free from unwarranted coercion.[120] They are those interests in goods and conditions that we all need independent of our individual

---

113   Feinberg, Vol. I, *op. cit. supra*, fn. 1 at p. 215.
114   *Id.* at pp. 33–34.
115   *Id.* at p. 36.
116   *Id.* at p. 34.
117   *Ibid.*
118   *Id.* at pp. 37, 207.
119   *Id.* at p. 37.
120   *Ibid.*

life plans. Everyone has a necessary stake in these kinds of interests, as they are the requisites of our well-being.[121]

Feinberg distinguishes important welfare interests from those interests that merely concern a person's more ulterior aims.[122] Our ulterior aims might include the goal to own a dream house, to have a prominent career as a movie star or as a politician, *etc*.[123] A person's more ultimate goals and wants (*e.g.*, building a dream house, gaining a political or professional position, solving some vital scientific question, raising a family, achieving spiritual grace, *etc*.) are not directly protected by the law.[124] 'If I have an interest in making an important scientific discovery, creating valuable works of art, or other personal achievements, the law will protect those aspirations by guarding my welfare interests that are essential to it. But given that I have my life, health, economic adequacy, liberty, and security, there is nothing more that the law (or anyone else, for that matter) can do for me; the rest is entirely up to me.'[125]

Ulterior interests that extend elements of welfare beyond minimal levels are also protected, however.[126] The law against burglary not only protects the welfare of the indigent person who might face starvation if burgled, but it also protects the billionaire whose welfare might not be directly affected by the theft of a Caravaggio painting that she had forgotten she owned.[127] Even though certain types of harm only have a trivial impact on the interests of certain individuals, they can have an accumulative impact. Hence, it is not only the ulterior interests of billionaires that are protected, 'but also their interests in liberty (the interest in being the person who decides how the accumulated funds are to be spent) and security (even his welfare interests might be threatened by the act that invades

---

121   *Ibid.*

122   *Ibid.*

123   'But in respect at least to welfare interests, we are inclined to say that what promotes them is good for the person in any case, whatever his beliefs or wants may be ... [T]here may be correspondence between interest and want, but the existence of the former is not dependent upon, nor derivative from, the existence of the latter.' *Id*. at p. 42.

124   *Id*. at p. 62.

125   'In my highest pecuniary accumulation as such, or in such uses of wealth as the purchase of a yacht or a dream house, the law can protect that interest indirectly by protecting me from burglary and fraud, but it cannot protect me from bad investment advice, personal imprudence, the unpredictable dependencies of others, the lack of personal diligence or ingenuity, and so on.' *Ibid.*

126   '[U]lterior interests are only indirectly invadable. The usual way of harming one of another person's ulterior interests is by invading one of the welfare interests whose maintenance at a minimal level is a necessary condition for the advancement of any other interests at all ... At least one class of ulterior interests are directly vulnerable: those that consist of the extension of welfare interests to transminimal levels. The rich man is wronged by indefensible acts of theft just as much as the poor man is, though he will not be harmed as much.' *Id*. at p. 112.

127   *Id*. at p. 63.

his financial interest, especially if the invasive act employs force or coercion, or seems likely to be frequently repeated).'[128] Coupled with this, even minor setbacks to the financial interests of others 'threaten ... the general security of property, and the orderliness and predictability of financial affairs in which everyone has an interest, however small.'[129] Those security interests that cushion our welfare interests are protectable.[130] For instance, common assaults are criminalized to protect our elementary sense of security.[131] In a similar vein, our accumulative interests are those non-essential interests that we have in the various good things in life.[132] The theft of a billionaire's yacht or Caravaggio would not necessarily deprive her of her livelihood or of her margin of security above the minimum, but it would invade her accumulative resources.[133] If left unchecked, it would also destabilize the entire property system in which we all have an interest.

Feinberg distinguishes mere wants from cognizable interests. It would be implausible to classify strong wants as interests. For example, Lucy, a devoted fan of the Yankees, might have a fervent desire to see the Yankees win, but that alone would hardly ground a case for claiming an interest in a Yankees victory.[134] Feinberg argues that:[135] 'Some of our most intense desires then are not of the appropriate kind to ground ulterior interests since (like a sudden craving for an ice cream cone) they are unlinked to our longer range purposes, or they are insufficiently stable and durable to represent any investment of a stake.' The harm principle is a measure that helps protect personal autonomy.[136] A person is harmed when his or her opportunities for enjoying or pursuing the good life are thwarted or diminished.[137] Harm occurs when a person's personal or proprietary resources are impaired, because our resources are needed to enable us to realize our other opportunities.[138]

---

128   Ibid.
129   Ibid. In this sense, Feinberg seems to have social cooperation in mind.
130   Id. at p. 207.
131   'Beyond the bare minimum of health and economic well-being required to pursue his aims, a person requires a certain additional safety margin. Without that margin, that person may be able to function, but only barely so—and with much reason for apprehension.' Andrew von Hirsch, 'Injury and Exasperation: An Examination of Harm to Others and Offense to Others,' (1985–1986) 84 Michigan Law Review 700 at p. 703.
132   Ibid.
133   Id. at p. 704.
134   Feinberg, Vol. I, op. cit. supra, fn. 1 at p. 42.
135   Id. at p. 43.
136   'Such a rationale explains why a minimum of political liberty is a welfare interest. It is not that one cannot subsist without liberty. It is instead, that one cannot formulate, select, and pursue one's own purposes where there is excessive outside interference with one's choices, associations, and expressions': von Hirsch, op. cit. supra, fn. 131 at p. 705.
137   Simester and von Hirsch, op. cit. supra, fn. 38 at p. 281.
138   Ibid.

Feinberg's formulation of the harm principle has its problems, but it generally provides a fairly convincing account of the wrongness of certain harms both in the primitive and conventional sense. If we return to the example of x lightly scratching the paintwork on y's Rolls-Royce, we can see that the bad consequence is conventionally constructed, it does not *necessarily* damage y's livelihood—nor does it *automatically* impact y's accumulative interests, which would ultimately affect the orderliness and predictability of financial affairs in which we all have an interest. It only impacts y's accumulative interests because she has been socialized to perceive the scratch on her car's original paintwork as an act of vandalism. It is the way in which y has been socialized that causes her to be offended by the aesthetics of the altered paintwork. Y is wronged, however, because x interfered with her autonomy (freedom of choice) by scratching her car without consent; and the wrong stands even though y's resentment hinges on the fact that she has been socialized to dislike the car's altered appearance. She feels compelled to use her accumulated resources to have it restored to its original condition and thus gain control over how her property will be used. This type of harm is not universally harmful in objective terms—and certainly not in a realist sense. In most modern contexts, a car is not a necessity. Coupled with this, y's car is still fully functional. Her accumulated resources have not necessarily been diminished (her overall livelihood—in the primitive sense, basic food, shelter, physical security, *etc.*),[139] because she can still gain full use from her car regardless of its altered paintwork. Feinberg draws on conventional property rights and argues that one should have the right to protect accumulated resources, even if those resources are unearned (as might be the case with celebrities who are often paid way beyond what a person could possibly earn using the labor and skill of a single human) because this is harmful in a normative sense. I think the protection of unearned wealth and excessive wealth surely has to rest on conventional notions of property rights.

Let us return to our example; because of y's socialization she will feel compelled to have the paintwork on her Rolls restored to its original form. In doing this she is asserting her right to decide how her property will be used. She will be harmed to the extent that she will have to draw on her accumulated resources to restore the car. Conventionally, it is arguable that it would be impossible for many people to live together cooperatively and seek the benefit of cooperative living without also accepting reasonable compromises. A person is expected to accept a compromise to her freedom, when exercising her freedom has avoidable (unjustifiable/ inexcusable) bad consequences for others, even if those bad consequences are conventionally contingent. People queue when they are waiting to be served at the grocers or bank, as this compromise allows each queue member to benefit from a fair distribution of the burdens and benefits that arise from cooperative living. The

---

139 Arguably, the right to accumulate resources well beyond what is needed to survive in modern societies is an extension of the primitive idea of accumulating to safeguard one's chances of survival during hard times (drought, floods, *etc.*).

criminal law is used in more serious cases to coerce[140] those who are unwilling to accept reasonable compromises. If everyone were allowed to scratch the cars of others, this would unnecessarily threaten the general cooperative system of living (community/society) in which everyone has an interest. By scratching the car, x does not act in a way that is acceptable to rational agents who are trying to work together in a co-operative system.[141] Communally situated agents would outlaw this type of conduct, because the goal of respecting property rights is sharable by them all.

Criminalization in this context is designed to facilitate a fair distribution of the benefits and burdens that arise from cooperative communal living. The harm-doer is not asked to accept an unreasonable compromise to her freedom, as the freedom to *wantonly* invade the property rights of others is not a fundamental freedom and is thus an avoidable violation of the freedom of others. The underlying social norms play a significant role in explaining why a person might feel compelled to maintain the appearance of a motorcar and thereby suffer a setback to her accumulated resources in order to restore her property.

The Conventional Badness of Offending Others

The conventional contingency of badness and ultimately wrongness is even more evident in the case of offense to others,[142] as its badness varies depending on the conventions adopted by the given community. Feinberg asserts that:[143] 'It is always a good reason in support of a proposed criminal prohibition that it is probably necessary to prevent serious offense to persons other than the actor and would probably be an effective means to that end if enacted.' Feinberg argues that a separate offense principle is needed because ephemeral annoyances, disappointments, disgusts, embarrassments, and detested conditions, such as fear, anxiety, and trifling (harmless) aches and pains do not necessarily result in harm. Some offensive encroachments (interferences) might set back our interests and thus come within the purview of the harm principle, but most forms of offense do not result in harm. Even gross offenses such as public displays of earrings made from human fetuses,[144] vomit eating in front of others in the confines of a public

---

140 More generally, Max Weber, *Law in Economy and Society*, Max Rheinstein (ed.), trans. Edward Shils and Max Rheinstein (Cambridge, MA: Harvard University Press, 1954).

141 Cf. the procedural realism presented by Korsgaard in Christine M. Korsgaard, *The Sources of Normativity* (Cambridge: Cambridge University Press, 1996) at pp. 131–166.

142 Like Feinberg, I assert that there is a conceptual distinction between offending others and harming others, but I think this distinction can be made in objective terms by drawing on our deep conventional understandings of harm and offense.

143 Feinberg, Vol. II, *op. cit. supra*, fn. 1 at p. 1.

144 *R. v. Gibson* [1991] 1 All E.R. 649.

bus, copulating in public spaces and so forth do not amount to harm. Since, '[harm] even in the broad un-technical sense rules out mere transitory disappointments, minor physical and mental "hurts", and a miscellany of disliked states of mind, including various forms of offendedness, anxiety, and boredom as harms, since harm in the broad sense is any setback of an interest, and there is (typically) no interest in the avoidance of such states.'[145] Feinberg uses the concept of culpable offense to provide a critical moral reason for criminalizing those harmless but offensive acts that are 'offenses proper (*e.g.*, revulsion and disgust) hurts (*e.g.*, "harmless" throbs and pangs), and "others" (*e.g.*, shame and embarrassment).'[146]

We need to examine two questions: (1) what makes offending others wrong; and (2) what are the criminalizable *bad* consequences of this type of wrongdoing? Offense is assessed almost entirely in accordance with community mores, which differ from community to community, from generation to generation. For example, public nudity is not universally offensive. In many African and tropical regions it is common for the tribespeople to go unclothed. Public nudity is also common on many European beaches. Similarly, a tramp swearing at another tramp in the Bronx would not have the same social meaning as a philosophy student swearing at a professor in the corridor of the Princeton philosophy department. The sight of two men or women kissing in public might cause profound affront in some parts of Russia, the Middle East or even in some parts of the United States,[147] but might go unnoticed in London, New York or Stockholm. Offense is predominantly a subjective sensation, some forms of communication will offend the old but not the young, some forms of communication will offend women but not men and some displays will offend Christians but not atheists, and vice versa.

What makes disgust objectively wrong? Underlying the wrongdoing involved in some forms of offense doing stands the idea of disrespect. Respect in its non-Kantian formulation would provide neutral reasons for tolerance and compromise. 'Respect people's sensibilities about the appropriate and acceptable appearance of fellow humans by conforming to established rules of proper modesty.'[148] Simester and von Hirsch,[149] drawing on the idea of respect and consideration for others, argue that the wrongness (and according to them, criminalizableness) of offensive behavior can be explained in terms of disrespectfulness and inconsiderateness. They argue that everyone has a right to be treated with a minimum degree of respect and consideration as self-determined morally responsible human beings. According to their analysis, certain offensive acts are impermissible because they treat others with a gross lack of respect and consideration as autonomous choosing agents. 'The wrongdoing requirement calls upon the proponent of criminalization to put forward reasons why the conduct is wrong—namely, under our proposed account, why the

---

145 Feinberg, Vol. I, *op. cit. supra*, fn. 1 at p. 48.
146 Feinberg, Vol. II, *op. cit. supra*, fn. 1 at p. 1.
147 *Lawrence v. Texas*, 539 U.S. 558 (2003).
148 Rescher, *op. cit. supra*, fn. 94 at p. 143.
149 Simester and von Hirsch, *op. cit. supra*, fn. 38 at p. 291.

conduct treats others with a gross lack of consideration or respect.'[150] However, von Hirsch and Simester provide a conventional case for criminalizing certain offensive acts. They refer to particular bad consequences such as insults, inverse-privacy and anonymity losses, rather than offense *per se*, to explain disrespect and inconsideration. I think a better approach would have been for them to test the boundaries of privacy violations as a *conventional* bad act/consequence and to argue that the union of this bad act with culpability equals wrongness.

Von Hirsch and Simester[151] postulate that the criminalizableness of exhibitionism might be drawn from:

> Nagel's conception of 'reticence', regarding obligations of mutual restraint concerning a person's private (and especially their intimate sphere). Notions of reticence include an entitlement to privacy—to exclude others from one's personal domain. But the obverse should also obtain: we are entitled not to be involuntarily included in the personal domain of others—particularly, to be spared certain intimate revelations. It is the wrongfulness of that involuntary inclusion that, arguably, makes exhibitionism a matter of treating others without consideration.

Does the bad consequence of having your privacy violated provide a principled justification for invoking the criminal law? There are deep conventional understandings concerning privacy in Western society and there is no doubt that gross privacy violations can have *bad* consequences for those affected. If a man films up a lady's skirt and thereafter posts the images on the Internet, it is not difficult to envisage the conventionally bad result that this will have for the victim. Any psychological distress would depend on the way the victim has been socialized to feel shame, as she would not complain if someone took a photo of her face. However, this type of conventionally contingent bad consequence is real and should be criminalized because it is violative of the victim's freedom; and the defendant has no great liberty interest in filming up the skirts of others. The issue becomes considerably more complex, however, when we move the focus onto encroachments—that is situations where people force others to receive their personal information in public contexts, as may be the case with the exhibitionist.

Let us consider the idea of privacy as a conventional justification for invoking the criminal law. Privacy as defined by Gavison involves three independent components: 'in perfect privacy no one has any information about X, no one pays attention to X, and no one has physical access to X.' A loss of privacy can result from people obtaining information about another, or paying attention to her, or gaining

---

150   Von Hirsch and Simester, 'Penalizing Offensive Behavior: Constitutive and Mediating Principles,' in von Hirsch and Simester, *op. cit. supra*, fn. 73 at p. 120. However, von Hirsch and Simester are well aware of the important role that convention must play.
151   Ibid.

access to her. These elements of secrecy, anonymity, and solitude are interrelated and all form a part of the complex fabric of the concept of privacy. A person would suffer a proximity and anonymity loss when an uninvited stranger sits at her table in a restaurant or sits next to her on the train even though the carriage is full of empty seats. In this sense we are referring to physical access (physical proximity). This means physical proximity in the sense of a person gaining the sort of access that would allow her to get close enough to touch or observe the captive viewer through the normal uses of her senses.

Gavison[152] provides a number of examples to demonstrate how certain privacy losses can be understood in terms of physical access. For example, if a stranger gains entrance to a woman's home on false pretences in order to watch her giving birth it is the proximity violation that causes the loss of privacy. Similarly, if a stranger 'chooses to sit on "our" bench, even though the park is full of empty benches' it is the proximity violation (physical access) that causes the loss of privacy in this context. In both of these cases 'the essence of the complaint is not that more information about us has been acquired or that more attention has been drawn to us, but that our spatial aloneness has been diminished.'[153] The context and underlying social norms are important. A person would not violate another's privacy by standing right next to her in a crowded train. Two people may be forced to sit next to each other on a crowded train, but they do not violate the other's territory, as they have a conventional understanding about the right to sit near each other in this context. It is the norm for people to use the shared space in a public train. If the train is totally crowded then people are expected to sit and stand closely together. The passengers expect this from experience. A person does not subject a fellow passenger to unwanted attention simply by sitting next to her.

I now want to turn my attention to the second and third types of privacy losses referred to by Gavison—that is: 'no one pays attention to x, and no one has physical access to x.' What are the bad consequences of exhibitionism? I have in mind the copulating couple in Feinberg's[154] hypothetical public bus. People have a right to be able to copulate, but should members of the public be forced to see the intimate details of the couple's copulation in a public place. If a couple copulate in Harvard Square, the non-consenting passers-by might have a right to be let alone and not to receive this kind of intimate information. Unwanted information, such

---

152 Ruth Gavison, 'Privacy and the Limits of Law,' (1980) 89(3) *Yale Law Journal* 421 at p. 428.
153 *Ibid*.
154 Feinberg, Vol. II, *op. cit. supra*, fn. 1 at pp. 10–13.

as nude displays, are obtrusions into domains.[155] Goffman[156] notes that wrongful encroachments can come about either through an intrusion or an obtrusion. X might intrude into y's physical space by taking y's private information or entering y's private home; or even by getting too close to y in a public park. Meanwhile, a wrongful obtrusion comes about when 'an individual makes what are taken as *over-extensive* claims to personal space of those adjacent to him or her on areas felt to be public in the sense of being non-claimable.'[157] For instance, if x were to plug a speaker into her iPod and play music at full volume while riding in a public bus, she would disturb the comfort of those who want silence or a reasonably minimum level of noise.

In *The Territories of the Self*,[158] Goffman defines a territory as a 'field of things' or a 'preserve,' which individuals have *claims* over. In the situational sense the individual would have an entitlement to control, use or possess the demarcated territory. In the egocentric sense there are 'preserves which move around with the claimant, he being in the centre.'[159] Territories are not determined by objective factors, but rather the determiners are contextual. Their contours have a socially determined variability and are defined according to such 'factors as local population density, purpose of the approacher, fixed seating equipment, character of the social occasion and so forth.'[160] Goffman's territories of self are defined by contextual and conventional factors rather than by objective criteria. Accordingly, he defines personal space as the 'space surrounding an individual, and where within which an entering other causes the individual to feel encroached upon, leading him to show displeasure and sometimes to withdraw.'[161] The contours of personal space are generally determined according to social norms,[162] so whether there is an objective violation of privacy depends on context and convention. For example, if a person is the only passenger in the train wagon and someone sits next to her, she might find this invasive. If the person who sits next to her is of the opposite sex, this might add dimension to her concern and discomfiture.[163] This sort of harassment has the potential to violate the train passenger's right to be let alone and remain anonymous. Likewise, if a man goes to an almost empty beach and sits within a foot of a young woman, his propinquity would violate her right to be let alone. He

---

155   Gavison rightly asserts that: 'a number of situations sometimes said to constitute invasions of privacy will be seen not to involve losses of privacy per se ... These include exposure to unpleasant noises, smells, and sights ... insulting, harassing, or persecuting behavior, presenting people in a "false light"; unsolicited mail and unwanted phone calls' and so on. Gavison, *op. cit. supra*, fn. 152 at p. 436.
156   Goffman, *op. cit. supra*, fn. 97 at pp. 50–51.
157   *Id.* at p. 51.
158   *Id.* at p. 29.
159   *Ibid.*
160   *Id.* at p. 31.
161   *Id.* at pp. 31–33.
162   *Ibid.*
163   *Id.* at p. 31.

is in her private domain—her territory. This would be an unjustifiable invasion of her personal space, which she has a claim over.

Egocentrically, a person's personal space moves around with her, '[she] being in the centre.'[164] She is entitled to exclude others from her territory. If the beach was absolutely packed, then keeping a distance of a foot might go unnoticed, as he is merely asking her to share the public beach, which is a permissible demand. Beach-goers consent to the crowding by making the decision to use the crowded beach and they share the common end of using the beach for recreational purposes. Goffman notes that: 'on the issue of will and self-determination turns the whole possibility of using territories of the self in a dual way, with comings-into-touch avoided as a means of maintaining respect and engaged in as a means of establishing regard. And on this duality rest the possibility of according meaning to territorial events and the practicality of doing so. It is no wonder that felt self-determination is crucial to one's sense of what it means to be a fully-fledged person.'[165] The conventional badness of an inverse-privacy violation can be understood as an autonomy violation. The privacy (and autonomy) violation is *objectively* bad to the extent that Western society values privacy and space. It is arguable that we all have an interest in maintaining a minimum degree of privacy, given the conventional and socialized makeup of moral agents in complex plural societies.

It is arguable that unreasonable autonomy losses occur when the wrongdoer's private (non-public) information is forced upon non-consenting spectators in the public domain. The bad consequence of exhibitionism is simply that the witness is denied the opportunity to choose whether to receive very intimate information: the opportunity to avoid being included in the exhibitionist's private domain. The unwanted information could be obtrusive without necessarily having an obscene or indecent content, for example, if a person plays an iPod in the confines of a public bus at its highest volume, she forces her way into the personal domains of the other passengers.[166] The loud decibels resonating from the iPod in the public bus would restrict the choices of the other passengers by preventing them from choosing between loud music and silence, or between the loud music and conversation with other passengers as features of their immediate ends. Feinberg[167] argues that: 'In being made to experience and to be occupied in certain ways by outsiders, and having had no choice in the matter whatever, the captive passengers suffer a violation of their autonomy.'

However, because the unwanted consequence is of a trivial nature any criminal regulation should be enforced with fines rather than jail terms. The justification for criminalizing this type of wrongdoing has nothing to do with critical morality. Even the conventional case for criminalization is exceptionally weak. There is no deep agreement about the need to limit offensive behavior in public places or about what

---

164 *Ibid.*
165 *Id.* at pp. 60–64.
166 Von Hirsch and Simester, *op. cit. supra*, fn. 73 at p. 125.
167 Feinberg, Vol. II, *op. cit. supra*, fn. 1 at p. 23.

is offensive. Certainly, many people would not be concerned about exhibitionism in open public places such as nude beaches and parks. If a person goes to a nude beach, she consents to what she might see. Von Hirsch and Simester[168] argue that if the offense is readily avoidable then it should not be criminalized. Certain types of offensive conduct violate the autonomy and privacy rights of non-consenting audiences in public places, so they are subject to a ready avoidability requirement, that is, such activities will be criminalized when others are not able to readily avoid them without unwarranted restriction of their own liberty.[169]

Similarly, a loose conventional argument for criminalizing traditional privacy violations might go as follows. Because of social conditioning, citizens living in Western societies have deep feelings about privacy. Revealing another person's very intimate information could cause them grave distress because of their social beliefs and the shaming norms in our society. People are made to feel ashamed of certain things and therefore require privacy. Privacy violations are clearly only bad in a conventionally contingent sense, but may cause genuine psychological distress. Modern technology has made it particularly easy to access and distribute private information via the Internet. In some cases, computer repairmen have discovered very private information (obscene images) on computers belonging to their celebrity customers and have uploaded the information onto the Internet without the customer's consent.[170] In these cases the privacy violation is grave enough to result in conventionally contingent harm. In perfect privacy no one has any information about the non-consenting party. But there is no such thing as perfect privacy. We all give up some privacy by entering the public domain to do our daily business: entering the public domain means public surveillance. But we have deep conventional understandings about privacy and a person is entitled to keep certain *intimate* information private regardless of whether she is a public figure or not.

When a person uploads obscene images of non-consenting adults onto the Internet, she causes a grave loss of privacy. This type of direct privacy violation could come within the purview of the criminal law when the material is of an exceptionally private and intimate nature. But the material would have to be *exceptionally intimate* in those cases involving public figures, because they gain benefits from public prominence and must expect more public scrutiny than the average citizen. If a person puts herself in the public spotlight, then she has to expect a much greater degree of media scrutiny than non-celebrities receive. But there are limits. Culpably distributing photos and movies of celebrities or of ex-partners copulating without their consent is *prima facie* criminalizable, because

---

168   Von Hirsch and Simester, *op. cit. supra*, fn. 73.
169   *Id.* at pp. 124–130.
170   See for example the recent scandal in Hong Kong, where obscene photos of celebrities were taken from a star's computer that had been sent for repair. The photos were subsequently uploaded onto the World Wide Web. Keith Bradsher, *Internet Sex Video Case Stirs Free-Speech Issues in Hong Kong* (New York: *New York Times*, February 13, 2008).

it has bad consequences for the non-consenting parties. Trivial or moderate privacy violations should not be criminalized, as the civil law provides adequate remedies.[171]

There are limitations on the types of information that can be disclosed without consent. When a person distributes private images of a celebrity (or of anyone) that is of an obscene nature, the public has no interest in seeing it, and the non-consenting party is entitled to have his or her privacy protected by use of the criminal law. It is one thing to report that a public figure is having a love affair, but it would be something entirely different to publish private *images* of that person having actual intercourse or of that person in the nude. Modern technology makes it so easy to (covertly or otherwise) film, record, photograph and circulate such materials, so the criminal law seems the most effective way to protect privacy in such cases. It would not be reasonable to expect the affected party to take proceedings on her own responsibility to put a stop to it. However, since freedom of expression is such a cardinal value, the criminal law should only be used to protect the most sensitive information, that is, information of a visually obscene or indecent kind. The criminal law protection of privacy cannot be extended to other forms of intimate information (*i.e.*, written or oral mention of the sensitive information, *etc.*) involving celebrities, because this would be too great a restriction on freedom of expression and too great an extension of the criminal law. Mere verbal or written mention (or non-obscene images) of a celebrity love affair would not be enough to justify invoking the criminal law.

Similarly, tacit consent will be sufficient to waive the right to privacy. If a celebrity (or anyone else for that matter) goes to a public nude beach, then he or she makes her intimate information public. If the paparazzi takes photos or movies of the display and distributes it to the tabloids, then the affected party cannot claim her privacy has been violated because she has made the information public by presenting it in the public domain. There is, however, a distinction between public and quasi-public places. If a journalist or photographer gains access to a locker room and takes a photo of a famous actor or footballer in the nude, she could hardly claim that the victim tacitly consented to his intimate information being made public.[172] Where a celebrity intentionally or indifferently exposes her posterior in public, then she could hardly complain about a loss of privacy.[173]

---

171 See *Douglas & Ors. v. Hello! Ltd & Ors.* [2003] EWHC 786. Cf. *Ettingshausen v. ACP* (1993) A. Def. R. [51,065] SC (N.S.W.) where the violation clearly could have been criminalized.

172 See *Ettingshausen v. ACP* (1993) A. Def. R. [51,065] SC (N.S.W.), where a photo that had been taken in a communal locker room, of a famous footballer in the nude, was published in a magazine. The non-consenting footballer successfully sued for civil damages.

173 See Robert Stansfield, '*Britney's VPL*' (London: *The Daily Mirror*, 4 December 2006), noting that Britney Spears got out of a car in a public place without any underwear thereby exposing (either recklessly or accidentally) her person.

Principled Criminalization and Conventionally Contingent Wrongs

Given that the objective badness of privacy losses is conventional, is it possible to build a principled case for criminalizing such wrongs. People in remote parts of Africa and Papua New Guinea have been socialized not to value privacy nor to perceive public nudity as intimate and unwanted information. Unlike the bad consequence of harm to others (basically an uncontested bad consequence in the primitive sense of harm), there is much less agreement about the badness of many forms of privacy violations. Measuring the justice of criminalization acts exclusively in terms of their impact on human values and experience does not mean that we cannot distinguish unprincipled criminalization from principled criminalization. It is by drawing on those values and experiences that we are able to identify conduct that is worthy of criminalization. Feinberg's harm principle can be grounded on a conventionalist account of harm and culpability. What we are able to do is draw on sociological and scientific evidence to make our harm claims objective within conventional paradigms.

There is no need to claim that our conceptualizations of harm and offense are correct according to some universal or correct standard. Our harm and offense claims can be tested against our core conventional and scientific understandings of harm. Harm is universal in the sense that all cultures recognize harm as a bad thing. Where societies differ is not on the notion that harm is bad, but on what counts as harm. At the base point, there are primitive harms that empirically and biologically affect all humans in the same way. For instance, torture will result in physical pain regardless of where the victim might be culturally situated. When a rogue state uses torture to obtain information from captured soldiers, it does so because torture is bad and harmful; if it were not, the captors would use some other method to obtain the information. Once we move away from the most primitive harms, it becomes more difficult to identify the types of harms that would ground principled criminalization. Nonetheless, there is plenty of agreement about many conventionally contingent harms. Given that criminalization is very harmful for those who are criminalized, it should not generally be used to deter soft harms and offenses.[174] We have conventional understandings about the psychological distress caused by grossly offensive acts. We can also supply justifications for criminalizing certain forms of offense. If these justifications are able to withstand detached scrutiny of communally situated agents then they will be objective.

In Western societies privacy is considered to be a cardinal value. Privacy violations in the traditional sense present a stronger case for principled criminalization, as the victim might be left rather traumatized by having her private acts uploaded onto the Internet. Because of the social makeup of citizens living in competitive and sophisticated modern societies, privacy has evolved as

---

174 Dennis J. Baker, 'Constitutionalizing the Harm Principle,' (2008) 27(2) *Criminal Justice Ethics* 3.

a cardinal *want*. When *x* uses a hidden camera to film up *y*'s skirt[175] he violates *y*'s autonomy by deciding how her private information will be used. Stanley Benn[176] rightly argues that such a violation is wrong because it treats its victim with a lack of respect as a person. Benn argues that covert surveillance is morally wrongful because it 'deliberately deceives a person about his [or her] world: It thwarts, on the basis of reasons that are not his [or her] own, the agent's attempts to make rational choices.'[177] This type of violation is wrong even though the information (movie, photos, *etc.*) might never be made public, not merely because the clandestine spying would hurt the victim's feelings, but because the wrongdoer uses the unsuspecting woman as a mere means to serve his end. Keeping the spying secret so that the victims do not find out might inadvertently spare the victims' feelings, but it would also add dimension to the wrongness of the spying because it falsifies the victims' self-perception. The victims might, acting on the false belief that they are in control of their private world, act even more 'intriguingly for [their] manipulator's ends.'[178] Benn goes on to assert that:[179] 'One cannot respect someone as engaged in an enterprise worthy of consideration if one knowingly and deliberately alters his conditions of action while concealing the fact from him.'[180] Benn uses Kantian terminology, but his account of wrongful privacy violations fairly well encapsulates our conventional understanding of the wrongness of privacy violations.

Those who learn about the covert spying would feel resentment and would be offended within Feinberg's wide definition of offense. The short-lived anger and psychological distress would not be enough to set back their interests, but the loss of privacy and anonymity would cause profound distress and resentment. This type of wrongdoing is criminalizable not only because it causes major distress, but because it also results in a *culpable violation* of the victim's autonomy and privacy rights. The privacy loss is an independent bad consequence, which can be used to give the legislature guidance and justification for invoking the criminal law. It is a consequence that is inter-subjectively accepted as bad by communally situated agents. What is also important is that the violator has no liberty interest in taking this type of private information from others. The distressfulness of this type of violation is conventionally contingent: in some cultures people might not care less if someone films them in a state of undress.

Nonetheless, the case for criminalization is exceptionally weak when the defendant is not *taking* another's private information, but rather is forcing another to *access* her own private information. *X* might claim that she has suffered an autonomy loss when she is forced to receive offensive information in a public

---

175 See the facts in *R. v. Hamilton* [2007] EWCA Crim. 2062.
176 Stanley I. Benn, *A Theory of Freedom* (Cambridge: Cambridge University Press, 1988) at p. 275.
177 Ibid.
178 Ibid.
179 Ibid.
180 Ibid.

context, because she is denied the opportunity to avoid receiving the unwanted information. However, given our conventional understanding about the importance of pluralism, toleration and free speech, the case for criminalizing those who offend others cannot be strong if it is to be principled. The offended party could no doubt claim she was disgusted and shocked by the display of a copulating couple, but so might those who have been socialized to find same-sex couples disgusting. They also could claim that being confined in a public bus where same-sex couples are merely *kissing* is a bad consequence for them as it is something they do not want to see. What if a woman is topless on the bus, does this differ to a man being topless on the bus? Such a law would violate our deeply held conventions about equality. Thus, if a law were to ban all kissing on public buses regardless of sexual orientation it might be permissible if it were really needed to prevent some type of bad consequence. Similarly, a law preventing women only from going topless in public would be discriminatory.

What makes forcing members of the public to deal with offensive information wrong? The offense is subjectively taken in all cases, because some passengers on a bus might be voyeurs and might not mind seeing copulating couples. Meanwhile, same-sex couples merely kissing would not offend many others. If it is merely the union of culpability and the consequence of the offended party being forced to receive information that she subjectively does not want to receive[181] that justifies criminalization, then we have no way of dealing with the problem of unprincipled criminalization beyond referring to core harms where there is deep agreement. I am of the view that, once we move away from culpable harm criteria, the case for criminalization becomes substantially weaker. Having said that, the gross privacy violations involved in uploading private information onto the Internet could come within the purview of the harm concept.[182] The latter is distinguishable because people have a *stronger liberty* interest in protecting their own information. The liberty interest in not receiving other peoples' private information in public contexts is not great, as free speech is a much more cardinal liberty.

One justification for criminalizing the copulating couple on the public bus would be that their actions are unhygienic—other people want to use the public bus seats without sitting where the couple once did their act. Likewise, a person would not want to sit on a restaurant seat if a nudist has just been sitting on it. The harm principle might be invoked in such cases. Similarly, uncovered nudists would not be welcome around the buffet in a restaurant. This would be a soft harm. However, if these people were on an open beach or in an open park the case for criminalization seems hard to sustain. Women wearing the burka in a public

---

181   There is a difference between wrongness (moral impermissibility—the union of bad act and culpability) and mere wrongfulness (culpableness). Mere intention does not necessarily equal wrongness—*x* might intentionally bring about good or neutral consequences, for example, she might intentionally help a little old lady to cross the road, but she would be morally praiseworthy not criminally censurable for her deed.

182   Feinberg, Vol. I, *op. cit. supra*, fn. 1 at p. 26.

place might cause offense to different people for different reasons,[183] but we would not want to use the criminal law to tell people how they should dress in public. Therefore, there is no strong case for criminalizing exhibitionism in open public places where food is not being served or where public seating is not involved. This probably explains why exhibitionism is not criminalized on beaches and in parks in most of Europe.

To the extent that people claim that they have a right not to see same-sex couples kissing, women wearing burkas, nudists on a beach and so on, the criminal law has no role to play. Feinberg cites the reasonableness of such offensive displays[184] as a reason for toleration, but the better justification for tolerating such conduct is that it is does not wrong others in a conventional sense, because there is deep agreement about the need to tolerate diversity in modern societies. Likewise, the deep offense caused to some by knowing that books such as Salman Rushdie's *The Satanic Verses* or Philip Roth's *Portnoy's Complaint* exist does not provide a justification for outlawing such literature. To the extent that people are offended by the bare knowledge of knowing that such activities are taking place behind closed doors or that such books exist, Murphy rightly notes:

> We must remember *ex hypothesi* the acts in question are performed in private by consenting adults. Thus the only thing to which the complainant could object to is the bare knowledge that something of which he disapproves is going on in private. The question, then, is this: Is freedom from knowledge that some disapproved activity is taking place a right that ought to be recognized? Hart argues convincingly not.[185]

Unless a person is forced to watch or read the offensive film or book, she could hardly claim she had been wronged. Would denying the Cambodian genocide or the Nanking Massacre at Speaker's Corner in London's Hyde Park violate a passing survivor's right not to receive such information? This type of speech clearly treats passers-by with a gross lack of consideration. But this type of political dialogue belongs in the public arena, even though it is factually wrong and offensive, because it is enlightening to the extent it allows the public to understand that there are some very disturbing views in existence and leads to informed debate, which allows the record to be put straight. People have an interest in knowing that these types of awful views exist in the real world and have a responsibility to publicly denounce such views.[186] This type of information is public information not private

---

183 Charles Bremner, 'France Goes from Burkas to Burgers in Latest Muslim Row' (London: *The Times*, February 19, 2010).

184 Feinberg, Vol. II, *op. cit. supra*, fn. 1 at p. 26.

185 Jeffrie G. Murphy, 'Another Look at Legal Moralism,' (1966) 77 *Ethics* 50 at p. 54.

186 Jeremy Waldron, 'Homelessness and Community,' (2000) 50 *University of Toronto Law Journal* 371, at pp. 391–392.

information and therefore it does not violate the rights of those who are forced to receive it. Such receivers consent to receiving this information by choosing to visit public places. People give up a certain amount of privacy and autonomy as soon as they walk out of their front door, and in doing this they cannot expect to be sheltered from the real world. This is not the type of sensitive and private information that a person could claim a right to be sheltered from. *Per contra*, copulation in a public bus does not serve a similar purpose and the intimate display is of no benefit to those who do not want to endure this type of up close and unavoidable encounter. But if it did occur, the public would have an interest in hearing or reading about it in the news, as it informs them about what is going on in the world.

The freedom of expression right protects this interest by creating an environment that facilitates the free flow of information. Waldron[187] points out that beggars cause offense to some passers-by as they may be distressed by the message conveyed by homeless people, but that distress is beneficial for both the offended auditor and the homeless person.[188] Firstly, the auditor might say: 'This is awful. I am glad I have found out about this'—additionally, the encounter might even motivate the auditor to do something about it. Such an encounter is a good consequence not a bad consequence (to the extent it is not aggressive: aggressively targeting passers-by is a form of harassment and would most likely come within the purview of the harm principle), because it forces society to acknowledge and respond to the harsh realities of indigence.[189] Unwanted speech that captures the public's attention is usually seen as a detriment, but it should not be seen as a detriment from the audience's point of view. 'As Mill rightly emphasized, there is significant benefit in being exposed to ideas and attitudes different from one's own, though this exposure may be unwelcome.'[190] The panhandler, the conservative, the liberal and the bigot all have an interest in articulating their views and in hearing the views of their adversaries. The consequence of being forced to deal with public political discussion is somewhat different to having a copulating couple's live presentation of their private affairs forced upon you in the *confines* of a public bus.

Feinberg correctly asserts that offense would hardly ever outweigh the value of free speech.[191] It appears that only a very narrow range of very intimate displays (copulating in a bus or physical intrusions such as accessing people for prolonged periods in certain contexts in public places, *etc.*) would be sufficiently bad to justify a criminal law response. Such activities interfere with the auditor's right to be let alone (right not to be proximately included in the very private affairs of others in confined public contexts). However, only a weak case can be made

---

187 *Id.* at p. 379.
188 A large minority would also be offended by the fact that some people find beggars offensive. It seems almost shocking that homeless people offend some people.
189 Waldron, *op. cit. supra*, fn. 186 at p. 379.
190 *Loper v. New York City Police Dept.* 802 F. Supp. 1029, 1043 (S.D.N.Y. 1992).
191 Feinberg, Vol. II, *op. cit. supra*, fn. 1 at pp. 38–39 *et passim*.

for criminalizing exhibitionism more generally, because the bad consequence is conventionally variable and barely could be said to have significant consequences for others when carried out in open spaces as opposed to confined public places.

Conclusion

There are established human values and conventions. There are also recognized standards of rational argument. McDowell[192] takes the view that moral values are both anthropocentric and real. He also argues that objectivity claims are to be made from the internal perspective of our actual practices. We might draw on our best theories of thought and language and so on, but this does not really tell us whether our claims of wrongness are truly objective. In this chapter, I have argued that principled criminalization does not have to rely on critical objectivity—in the sense of producing transcultural and truly correct standards. I have argued that Feinberg's harm principle can be supported with conventional accounts of harm. The best that we can do is scrutinize our conventional conceptualizations of harm and badness, but that scrutiny is constrained by the limits of epistemological enquiry and our capacity for rationality at any given point in time. The conflicts that arise from communal living inevitably lead to some kind of political philosophy. Many acts are criminalizable because they violate conventions that are sharable by communally situated agents.

I have noted there is no deep inter-subjective agreement about the badness of exhibitionism and the like. Nor is it clear that we have a sharable end in outlawing it. The offended group itself will only follow norms against it while it continues to collectively 'retain certain attitudes and beliefs about them.'[193] We might criminalize some soft harms such as privacy violations to prevent those who have been socialized to value privacy for suffering humiliation and psychological distress. But if that distress arises from other forms of offense, such as exhibitionism or hate speech, the cardinal value of freedom of expression would most likely override the victim's liberty interest in avoiding offense. As noted above, offense can stimulate debate and tolerance. The difference with exhibitionism is that the offending party has an overriding liberty interest, unless his or her exhibitionism occurs in a context where it raises hygiene issues or targets a captive spectator, as might be the case in a public bus. The bad consequence of *privacy loss* is conventionally contingent—it is contingent on the way the victim as been socialized.

The gravity of rape also hinges on socialization and convention. It is not too difficult to imagine a society where people might be socialized from a young age

---

192   McDowell, *op. cit. supra*, fn. 107.
193   Matthew H. Kramer, *Objectivity and the Rule of Law* (Cambridge: Cambridge University Press, 2007) at p. 17. Gardner, too, notes that in the end it is necessary to appeal to the harm principle or some similar principle of toleration. John Gardner, 'Prohibiting Immoralities,' (2007) 28(6) *Cardozo Law Review* 2613.

to believe that it is a great honor to be used as a sex object by an old man.[194] Obviously, in such a society the psychological harm would differ to that faced by rape victims in modern Western society. What is undeniable is that socialization means that rape not only results in physical harm in modern societies but also genuine psychological harm and trauma. There is deep agreement about the need to criminalize rape because of its psychological and physical badness. Because of the way people are socialized, some forms of sexual use seem to be tolerated in modern society. For instance, it is arguable that to some extent people are socialized to tolerate sexual use from celebrities and other powerful figures. It is doubtful that Tiger Woods,[195] a celebrity golfer, would have managed to convince so many women that they should be used by him for sex, if he had been a normal laborer rather than a skilled laborer—after all golf is merely physical work is it not?[196] As J.L. Mackie notes:

> Only some kinds of harm are socially, cooperatively, resented, and cooperation in gratitude is even more restricted. Again we must seek and can find sociological reasons for these differences: only with particular kinds of harm are the conditions favorable for the growth of a convention of cooperative hostility to them, so only some kinds of harm are seen as wrong and as calling for general resentment and punishment ... Though retributive principles cannot be defended, with any plausibility, as allegedly objective moral truths, retributive attitudes can be readily understood and explained as sentiments that have grown up and

---

194 In China women were socialized (Daoist theory, among other socializing tools, was used to help convince up to 20,000 young women to be on call to the emperor) into believing it was a great honor to be chosen to be a concubine (some would suggest a sexual object of use) for the emperor. By the Qing Dynasty there were up to 20,000 kept in the Forbidden City. See generally, Bernard Llewellyn, *China's Court and Concubines: Some People in Chinese History* (London: Allen & Unwin, 1956). 'How sad is it to be a woman! Nothing on earth is held so cheap, lamented the 3rd-century Chinese Poet Fu Xuan.' Quoted in Elizabeth Abbott, *A History of Mistresses* (Toronto: Harper Flamingo, 2003) at p. 34. It is incorrect to assume oppression rather than socialization was used to achieve such aims in all cases.

195 Woods is a celebrity golfer who has allegedly slept with numerous women, but his wife seems to be tolerating it. Sam Tanenhaus, 'Tiger Woods and the Perils of Modern Celebrity,' (New York: *New York Times*, December 12, 2009).

196 Baker and Hacker note: '[S]ocial behavior, viewed externally, in ignorance of the norms which inform it, may seem altogether unintelligible. A story is told of a Chinese mandarin passing through the foreign legations' compound in Peking. Seeing two of the European staff playing tennis, he stopped to watch. Bemused, he turned to a player and said, "If it is, for some obscure reason, necessary to hit this little ball back and forth thus, would it not be possible to get the servants to do it?"' Baker and Hacker, *op. cit. supra*, fn. 110 at pp. 257–258.

are sustained partly through biological processes, and partly through analogous sociological ones.[197]

Even our best sociological and biological conceptualizations of harm do not cover mere umbrage. We might invoke Lord Devlin's argument and hold that if the majority, 'do not like it then criminalize it,' but that would allow anything to be criminalized. The perseveration of social harmony argument is weaker in the case of personal space violations[198] than it is in the case of those violations that are likely to have deeper psychological consequences as rape or filming up a lady's skirt might do. When the conduct involves soft harms the criminal law should be used only as last resort.

It is possible to have a principled criminal law, but this would mean accepting deeply held conventional accounts of harm (and of soft harm) and offense. It would also mean accepting that something that is considered as a soft harm now might not be considered as one in the future or in some other cultural context. There is a clear case for criminalizing harms of a more primitive kind. There are strong conventions telling us not to rape, murder, steal and so on. There are also clear conventional understandings about the humiliation and psychological distress that might flow from privacy violations. It is essential for us to scrutinize soft harms and offensive acts much more than is necessary for primitive harms and in doing this we should be able to reduce unprincipled criminalization. This cannot provide a perfect solution, but it provides more guidance than critical morality does.

There may be an argument for the critically objective (variable) conventional beliefs, but I have not been able to identify it. I have aimed to identify some of the preliminary issues that have to be sorted out before more work can be done. Some might argue that, apart from 'primitive' harms common to all societies, my criterion of wrong is whatever is inter-subjectively considered wrong by agents seen as culturally situated. The question then is how this differs from positive morality? It does not, except that it requires us to really scrutinize the justifications we put forward for criminalizing soft harms and offensive acts. I would hope that modern thinkers would subject our conventional practices to greater scrutiny than Lord Devlin did. Finally, I note that the problem for those who want transcultural accounts of harm and offense is that procedural realism is not convincing as a method for grounding such standards.[199] Procedural realism

---

197 Mackie, *op. cit. supra*, fn. 62 at p. 684.

198 We have been socialized into tolerating gross violations of our personal space in certain contexts such as on the New York metro where, daily, the commuters are literally pushed against each other in a smelly, poorly ventilated carriage for long periods of time.

199 I have combed through the work of critical moralists and that of moral realists, but was unable to find anything solid which might have helped me with the questions presented above. Likewise, the work of Putnam is some of the most interesting I have read, but his latter work seems to be pushing towards procedural realism. See Gil Martin, *et al.*,

has greater potential as a mechanism for scrutinizing conventional standards, but it would have to accept that the deliberators are merely human agents who are communally situated.

'Truth and Moral Objectivity Procedural Realism in Putnam's Pragmatism,' (2008) 95(1) *Poznan Studies in the Philosophy of the Sciences and the Humanities* 265.

Chapter 7
Conclusion

Fine Tuning Criminalization Determinations: Tolerance and Pluralism

The original and significant proposal put forward in this book is that everyone has a right not to be unfairly criminalized. I have argued that the proportionality constraint as expressed in the Eighth Amendment of the United States Constitution and the more general proportionate legislative response provision found in the personal autonomy-type provisions could be used to ensure that wrongs are appropriately labeled as either criminal or non-criminal; and as serious or non-serious from the *ex ante* criminalization perspective. Governments would be forced to consider the potential constitutional consequences of enacting criminal laws. Proportionality and justice require the lawmaker to consider the harmfulness or badness of the potential consequences that are being criminalized along with the potential degrees of culpability that may be involved.

The Eighth Amendment incorporates a cardinal right: the right not to be subjected to unjust state punishment and criminalization. The Supreme Court could use *harm* as a criterion when considering the proportionate fairness of criminalization. Will act *x* harm society or given victims sufficiently to justify criminalization? Laws carrying disproportionate prison sentences could be struck down, as could laws that are a disproportionate response for dealing with the social problem at issue, such as those that criminalize begging, possessing sex toys, attending strip clubs, ingesting trans fats and so on. The fact that exhibitionism is not harmful would give the courts some indication as to the type of punishment that would be proportionate and fair. In borderline cases such as exhibitionism, the higher courts are not likely to judicially review the penalty unless it is patently excessive. Harm to others is not the only justification for criminalization, because exhibitionism and many other harmless bad consequences might require state regulation. However, harm to others is the only justification of sufficient weight for jailing wrongdoers.

A pecuniary fine would have to be patently excessive to warrant the Supreme Court intervening. The Supreme Court could not be expected to second-guess every borderline case, but it should consider those cases where injustice is evident. The gravity of the harm involved in being imprisoned means judicial review is a basic human right that should be available to make sure that any sentence is proportionate with the offender's wrongdoing. The constitutional courts would not be able to deal with borderline injustices, as it is not possible to decide a fair sentence length with any degree of exactitude. If *x* has raped *y* the state does not have *y* raped in order to punish him, instead it tries to substitute one type of harm with another type of harm (*i.e.*, it considers the seriousness of the grave physical and psychological harm caused to the rape victim and then attempts to determine how much harm to inflict on the rapist by way of years in jail). Obviously, using a completely different kind of harm to punish the wrongdoer makes it nearly impossible to come up with a fair sentence right to the decimal point. In cases of serious harm-doing a sentence could be out by a number of years before the courts would have grounds to get involved. For instance, if we accept, depending on the aggravating factors, that it is fair to impose sentences of around 10 to 12 years for rape, then a rape sentence might have to be around 16 to 18 years before the injustice would be sufficiently apparent and measurable to warrant the courts intervening. Likewise, if x is given a six year sentence for robbery and y is given four years for the exact same type of robbery, then the Supreme Court is not likely to intervene. There is no clear injustice in such cases, because the excessiveness is not manifest.

The appropriate approach would be to follow *Solem v. Helm* where the Supreme Court said the analysis should not only consider the 'gravity of the offense and the harshness of the penalty,' but also 'the sentences imposed on other criminals in the same jurisdiction, that is, whether more serious crimes are subject to the same penalty or to less serious penalties; and the sentences imposed for commission of the same crime in other jurisdictions.'[1] The justice criteria are harm, culpability, past practice and sentences for similar crimes in other jurisdictions. The latter should involve a global analysis. The judge should start by considering sentences for the most harmful crimes such as murder, terrorism, rape, *etc.*, then work her way down the seriousness ladder and consider all the relevant variables. I am of the opinion that the right not to be criminalized, to the extent that it is constitutionalized through the proportionality constraint, is likely to be more effective in those cases where there is no obvious basis for criminalization. For instance, laws criminalizing harmless activities, such as feeding homeless people, could be struck down without requiring a controversial analysis; so might those other offenses that unjustly penalize harmless conduct such as those outlawing non-aggressive begging, attending strip shows, selling food containing trans fats, purchasing sex toys, *etc.*

The U.S. Supreme Court has already used the Eighth Amendment to strike down laws that have made innocuous acts criminal. In *Robinson v. California*[2] the Court held that a law criminalizing the innocuous activity of existing with the condition of drug addiction was contrary to the Eighth Amendment. Justice Douglas noted that: 'The addict is a sick person. He may of course, be confined for treatment or for the protection of society. Cruel and unusual punishment results not from confinement, but from convicting the addict of a crime.' 'Even one day in prison would be a cruel and unusual punishment for the "crime" of having a

---

1   *Solem v. Helm*, 463 U.S. 277, 290–292 (1983).
2   370 U.S. 660, 676 (1962).

common cold.'³ Another area where the right could have a significant impact is in those cases where the prison sentence is grossly disproportionate in comparison with the harmfulness of the offender's wrongdoing. As we have seen, in *Solem v. Helm* the criminalization was grossly unjust as the respondent merely uttered a 'no account' check for $100, but was sentenced to life imprisonment without possibility of parole under South Dakota's recidivist statute because he had prior convictions. As I noted above, the Supreme Court held that: 'In light of the relevant objective criteria [*i.e.*, harm, culpability and sentences for similar crimes], the respondent's sentence of life imprisonment without possibility of parole [was] significantly disproportionate to his crime, and is therefore prohibited by the Eighth Amendment.'⁴ A progressive Supreme Court could make many crimes that are currently on the statute books meaningless by holding that the penalties involved are contrary to the Eighth Amendment.

Criminalization results in harm, stigmatization and hard treatment for those who are brought within its purview, regardless of whether an offense carries a jail term. Therefore, justice requires the lawmaker to produce sound justifications for invoking the criminal law. There are many crimes that clearly do not meet the requirements of justice. The real challenge for legal philosophers, judges and politicians will be to decide where to draw the line. In many borderline cases it will not be easy to ascertain whether the potentially bad consequences are worthy of criminal condemnation. In those cases where the bad consequence is harmful, Feinberg's balancing approach⁵ and the common sense balancing approach taken by the Canadian courts in *Malmo-Levine*⁶ would be useful for determining where to draw the line. Von Hirsch's and Simester's mediating principle, based on ready avoidability would be useful for determining where to draw the line in those cases where the potentially bad consequence is not harmful. In some cases it will not be difficult to draw a line at all. For example, the crime of feeding homeless people with its maximum penalty of $1,000 and a six month jail term is clearly unconstitutional. It is clear that feeding a homeless person does not bring about bad consequences for anyone. Instead, it is conduct that aims at bringing about good consequences.⁷ There is no moral justification for invoking the criminal law in such situations.

---

3   *Robinson v. California*, 360 U.S. 660, 667 (1962).

4   *Solem v. Helm*, 463 U.S. 277, 295–303 (1983).

5   Joel Feinberg, *The Moral Limits of the Criminal Law: Harm to Others* (New York: Oxford University Press, 1984) at pp. 215–216.

6   *R. v. Malmo-Levine* [2000] B.C.C.A. 335. See also the dissenting judgment of Justice Arbour in *Malmo-Levine* [2003] S.C.C. 74. As I noted in Chapter 2, the *majority* in the Supreme Court of Canada in that case did not carry out a harms analysis, but rather pointed to old offenses such as incest and bestiality, which had been (and continue to be) mislabeled as very serious crimes to justify upholding the marijuana prohibition.

7   Georg Henrik von Wright, *The Varieties of Goodness* (Routledge & Kegan Paul, 1963) at pp. 114–135.

What about those situations where a homeless person exposes herself to urinate in public because she does not have a bathroom of her own? I noted above that we have a right not to be exposed to certain private information in public places. Von Hirsch and Simester propose a mediating principle that makes provision for tolerating certain forms of behavior that is *prima facie* criminalizable. They propose two core justifications for tolerating certain invasions in public places. Firstly, obtrusive displays should be tolerated if they are readily avoidable. As I noted above, this principle strikes a balance between minority and majority interests. Licensing and zoning regulations restrict the practice of potentially offensive acts to private areas to limit the minority's impact on the ethical environment in proportion to what its numbers and tastes justify.[8] A balance is struck between majoritarian claims and minority claims so that minorities are able to have some impact in our plural society.[9] It is unacceptable to force the public to receive certain types of non-public information, unless the information is readily avoidable because others should be able to avoid certain displays 'without undue restriction of their own liberty.'[10]

Exhibitionism is a wrong not because of the natural content of the exhibit, but because x's nudity forces y to enter x's private domain: it is a wrongful inclusion. People should be able to be spared from witnessing certain intimate revelations.[11] Exhibitionism may violate our right to be let alone (be spared intimate revelations), but it will not always be criminalizable. In Europe many designated nudists' areas are only partially segregated in the parks: people can see the nudists and are usually aware of such areas or at least can see them from a distance. Under the ready avoidability principle, this kind of nudity is tolerable, because members of the public are provided with ample warning about the presence of the nudity and are afforded a reasonable opportunity to avoid it, if they wish to do so. Exhibitionism in places that are essentially private (private homes) or quasi-private (strip clubs) does not involve moral wrongdoing. Those who attend the strip club consent to the display and any affront to their sensibilities would be totally avoidable. Their rights are not violated as they consent. Nude beaches are distinguishable in that they are public places. Nevertheless, exhibitionism on a nude beach is tolerable as it would be readily avoidable. Those who do not want to receive this type of intimate information can easily avoid receiving it by avoiding nude beaches. Avoiding such places would not restrict their freedom of movement or place undue burdens on them, because there are plenty of other beaches.

If the exhibitionist takes care to only disrobe in the nudist area her conduct would be tolerable, because she does not subject others to an unavoidable display

---

8   Ronald Dworkin, *Sovereign Virtue* (Cambridge, MA: Harvard University Press, 2000) at p. 214.

9   *Ibid.*

10   Andrew von Hirsch and Andrew P. Simester, *Incivilities: Regulating Offensive Behaviour* (Oxford: Hart Publishing, 2006) at pp. 125–128.

11   *Ibid.*

of nudity. She is not forcing the violated witness to take in her display, as the witness is only subjected to nudity in this context when she chooses to enter the designated nudist area. I noted above that most open public places would probably also be available to the nudist, if we accept the state has not right to tell people how to dress. The reverse would be the case in the confines of a public bus where the audience is held completely captive. What about nude protests and public art exhibitions that are not totally avoidable? Feinberg would start by arguing that this type of nudity has an independent social value, because it is of personal importance to the nude models, the artists or nude protestors. It would also involve free expression. Seventeen hundred naked people walked across the Millennium Bridge in Newcastle as a part of an art project. Notably, it was done at 4 *a.m.* in the morning so that members of the public would have a reasonably high chance of avoiding it, but it was done during the summer daylight hours. Arguably, people would be expected to tolerate this kind of public nudity in a plural society because it would be readily avoidable. Hardly anyone would be roaming the streets at 4 *a.m.* in the morning. But this kind of display would not be readily avoidable, if it took place at midday in a food court in a shopping mall. In this context it would involve hygiene issues and would also force non-consenting witnesses to receive unwanted intimate information in a confined public place. Ready avoidability is not merely about captivity, it is about having a reasonable chance of avoiding the unwanted information.

Feinberg might argue that this kind of public nudity is mediated by the fact that it cannot take place in an alternative location as the public arena is needed for the shock effect (as might be the case with nude war protests)[12] that these kinds of activities are designed to achieve. Feinberg's limits also incorporate wider normative reasons for tolerating certain kinds of offenses. These types of considerations come within the purview of the social tolerance principle,[13] which could be invoked, as nude art exhibitions and nude protests have an independent social value and are uncommon in public places. The germane reason for tolerance is that offensive display is readily avoidable and has some social value. It would be difficult to argue that readily avoidable displays of an intimate kind should be criminalized in a modern plural society. The ready avoidability counteracts the apparent privacy violation that generally stems from these types of displays.

I do not intend to recast Feinberg's mediating maxims. Notwithstanding that Feinberg failed to establish a clear account of the objective wrongness of offending others, his 'reasonableness' mediating maxims are reconcilable with those proposed by von Hirsch and Simester.[14] The ready avoidability justification does not add much to the case for overriding the criminalization of the intimate

---

12   See for example, Feinberg's comments on the value of 'shock effect' words, which are used to convey political messages. Joel Feinberg, *The Moral Limits of the Criminal Law: Offense to Others* (New York: Oxford University Press, Vol. II, 1985) at pp. 216–217.

13   Von Hirsch and Simester, *op. cit. supra*, fn. 10 at pp. 125–126.

14   *Ibid.*

activities carried out by homeless people in public places, because these types of activities are often carried out in public parks and cannot be avoided unless the spectator waives her right to use the public park. If a person goes to Central Park, surely she has the right to enjoy her sandwiches without being included in the homeless person's intimate domain—*i.e.*, being forced to witness a homeless person's most intimate actions such as urinating, bathing and so forth. While these types of activities are *prima facie* criminalizable, von Hirsch and Simester argue that in certain contexts we have to tolerate conflicting lifestyles. To tolerate is to put up with something that a person does not really approve of.[15] '[T]oleration requires a positive "acceptance component", which does not cancel out the negative judgment but gives certain positive reasons which trump the negative ones in the relevant context.'[16] It is more plausible to raise the idea of tolerance in the context of harmless bad consequences than in the harm context.[17] A person who enters the crowded evening bus with a portable wireless blaring loudly might invade the personal space of others, even though this may not be her intention. Should she be prevented from enjoying her lifestyle, which includes using a portable 'boom-box' in confined public places, such as city buses? The other bus passengers might include tired workers who may wish to enjoy their evening newspapers without being bombarded with loud gangster rap music. Von Hirsch and Simester emphasize the importance of tolerating the different ways in which people choose to present themselves and live their lives.[18] They note that: '[p]lural society is not just a present social fact (that people have different lifestyles) that need to be "managed". It is also a normative matter: we *ought* to encourage varying and sometimes even conflicting lifestyles.'[19]

In the wider sense social tolerance is about tolerating aspects of others' lifestyles that you do not agree with. The Muslim might be asked to tolerate homosexuals, the Westerner might be asked to tolerate the Muslim head veil, the conservative might be asked to tolerate the punk with pink spiked hair and so forth. In the aforementioned examples no one is asked to tolerate wrongful conduct, as the conduct, if it is violative at all, is only violative according to *rapidly*[20] evolving

---

15   See Thomas Nagel, *Equality and Partiality* (New York: Oxford University Press, 1991) at pp. 144–168. See also Peter King, *Toleration* (London: Frank Cass, 2nd ed. 1998) at p. 21.

16   Rainer Forst, 'Toleration, Justice and Reason,' in Catriona McKinnon and Dario Castiglione, *The Culture of Toleration in Diverse Societies* (Manchester: Manchester University Press, 2003) at p. 72.

17   '[T]he absence of setbacks to their interests tends to give the wrongdoing [involved in privacy violations *per se*] a less serious character—and thus leaves more scope for countervailing concerns such as the importance of self-preservation': von Hirsch and Simester, *op. cit. supra*, fn. 10 at p. 125.

18   *Ibid.*

19   *Ibid.*

20   These customs change each decade in Western society, and differ to those conventions that are deeply held (long held) as serving some legitimate social goal.

social customs. In our case, we are asking whether people should tolerate conduct that is *prima facie* criminalizable. 'The concept of toleration entails the idea of certain "limits of toleration". They lie at the point where reasons for rejection become stronger than the acceptance reasons.'[21] In our case, we are focusing on a homeless person's right to exist as opposed to the right of others to be let alone and avoid receiving what is non-public information. Does the homeless person have a greater normative claim than the affected spectator? The social tolerance principle is about constructing sound normative reasons to counteract a *prima facie* case for criminalization.

Waldron[22] presents a strong case for tolerating the intimate displays that are forced onto non-consenting audiences because of the homeless person's lifestyle. He argues that many of the intimate displays that resonate from homelessness such as homeless people urinating in public and bathing in public, ought to be tolerated since most vagrants do not have any choice but to expose themselves in public for such purposes. Such people are more or less forced to live on a public stage—in a fish bowl. Homeless people are forced to live their lives in the public arena under public surveillance 24 hours a day. Is this an empirical fact? Ought we tolerate what homeless people are forced to display? Does this not require us to tolerate the intrusive displays that emanate when a homeless person is forced to defecate, urinate or bathe in public? Arguably, this provides us with a reason for tolerating what are clearly bad consequences for us if we want to enjoy the park for recreational purposes. Social tolerance is a cardinal virtue[23] and a moral matter.[24] We are expected to encourage and tolerate different and often conflicting lifestyles.[25] The lifestyle of the homeless is markedly different from that of the majority. The dysfunctional drug addict may be forced to beg for alms, defecate, urinate, sleep, vomit, and eat under total and unrelenting public surveillance.[26]

Waldron asserts that homeless people are forced to carry out everyday activities in public places, as they have no private place of their own. A distinction needs to be made between those acts that do involve moral wrongdoing and those that do not, because the focus is on overriding criminalization. Sleeping and eating in public are not my concern, as they are not *prima facie* wrong. I am interested in those acts that have bad consequences for others because of their publicness.

---

21   Forst, *op. cit. supra*, fn. 16 at p. 72.
22   Cf. Jeremy Waldron, *Liberal Rights, Collected Papers 1981–1991* (Cambridge: Cambridge University Press, 1993) at pp. 63–87. See also Jeremy Waldron, 'Toleration and Reasonableness,' in McKinnon and Castiglone, *op. cit. supra*, fn. 16.
23   Will Kymlicka, *Liberalism, Community and Culture* (Oxford: Clarendon Press, 1989) at pp. 9–10.
24   Joseph Raz, *Ethics in the Public Domain* (Oxford: Clarendon Press, 1995) at pp. 162 *et seq*.
25   King, *loc. cit. supra*, fn. 15.
26   Jeremy Waldron, 'Homelessness and Community,' (2000) 50 *University of Toronto Law Journal* 371 at pp. 309–338.

For instance, nudity or copulation does not involve moral wrongdoing when it occurs in private. There is nothing wrong with copulating or being naked to bathe, to defecate or urinate so long as it is done in the privacy of a person's home. Nonetheless, if these acts are carried out in public places they interfere with the rights of others to be let alone and to enjoy the public places that are there for everyone.[27] Defecating, urinating or copulating in front of members of the public (and fouling up those public areas we all have an interest in using and in keeping clean) would affect the rights of others to use and enjoy such places. No one would choose to eat a sandwich in a park (or otherwise use a public area) that reeks of urine and is littered with rubbish and human feces, *etc.* Nor would a person choose to see the exposed homeless person defecating, bathing, copulating or urinating in the park. Waldron claims that if we choose (tolerate) the economic system and property rules that force people to live in public places, then their claim to exist in this way may outweigh our right to avoid the bad side-effects.[28]

Waldron thinks that if we are willing as a nation to tolerate a social and legal structure that forces some people to use public places as a bathroom or otherwise, then surely we have to tolerate the bad consequences.[29] Waldron argues that, at least in the United States, the homeless person is forced to urinate and defecate in public as a matter of necessity because they have no private place (home) of their own.[30] Furthermore, homeless people are usually barred from using the lavatories in private establishments, such as restaurants and hotels.[31] According to Waldron: 'The rules of property prohibit the homeless person from doing any of these acts in private, since there is no private place that he has a right to be. And the rules governing public places prohibit him from doing any of these acts in public, since that is how we have decided to regulate the use of public places.'[32] Urinating, defecating and sleeping are necessary and quotidian acts that a person cannot

---

27 Someone reading this 50 years from now may find this statement relativistic rather than objective, as mainstream attitudes are shifting with respect to nudity and sex scenes, *etc.* People are wearing less and less. Furthermore, movies, mainstream newspapers, the World Wide Web, YouTube, and so on contain a plethora of images of nudity and sex scenes. However, a real live encounter with someone engaging in this type of private activity is different and the objective idea of personal space is likely to become increasingly important in an overpopulated world.

28 The displays are side-effects as clearly the homeless person does not aim to wrong others. The situation is less acute in England, Canada and Australia where welfare is plentiful. The situation in those jurisdictions is more likely to be countered by providing more drug and alcohol rehabilitation centers and mental health care programs as the homeless people in those jurisdictions are predominantly those who are too dysfunctional to collect their welfare payments. See generally, Hartley Dean, *Begging Questions: Street-Level Economic Activity and Social Policy Failure* (Bristol: The Policy Press, 1999).

29 Waldron, *op. cit. supra*, fn. 26 at pp. 325–330.

30 *Ibid.*

31 *Id.* at p. 326.

32 *Id.* at p. 328.

refrain from performing. If we, as a society, choose not to provide sufficient numbers of public bathrooms, mental healthcare programs, and homeless hostels, then arguably we should not punish those who are forced to defecate and urinate in public. The right to exist and use public places for such purposes has to be reconciled with other competitive claims; that is, with the wider public's right to use and enjoy the same space. The homeless person would have a right to survive or exist, urinate, defecate and bathe in general. This is a basic human right, which no one can be excluded from exercising. Punishing homeless people under these circumstances would be wrongful.

The empirical evidence would have to be exceptionally convincing. If the empirical evidence could prove that homeless people have no choice but to urinate and so on in public, then this would provide us with reason for tolerating this kind of offense. The right (and need) to defecate, urinate and bathe is a freedom shared by everyone.[33] Such acts have to be committed somewhere and for some this will have to be in public. The issue is not only about the fulfillment of these *a*societal needs, but also about having the freedom to choose to do so in private. King[34] draws on O'Neill's[35] constructivism and Waldron's idea of basic freedom, to argue that everyone has a right to housing. 'Housing rights exist because of the institutions that convert imperfect duties into special perfect obligations. This arrangement is justified because of the belief that all individuals need a place where they can undertake those functionings necessary for any form of life.'[36] If the government has no primary obligation to provide adequate public bathrooms and very basic homeless hostels,[37] then it ought to tolerate the side-effects of homelessness. In America there is only a small minority of homeless people who are too dysfunctional to access the welfare and housing that is available. Nevertheless, the fact that a homeless person has not been able to use the capitalist system productively to provide for themselves does not give them *carte blanche* to deliberately expose themselves in public parks and to foul up such places. A balanced approach would support tolerance in a very narrow range of situations,

---

33 Ibid.
34 Peter King, 'Conceptualizing Housing Right,' (London: C.C.H.R. Conference Paper, 2001). See also Peter King, *Private Dwelling: Contemplating the Use of Housing* (London: Routledge, 2003); Peter King, *The Common Place: In the Midst of the Ordinary* (Aldershot: Ashgate, 2005); and Peter King, *Housing, Individuals and the State: The Morality of Government Intervention* (London: Routledge, 1998).
35 Onora O'Neill, *Towards Justice and Virtue: A Constructive Account of Practical Reasoning* (Cambridge: Cambridge University Press, 1996) at pp. 122–153.
36 King, *op. cit. supra*, fn. 34.
37 I do not agree with King's claim that everyone has a right to housing. However, it does seem reasonable to provide basic hostels so that those who are temporarily too dysfunctional to collect their welfare or to work can be given somewhere to stay until they get their act together. Some of these people may have chronic conditions and may need long-term support.

that is, in those contexts where there are no public bathrooms within reasonable proximity and the person is genuinely homeless.

At the edges the criminalizability of borderline bad consequences is not easy to determine. There will always be a range of countervailing considerations. Even in those cases where the unwanted conduct involves objective harm, the lawmaker will have to balance a range of considerations before making a final decision about whether to invoke the criminal law to prevent the harm-doing. There is no easy method for deciding such cases. The best way to proceed is to recognize the right not to be criminalized as a constitutional right by using the proportionality constraint as far as possible to strike down offenses with disproportional sentences and those that jail people for engaging in conduct that has purely neutral or good consequences (*i.e.*, crimes that are disproportional given the nature and gravity of the societal problem being dealt with). Recognizing harm as a constitutional proportionality standard will prevent the state from criminalizing many innocuous acts and will allow many criminal laws that carry unjust prison sentences to be struck down. The state might redraft the laws to remove the jail sentences, but such laws would lack any bite[38] and might be subject to further analysis under the general personal autonomy provision. It is hoped that the deeper analysis provided in this book will initiate further debate and discussion on this very important topic and offer some guidance for future developments in this area.

Proposals

In this book I have examined the legal limits of the substantive criminal law. In doing so, I have formulated a constitutional right not to be criminalized. I have argued that right can only be overridden when the state can produce a compelling justification for overriding it. If the criminalization involves jail time, the compelling justification for overriding the right would have to be that the offender's conduct results in harms for others.

The crux of the retributive justification for overriding a person's right not to be criminalized is that those who harm others (or otherwise violate their rights) deserve criminal condemnation. It is the wrongdoer's bad acting that the criminal law aims to prevent and punish. The lawmaker needs to be able to say in advance that those who deliberately bring about bad consequences for others (for example, the resultant situation that flows from stealing another's property), will be labeled as criminals and punished in proportion with the seriousness of their offending.[39]

---

38 See T.A. Turk, *Criminology and Legal Order* (Chicago: Rand McNally, 1969), where the author discusses decriminalization due to a lack of enforcement.

39 The sentence would be set in advance and would be rather severe for this kind of act depending whether it was a case of robbery or mere theft. The sentence and label might also be adjusted depending on whether the theft was successful or was a mere attempt. Of course, at the *ex post* trial stage the judge would have some discretion to consider mitigating

The lawmaker says in advance that it is wrong for anyone to deliberately bring about bad consequences for others and this provides potential wrongdoers with a reason for resisting the temptation to do so. If x intentionally robs y at gunpoint, criminalization communicates to x in terms that both she and everyone else in society can understand, that x deserves to be censured and punished for her harmful choice. The objective reasons we can offer to x to explain why it is just and fair to criminalize her for robbing others are clear. She deserves censure for choosing to rob because she knew that she was bringing about bad consequences for y (harm), and the gradation of that offense as a serious crime can be dialectically defended.[40]

There is global agreement that harm is bad, but what counts as harm is another question. The harmfulness of a given act often depends on conventional conceptualizations of harm, social norms and socialization. Primitive harms are of a more universal nature, but almost always accord with our deep conventional understanding of harm as well. I have tried to channel the concept of harm to make it more workable as a yardstick for determining when the right not to be criminalized can be overridden. The following conclusions were reached:

- The seriousness of the harm is a core yardstick for determining whether to criminalize the harm.
- Criminalization is not optional when the harm is serious and clearly warrants state action (*i.e.*, marital rape and serious corporate negligence should not be left to the parties involved to resolve).
- Wantonly harming animals can be brought within the reach of the harm concept.
- Harm has to be fairly imputed to the person being held responsible for it.
- There are limits to how much harm a person can consent to.
- It is almost impossible to claim that something is harmful as a matter of truth or in a purely objective sense, but it is possible to claim that something is objectively harmful by drawing on scientific and deeply held conventional understandings of harm.
- Many criminalization decisions are unjust when measured against Western conceptualization of justice, badness, harmfulness and wrongness.

---

factors, but this would not alter the *prima facie* labeling of this type of wrongful harm according to its category of seriousness. The words theft and robbery do little to label an offense, because in the end it is the level of punishment that labels an offense.

40 'To pursue objectivity in practice means doing the best we can to assure the rationality of our own proceedings, to seek to do what other reasonable people would do in our situation. And there is no more effectively practicable way to achieve this than by entering into a communicative commerce with them that enables us to learn by study—and even interrogation—how other sensible people manage those affairs.' Nicholas Rescher, *Objectivity: The Obligations of Impersonal Reason* (Notre Dame, IL: University of Notre Dame Press, 1997) at p. 87.

Therefore, it seems odd that we ask non-Western states to comply with our deeply held conventional understandings of justice when we do not.
- If soft harms, such as those that merely cause umbrage, are to be criminalized, then jail sentences should not be used as a penalty. The exhibitionist and her kind should not be sent to jail, but should be fined and so on. Given that many of these acts are not harmful and are only wrong in a very conventional sense, excluding jail terms as a form of punishment seems to strikes a sensible balance. It allows conduct to be regulated in our plural society, so that people can enjoy public spaces without being involved in unnecessary social conflicts, but also ensures that severe punishment is not used to regulate such trivial conflicts.
- Offending others does not provide a principled justification for criminalization. However, if the umbrage also causes a privacy loss or creates an intolerable social conflict because society is not yet willing to accept a particular kind of behavior, it may be regulated so long as it does not unreasonably interfere with the rights of the alleged wrongdoer.

Firstly, people should not be criminalized for inadvertently influencing the criminal choices of others. A person cannot be held responsible for someone else's harm-doing. A person can only be held responsible for harm, if that harm can be fairly imputed to her because of something she did. It is not fair to punish people for the inadvertent and very remote consequences of their actions. Secondly, the harm principle cannot be replaced with a dignity principle or some other loose sense of freedom, as it is not possible to measure freedom in any practical sense. Thirdly, the wrongness of *grossly harming* human beings cannot be annulled through consent. Consent cannot be used to annul wrongdoing and harm in all cases. Consent has its limits in a humane society that cares about its members. The gravity and irreparable nature of the harm involved wantonly killing, blinding, amputating limbs, and so on is intolerable in a civilized society. Our deeply held conventional understandings of human dignity mean that the right to life is inalienable. Similarly, the right to maintain a minimal level of health and psychological stability is also inalienable. We do not criminalize self-harm, but we also do not provide a defense of consent to those who rely on consent to inflict such atrocities against their fellow human beings. A part of the rationale for limiting consent as a defense is that we do not want to desensitize members of our society into thinking that such conduct is good merely because the victim consents.

There are a number of original ideas presented in this book, including the issue of the freedom criterion not providing a feasible alternative to the harm criterion as a measure for the justice of criminalization decisions, the mandatory requirement that harm be fairly imputed to the person being held responsible for it, and the limits of consent as a defense. However, the most significant ideas presented were: (1) the idea that there is a constitutional right not to be criminalized; (2) that it might not be possible to claim that a particular bad consequence is objectively bad or harmful. The difficulty of objectivity claims is most patently exposed in the discussion on the bad consequence of umbrage. I tackled this issue in Chapter 6. In that chapter I argued that 'umbrage' is a fairly empty concept for the purpose of providing objective criteria for guiding criminalization decisions.

It was noted that the wrongness of some offensive acts is purely conventional in that the conduct is wrong because it violates some convention which people have been socialized into believing is highly valuable. For instance, when x films up y's skirt and then uploads it onto the Internet, y might suffer genuine psychological distress because of the way in which she has been socialized to need privacy. In a different culture such a violation might not even be noticed. I held that this type of wrong is genuinely wrong and is worthy of regulation. However, this highlights the enormous difficulty involved in trying to distinguish genuine conventional wrongs from those that rest purely in prejudice. This issue is of cardinal importance, as most of the controversy concerning unjust criminalization decisions concerns borderline conduct, not obvious harms where there is deep agreement about the harmfulness of the conduct being criminalized. A good book should raise as many questions as it answers and I think Chapter 6 certainly raises many questions. It is hoped that the discussion in this book will stimulate further debate on this issue and encourage philosophers to do more to demonstrate the objectiveness of conventionally contingent umbrages and soft harms. This is of cardinal importance, because a sound account of the act's objective badness is an important limiting factor, because it will be either badness or harmfulness of the particular consequence that will provide the lawmaker with guidance as to whether it should be criminalized.

Harm-doing provides the only sound justification for depriving a person of his or her liberty through *imprisonment*. Such an approach leaves the state with ample discretion to enact a wide range of other regulatory offenses regardless of harm, but prevents it from using jail terms to enforce these offenses. It might not be able to determine harmfulness claims with exact precision, but lawmakers could do enough to make recognizing the harm criterion as a constitutional yardstick worthwhile. In the current climate of penal populism the harm criterion has to be taken out of the academic literature and constitutionalized, if it is to be taken seriously.

In conclusion, it is worth noting that harm can only be taken seriously as a fairness constraint, if we distinguish objective harm from non-objective harm, compel lawmakers to criminalize serious harm, constitutionalize the harm criterion and also explain the culpableness of wantonly harming animals.

Bibliography

Abbey, R., 'Rawlsian Resources for Animal Ethics,' (2007) 12(1) *Ethics & The Environment* 1.
Abbott, E., *A History of Mistresses* (Toronto: Harper Flamingo, 2003).
Alexander, L., 'Harm, Offense, and Morality,' (1994) 7 *Canadian Journal of Law and Jurisprudence* 199.
——, 'The Enforcement of Morality,' in Frey, R.G. and Wellman, C.H. (eds), *A Companion to Applied Ethics* (Oxford: Blackwell Publishing, 2003).
——, 'When Are We Rightfully Aggrieved?,' (2005) 11(3) *Legal Theory* 325.
Allen, A., *Uneasy Access* (Totowa, NJ: Rowman & Littlefield, 1988).
Allen, C.K., *Legal Duties* (Oxford: Clarendon Press, 1931).
Archbold Hong Kong, *Criminal Law, Pleading, Evidence and Practice* (Hong Kong: Sweet & Maxwell Asia, 2007).
Archibold, R.C., 'Las Vegas Makes it Illegal to Feed Homeless in Parks,' (New York: *New York Times*, July 28, 2006).
Arlidge, A., Eady, D. and Smith, A.T.H., *Eady, Arlidge and Smith on Contempt* (London: Thomson Professional, 2nd ed., 1999).
Arneson, R.J., 'Liberalism, Freedom, and Community,' (1990) 100 *Ethics* 368.
——, 'Joel Feinberg and the Justifications of Hard Paternalism,' (2005) 11(3) *Legal Theory* 259.
Ashworth, A., 'Taking the Consequences,' in Shute, S., Gardner, J. and Horder, J. (eds), *Action and Value in Criminal Law* (Oxford: Clarendon Press, 1993).
——, 'Is the Criminal Law a Lost Cause?,' (2000) 116 *The Law Quarterly Review* 225.
——, *Principles of Criminal Law* (Oxford: Oxford University Press, 4th ed., 2003).
—— and Blake, M., 'The Presumption of Innocence in English Criminal Law,' (1996) *Criminal Law Review* 306.
Atkinson, C.M., *Bentham's Theory of Legislation* (London: Oxford University Press, Vol. I, 1914).
Aune, B., *Kant's Theory of Morals* (Princeton NJ: Princeton University Press, 1979).
Austin, J., *The Province of Jurisprudence Determined*, 1832 (London: Weidenfeld and Nicolson, republished ed., with an introduction by H.L.A. Hart, 1954).
Austin, J.L., 'A Plea for Excuses,' (1956–1957) *Proceedings of the Aristotelian Society* 1.
Baier, K., *The Moral Point of View* (Ithaca: Cornell University Press, 1964).

Baker, C.E., *Human Liberty and Freedom of Speech* (New York: Oxford University Press, 1989).

Baker, D.J., 'The Moral Limits of Criminalizing Remote Harms,' (2007) 10(3) *New Criminal Law Review* 370.

———, 'Consensual Harm Doing,' (2008) 12 *UWS Law Review* 21.

———, 'Constitutionalizing the Harm Principle,' (2008) 27(2) *Criminal Justice Ethics* 3.

———, 'The Harm Principle vs. Kantian Criteria for Ensuring Fair, Principled and Just Criminalization,' (2008) 33 *Australian Journal of Legal Philosophy* 66.

———, 'The Sense and Nonsense of Criminalizing Transfers of Obscene Materials,' (2008) 26 *Singapore Law Review* 126.

———, 'A Critical Evaluation of the Historical and Contemporary Justifications for Criminalising Begging,' (2009) 73(3) *Journal of Criminal Law* 212.

———, 'Collective Criminalization and the Constitutional Right to Endanger Others,' (2009) 28(2) *Criminal Justice Ethics*.

———, 'The Moral Limits of Consent as a Defense in the Criminal Law,' (2009) 12(1) *New Criminal Law Review* 93.

———, 'Punishment Without a Crime: Is Preventive Detention Reconcilable with Justice?,' (2009) 34 *Australian Journal of Legal Philosophy* 120.

———, 'Omissions Liability for Homicide Offences: Reconciling *R. v. Kennedy* (No. 2) with *R. v. Evans*,' (2010) 74(4) *Journal of Criminal Law* 80.

———, 'Complicity, Proportionality and the Serious Crime Act,'(2011) 14(3) *New Criminal Law Review*.

——— and Xia Zhao, L., 'Responsibility Links, Fair Labeling and Proportionality in China: A Comparative Analysis,' (2010) 15 *UCLA Journal of International Law & Foreign Affairs* 274.

Baker, G.P. and Hacker, P.M.S., *Language, Sense and Nonsense: A Critical Investigation into Modern Theories of Language* (Oxford: Basil Blackwell, 1984).

Baker, S.J., *Measuring the Explosive Growth of Federal Crime Legislation* (Washington, D.C.: Federalist Society for Law and Policy Studies, Crime Report, 2004).

———, 'Jurisdictional and Separation of Powers Strategies to Limit the Expansion of Federal Crimes,' (2005) 54 *American University Law Review* 545.

Baldwin, R., 'The New Punitive Regulation,' (2004) 67 *Modern Law Review* 351.

Balkin, J.M. and Levinson, S., 'Understanding the Constitutional Revolution,' (2001) 87(6) *Virginia Law Review* 1045.

Barendt, E., 'Threats to Freedom of Speech in the United Kingdom,' (2005) 28 *University of New South Wales Law Journal* 895.

Barkham, P., 'Australian Government Rocked by Phonecard Sleaze Row' (London: *Guardian Unlimited*, October 30, 2000).

Barnett, R.E., 'Justice Kennedy's Libertarian Revolution: *Lawrence v. Texas*,' (2002–2003) *Cato Supreme Court Review* 21.

———, 'The Proper Scope of the Police Power,' (2004) 79 *Notre Dame Law Review* 429.
Bartholomew, A.A., 'Vagrancy: Insufficient Lawful Means of Support,' (1971) 4(2) *Australian and New Zealand Journal of Criminology* 65.
Beale, S.S., 'The Many Faces of Overcriminalization: From Morals and Mattress Tags to Over-federalization,' (2005) 54 *American University Law Review* 747.
Beccaria, C., *On Crimes and Punishments* (Indianapolis, IN: Hackett Publishing, 1986).
Becker, H.S., *Outsiders* (Glencoe, IL: The Free Press, 1963).
Becker, L.C., 'Crimes Against Autonomy: Gerald Dworkin on the Enforcement of Morality,' (1999) 40 *William & Mary Law Review* 959.
Becker, S.L. et al., 'Young H.I.V.-Infected Adults Are at Greater Risk for Medication Nonadherence,' (2002) 4(3) *Medscape General Medicine* 21.
Beetham, D., *The Legitimation of Power* (Basingstoke, U.K.: Macmillan, 1991).
Benn, S.I., 'Individuality, Autonomy, and Community: An Essay in Mediation,' (1978) *Bulletin of the Australian Society of Legal Philosophy* 1.
Benson, C., *A Theory of Freedom* (Cambridge: Cambridge University Press, 1988).
———, 'Privacy, Freedom, and Respect for Persons,' in Wacks, R. (ed.), *Privacy* (Aldershot: Dartmouth, 1993).
——— and Matthews, R., 'Street Prostitution: Ten Facts in Search of a Policy,' (1995) 23 *International Journal of the Sociology of Law* 395.
Berenson, F., 'Understanding Art and Understanding Persons,' in S.C. Brown (ed.), *Objectivity and Cultural Divergence* (Cambridge: Cambridge University Press, 1984).
Bergelson, V., 'Conditional Rights and Comparative Wrongs: More on the Theory and Application of Comparative Criminal Liability,' (2004–2005) 8 *Buffalo Criminal Law Review* 567.
———, 'Victims and Perpetrators: An Argument for Comparative Liability in Criminal Law,' (2004–2005) 8 *Buffalo Criminal Law Review* 385.
Bernd, B. and Gesa, H., 'Zero Tolerance for the Industrial Past and Other Threats: Policing and Urban Entrepreneurialism in Britain and Germany,' (2003) 40(9) *Urban Studies* 1845.
Beyleveld, D. and Brownsword, R., 'Human Dignity, Human Rights, and Human Genetics,' (1998) 61(5) *Modern Law Review* 661.
——— and ———, *Human Dignity in Bioethics and Biolaw* (Oxford: Oxford University Press, 2001).
Bhalla, K. et al., 'A Risk-Based Method for Modeling Traffic Fatalities,' (2007) 27(1) *Risk Analysis* 125.
Black, D. *The Behavior of Law* (New York: Academic Press, 1968).
Blackstone, W., *Commentaries on the Laws of England* (London: Sweet & Maxwell, Vol. 4, 21st ed., 1844).
Blackstone, W.T., 'On the Meaning and Justification of the Equality Principle,' (1967) 77(4) *Ethics* 239.

Bloustein, E., 'Privacy as an Aspect of Human Dignity: An Answer to Dean Prosser,' (1964) 39 *New York University Law Review* 962.
Bludner, A., 'A Theory of Necessity,' (1987) 7 *Oxford Journal of Legal Studies* 339.
Bodenhamer, D.J. and Ely, J.W., *The Bill of Rights in Modern America* (Bloomington, IN: Indiana University Press, 1993).
Bottoms, A.E., 'The Philosophy and Politics of Punishment and Sentencing,' in Clarkson, C.M.V. and Morgan, R. (eds), *The Politics of Sentencing Reform* (Oxford: Clarendon Press, Oxford, 1995).
——, 'Five Puzzles in von Hirsch's Theory of Punishment,' in Ashworth, A. and Wasik, M. (eds), *Fundamentals of Sentencing Theory: Essays in Honor of Andrew von Hirsch* (Oxford: Clarendon Press, 1998).
——, 'Incivilities, Offence, and Social Order in Residential Communities,' in Hirsch, A. von and Simester, A.P., *Incivilities: Regulating Offensive Behaviour* (Oxford: Hart Publishing, 2006).
—— and Light, R., *Problems of Long-Term Imprisonment* (Aldershot: Gower, 1987).
Bowie, N.E. and Simon, R.L., *The Individual and the Political Order* (New York: Rowman and Littlefield, 1998).
Bowling, B., 'The Rise and Fall of New York Murder: Zero Tolerance or Crack's Decline,' (1999) 39 (4) *British Journal of Criminology* 531.
Bradsher, K., 'Internet Sex Video Case Stirs Free-Speech Issues in Hong Kong,' (New York: *New York Times*, February 13, 2008).
Bratton, W.J., 'The New York City Police Department's Civil Enforcement of Quality-of-Life Crimes,' (1995) *Journal of Law & Policy* 447.
Bremner, C., 'France Goes from Burkas to Burgers in Latest Muslim Row,' (London: *The Times*, February 19, 2010).
Brems, E., *Human Rights: Universality and Diversity* (The Hague: Martinus Nijhoff Publishers, 2001).
Brett, P., *An Inquiry into Criminal Guilt* (London: Sweet & Maxwell Ltd., 1963).
British Medical Journal, 'Success in Gun Law Reform in Australia,' (2007) 334 *British Medical Journal* 284.
Britten, N., 'Pensioner's Body Stolen by Animal Rights Group is Found,' (London: *The Daily Telegraph*, May 4, 2005).
Brown, L.R., *Outgrowing the Earth: The Food Security Challenge in an Age of Falling Water Tables and Rising Temperatures* (New York: W.W. Norton & Company, 2005).
Bruni, L. and Sugden, R., 'Fraternity: Why the Market Need Not Be a Morally Free Zone,' (2008) 24 *Economics and Philosophy* 35.
Buchholz, R.A., 'The Protestant Ethic as an Ideological Justification of Capitalism,' (1983) 2(2) *Journal of Business Ethics* 51.
Burke-Hopkins, R., 'The Regulation of Begging and Vagrancy: A Critical Discussion,' (2000) 2 *Crime Prevention and Community Safety: An International Journal* 43.

———, *Zero Tolerance Policing* (Leicester: Perpetuity Press, 2001).
Butt, P., Eagleson, R.D. and Lane, P., *Mabo, Wik and Native Title* (Sydney: The Federation Press, 4th rev. ed., 2001).
Calhoun, G.M., *The Growth of Criminal Law in Ancient Greece* (Berkeley, CA: University of California Press, 1927).
Callahan, J.C., 'On Harming the Dead,' (1989) 97(2) *Ethics* 342.
Card, C., *The Atrocity Paradigm: A Theory of Evil* (Oxford: Oxford University Press, 2002).
Carruthers, P., *The Animal Issue: Moral Theory in Practice* (Cambridge: Cambridge University Press, 1992).
Carter, I., *A Measure of Freedom* (Oxford: Oxford University Press, 1999).
Caughey, M.S., 'Note: Criminal Law—The Principle of Harm and its Application to Laws Criminalizing Prostitution,' (1974) 51 *Denver Law Journal* 235.
Caygill, H., *A Kant Dictionary* (Oxford: Blackwell Publishers, 1999).
Chambliss, W.J., 'A Sociological Analysis of the Laws of Vagrancy,' in Carson, W.G. and Wiles, P. (eds), *The Sociology of Crime and Delinquency in Britain* (Oxford: Martin Robinson, 1981).
——— and Seidmann, R., *Law, Order, and Power* (Reading, MA: Addison-Wesley, 1982).
Charlesworth, L., 'Why Is it a Crime to Be Poor,' (1999) 21 *Liverpool Law Review* 149.
Cheh, M.M., 'Constitutional Limits on Using Civil Remedies to Achieve Criminal Law Objectives: Understanding and Transcending the Criminal Civil Law Distinction,' (1990–1991) 42 *Hastings Law Journal* 1325.
Chevigny, P.G., 'Begging and the First Amendment: *Young v. New York City Transit Authority*,' (1991) 57 *Brooklyn Law Review* 525.
Cochrane, A., 'Animal Rights and Animal Experiments: An Interests-Based Approach,' (2007) 13 *Res Publica* 293.
Coffee, J.C., 'Does "Unlawful" Mean "Criminal"?: Reflections on the Disappearing Tort/Crime Distinction in American Law,' (1991) 71 *Boston University Law Review* 193.
Cohan, J., 'Seditious Conspiracy, the Smith Act, and Prosecution for Religious Speech Advocating the Violent Overthrow of the Government,' (2003) 17 *St John's Journal of Legal Commentary* 199.
Cohen, M.R., 'Moral Aspects of the Criminal Law,' (1940) 49 *Yale Law Journal* 987.
Cook, P.J. and Ludwig, J., *Gun Violence: The Real Costs* (New York: Oxford University Press, 2000).
Corning, P.A., '"Fair Shares": Beyond Capitalism and Socialism, or the Biological Basis of Social Justice,' (2003) 22(2) *Politics and the Life Sciences* 12.
Cullinane, S., 'Hong Kong's Low Car Dependence: Lessons and Prospects,' (2003) 11(1) *Journal of Transport Geography* 25.
Cutler, D.M. *et al.*, 'An Ageing Society: Opportunity or Challenge?,' (1990) 1 *Brook Papers Economic Activity* 1–73.

Dahl, N.O., *Practical Reason, Aristotle, and Weakness of the Will* (Minneapolis, MN: University of Minnesota Press, 1984).

Dalton, H.L., 'Disgust and Punishment,' (1986–1987) 96 *Yale Law Journal* 883.

Dan-Cohen, M., 'Defending Dignity,' (2002) *Boalt Working Papers in Public Law*, Paper 99 (Berkeley, CA: University of California).

Dancy, J., *Normativity* (Oxford: Blackwell Publishers, 2000).

Davis, L.W., 'The Effect of Driving Restrictions on Air Quality in Mexico City,' (2008) 116(1) *The Journal of Political Economy* 38.

Dean, H. (ed.), *Begging Questions: Street-Level Economic Activity and Social Policy Failure* (Bristol: Policy Press, 1999).

Dean, R., 'What Should We Treat as an End in Itself,' (1996) 77(4) *Pacific Philosophical Quarterly* 268.

DeGrazia, D., *Taking Animals Seriously: Mental Life and Moral Status* (Cambridge: Cambridge University Press, 1996).

Dempsey, M.M., 'Rethinking Wolfenden: Prostitute Use, Criminal Law, and Remote Harm,' (2005) *Criminal Law Review* 444.

Devlin, P., *The Enforcement of Morals* (Oxford: Oxford University Press, 1965).

Diamond, A.S., *Primitive Law: Past and Present* (London: Methuen & Co. Ltd., 1971).

Dirie, M.A. and Lindmark, G., 'The Risk of Medical Complications after Female Circumcision,' (1992) 69(9) *East African Medical Journal* 479.

Dorf, M.C., 'Truth, Justice, and the American Constitution,' (1997) 97 *Columbia Law Review* 133.

Dressler, J., 'Reassessing the Theoretical Understandings of Accomplice Liability: New Solutions to an Old Problem,' (1985) 37 *Hastings Law Journal* 91.

———, *Understanding Criminal Law* (Newark, NJ: LexisNexis, 2006).

Dripps, D.A., 'Overcriminalization, Discretion, Waiver: A Survey of Possible Exit Strategies,' (2004–2005) 109 *Penn. State Law Review* 1155.

Dubber, M.D., 'Towards a Constitutional Law of Crime and Punishment,' (2003–2004) 55 *Hastings Law Journal* 509.

Dubin, G.V. and Robinson, R.H., 'The Vagrancy Concept Reconsidered: Problems and Abuses of Status Criminality,' (1962) 37 *New York University Law Review* 102.

Duff, R.A., *Intention, Agency and Criminal Liability* (Oxford: Basil Blackwell, 1990).

———, *Criminal Attempts* (Oxford: Clarendon Press, 1996).

———, 'Harms and Wrongs,' (2001–2002) 5 *Buffalo Criminal Law Review* 13.

———, 'Criminalizing Endangerment,' in Duff, R.A. and Green, S.P. (eds), *Defining Crimes: Essays on the Special Part of the Criminal Law* (Oxford: Oxford University Press, 2005).

Dworkin, R., *Taking Rights Seriously* (King's Lynn: Duckworth, 1977).

———, *A Matter of Principle* (Cambridge, MA: Harvard University Press, 1985).

———, *Life's Dominion: An Argument About Abortion, Euthanasia, and Individual Freedom* (New York: Knopf, 1993).

———, *Freedom's Law: The Moral Reading of the American Constitution* (Oxford: Oxford University Press, 1996).

———, 'Objectivity and Truth: You'd Better Believe It,' (1996) *Philosophy and Public Affairs* 87.

———, *Sovereign Virtue* (Cambridge, MA: Harvard University Press, 2000).

———, *Is Democracy Possible Here?* (Princeton, NJ: Princeton University Press, 2006).

———, *Justice in Robes* (Cambridge, MA: Harvard University Press, 2006).

Eddin-Taqi, K. and Macallair, D., 'Shattering "Broken Windows": An Analysis of San Francisco's Alternative Crime Policies,' Centre on Juvenile and Criminal Justice (San Francisco, 2002): available online at <http://www.prisonpolicy.org/scans/windows.pdf>.

Eggleston, E., *Fear, Favor of Affection* (Canberra: Australian National University Press, 1976).

Ellickson, R.C., 'Controlling Chronic Misconduct in City Spaces: Of Panhandlers, Skid Rows, and Public-Space Zoning,' (1995–1996) 105 *Yale Law Journal* 1165.

Ellis, E., *The Principle of Proportionality in the Laws of Europe* (Oxford: Hart Publishing, 2000).

Elwell, F.W., *A Commentary on Malthus's 1798 Essay on Population as Social Theory* (Lewiston, NY: Edwin Mellen Press, 2001).

Emsley, C., 'The History of Crime and Crime Control Institutions,' in Maguire, M. et al. (eds), *The Oxford Handbook of Criminology* (Oxford: Oxford University Press, 3rd ed., 2003).

Epstein, R., 'The Harm Principle—And How It Grew,' (1995) 45(4) *Toronto Law Journal* 369.

Erskine, A. and McIntosh, I., 'Why Begging Offends: Historical Perspectives and Continuities,' in Dean, H. (ed.), *Begging Questions: Street-Level Economic Activity and Social Policy Failure* (Bristol: The Policy Press, 1999).

Evans, E.P., *The Criminal Prosecution and Capital Punishment of Animals* (London: Faber and Faber, 1987).

Evans, L.T., *Feeding the Ten Billion—Plants and Population Growth* (Cambridge: Cambridge University Press, 1998).

Falls, M.M., 'Retribution, Reciprocity, and Respect for Persons,' (1987) 6 *Law and Philosophy* 25.

Fehr, E. and Schmidt, K.M., 'A Theory of Fairness, Competition, and Cooperation,' (1999) 114(3) *The Quarterly Journal of Economics* 817.

Feinberg, J., *Doing and Deserving* (Princeton, NJ: Princeton University Press, 1970).

———, 'The Rights of Animals and Unborn Generations,' in Blackstone, W.T. (ed.), *Philosophy and Environmental Crisis* (Athens, GA: University of Georgia Press, 1974).

———, *The Moral Limits of the Criminal Law: Harm to Others* (New York: Oxford University Press, Vol. I, 1984).

———, *The Moral Limits of the Criminal Law: Offense to Others* (New York: Oxford University Press, Vol. II, 1985).

———, *The Moral Limits of the Criminal Law: Harm to Self* (New York: Oxford University Press, Vol. III, 1986).

———, *The Morals Limits of the Criminal Law: Harmless Wrongdoing* (New York: Oxford University Press, Vol. IV, 1988).

———, 'In Defence of Moral Rights,' (1992) 12(2) *Oxford Journal of Legal Studies* 149.

Feldbrugge, F.J.M., *The Law's Beginnings* (Leiden: Brill Academic Publishing, 2003).

Ferrajoli, L. and Zolo, D., 'Marxism and the Criminal Question,' (1985) 4 *Law and Philosophy* 71.

Findlay, M. et al., *Australian Criminal Justice* (Melbourne: Oxford University Press, 1999).

Finkelstein, C., 'Positivism and the Notion of an Offence,' (2000) 88 *California Law Review* 335.

———, 'Is Risk Harm?' (2002–2003) 151 *University of Pennsylvania Law Review* 963.

———, 'Responsibility for Unintended Consequences,' (2005) 2 *Ohio State Journal of Criminal Law* 579.

Finn, J., 'Culpable Non-Intervention: Reconsidering the Basis for Party Liability by Omission,' (1994) 18 *Criminal Law Journal* 90.

Finnis, J., *Natural Law and Natural Rights* (Oxford: Clarendon Press, 1979).

———, *Fundamentals of Ethics* (Oxford: Clarendon Press, 1983).

———, 'Intention and Side-Effects,' in Frey, R.G. and Morris, C.W. (eds), *Liability and Responsibility* (Cambridge: University Press, 1991).

Fish, S., *There's No Such Thing as Free Speech and It's a Good Thing Too* (New York: Oxford University Press, 1994).

Fitzgerald, P.J., *Criminal Law and Punishment* (Oxford: Clarendon Press, 1962).

Fletcher, G.P., *Rethinking the Criminal Law* (Boston: Little, Brown and Company, 1978).

———, *Basic Concepts of Legal Thought* (New York: Oxford University Press, 1996).

———, *Basic Concepts of Criminal Law* (New York: Oxford University Press, 1998).

Flikschuh, K., 'Kantian Desires,' in Timmons, M. (ed.), *Kant's Metaphysics of Morals: Interpretative Essays* (Oxford: Oxford University Press, 2002).

Forst, R., 'Toleration, Justice and Reason,' in McKinnon, C. and Castiglione, D. (eds), *The Culture of Toleration in Diverse Societies* (Manchester: Manchester University Press, 2003).

Foscarinis, M., 'Out of Sight–Out of Mind?: The Continuing Trend Toward the Criminalization of Homelessness,' (1999) 6 *Georgetown Journal of Poverty Law and Policy* 145.

Fougère, M. and Mérette, M., 'Population Ageing and Economic Growth in Seven OECD Countries,' (1999) 16(3) *Economic Modeling* 411.

Frankfurt, H., 'Freedom of the Will and the Concept of a Person,' (1971) 68 *Journal of Philosophy* 1.

Frase, R.S., 'State Sentencing Guidelines Still Going Strong,' (1994–1995) 78 *Judicature* 173.

Fried, C., *Right and Wrong* (Cambridge, MA: Harvard University Press, 1979).

Friedrich, C.J., *The Philosophy of Kant: Immanuel Kant's Moral and Political Writings* (New York: The Modern Library, 1949).

Galligan, D.J., 'The Return to Retribution in Penal Theory,' in Tapper, C.F.H. (ed.), *Crime, Proof and Punishment: Essays in Memory of Sir Rupert Cross* (London: Butterworths, 1981).

Galtung, J., 'Cultural Violence,' (1990) 27(3) *Journal of Peace Research* 291.

Gardner, J., 'Nearly Natural Law,' (2007) 52 *The American Journal of Jurisprudence* 1.

———, 'Prohibiting Immoralities,' (2007) 28(6) *Cardozo Law Review* 2613.

——— and Shute. S., 'The Wrongness of Rape,' in Horder, J. (ed.), *Oxford Essays in Jurisprudence* (Oxford: Oxford University Press, 4th Series, 2000).

Gaus, G.F., 'Respect for Persons and Environmental Values,' in Kneller, J. and Axinn, S. (eds), *Autonomy and Community: Readings in Contemporary Kantian Social Philosophy* (New York: State University of New York Press, 1998).

Gauthier, D., *Morals by Agreement* (Oxford: Clarendon Press, 1986).

Gavison, R., 'Privacy and the Limits of Law,' (1980) 89(3) *Yale Law Journal* 421.

Geras, N., *Solidarity in the Conversation of Humankind: The Ungroundable Liberalism of Richard Rorty* (London: Verso, 1995).

Gobert, J. and Punch, M., *Rethinking Corporate Crime* (London: Butterworths LexisNexis, 2003).

Goffman, E., *Relations in Public, Microstudies of Public Order* (London: Penguin Press, 1971).

Goldsmith, A. *et al.* (eds), *Crime and Justice: A Guide to Criminology* (Sydney: Thomson Lawbook Co., 3rd ed., 2006).

Goldstein, B.J., 'Panhandlers at Yale: A Case Study in the Limits of Law,' (1993–1994) 27 *Indiana Law Review* 295.

Goss, K.A., *The Missing Movement for Gun Control in America* (Princeton, NJ: Princeton University Press, 2006).

Gotsch, K.D., Annest, J.L., Mercy, J.A. and Ryan, G.W., 'Surveillance for Fatal and Nonfatal Firearm Related Injuries – United-States 1993–1998,' in CDC Surveillance Summaries (April 13, 2001, No. SS-2): available online at <http://www.cdc.gov./mmwr/pdf/ss/ss5002.pdf>.

Grasmick, H.G. and Green, D.E., 'Legal Punishment, Social Disapproval, and Internalization as Inhibitors of Illegal Behaviour,' (1980) 71 *Criminal Law and Criminology* 325.

Green, L., 'Tort Law Public Law in Disguise,' (1959–60) 38 *Texas Law Review* 257.
Greenwood, P.W. *et al.* (eds), *Three Strikes and You're Out: Estimated Benefits and Costs of California's New Mandatory-Sentencing Law* (Santa Monica, CA: Rand, 1994).
Griffin, J., *On Human Rights* (Oxford: Oxford University Press, 2008).
Gross, H., *A Theory of Criminal Justice* (New York: Oxford University Press, 1979).
Grover, D., 'Posthumous Harm,' (1989) 39(156) *The Philosophical Quarterly* 334.
Gusfield, J.R., *Symbolic Crusade* (Urbana, IL: University of Illinois Press, 2nd ed., 1986).
Haas-Wilson, D., 'The Economic Impact of State Restrictions on Abortion: Parental Consent and Notification Laws and Medicaid Funding Restrictions,' (1993) 12(3) *Journal of Policy Analysis and Management* 498.
Haiman, F.S., 'Is There a Right Not to Be Spoken to?,' (1972) 67 *Northwestern University Law Review* 153.
Hall, J., *General Principles of Criminal Law* (Indianapolis, IN: Bobbs-Merrill Co., 2nd ed., 1960).
Hall, W., Solowij, N., Lemon, J. *et al.*, *The Health and Psychological Consequences of Cannabis Use* (Canberra: Australian Government Publishing Service, National Drug Strategy, 1994).
Hampton, J., 'The Nature of Morality,' (1989) 7(1) *Social Philosophy & Policy* 22.
———, 'Mens Rea,' (1990) 7(2) *Social Philosophy & Policy* 1.
———, 'Liberalism, Retribution and Criminality,' in Coleman, J.L. and Buchanan, A. (eds), *In Harm's Way: Essays in Honor of Joel Feinberg* (Cambridge: Cambridge University Press, 1994).
———, 'Retribution and the Liberal State,' (1994) 5 *Journal of Contemporary Legal Issues* 117.
———, *The Authority of Reason* (Cambridge: Cambridge University Press, 1998).
Harcourt, B.E., 'Reflecting on the Subject: A Critique of the Social Influence Conception of Deterrence, the Broken Windows Theory, and Order Maintenance Policing New York Style,' (1998) 97 *Michigan Law Review* 291.
———, 'Collapse of the Harm Principle,' (1999–2000) 90 *Journal of Criminal Law and Criminology* 109.
———, *Illusion of Order, The False Promise of Broken Windows Policing* (Cambridge, MA: Harvard University Press, 2001).
———, 'Joel Feinberg on Crime and Punishment: Exploring the Relationship Between the Moral Limits of the Criminal Law and the Expressive Function of Punishment,' (2001–2002) 5 *Buffalo Criminal Law Review* 145.
———, 'Policing Disorder: Can We Reduce Serious Crime by Punishing Petty Offenses?,' (2002) *Boston Review*, April/May.
——— and Ludwig, J., 'Broken Windows: New Evidence from New York City and a Five City Social Experiment,' (2006) 73(1) *University of Chicago Law Review* 271.

Hare, I., 'Method and Objectivity in Free Speech Adjudication: Lessons from America,' (2005) 54 *International and Comparative Law Quarterly* 49.

Hargrove, E.C., *The Animal Rights: Environmental Ethics Debate* (New York: State University of New York Press, 1992).

Hart, H.L.A., 'Are There Any Natural Rights,' (1955) 64 *The Philosophical Review* 175.

———, *Law, Liberty and Morality* (London: Oxford University Press, 1963).

———, *The Morality of the Criminal Law* (Oxford: Oxford University Press, 1965).

———, *Punishment and Responsibility: Essays in the Philosophy of Law* (Oxford: Clarendon Press, 1968).

———, 'Between Utility and Rights,' (1979) 79 *Columbia Law Review* 828.

———, *Essays in Jurisprudence and Philosophy* (Oxford: Clarendon Press, 1983).

———, 'Liberty, Utility, and Rights,' in *Essays in Jurisprudence and Philosophy* (Oxford: Clarendon Press, 1983).

———, 'Social Solidarity and the Enforcement of Morality,' in *Essays in Jurisprudence and Philosophy* (Oxford: Clarendon Press, 1983).

Hart, H.M., 'The Aims of the Criminal Law,' (1958) 23 *Law & Contemporary Problems* 401.

Hayek, F.A. von, *The Constitution of Liberty* (Chicago: University of Chicago Press, 1978).

Hemenway, D., 'The Public Approach to Reducing Firearm Injury and Violence,' (2006) 17 *Stanford Law & Policy Review* 635.

Henkin, L., 'Privacy and Autonomy,' (1974) 74 *Columbia Law Review* 1410.

Herring, J., *Criminal Law: Text, Cases and Materials* (Oxford: Oxford University Press, 2005).

Hershkoff, H. and Cohen, A.S., 'Begging to Differ: The First Amendment and the Right to Beg,' (1991) 104 *Harvard Law Review* 896.

Hershovitz, S., *Exploring Law's Empire: The Jurisprudence of Ronald Dworkin* (New York: Oxford University Press, 2006).

Hill, T.E., 'Humanity as an End in Itself,' (1980–1981) 91 *Ethics* 84.

———, *Autonomy and Self-Respect* (Cambridge: Cambridge University Press, 1991).

Hills, J. and Lelkes, O., 'Social Security, Selective Universalism and Patchwork Redistribution,' in Jowell, R. *et al.* (eds), *British Social Attitudes*, Report 16 (Aldershot: Ashgate, 1999).

Hirsch, A. von, 'Injury and Exasperation: An Examination of Harm to Others and Offense to Others,' (1985–1986) 84 *Michigan Law Review* 700.

———, *Censure and Sanctions* (Oxford: Oxford University Press, 1993).

———, 'Extending the Harm Principle: "Remote" Harms and Fair Imputation,' in Simester, A.P. and Smith, A.T.H. (eds), *Harm and Culpability* (Oxford: Clarendon Press, 1996).

———, 'The Ethics of Public Television Surveillance,' in Hirsch, A. von, Garland, D. and Wakefield, A., *Ethical and Social Perspectives on Situational Crime Prevention* (Oxford: Hart Publishing, 2000).

———, 'Toleranz als Mediating Principle,' in Hirsch, A. von, Seelmann, K. and Wolfgang, W. (eds), *Mediating Principles* (Baden-Baden: Nomos Verlagsgesellschaft, 2006).

———, 'Varieties of Remote Harms and Rationales for their Criminalization' (Cambridge University, Unpublished Mimeo, 2006).

——— and Ashworth, A., *Proportionate Sentencing: Exploring the Principles* (Oxford: Oxford University Press, 2005).

——— and Jareborg, N., 'Gauging Crime Seriousness: A "Living Standard" Conception of Criminal Harm,' in Hirsch, A. von and Ashworth, A., *Proportionate Sentencing: Exploring the Principles*, (Oxford: Oxford University Press, 2005).

——— and Simester, A.P., *Incivilities: Regulating Offensive Behaviour* (Oxford: Hart Publishing, 2006).

——— and ———, 'Penalizing Offensive Behavior: Constitutive and Mediating Principles,' in Hirsch, A. von and Simester, A.P., *Incivilities: Regulating Offensive Behaviour* (Oxford: Hart Publishing, 2006).

Hirschman, A.O., 'Rival Interpretations of Market Society: Civilizing, Destructive, or Feeble?' (1982) 20 *Journal of Economic Literature* 1463.

Home Office, Report of the Committee on Homosexual Offences and Prostitution (London: Home Office, Cmnd 247, 1957).

———, Working Party Report of the Working Party on Vagrancy and Street Offences (London: Home Office, 1976).

———, Respect and Responsibility—Taking a Stand Against Anti-Social Behaviour (London: Home Office, White Paper Cm 5778, 2003).

———, Paying the Price: A Consultation Paper on Prostitution (London: Home Office, 2004).

———, *Together*, Action Plan (London: Home Office, 2003).

Honoré, T.M., 'Social Justice,' in Summers, R.S. (ed.), *Essays in Legal Philosophy* (Oxford: Basil Blackwell, 1968).

Hörnle, T., 'Offensive Behaviour and German Penal Law,' (2001–2002) 5 *Buffalo Criminal Law Review* 255.

Hruschka, J., 'Imputation,' (1986) *B.Y.U. Law Review* 669.

Hume, D., *A Treatise of Human Nature*, Norton, D.F. and Norton, M.J. (eds), (Oxford: Oxford University Press, 2007).

Hurd, H., 'Justification and Excuse, Wrongdoing and Culpability,' (1999) 74 *Notre Dame Law Review* 1551.

Hurley, D., 'On Crime as Science (A Neighbour at a Time),' (New York: *New York Times*, January 6, 2004).

Husak, D.N., *Philosophy of Criminal Law* (New York: Rowman & Littlefield, 1987).

———, 'The Nature and Justifiability of Nonconsummate Offenses,' (1995) 37 *Arizona Law Review* 151.

———, 'Limitations on Criminalization,' in Shute, S. and Simester, A.P., *Criminal Law Theory: Doctrines of the General Part* (Oxford: Oxford University Press, 2002).

———, 'Guns and Drugs: Case Studies on the Principled Limits of the Criminal Sanction,' (2004) 23 *Law and Philosophy* 437.

———, 'Malum Prohibitum and Retribution,' in Duff, R.A. and Green, S.P. (eds), *Defining Crimes: Essays on the Special Part of the Criminal Law* (Oxford: Oxford University Press, 2005).

———, 'Disgust: Metaphysical and Empirical Speculations,' in Hirsch, A. von and Simester, A.P., *Incivilities: Regulating Offensive Behaviour* (Oxford: Hart Publishing, 2006).

———, *Overcriminalization: The Limits of the Criminal Law* (New York: Oxford University Press, 2008).

——— and Marneffe, P. de, *The Legalization of Drugs: For and Against* (Cambridge: Cambridge University Press, 2005).

Inness, J.C., *Privacy, Intimacy, and Isolation* (Oxford: Oxford University Press, 1992).

Irish Law Reform Commission, *Report on Vagrancy and Related Offences*, Report L.R.C. 11, 1985.

Johnson, A., 'Note, The Second Circuit Refuses to Extend Beggars a Helping Hand: *Young v. New York City Transit Authority*,' (1991) 69 *Washington University Quarterly* 969.

Jolowicz, J.A., *Lectures on Jurisprudence* (London: Athlone Press, 1963).

Jones, R.K., 'Abortion in the United States: Incidence and Access to Services, 2005,' (2008) 40 *Perspectives on Sexual and Reproduction Health* 6.

Jordan, W.K., *Philanthropy in England 1480–1660* (London: Allen & Unwin, 1959).

Joyce, R., *The Myth of Morality* (New York: Cambridge University Press, 2001).

Junker, M.J., 'Criminalization and Criminogenesis,' (1971–1972) 19 *U.C.L.A. Law Review* 697.

Kadish, S.H., 'The Crisis of Overcriminalization,' (1967) 374 *The Annals of the American Academy* 157.

———, 'More on Overcriminalization: A Reply to Professor Junker,' (1971–1972) 19 *U.C.L.A. Law Review* 719.

———, 'Complicity, Cause and Blame: A Study in the Interpretation of Doctrine,' (1985) 73 *California Law Review* 323.

———, 'Criminal Law: Reckless Complicity,' (1997) 87 *Journal of Criminal Law and Criminology* 369.

——— et al., *Criminal Law and its Processes: Cases and Materials* (New York: Aspen Publishers, 2007).

Kahan, D.M., 'Social Influence, Social Meaning, and Deterrence,' (1997) 83 *Virginia Law Review* 349.

Kant, I., *Groundwork of the Metaphysics of Morals*, 1785, translated from the German by Paton, H.J., *The Moral Law* (London: Hutchinson University Library, 1972).

———, *The Philosophy of Law: An Exposition of the Fundamental Principles of Jurisprudence as the Science of Right*, 1796, translated from the German by Hastie, W., *The Philosophy of Law* (Edinburgh: T. & T. Clark, 1887).

———, *Metaphysics of Morals*, 1797, translated from the German by Gregor, M.J., *Practical Philosophy: The Cambridge Edition of the Works of Immanuel Kant* (Cambridge: Cambridge University Press, 1999).

Kaplan, J., 'The Role of the Law in Drug Control,' (1971) *Duke Law Journal* 1065.

Kaufman, S.M., 'Comment, First Amendment Protection of Begging in Subways,' (1991) 79 *Georgetown Law Journal* 1803.

Kelling, G., 'Broken Windows, Zero Tolerance and Crime Control,' in Francis, P. and Fraser, P., *Building Safer Communities* (London: Centre for Criminal Justice Studies, 1999).

——— and Coles, C.M., *Fixing Broken Windows: Restoring Order and Reducing Crime in our Communities* (New York: Simon and Schuster, 1996).

Kellogg, T., 'Legislating Rights: Basic Law Article 23, National Security, and Human Rights in Hong Kong,' (2004) 17 *Columbia Journal of Asian Law* 307.

Kelsen, H., *What is Justice?* (Los Angeles: University of California Press, 1971).

Kiflik, A., 'The Inalienability of Autonomy,' (1984) 13(4) *Philosophy & Public Affairs* 271.

———, 'The Utilitarian Logic of Inalienable Rights,' (1986) 97 *Ethics* 75.

King, P., *Housing, Individuals and the State: The Morality of Government Intervention* (London: Routledge, 1998).

———, *Toleration* (London: Frank Cass, 2nd ed., 1998).

———, 'Conceptualizing Housing Right,' (London: C.C.H.R. Conference Paper, 2001).

———, *Private Dwelling: Contemplating the Use of Housing* (London: Routledge, 2003).

———, *The Common Place: In the Midst of the Ordinary* (Aldershot: Ashgate, 2005).

Kingston, M., 'More on the Reith Telecard Affair' (Sydney: *Sydney Morning Herald*, October 30, 2000).

Kleck, G., *Point Blank: Guns and Violence in America* (Hawthorne, NY: Aldine de Gruyter, 1991).

———, *Targeting Guns: Firearms and their Control* (Piscataway, NJ: Aldine Transaction, 1997).

Kleinig, J., 'Criminally Harming Others,' (1986) 5 *Criminal Justice Ethics* 3.

Klimchuk, D., 'Three Accounts of Respect for Persons in Kant's Ethics,' (2003) 7 *Kantian Review* 38.

Koehlinger, J.S. 'Substantive Due Process Analysis and the Lockean Liberal Tradition: Rethinking the Modern Privacy Cases,' (1990) 65 *Indiana Law Journal* 723.

Kolnai, A., 'The Standard Modes of Aversion: Fear, Disgust and Hatred,' (1998) 107 *Mind* 581.
Korsgaard, C.M., 'The Reasons We Can Share: An Attack on the Distinction Between Agent-Relative and Agent-Neutral Values,' (1993) 10(1) *Social Philosophy and Policy* 24.
———, *Creating the Kingdom of Ends* (Cambridge: Cambridge University Press, 1996).
———, *The Sources of Normativity* (Cambridge: Cambridge University Press, 1996).
Kramer, M.H., *Rights, Wrongs and Responsibilities* (Chippenham, Wiltshire: Palgrave, 2001).
———, *Where Law and Morality Meet* (Oxford: Oxford University Press, 2004).
———, *Objectivity and the Rule of Law* (Cambridge: Cambridge University Press, 2007).
Kraut, R., *What is Good and Why: The Ethics of Well-Being* (Cambridge, MA: Harvard University Press, 2007).
Kretschmann, P.M., 'An Exposition of Kant's Philosophy of Law,' in Whitney, G.T. and Bowers, D.F. (eds), *The Heritage of Kant* (Princeton NJ: Princeton University Press, 1939).
Kruschke, E.R., *Gun Control: A Reference Book* (Santa Barbara, CA: ABC-CLIO, 1995).
Kugler, I., *Direct and Oblique Intention in the Criminal Law: And Inquiry into Degrees of Blameworthiness* (Aldershot: Ashgate, 2002).
Kymlicka, W., *Liberalism, Community and Culture* (Oxford: Clarendon Press, 1989).
Lacey, N., 'Criminalization as Regulation: The Role of Criminal Law,' in Parker, C. *et al.* (eds), *Regulating Law* (Oxford University Press, 2004).
———, Wells, C. and Quick, O., *Reconstructing Criminal Law* (London: LexisNexis, 3rd ed., 2003).
Lahan, P.M., 'Comments: Trends in the Law of Vagrancy,' (1968) 1 *Connecticut Law Review* 350.
Lanham, D., 'Danger Down Under,' (1999) *Criminal Law Review* 961.
Law Commission of Canada, What is a Crime? Discussion Paper (2003).
Law Commission of England and Wales, *Consent in the Criminal Law*, Consultation Paper No. 139 (London: H.M.S.O., 1995).
Lee, H.N., 'Morals, Morality, and Ethics: Suggested Terminology,' (1928) 38(4) *International Journal of Ethics* 450.
Leiter, B., *Objectivity in Law and Morals* (Cambridge: Cambridge University Press, 2001).
Leonardatos, C., Blackman, P.H. and Kopel, D.B., 'Smart Guns/Foolish Legislators: Finding the Right Public Safety Laws, and Avoiding the Wrong Ones,' (2001) 34 *Connecticut Law Review* 157.
Levenbook, B.B., 'Harming Someone After His Death,' (1984) 94(3) *Ethics* 407.

Levitt, A., 'The Origin of the Doctrine of Mens Rea,' (1922–1923) 17 *Illinois Law Review* 117.
Lewis, D., *Convention: A Philosophical Study* (Oxford: Blackwell Publishing, 2002).
Livingston, D., 'Police Discretion and the Quality of Life in Public Places: Courts, Communities, and New Policing,' (1997) 97 *Columbia Law Review* 551.
Llewellyn, B., *China's Court and Concubines: Some People in Chinese History* (London: Allen & Unwin, 1956).
Locke, J., *An Essay Concerning Human Understanding*, Nidditch, P.H. (ed.) (Oxford: Clarendon Press, 1974).
Lott, J.R., *More Guns, Less Crime: Understanding Crime and Gun Control Laws* (Chicago: University of Chicago Press, 1998).
Lucas, J.R., *On Justice* (Oxford: Clarendon Press, 1980).
———, *Responsibility* (Oxford: Clarendon Press, 1993).
Luna, E., 'Overextending the Criminal Law,' (December 2003) XXV(6) *CATO Policy Report*.
———, 'The Overcriminalization Phenomenon,' (2005) 54 *American University Law Review* 703.
Luoma, J. and Sivak, M., 'Characteristics and Availability of Fatal Road-Crash Databases in 20 Countries Worldwide,' (2007) 38(3) *Journal of Safety Research* 323.
Lyall, S., 'British MPs Say Speaker Has Lost Moral Authority,' (*New York Times*, May 19, 2009, p. A12).
MacCormack, G., *The Spirit of Traditional Chinese Law* (Athens, GA: University of Georgia Press, 1996).
MacCormick, N., *H.L.A. Hart* (Stanford, CA: Stanford University Press, 1981).
MacFarlane, A.D.J., 'Witchcraft in Tudor and Stuart Essex,' in Cockburn J.S. (ed.), *Crime in England 1550–1800* (Cambridge: Methuen & Co., 1977).
MacIntyre, A., *After Virtue: A Study in Moral Theory* (Notre Dame, IN: University of Notre Dame Press, 1984).
Mackie, J.L., *Ethics: Inventing Right and Wrong* (London: Penguin Books, 1977).
———, 'Morality and the Retributive Emotions,' (1982) 1 *Criminal Justice Ethics* 3.
———, 'Retributivism: A Test Case for Ethical Objectivity,' in Feinberg, J. and Gross, H., *Philosophy of Law* (Belmont, CA: Wadsworth Publishing Company, 1991).
MacKinnon, C.A., *Toward a Feminist Theory of the State* (Cambridge, MA: Harvard University Press, 1989).
Macklin, R. and Sherwin, S., 'Experimenting on Human Subjects: Philosophical Perspectives,' (1975) 25 *Case Western Reserve Law Review* 434.
Maguire, M. and Bennett, T., *Burglary in a Dwelling* (London: Heinemann, 1982).
——— and Kynch, J., *Public Perceptions and Victims' Experiences of Victim Support* (London: H.M.S.O., 2000).
Malcolm, J.L., *To Keep and Bear Arms: The Origins of an Anglo-American Right* (Cambridge, MA: Harvard University Press, 1994).

Mann, K., 'Punitive Civil Sanctions: The Middleground Between Criminal and Civil Law,' (1991–1992) 101 *Yale Law Journal* 1795.

Manson, N.C. and O'Neill, O., *Rethinking Informed Consent in Bioethics* (Cambridge: Cambridge University Press, 2007).

Marby, C.A., 'Brother Can You Spare Some Change? – And Your Privacy Too?: Avoiding a Fatal Collision Between Public Interests and Beggars' First Amendment Rights,' (1996) 28 *University of San Francisco Law Review* 309.

Marmor, A., 'On the Limits of Rights,' (1997) 16(1) *Law and Philosophy* 1.

Marshall, S.E. and Duff, R.A., 'Criminalization and Sharing Wrongs,' (1998) 11 *Canadian Journal of Law and Jurisprudence* 7.

Martin, G. *et al.*, 'Truth and Moral Objectivity Procedural Realism in Putnam's Pragmatism,' (2008) 95(1) *Poznan Studies in the Philosophy of the Sciences and the Humanities* 265.

Matthews, R., 'Regulating Street Prostitution and Kerb Crawling: A Reply to John Lowman,' (1992) 32(1) *British Journal of Criminology* 18.

—— and Young, J., *Issues in Realist Criminology* (London: Sage Publications, 1992).

McConnell, T., *Inalienable Rights: The Limits of Consent in Medicine and Law* (Oxford: Oxford University Press, 2000).

McDowell, J., *Mind Value and Reality* (Cambridge, MA: Harvard University Press, 1998).

McGowan, M.O., 'Outlaws to Ingroup: Romer, Lawrence, and the Inevitable Normativity of Group Recognition,' (2004) 88 *Minnesota Law Review* 1312.

McKinnon, C. and Castiglone, D., *The Culture of Toleration in Diverse Societies* (Manchester: Manchester University Press, 2003).

Metcalf, H. *et al.*, *Barriers to Work for Offenders and Ex-Offenders* (London: Department of Work and Pensions, Research Report 155, 2001).

Meyers, D.T., *Inalienable Rights: A Defense* (New York: Columbia University Press, 1985).

Miles, D., 'Modeling the Impact of Demographic Change Upon the Economy,' (1999) *The Economic Journal* 109.

Mill, J.S., *On Liberty and Other Essays* (Oxford: Oxford University Press, 1991).

Miller, E.M., 'The United States,' in Davis, NJ (ed.), *Prostitution: An International Handbook on Trends, Problems and Policies* (Westport, CT: Greenwood Press, 1993).

Miller, S. and Selgelid, M.J., 'Ethical and Philosophical Consideration of the Dual-Use Dilemma in the Biological Sciences,' (2007) 13(4) *Science and Engineering Ethics* 523.

Millich, N.A., 'Compassion Fatigue and the First Amendment: Are the Homeless Constitutional Castaways?' (1994) 27 *University of California, Davis Law Review* 225.

Milo, R.D., *Immorality* (Princeton, NJ: Princeton University Press, 1984).

Moore, M., 'Justifying Retributivism,' (1993) 27 *Israel Law Review* 15.

———, 'The Independent Moral Significance of Moral Wrongdoing,' (1994) 5 *Journal of Contemporary Legal Issues* 237.
———, *Placing Blame: A General Theory of the Criminal Law* (Oxford: Clarendon Press, 1997).
Morris, A.A., 'Overcriminalization and Washington's Revised Criminal Code,' (1972–1973) 48 *Washington Law Review* 5.
Morris, N. and Hawkins, G., *The Honest Politician's Guide to Crime Control* (Chicago: Chicago University Press, 1970).
Murphy, J.G., 'Another Look at Legal Moralism,' (1966) 77(1) *Ethics* 50.
———, 'Does Kant Have a Theory of Punishment,' (1987) 87 *Columbia Law Review* 509.
———, *Retribution Reconsidered* (Dordrecht: Kluwer Academic Publishers, 1992).
——— and Coleman, J.L., *Philosophy of Law: An Introduction to Jurisprudence* (Boulder, CO: Westview Press, 1990).
Nagel, T., *The View From Nowhere* (New York: Oxford University Press, 1986).
———, *Equality and Partiality* (New York: Oxford University Press, 1991).
———, *The Last Word* (New York: Oxford University Press, 1997).
———, 'Concealment and Exposure,' (1998) 27 *Philosophy & Public Affairs* 3.
National Center for Health Statistics, *Trend C Table 292: Deaths for 282 Selected Causes* (1888): available online at <http://www.cdc.gov/nchs/data/statab/gm292_3.pdf.>.
National Center for Policy Analysis, 'Involved Neighbors Reduce Crime,' (Washington, D.C.: January 9, 2004): available online at <http://www.n c p a.org/iss/cri/>.
National Coalition for the Homeless, 'Illegal to be Homeless: The Criminalization of Homelessness in the United States,' *National Coalition for the Homeless Report*, (Washington, D.C.: 2003).
Naylor, R.T., 'The Underworld of Ivory,' (2004) 42 *Crime, Law & Social Change* 261.
Nemerson, S.S., 'Note: Criminal Liability Without Fault: A Philosophical Perspective,' (1975) 75 *Columbia Law Review* 1517.
New York Times, 'Bicyclists Ride in Protest, and in Little Else,' (New York: *New York Times*, June 12, 2005).
———, 'British Couple Appealing Dubai Kiss Conviction,' (New York: *New York Times*, March 14, 2010).
Nichols, P., 'The Panhandler's First Amendment Right: A Critique of *Loper v. New York City Police Department* and Related Academic Commentary,' (1996–1997) 48 *South Carolina Law Review* 268.
Nissenbaum, H., 'Protecting Privacy in an Information Age: The Problem of Privacy in Public,' (1998) 17 *Law and Philosophy* 559.
Nozick, R., *Anarchy, State, and Utopia* (New York: Basic Books, 1974).
———, *Philosophical Explanations* (Oxford: Clarendon Press, 1981).
O'Connell, D., *Prostitution, Power and Freedom* (Cambridge: Polity Press, 1998).

O'Doherty, S., 'The Emergence of Criminal Laws,' (1999) 163 *Justice of the Peace* 528.
Odujirin, A., *The Normative Basis of Fault in Criminal Law: History and Theory* (Toronto: University of Toronto Press, 1998).
O'Neill, O., *Constructions of Reason: Explorations of Kant's Practical Philosophy* (Cambridge: Cambridge University Press, 1989).
———, *Towards Justice and Virtue: A Constructive Account of Practical Reasoning* (Cambridge: Cambridge University Press, 1996).
———, 'Kant and the Social Contract Tradition,' in Duchesneau, F., Lafrance, G. and Piché, C., (eds), *Kant Actuel: Hommage à Pierre Laberge* (Montréal: Bellarmin, 2000).
———, 'Public Health or Clinical Ethics: Thinking Beyond Borders,' (2002) 16(2) *Ethics & International Affairs* 35.
Ormerod, D., *Smith & Hogan: Criminal Law* (Oxford: Oxford University Press, 12th ed., 2008).
Ost, S., *Child Pornography and Sexual Grooming: Legal and Societal Responses* (Cambridge: Cambridge University Press, 2009).
Packer, H.L., *The Limits of the Criminal Sanction* (Stanford, CA: Stanford University Press, 1968).
Panichas, G.E., 'The Structure of Basic Human Rights,' (1985) 4 *Law and Philosophy* 343.
Parent, W., 'Privacy, Morality and the Law,' (1983) 12 *Philosophy and Public Affairs* 269.
Perkins, R.M., 'A Rationale of Mens Rea,' (1939) 52(6) *Harvard Law Review* 905.
——— and Boyce, R.N., *Criminal Law* (New York: The Foundation Press, Inc., 3rd ed., 1982).
Perry, M., 'Moral Knowledge, Moral Reasoning, Moral Relativism: A "Naturalist" Perspective,' (1985–1986) 20 *Georgia Law Review* 995.
Perry, S.R., 'Corrective v. Distributive Justice,' in Horder, J.(ed.), *Oxford Essays in Jurisprudence* (Oxford: Oxford University Press, 4th series, 2000).
Pettit P., 'Two Sources of Morality,' 18(2) *Social Philosophy & Policy* 102 (2001).
——— and Smith, M., 'The Truth in Deontology,' in Wallace, R.J. et al. (eds), *Reason and Value: Themes from the Moral Philosophy of Joseph Raz* (Oxford: Clarendon Press, 2004).
Pilon, R., 'Capitalism and Rights: An Essay Toward Fine Tuning the Moral Foundations of the Free Society,' (1982) 1(1) *Journal of Business Ethics* 29.
Pollock, F., *A First Book of Jurisprudence* (London: Macmillan & Co., 1929).
——— and Maitland, F.W., *The History of English Law Before the Time of Edward I* (Cambridge: Cambridge University Press, Vol. II, 1923).
Posner, R.A., *Law, Pragmatism, and Democracy* (Cambridge, MA: Harvard University Press, 2003).
Postema, G.J., 'Objectivity Fit for Law,' in Leiter, B. (ed.), *Objectivity in Law and Morals* (Cambridge: Cambridge University Press, 2001).

———, 'Politics is about Grievance: Feinberg on the Legal Enforcement of Morals,' (2005) 11 *Legal Theory* 293.

———, 'Salience Reasoning,' (2008) 27 *Topoi* 41.

Pound, J., *Poverty and Vagrancy in Tudor England* (Harlow, U.K.: Longman, 1971).

Putman, H., 'The Meaning of "Meaning,"' in *Mind, Language, and Reality* (Cambridge: Cambridge University Press, 1975).

Quinney, R., *The Critique of Legal Order* (Boston: Little Brown, 1974).

Rainbolt, G.W., 'Two Interpretations of Feinberg's Theory of Rights,' (2005) 11 *Legal Theory* 227.

Raphael, D.D., *British Moralists 1650–1800* (Oxford: Oxford University Press, 1969).

Rawls, J., *A Theory of Justice* (Cambridge MA: Harvard University Press, 1971).

———, *Lectures on the History of Moral Philosophy* (Cambridge, MA: Harvard University Press, 2000).

———, 'Two Concepts of Rules,' in Foot, P., *Theories of Ethics* (Oxford: Oxford University Press, 2002).

Ray, J.J., *Conservatism as Heresy* (Sydney: A.N.Z. Book Co., 1974).

Raz, J., *The Morality of Freedom* (Oxford: Clarendon Press, 1986).

———, *Ethics in the Public Domain* (Oxford: Clarendon Press, 1995).

———, *The Practice of Value* (Oxford: Clarendon Press, 2003).

Reiman, J., *The Rich Get Richer and the Poor Get Prison* (Boston, MA: Allyn and Bacon, 4th ed., 1995).

Reiss, H. and Nisbet, H.B., *Kant's Political Writing* (Cambridge: Cambridge University Press, 1970).

Rescher, N., *Objectivity: The Obligations of Impersonal Reason* (Notre Dame, IN: University of Notre Dame Press, 1997).

Rhinehart, L.K., 'Would Workers Be Better Protected if They Were Declared Endangered Species? A Comparison of Criminal Enforcement Under the Federal Workplace Safety and Environmental Protection Laws,' (1994) 31 *American Criminal Law Review* 351.

Ribton-Turner, C.J., *A History of Vagrants and Vagrancy and Beggars and Begging* (London: Chapman and Hall, 1887).

Richards, D.A.J., 'Human Rights and the Moral Foundations of the Substantive Criminal Law,' (1979) 12 *Georgia Law Review* 1395.

———, 'Drug Use and the Rights of the Person: A Moral Argument for Decriminalization of Certain Forms of Drug Use,' (1980–1981) 33 *Rutgers Law Review* 607.

———, *Sex, Drugs, Death and the Law: An Essay on Human Rights and Overcriminalization* (Totowa, NJ: Rowman and Littlefield, 1982).

Ripstein, A., 'Authority and Coercion,' (2004) 32(1) *Philosophy & Public Affairs* 1.

———, 'Beyond the Harm Principle,' (2006) 34(3) *Philosophy & Public Affairs* 215.

Roberts, J. et al., *Populism and Public Opinion: Lessons from Five Countries* (Oxford: Oxford University Press, 2003).

Roberts, P., 'Privacy, Autonomy and Criminal Justice Rights: Philosophical Preliminaries,' in Alldridge, P. and Brants, C.H. (eds), *Personal Autonomy, The Private Sphere and Criminal Law* (Oxford: Hart Publishing, 2001).

Robinson, P. H., 'A Theory of Justification: Societal Harm as a Prerequisite for Criminal Liability,' (1975) 23 *UCLA Law Review* 266.

——, 'Supreme Court Review: Foreword: The Criminal–Civil Distinction and Dangerous Blameless Offenders,' (1993) 83 *Journal of Criminal Law and Criminology* 693.

—— and Cahill, M.T., 'Can a Model Penal Code Second Save the States from Themselves?,' (2003) 1 *Ohio State Journal of Criminal Law* 169.

Rorty, R., *Consequences of Pragmatism* (Minneapolis, MN: University of Minnesota Press, 1982).

——, *Objectivity, Relativism, and Truth: Philosophical Papers* (Cambridge: Cambridge University Press, Vol. I, 1991).

Rose, J.A., 'The Beggar's Free Speech Claim,' (1989–1990) 65 *Indiana Law Review* 191.

Ross, W.D., *The Right and the Good* (Oxford: Oxford University Press, 1930).

Sampson, R.J. and Raudenbush, S.W., 'Systematic Social Observation of Public Spaces: A New Look at Disorder in Urban Neighborhoods,' (1999) 105(3) *American Journal of Sociology* 603.

——, —— and Earls, F., 'Neighborhoods and Violent Crime: A Multilateral Study of Collective Efficacy,' (1997) 277 *Science, New Series* 918.

Saul, B., 'Speaking of Terror: Criminalizing Incitement to Violence,' (2005) 28 *University of New South Wales Law Journal* 868.

Sayre, F.B., 'Criminal Responsibility for the Acts of Another,' (1930) 43 *Harvard Law Review* 689.

——, 'Mens Rea,' (1932) 45(6) *Harvard Law Review* 974.

Scambler, G. and Scambler, A. (eds), *Rethinking Prostitution: Purchasing Sex in the 1990s* (London: Routledge, 1998).

Scanlon, T.M., 'A Theory of Freedom of Expression,' (1971–1972) 1 *Philosophy and Public Affairs* 204.

——, *What We Owe to Each Other* (Cambridge, MA: Harvard University Press, 2000).

Schackman, B.R. et al., 'The Lifetime Cost of Current H.I.V. Care in the United States,' (2006) 44(11) *Medical Care* 990.

Schneewind, J.B., *The Invention of Autonomy* (Cambridge: Cambridge University Press, 1998).

Schonsheck, J., *On Criminalization* (London: Kluwer Academic Publishers, 1994).

Schwartz, L.B., 'Morals, Offenses and the Model Penal Code,' (1963) 63 *Columbia Law Review* 669.

Schwartz, R.G., 'Criminalizing Occupational Safety Violations: The Use of "Knowing Endangerment" Statutes to Punish Employers Who Maintain Toxic Working Conditions,' (1990) 14 *Harvard Environmental Law Review* 487.

Scott, M.S., *Panhandling*, Problem-Oriented Guides for Police, Problem-Specific Guides Series No. 13, U.S. Dept. of Justice.

Sefton, T., 'What We Want from the Welfare State,' in Park, A. et al. (eds), *British Social Attitudes* (London: Sage Publications, Report 20, 2003).

Seidman, L.M., 'Soldiers, Martyrs, and Criminals: Utilitarian Theory and the Problem of Crime Control,' (1984) 94 *Yale Law Journal* 315.

Shafer-Landau, R., 'Liberalism and Paternalism,' (2005) 11(3) *Legal Theory* 169.

Shapin, S., *A Social History of Truth: Civility and Science in Seventeenth-Century England* (Chicago, IL: University of Chicago Press, 1994).

Shute, S., 'With and Without Constitutional Restraints: A Comparison Between the Criminal Law of England and America,' (1998) 1 *Buffalo Criminal Law Review* 329.

Silverman, E.B., *NYPD Battles Crime: Innovative Strategies in Policing* (Boston, MA: Northeastern University Press, 1999).

Simester, A.P. and Hirsch, A. von, 'Rethinking the Offense Principle,' (2002) 8 *Legal Theory* 269.

—— and Sullivan, G.R., *Criminal Law: Theory and Doctrine* (Oxford: Hart Publishing, 2nd ed. revised, 2004).

Simons, K.W., 'Criminal Law: When Is Strict Criminal Liability Just,' (1997) 87(4) *Journal of Criminal Law and Criminology* 1075.

Skogan, W., 'Disorder, Crime and Community Decline' in Hope, T. and Shaw, M. (eds), *Communities and Crime Reduction* (London: H.M.S.O., 1988).

——, *Disorder and Decline* (New York: Free Press, 1990).

Skolnick, J.H., 'Criminalization and Criminogenesis: A Reply to Professor Junker,' (1971–1972) 19 *U.C.L.A. Law Review* 715.

Smith, C.J., *China in the Post-Utopian Age* (Boulder, CO: Westview Press, 2000).

Smith, K.J.M., 'Liability for Endangerment: English Ad Hoc Pragmatism and American Innovation,' (1983) *Criminal Law Review* 127.

Smith, S.D., 'The Hollowness of the Harm Principle,' Paper 17, *Public Law and Legal Theory Research Paper Series*, No. 05-07 (University of San Diego School of Law, 2004).

Snyder, O.C., *An Introduction to Criminal Justice, Text and Cases* (New York: Prentice-Hall, 1953).

——, 'Criminal Responsibility,' (1962) 11 *Duke Law Journal* 204.

Snyman, C.R., 'The Normative Concept of Mens Rea—A New Development in Germany,' (1979) *International and Comparative Law Quarterly* 211.

Sparks, R., 'Reason and Unreason in "Left Realism": Some Problems in the Constitution of the Fear of Crime,' in Matthews, R. and Young, J., *Issues in Realist Criminology* (London: Sage Publications, 1992).

Spencer, J.R., 'Liability for Reckless Infection,' (2004) *New Law Journal* 448.

Spitzer, R.J., *The Politics of Gun Control* (Chatham, NJ: Chatham House Publishers, 1995).
Squires, P., *Gun Culture or Gun Control* (London: Routledge, 2000).
Stansfield, R., 'Britney's VPL' (London: *The Daily Mirror*, December 4, 2006).
Stapleton, J., 'Cause-in-Fact and the Scope of Liability for Consequences,' (2003) 119 *Law Quarterly Review* 388.
Stell, L.K., 'Dueling and the Right to Life,' (1979) 90(1) *Ethics* 7.
———, 'Gun Control,' in Frey, R.G. and Wellman, C.H. (eds), *A Companion to Applied Ethics* (Oxford: Blackwell Publishing, 2003).
Stephen, J.F., *Liberty, Equality, Fraternity* (London: Smith, Elder, & Co., 1873).
———, *A History of the Criminal Law in England* (New York: Burt Franklin, Vol. II, 1883).
———, *Liberty, Equality, Fraternity*, Stuart D. Warner (ed.), (Indianapolis, IN: Liberty Fund, 1993).
Stewart, H., 'Harms, Wrongs, and Set-Backs in Feinberg's Moral Limits of the Criminal Law,' (2001–2002) 5 *Buffalo Criminal Law Review* 47.
Strong, G., 'Fault, Threat and the Predicates of Criminal Liability,' (1980) *Wisconsin Law Review* 441.
Stuart, D., *Charter Justice in Canadian Criminal Law* (Toronto: Thomson Carswell, 2005).
Stuntz, W.J., 'The Pathological Politics of Criminal Law,' (2001–2002) 100 *Michigan Law Review* 505.
Sugden, S., 'The Role of Inductive Reasoning in the Evolution of Conventions,' (1998) 17(4) *Law and Philosophy* 377.
Sullivan, R.J., *Immanuel Kant's Moral Theory* (Cambridge: Cambridge University Press, 1989).
Summer, C., *Censure, Politics and Criminal Justice* (Milton Keynes, U.K.: Open University Press, 1990).
Swanson, J.A., *The Public and the Private in Aristotle's Political Philosophy* (Ithaca, New York: Cornell University Press, 1992).
Tanenhaus, S., 'Tiger Woods and the Perils of Modern Celebrity' (New York: *New York Times*, December 12, 2009).
Tardos, V., 'Recklessness and the Duty to Take Care,' in Shute, S. and Simester, A.P., *Criminal Law Theory: Doctrines of the General Part* (Oxford: Oxford University Press, 2002).
Tarling, R. and Davison, T., *Victims of Domestic Burglary: A Review of the Literature* (London: H.M.S.O., 2000).
Tasioulas, J., 'Crimes of Offense,' in Hirsch, A. von and Simester, A., *Incivilities: Regulating Offensive Behavior* (Oxford: Hart Publishing, 2006).
———, 'Punishment and Repentance,' (2006) 81 *Philosophy* 279.
Taylor, I., *Crime in Context, A Critical Criminology of Market Societies* (Boulder, CO: Westview Press, 1999).
Taylor, P.W., *Respect for Nature: A Theory of Environmental Ethics* (Princeton, NJ: Princeton University Press, 1986).

Teir, R., 'Maintaining Safety and Civility in Public Spaces: A Constitutional Approach to Aggressive Begging,' (1993) 54 *Louisiana Law Review* 285.

TenBroek, J., 'California's Dual System of Family Law: Its Origin, Development, and Present Status,' (1964) 16 *Stanford Law Review* 257.

Timmons, M. (ed.), *Kant's Metaphysics of Morals: Interpretative Essays* (Oxford: Oxford University Press, 2002).

———, 'Motive and Rightness in Kant's Ethical System,' in Timmons, M. (ed.), *Kant's Metaphysics of Morals: Interpretative Essays* (Oxford: Oxford University Press, 2002).

Tonry, M. and Frase, R.S. (eds), *Sentencing and Sanctions in Western Countries* (Oxford: Oxford University Press, 2001).

Trewavas, A., 'Malthus Foiled Again and Again,' (2002) 418 *Nature* 668.

Turk, T.A., *Criminology and Legal Order* (Chicago: Rand McNally, 1969).

Turner, G.M., 'HIPAA and the Criminalization of American Medicine,' (2002) 22(1) *Cato Journal* 121.

Tyler, T., *Why People Obey the Law* (New Haven, CT: Yale University Press, 1990).

Velleman, 'A Right to Self-Termination?' (1999) 109 *Ethics* 612.

Violence Policy Center, *When Men Murder Women: An Analysis of 2004 Homicide Data*, 3 (2006): available online at <http://.vpc.org/studies/wmmw2006.pdf.>.

Wacks, R., 'National Security and Fundamental Freedoms: Hong Kong's Article 23 under Scrutiny—A Review,' (2006) *Public Law* 180.

Waldron, J., *Liberal Rights, Collected Papers 1981–1991* (Cambridge: Cambridge University Press, 1993).

———, 'Homelessness and Community,' (2000) 50 *University of Toronto Law Journal* 371.

———, 'Toleration and Reasonableness,' in McKinnon C. and Castiglione, D. (eds), *The Culture of Toleration in Diverse Societies* (Manchester: Manchester University Press, 2003).

———, 'Moral Autonomy and Personal Autonomy,' in Christman, J. and Anderson, J. (eds), *Autonomy and the Challenges to Liberalism* (Cambridge: Cambridge University Press, 2005).

Walker, G., *Moral Foundations of Constitutional Thought* (Princeton, NJ: Princeton University Press, 1990).

Walker, N., *Punishment, Danger and Stigma* (Oxford: Basil Blackwell, 1980).

———, *Crime and Criminology* (Oxford: Oxford University Press, 1987).

———, *Why Punish?* (Oxford: Oxford University Press, 1991).

Walsh, T., '"Waltzing Matilda" One Hundred Years Later: Interactions Between Homeless Persons and the Criminal Justice System in Queensland,' (2003) *Sydney Law Review* 5.

———, 'Defending Begging Offenders,' (2004) 4(1) *Queensland University of Technology Law Journal* 58.

Weait, M., 'Criminal Law and the Sexual Transmission of HIV: *R v Dica*,' (2005) 68(1) *Modern Law Review* 121.

———, 'Harm, Consent and the Limits of Privacy,' (2005) 13 *Feminist Legal Studies* 97.

Weber, M., *Law in Economy and Society*, Rheinstein, M. (ed.), translated from the German by Shils, E. and Rheinstein, M. (Cambridge, MA: Harvard University Press, 1954).

———, *Economy and Society*, translated from the German by Roth, G. and Wittich, C. (New York: Bedminster Press, 1968).

Weisberg, R., 'Reappraising Complicity,' (2000–2001) 4 *Buffalo Criminal Law Review* 217.

Wellman, C., 'The Inalienable Right to Life and the Durable Power of Attorney,' (1995) 14 *Law and Philosophy* 245.

Wellman, C.H., 'Feinberg's Two Concepts of Rights,' (2005) 11(3) *Legal Theory* 213.

Wells, C., *Corporations and Criminal Responsibility* (Oxford: Oxford University Press, 2nd ed., 2001).

Whitman, J.Q., 'Enforcing Civility and Respect: Three Societies,' (1999–2000) 102 *Yale Law Journal* 1280.

Wiggins, D., *Needs, Values, Truth* (Oxford: Oxford University Press, 1998).

———, *Ethics, Twelve Lectures on the Philosophy of Morality* (Cambridge, MA: Harvard University Press, 2006).

Williams, G.L., 'The Definition of a Crime,' (1955) 8 *Current Legal Problems* 107.

———, *Criminal Law: The General Part* (London: Stevens & Sons Ltd., 1961).

———, *Textbook of Criminal Law* (London: Stevens & Sons, 2nd ed., 1983).

———, 'Oblique Intention,' (1987) 46 *Cambridge Law Journal* 417.

———, 'Complicity, Purpose and the Draft Code – 1,' (1990*) Criminal Law Review* 4.

———, 'Complicity, Purpose and the Draft Code – 2,' (1990) *Criminal Law Review* 98.

———, 'Obedience to Law as a Crime,' (1990) 53 *Modern Law Review* 445.

Williams, K.S., *Textbook on Criminology* (Oxford: Oxford University Press, 2001).

Williamson, J.G., *Did British Capitalism Breed Inequality?* (London: Routledge, 2005).

Willigenburg, T. van, 'Reason and Love: A Non-Reductive Analysis of the Normativity of Agent-Relative Reasons,' (2004) 8 *Ethical Theory and Moral Practice* 45.

Wilson, J.Q. and Kelling, G., 'Broken Windows: The Police and Neighborhood Safety,' (1982) *Atlantic Monthly* 29.

Wolff, K.H., *The Sociology of George Simmel* (Glencoe, IL: The Free Press, 1950).

Wolff, R.P., Moore, B. and Marcuse, H., *A Critique of Pure Toleration* (Boston, MA: Beacon Press, 1965).

Wood, A.W., *Kant's Ethical Thought* (Cambridge: Cambridge University Press, 1999).

────── and O'Neill, O., 'Kant on Duties Regarding Nonrational Nature,' (1998) *Proceedings of the Aristotelian Society* 189.
Wright, G.H. von, *Norm and Action: A Logical Enquiry* (London: Routledge & Kegan Paul, 1963).
──────, *The Varieties of Goodness* (London: Routledge & Kegan Paul, 1963).
Young, J., *The Exclusive Society* (London: Sage Publications, 1999).
Yourow, H.C., *The Margin of Appreciation Doctrine in the Dynamics of European Human Rights Jurisprudence* (The Hague: Martinus Nijhoff Publishers, 1995).
Zimmerman, M.J., 'Sharing Responsibility,' (1985) 22(2) *American Philosophical Quarterly* 115.
──────, *An Essay on Moral Responsibility* (Totowa, NJ: Rowman & Littlefield, 1988).
Zimring, F.E., 'The Multiple Middlegrounds Between Civil and Criminal Law,' (1992) 101 *Yale Law Journal* 1901.
────── and Hawkins, G., *The Citizens Guide to Gun Control* (New York: Macmillan, 1992).
────── and ──────, *Crime Is Not the Problem: Lethal Violence in America* (Oxford: Oxford University Press, 1997).

Index

Note: numbers in brackets preceded by *n* refer to footnotes.

abortion 1, 2, 14, 15, 76, 79, 129–130, 133, 137
    and rights of fetus 161–163
accessories/accomplices 95, 120–121, 124–127
accumulative interests 42, 43–44, 223, 225, 226
actual bodily harm *see R. v. Brown*; *R. v. Konzani*
actus non facit reum nisi mens sit rea 53
actus reus 117
agency 22–25, 50, 149–150
aggregate harm 107–108, 115, 117–127, 129, 138–139
    fair imputation of 118–127
Allen, C.K. 75
American Law Institute 27
Amish people 15
amputation 20, 33, 174, 176, 189, 206–207
animality 147
animals, harm to 31, 32, 82, 255, 257
    and bad consequences 60, 61
    and Categorical Imperative 144, 158–163
    and culling 60(*n*109), 61
    extinctions of species 57–58
    and farming 56, 60, 61
    and Feinberg's Harm Principle 40, 41, 56–61
    foxhunting/bullfighting 2, 4, 57, 60, 158
    and human duties 59
    and human rationality 45–46
    and interests 46(*n*53), 56–57, 58, 161
    and lower/higher orders 60
    and respect for persons principle 144
    and scientific experiments 60
    wanton cruelty, as objective wrong 56, 58–59, 60, 161
animals, prosecution of 218(*n*95)
anti-competition laws 47–48
anti-gun lobby 101
apotemnophilia *see* self-harm
arbitrary detention 10, 14
Arbour, Justice 84, 94
armed robbery 90
art, willful damage to 20, 26–27, 221–222
ASBOs (Anti-Social Behavior Orders) 7–8
Ashworth, Andrew 6, 66, 73, 169(*n*116), 176–177, 203, 207
assault 89, 189
Australia 41(*n*22), 66–67, 95, 252(*n*28)
    firearm controls in 106–107
Australian Securities and Investments Commission v. Vizard [2006] 66
automobiles *see* car ownership/use; road accidents
autonomy *see* personal autonomy

bad acts/consequences 11–12, 20, 21–23, 30, 38, 68, 152, 212, 245, 247, 254–255
    and contingency 34–35
    and harm to animals 40, 45–46, 60, 61
    as justification for imprisonment 69, 70
    and moral culpability 52, 53–54, 55, 90
    and offense 35, 195–196, 202, 222
    and remote harm criminalization 103, 104, 118
    and wrongdoing 49, 216
Baker, C. Edwin 135(*n*161)

Barnes v. Glen Theatre, Inc. 4–5(*n*16)
Beatty v. Gillbanks (1892) 126(*nn*125, 128), 127
Beccaria, Cesare 37
begging 1, 4, 20, 39, 61, 239, 245, 246
    and broken window thesis 109–110, 114, 125
    decriminalization of 11, 76–77
    and freedom of speech 4(*n*10), 11, 77, 78
    and secondary liability theory 31
    see also homeless people, feeding
Benn, Stanley I. 151, 236
bestiality 82, 83
Bottoms, Anthony 114
Bowers v. Hardwick (1986) 16
Braidwood J.A. 81
bribery 92–93, 208
Britain (U.K.) 1, 25, 109–110, 137, 252(*n*28)
    ASBOs in 7–8
    corporate liability in 24
    criminalizing non-objective harm in 61
    human rights abuses in 19
    number of offences in 6
    oblique intention in 121, 122–123
    obscenity/indecency in 62(*n*120), 63
    parliamentary expenses scandal in 66–67(*n*144)
    proportionality in 85–86(*n*225), 86
    second chance mechanisms in 66
broken window thesis 7, 31, 109–115
    lack of evidence for 111–115
bullfighting 57, 60, 158
burglary 43, 167–169
    attempted, as inchoate offence 168–169
burka-wearing 237–238
'but for' cause 9, 63(*n*124), 115–117

Canada 98, 247, 252(*n*28)
    compelling state interest in 18
    freedom of speech in 11, 77
    personal autonomy in 13–14, 13(*n*46), 79
Canadian Charter of Rights and Freedoms 1, 10, 41(*n*22), 76

harm criterion in 80–85
cannibalism 82, 83, 174, 176(*n*12), 179, 180, 185, 186, 187, 189
capital punishment 68(*n*149), 87, 206
cardinal proportionality 95–96, 97
car ownership/use 102, 115, 128, 129, 133, 136
Categorical Imperative (Kant) 143, 145–152
    and abortion/rights of fetus 161–163
    aim of theory 145
    false promising exemplar in 150
    good will in 145–146, 148
    and harm to animals 144, 158–163
    humanity in 146–147, 148–149, 150–151, 159–160, 161–163
    means/ends in 146, 148–149, 150
    personal autonomy in 141, 144, 148, 149, 175(*n*8)
    and rape by deception 153, 156, 157
    reason/rationality in 146–148, 158, 159, 181
    respect for persons in 141, 144, 148–150, 151–152
    shortcomings of 150, 152, 157, 158–159
    things/persons distinction in 149
    and unfair/unprincipled criminalization 157
    universalizable maxims in 146, 186, 188
causation *see* proximate causation constraint
celebrities 48, 192, 226, 241
    and privacy violations 62(*n*118), 63, 233–234
Chicago (U.S.) 113–114
child pornography 134–146
child rearing 15, 79
China 76, 130, 241(*n*194)
civil wrongs/injunctions 7–8, 65–66, 73
    see also torts
class system 64–65
cocaine 19, 86
Coleman, Jules L. 108(*n*38)
Coles, Catherine M. 112
collective efficacy 113–114
collective interests 92, 94, 208

see also individual justice/collective good
common law 86, 87
Commonwealth v. Bonadio 16
community, harm to 74–75
community interests 92
compelling state interest 17–18
competition 46–49
    and culpability 47–49
    and unfairness 48
consent, moral limits of 33–34, 82–83, 143, 173–193
    and authenticity 179
    and degree of risk/recklessness 182–184
    and deliberate infection with disease *see R. v. Konzani*
    and Golden Rule 188
    and grave harm 174, 178–179, 183, 187, 192–193, 256
    and human dignity 173–174, 191–192
    and objectivity 173–177
    and plastic surgery 191–192
    and respect for persons 181–182, 189
    and sadomasochism *see R. v. Brown*
consequentialism 69–70, 102–103, 118, 130, 169(n116)
conspiracy 118, 119
contingency *see* conventional contingency
contraception 15, 76, 79
contracts, breaches of 73, 74, 195(n2)
conventional contingency 2, 12, 20, 26–27, 29, 34–35, 205
conventional objectivity 5, 34, 205, 206, 216
conventional wrongs 195–243
    and badness of offending others 227–234
    and contingent harms 223–227
    and critical morality 204–207, 213–222
    and legitimacy 208–213
    and mediating maxims 198–204
    and Offense Principle 195–207
    and principled criminalization 235–240
Cook, Philip J. 105

cooperation/cooperation problems 34, 208, 226–227
copulation, public *see* exhibitionism
copyright laws 48
core harms *see* primitive harms
corporate crime/liability 23–24, 39–40, 65–66, 72
corpses, interfering with 83–84
corruption/bribery 92–93
corruption of public morals 63
covert harm 32, 153–155
    see also under rape
crime labels 2, 4, 11–12, 19, 22–23, 34, 38, 134, 208
    and disadvantaged people 64
    and fairness/unfairness 52, 67
    and overcriminalization 3(n3), 9, 247(n6)
    proportionality of 96, 254
    see also categories/variables *under* harm
crime prevention 69–70
    see also broken window thesis
crime rates 112–115
criminal damage 20, 26–27, 221–222, 226–227
criminalization 2–6
    consequences of 2–3, 9
    and convention/legitimacy 208–213
    core prerequisites of 26
    and corporations/governments 65–66
    and fairness *see* proportionality
    over- *see* overcriminalization
    personal 23
    principled 26–29, 31–32
    regulatory 23–24
    retributive/preventative justification for 21–22, 69–70
    unprincipled *see* unprincipled criminalization
criminal policy 3
    and populism/expediency 4, 6–8
    proposals 254–257
criminal record 13, 13(n46)
criminal responsibility 101–104
critical morality 34–35, 57–58, 130, 134, 161, 173, 204–205, 207, 212

and bad consequence 216, 217, 218, 219, 220–221
and culpability 217–220
shortcomings of 213–222
cruelty 59, 60
cruel/unusual punishment 18–19, 41(*n*22), 77(*n*187), 85, 87
culling 60(*n*109), 61
culpability 11–12, 18, 22–23, 26, 30, 31, 71(*n*160), 154
    of accessories/accomplices 95, 120–121, 124
    of animals 217–218
    and competition 47–49
    continuum 68, 75
    and critical morality 217–220
    and endangerment 132–133
    and Harm Principle 38, 88–89
    moral *see* moral culpability
    and oblique intention 121–123
    principle 220
    and remote harm criminalization 101, 103, 104, 118, 119, 120
    three core grades of 88, 89
culpable involvement 120–121

Dan-Cohen, Meir 31–33, 141, 142, 143, 144, 158
    criticisms of Harm Principle 152–157, 171
danger *see* endangerment
decency, standards of 17(*n*71), 62, 76, 87–88
decriminalization 11, 15, 27, 76–77, 142
defamation 73, 74, 142
defecating *see* urinating/defecating in public
Dempsey, Michelle M. 134–135
deontological theory 30(*n*120), 32, 144, 152–153, 157
    see also Categorical Imperative
desert theory 21(*n*87), 22, 103–104
deterrence 21, 40, 69
Devlin, Patrick 27, 62, 204, 206, 207, 211, 212, 215, 222, 242
dignity principle 32, 141, 142
disease, deliberate transmission of 109(*n*40), 134, 178, 179

special case for 187–188
see also R. v.Konzani
disgust 34, 97, 195, 196, 197–198, 199, 202, 220(*n*106), 227, 228
    objective wrongness of 228–229
    reasonableness evaluation of 203
disorder-crime link *see* broken window thesis
disproportionate punishment 12, 18–19, 21, 76, 85–87, 98
District of Columbia v. Heller (2008) 86, 87, 139
Doctrine of Right (Kant) 32, 143(*n*7), 164
Dressler, Joshua 105(*n*16), 120, 121
drugs 1, 4, 63(*n*124), 94, 114, 246–247, 251
    inchoate criminalization of 108–109
    life sentence for 19, 86
    see also marijuana
due process *see* personal autonomy
Due Process Clause (U.S. Constitution) 10, 71, 78, 80
Duff, R.A. 74–75, 90, 169(*n*115), 180, 189
duty 59–60, 145, 146, 150(*n*53), 159
Dworkin, R. 28(*n*111), 77, 81, 135, 175, 176, 187

Earls, F. 113–114
E.C.H.R. (European Convention on Human Rights) 1, 10, 12, 19, 76
    personal autonomy in 13(*n*48), 79
    proportionality in 41(*n*22), 97
economic competition 46–49, 209, 217
economic harm 12, 18–19, 89–90, 221(*n*109)
education 15, 79
Eighth Amendment of U.S. Constitution 9, 10, 12, 39, 71
    evolving standards of decency in 17(*n*71), 76, 87–88
    proportionality in 18–19, 41, 85–88, 95, 96, 97, 98, 245
Ellickson, Robert 202
encroachments 196, 227, 229, 230–231
endangerment 90–91, 101, 104, 106–107, 118, 119, 128–139
    and creation of demand 134–136
    direct/indirect 132–133

distinct from harm 131(*n*146)
and Standard Harms Analysis 131–132, 135
time factor in 133
environmental crimes 57, 92, 208
see also littering
environmental degradation 92, 93, 129, 130, 136
see also global warming
equal freedom 32, 141, 142–143, 164
equality principle 220, 237
equal respect 34
Europe 1, 19, 76
human rights abuses in 12
European Convention on Human Rights *see* E.C.H.R.
euthanasia 179(*n*26), 185
evil 51
free-floating 57–58
evolutive interpretation 10, 97
ex ante/*ex post* criminalization 9, 23, 50–51, 53, 54–55, 69(*n*151), 154–155
exhibitionism 2, 4, 9, 20, 34–35, 70, 88–89, 96–97, 208, 216, 245
and degree of offense 199–200, 237–238, 240
and liberty interest 240
and reticence/personal domains 229, 230–231, 239–240, 248–249
see also public nudity
explosives 132–133
ex post blameworthiness 55
external freedom 164–165
extinctions of species 57–58

facilitation offenses 124
fair criminalization, Kantian criteria for 141–152
fairness constraints 31, 32, 153
fair punishment *see* proportionality
false promising 26, 49, 141, 146, 150, 152–153, 195(*n*2)
Feinberg, Joel 3(*n*5), 84, 92, 173
on consent 143, 176
on critical morality 204–205, 222
on interests *see* interests

Offense Principle of *see* Feinberg's Offense Principle
on paternalism 174
on positive morality 206
Feinberg's Harm Principle 29–30, 38, 40–55, 94(*n*255), 196, 230, 240
balancing process in 52(*n*74), 247
and *ex ante*/*ex post* criminalization 50–51, 53, 54–55
and harm to animals 40, 41, 56–61, 158
interests in *see* interests
and moral culpability 49–55, 198
shortcomings of 31, 40, 41, 50, 54, 56
and Standard Harms Analysis 131–132, 135
and sufficient condition requirement 39, 67, 73(*n*172), 142(*n*4)
three senses of harm in 41–42, 178–179, 223
ulterior aims in 42–43, 224, 226
wants in 44
wrongness theory in 56
Feinberg's Offense Principle 8–9, 29–30, 34, 35, 82, 97, 195–207
and conventionally contingent wrongs 236, 238, 239–240, 249
and critical morality 204–205, 207, 212–213
and extent/intensity of offense 199–201
Feinberg's justification for 196, 207, 222, 227–228
hollowness of 30, 195–198, 220(*n*106)
and mediating maxims/critical morality 198–207, 249
and norms 195(*n*2), 196, 197, 198, 200, 202, 204, 207
and objectivity 197, 201, 202, 228–229
reasonableness evaluation in 203
and unwanted information 238, 249
fetus
earrings made from 62(*n*119), 196, 222(*n*111), 227–228
rights of 161–163
fictitious legal entities 23–24

financial interests 43
  see also economic competition
Finnis, John 130–131(*n*145)
firearm deaths/injuries 105–106, 129, 133–134
firearm licencing/storage 139
firearm possession 31, 86, 87, 101–107
  and accomplice/accessory liability 120–121, 124–127
  and aggregate harm 107–108, 115, 117–127, 129, 138–139
  and culpability 101, 103, 104, 118, 119, 120–121, 127
  and direct harm 105–107
  endangerment approach to 101, 104, 106–107, 118, 119, 128–139
  and extent of risk 133–134
  and inchoate liability 109, 115, 118–119
  and objective harm 107, 108
  and oblique intention 121–123
  and proximate causation constraint 103, 104, 107, 118
  and recklessness 121–122, 123–124
  and remote harm 107–108, 127
  and remote harm criminalization 101–104, 115
  and right to bear arms 101, 136–137
  social value of 136–137, 138
  and substantial/unjustifiable risk 121–122, 123, 123(*n*119)
firearm sales 122, 123, 124
Formula of Autonomy (Kant) 147, 148
fornication 61, 70
foxhunting 2, 4, 57, 60, 158
fraud 98, 214
freedom of conscience 14, 25
freedoms 1, 10–11, 14, 186, 239, 256
  equal 32, 141, 142–143, 164
  external 164–165
  and interests 44(*n*46)
  mere/fundamental 17–18
freedom of speech 14, 77, 77(*n*187), 98, 133, 237
  and begging 4(*n*10), 11, 77, 78
  four values/two justifications of 135(*n*161)
free-floating evil 57–58

French Declaration of the Rights of Man 96
Fried, Charles 52(*n*72), 55(*n*85)

game theory 214
Gardner, John 49(*n*58), 131, 153, 154, 155–156, 240(*n*193)
Gavison, Ruth 229–230, 231(*n*155)
gladiatorial battles 143, 178, 184
global warming 93, 128, 129, 130, 133
Goffman, Erving 231–232
Golden Rule 188
Goldsmith, Andrew 66
good will 145–146, 148
governmental interests 92–93
Griswold v. Connecticut (1965) 79
Gross, Hyman 92
Groundwork of the Metaphysics of Morals (Kant) 32, 144, 145, 146
Guiliani, Rudolph 112
guns *see* firearm deaths/injuries; firearm possession; firearm sales

Hall, Jerome 37, 55(*n*83)
Hampton, Jean E. 22, 53–54(*nn*77, 78), 73
Harcourt, Bernard 8, 63–64, 112–113
harm 8, 11–12
  aggregate *see* aggregate harm
  categories/variables of 89–91
  and community/collective interests 92–94, 208
  as constitutional requirement 81–88
  contingent/perceived 7, 20–21, 222
  and convention/socialization 20, 221–222
  covert/hidden 32, 153–155
  crime defined by 37–38
  criminal/private law 72–75
  criterion 80–85, 88–96, 98–99
  direct/indirect 105, 208
  Feinberg's conception of 178, 196–197
  Feinberg's three senses of 41–42, 178–179, 223
  and interests *see* interests
  objective *see* objectivity constraint
  prevention 23, 26
  primitive/core *see* primitive harms

remote *see* remote harm
tangible 27
trans-cultural account of 11, 12
and wrongdoing 37–41
as yardstick, proposals for 255–256
Harmelin v. Michigan (1991) 19, 86–88, 98
harmfulness grid/ladder 89, 91–92
harmless wrongs 8–9, 12, 15, 16, 26, 61–64, 158, 227–228
and criminalization 30, 35, 68, 70–71, 141, 142, 215
wrongful harms classed as 32, 143
see also non-objective harm
harm prevention 21, 23, 30, 60, 70, 75, 132, 169
and endangerment 132
and inchoate liability 104, 119
Harm Principle 1, 1–2, 7–8, 16, 20(*n*85), 27, 28–32, 220
autonomy in 170
and Categorical Imperative, compared 152, 157
and civil wrongs 142
and constitutional rights 76–77
constitutionalizing 67–68
contingency of 2
and corporations/wealthy people 23–24, 39–40, 65–67
and culpability 38
Dan-Cohen's criticisms of 152–157
Feinberg's formulation of *see* Feinberg's Harm Principle
harm prevention/risk of harm in 167, 168, 169
as justification for imprisonment 31, 38–39, 54, 69–72
limits of 142, 184–185
and mere/fundamental liberties 18, 85
objective/non-objective conceptions 61–67, 205–206
and populism 8, 28, 31
and principled criminalization 31–32
as principle of fundamental justice 81
and Standard Harms Analysis 131–132, 135
and sufficient condition *see* sufficient condition requirement

worth defending 30, 171
Hart, H.L.A. 21, 26, 27, 29, 82, 122, 203, 205, 207, 212, 238
on economic competition 46–47
Hawkins, Gordon 105–106(*n*23)
health and safety regulations 24(*n*93), 66, 214
Hemenway, David 106, 107
hidden harm 32, 153–156
Hill, Thomas E. 185(*n*53), 186, 187
H.I.V. cases 33, 134, 177, 179, 193
and *R. v. Brown* 189–190
see also R. v. Konzani
HKSAR v. Hiroyuki Takeda [1998] 62
Hohfeldian correlativity theory 59–60
homeless people
feeding 4, 6(*n*22), 7, 12, 20, 98, 246, 247
and offense/tolerance 248, 250, 251, 252–254
see also begging
homosexuality 4, 15, 16, 27, 28, 200–201, 204(*n*51), 211
and moral culpability 52–53
and objectivity constraint 45
Hong Kong 62, 63, 128(*n*134), 233(*n*170)
Honoré, Tony M. 21(*n*87)
humanity/human dignity 9(*n*38), 34, 45, 173
and autonomy/freedom 174–176, 186–187, 192–193
degradation/alienation of 180–181, 182, 186–188
Kant's conception of 145, 146–147, 150–151, 159–160, 161–163, 164, 176, 180, 181
see also under R. v. Brown; R. v. Konzani
human rights 1, 9–11, 19–20, 253
abuses 12, 19, 21
and contemporary standards of justice 76, 77
and Harm Principle 76–77
moral dimensions of 75–79
waiving 173, 174–175
Human Rights, Universal Declaration of 41(*n*22)
hurts, physical/mental 45, 196, 228

Husak, Douglas 3(*n*3), 17, 20(*n*85), 22(*n*89), 29(*n*118), 104, 220(*n*106)

imprisonment 67–68, 257
   as harm 12, 21, 67, 83, 84, 245–246
   harmfulness criterion for 31, 38–39, 54, 69–72, 88–89
   length of *see* sentence, length of
   and proportionality 13–15
incest 82, 83, 98
inchoateness 90, 104, 108–109, 118–119, 168–169
incitement 118
individual justice/collective good 101, 102, 118, 119
inequity 48
infants' rights 56(*n*89)
insider trading 66
intentionality 51, 52, 55, 55(*n*83), 88, 92(*n*246)
   oblique 121–123
   and remote harm 125–126
   see also culpability
interests 41–45, 223–225
   accumulative 42, 43–44, 223, 225, 226–227
   and harm to animals 46(*n*53), 56–57, 58, 161
   majority/minority 248
   security 42, 43, 166–167, 223, 225
   setbacks of, harm as 41–42, 45, 50
   and ulterior aims 42–43, 224, 226
   and wants 44, 235–236
   welfare *see* welfare interests
international conventions 75
Internet 35, 62, 137, 233
inter-subjectivity 5, 81(*n*205), 173, 181, 206, 209–211, 212, 214, 215(*n*89), 216, 240
ivory poaching 135, 160

jail *see* imprisonment
Jauncey, Lord 177
judicial review 245–247
just deserts justification 40, 69–70, 103–104
justice constraint 1, 12, 38, 54, 96, 245–247

Kadish, Sandford 121, 123(*n*119)
Kant, Immanuel 5, 32, 96, 141–144, 209, 221
   autonomy in 141, 144, 148, 149, 169–170, 174–175
   external freedom in 164, 186
   fair criminalization in 141–152
   Golden Rule in 188
   rationality in 146–148, 174, 181
   see also Categorical Imperative
Kelling, George 7, 110–111, 112
Kennedy v. Louisiana (2008) 88
King, Peter 253
kissing in public 209(*n*67), 228, 237
Kleinig, John 72
Korsgaard, Christine 209, 221
Kramer, M.H. 59–60

Las Vegas (U.S.) 6(*n*22), 7
law enforcement costs 3–4
law as integrity 81
Lawrence v. Texas (2003) 16, 17, 204(*n*51)
legal limits of criminal law 1
legal moralism 26(*n*93), 29, 174, 177
legitimacy of criminal law 208–213
lesbianism *see* homosexuality
liberalism 57
liberties *see* freedoms
liberty interest 13–14, 16–18, 80–81, 85, 85(*n*221), 137, 240
   and privacy violations 229, 236, 237, 240
liberty, right to 9–10, 80–81, 240
Lieter, Brian 210(*n*70)
life imprisonment 12
   and three strikes and you're out policy 4, 98, 208(*n*63)
   see also Solem v. Helm
lifestyle choice 15–16, 250–251
littering 23(*n*92), 70, 75, 89, 91–92, 93
   and remote harm 116–117
Lockyer v. Andrade (2003) 98
Lott, John R. 102(*n*3)
Lucas, J.R. 28(*n*112), 74(*n*175)
Ludwig, Jens 105

McConnell, Terrance 179
McDowell, John 221(*n*107), 240

Mackie, J.L. 207, 213, 214, 241–242
Magna Carta 86
Malcolm, Joyce Lee 136–137
Malmo-Levine case (2003) 13–14, 80–85, 94–95, 98, 247
margin of appreciation 10
marijuana possession 1, 4, 15, 61
    Malmo-Levine case 13–14, 80–85, 94–95, 98, 247
markets *see* competition
Marmor, Andrei 60
Marshall, S.E. 74–75
means/ends 146, 148–149, 150, 157, 164, 181
    mere 151, 152, 154
media 6, 125–127, 135, 136
mediating principles 142, 198–207, 247–248, 249
medical negligence 65
mens rea 89, 142, 217
mental suffering 84
Mill, J.S. 1, 15(n55), 16, 25, 29, 79, 79(n196), 239
money laundering 108–109
Moore, Michael 69(n151), 70
moral autonomy 141, 144
moral culpability 47–48, 49–55, 51(n69), 88, 90, 118, 203, 204–205
    and homosexuality 52–53
    and responsibility/condemnability 53–54
    and torts/crimes 72, 73
    and wrongfulness/wrongness 51–52, 237(n181)
moral impermissibility 51
morality and law 213–214
moral law *see* Categorical Imperative
moral limits of criminal law 1, 4–5, 26(n97), 27–28, 29, 31, 32–33
murder 89
    attempted 91
    and oblique intention 121, 122–123
Murphy, Jeffrie G. 108(n38), 143, 238

Nagel, Thomas 51, 221, 229
negligence 40, 50, 51, 65(n133), 72, 74, 88
    assisting 123–124

corporate 74(n177)
and imprisonment 89
mere/gross 89
see also culpability
neighborhoods/neighborliness 113–114
New York City (U.S.) 110–111, 112–113
New Zealand 62(n120), 106
non-correlative duty theory 59
non-criminal regulation 25, 26, 39, 66, 130
non-objective harm 61–64
    obscenity/indecency 62–63
nudity *see* public nudity
nuisance behavior 7, 25, 64, 74(n176), 110–111
    and Offense Principle 199

objectivity 5, 30, 31, 33–34, 35, 39, 45, 54, 56, 61–67, 68, 70–72, 94, 97–98, 173, 221
    and inter-subjectivity 210(n70)
    and offense/umbrage 197, 201, 202, 228–229, 256–257
    and rationality 255(n40)
objectivity and consent 173–177, 180–191
    limits of 180–188
    and wanton use of humans 188–191
oblique intention 121–123
obscenity/indecency 62–63, 133
    and privacy violations 63, 233–234
Offences Against the Person Act [1861] 182, 190
offensive behavior 195, 196, 211
    conventional badness of 227–234, 235
    and literature/public speaking 238–239
    and mediating principle 248, 249
    and privacy *see* privacy
    subjectivity of 228, 232–233
    see also Feinberg's Offense Principle
one-child policy 129, 130
O'Neill, Onora 159–160, 179, 253
ordinal proportionality 95, 96, 97
organ donation 83
overcriminalization 3, 4–5, 39, 76, 246–247

parliamentary expenses scandal (U.K.) 66–67(n144)

paternalism 20–21, 29–30, 63(*n*124), 83, 174, 185
penal fines 23, 24, 54, 70, 96, 245
penal populism 4, 6–8, 28, 31, 40, 61
people-smuggling 184
personal autonomy 10, 12–18, 19, 26, 45, 71, 79, 173–177, 192–193, 215, 225
  ad hoc application of 76
  constraint 34, 44
  and human dignity 34, 174–176, 191
  Kant's conception of *see under* Kant
  and mere/fundamental liberty 17–18
  and opportunities 44(*n*50)
  and waiving of rights 173, 174–175
  see also privacy; self-determination
personal criminalization 23
personality, Kant's conception of 147, 148
personal space 231–232, 242, 248–249, 250
petty offences 23–24, 25, 39, 70–71
  see also broken window thesis
physical access 230–231
plastic surgery 191–192
pluralism 237, 245–254
police 110–111, 113
  unarmed 137(*n*164)
populism *see* penal populism
pornography 63(*n*124)
  child 134–135
positive morality 16(*n*65), 18(*n*76), 27–28, 204(*n*51), 205, 206, 212
  and inter-subjectivity 242–243
poverty 64–65, 113, 114
practicality constraint 75
primitive harms 20, 26, 35, 208–209, 212, 222, 242, 255
principled criminalization 26–29, 31–32, 204–205, 208, 209–210
  and conventional wrongs 235–240
prison riots 125, 127
privacy 13, 14, 15, 17, 77(*n*187), 78, 98, 211, 229–233, 235–236
  and consent 176–177(*n*12)
  three components of 229–230

privacy violations 9, 166–168, 195, 213, 229, 230–234, 235–237
  and Internet 35, 62, 233
  and liberty interest 229, 236, 237, 240
  and personal space 231–232, 242, 248–249, 250, 251–252
  and principled criminalization 235–236
private law *see* torts
procedural realism 242–243
promises, false/broken *see* false promising
property rights/interests 43–44, 44(*n*50), 210(*n*69), 221–222, 221(*n*109), 226
proportionality 9–14, 18–19, 21, 41, 54, 70–71, 80, 90–91, 245–246
  and culpability 30, 52, 55
  formula for 11
  as human right 41(*n*22), 80
  ordinal/cardinal 95–96, 97
  U.S. interpretation of *see under* Eighth Amendment of U.S.
  see also Solem v. Helm
prostitution 5, 27, 109, 114, 124, 211
proxies 56–57(*n*89)
proximate causation constraint 103, 104, 107, 118
psychological distress 154
public amenities 92, 93
public figures *see* celebrities
public nudity 4–5(*n*16), 203, 206, 211, 220–221, 228, 231, 237, 248–249, 252
  as art 249
  and public protest 135, 136, 215–216
public order policing 110–111
punishment 2
  populist *see* penal populism
  proportionate *see* fair punishment
punishment theory 69–70
purpose *see* intentionality

quality of life initiative (New York) 110–111, 112–113
Quod tibi non vis fieri (Golden Rule) 188

racial abuse 201–202
Rammel v. Estelle (1980) 98
rape 4, 20, 55, 71, 88, 103, 150–151, 245–246
   covert/by deception 32, 143, 153–156, 155(*n*73)
   and harm to community 74, 75
   harmless 153, 154, 155
   marital 39, 73–74, 142(*n*4)
   and socialization/convention 240–241
   and universal law 146
rational basis test 16, 17
rationality 214–216, 218–220, 255(*n*40)
   Kant's conception of 146–148, 174, 181
Raudenbush, S.W. 113–114
Ravin v. State (Alaska 1975) 15
Raz, Joseph 44, 46(*n*53), 59, 83(*n*214), 161, 214
reason *see* rationality
receiving stolen goods 136
recklessness 12, 31, 33, 50, 51, 53, 68, 71–72, 88, 92(*n*246)
   and corporations/governments 65
   and intention 121, 152
   subjective/extreme subjective 121–122, 123–124, 125
   see also culpability
regulatory criminalization 23–24
Reiman, J. 39, 64–65
Reith, Peter 66–67
remote harm 31, 63(*n*124), 94–95, 101–139
   accessory/accomplice liability 120–121, 124–127
   and aggregate harm 118–127, 129, 138–139
   and broken window thesis 109–113
   and collective efficacy 113–114
   and culpability 101, 103, 104, 105(*n*16), 109, 115, 118, 119, 120
   empirical evidence of 105–118
   endangerment approach to 101, 104, 106–107, 118, 119, 128–139
   and facilitation offenses 124–125
   and individual justice/collective good 101–104
   and recklessness 121–122, 123, 124–125
   and substantial/unjustifiable risk 121–122, 123, 123(*n*119)
   time factor in 133
repeat offending 4, 94, 208(*n*63)
   see also Solem v. Helm
Rescher, Nicholas 5, 71(*n*159), 217(*n*94), 255(*n*40)
respect for persons 141, 144, 148–149, 151–152, 181–182, 189
   and disgust 228–229
retribution 21–25, 69, 90–91, 94, 103, 104, 108, 207
Richards, David 3–4
riots/protests 125–127, 135
Ripstein, Arthur 31–33, 56(*n*86)
   sovereignty principle of *see* sovereignty principle
risk *see* endangerment; substantial/unjustifiable risk
road accidents 102, 128(*n*136), 129
robbery/theft 112, 114, 254–255
Roberts, Justice Owen J. 117
Robinson, Paul H. 131(*n*146)
Robinson v. California (1962) 246–247
Roe v. Wade (1973) 79
Russell, Bertrand 59
R. v. Brown [1994] 33, 173–174, 175–176, 189–191
   as borderline case 189, 191, 193
   and H.I.V. cases, compared 189–190
   human dignity/respect for persons in 189, 190–191
   private morality defense in 176–177
R. v. Bryce [2004] 122–123
R. v. Gibson [1991] 62(*n*119), 222(*n*111)
R. v. Konzani [2005] 33, 173–174, 175–176, 180–88
   degree of risk/recklessness in 182–184
   human dignity in 180, 184–185, 186–187
   and respect for persons 181–182

R. v. Malmo-Levine [2003] 13–14, 80–85, 94–95, 98, 247

sadomasochism 177, 178, 184, 188
   and human dignity 190–191, 192
   see also R. v. Brown
Salvation Army 127
Sampson, R.J. 113–114
San Fransisco (U.S.) 113, 114
Scalia, Justice 86–87, 101, 138–139
Schneider v. New Jersey (1939) 116–117
Second Amendment of U.S. Constitution 86, 87, 101, 136–137
second chance mechanisms 65–66
secondary liability theory 31
security interests 42, 43, 166–167, 223, 225
self-defense 55, 102
self-determination 15, 79(n196), 232
self-harm 20–21, 95, 108, 176, 184–185, 256
sentence, length of 89, 93–94, 95–96, 134, 245–247, 254–255(n39)
setbacks of interests, harm as 41–42, 45
sex toys 4, 18, 61, 98, 245, 246
sexual activities/freedom 1, 4, 16, 18
shoplifting 91, 91–92(n246), 97, 98, 209
Shute, Stephen 131, 153, 154, 155–156
Simester, Andrew P. 44, 177, 228–229, 233
   mediating principle of 247, 249, 250
Skogan, Wesley G. 111–112
slavery 33, 143, 179(n26)
social cohesion 113–114
social contract 213
social disintegration thesis 27
social functions of law 214
social norms 20, 26–27, 195(n2), 216, 220, 221–222, 241(n196), 250–251, 255
soft harms 2, 29, 211, 235, 237, 242, 256, 257
Solem v. Helm (1983) 18–19, 68(n149), 85–87, 88, 95–96, 246, 247
   objective criteria in 97
solicitation 119, 127
South Dakota (U.S.) 19, 247

sovereignty principle 141, 142–143, 144, 164–171
   freedom in 164–166, 169
   and inchoate offences 168–169
   lack of sophistiction of 171
   shortcomings of 167, 169–171
   trespass/security in 166–169
Standard Harms Analysis 131–132, 135
Stanley v. Georgia (1969) 63, 133
state/local criminalization 6
State v. Minkowski (1962) 153–154
Stephen, James Fitzjames 37
stigmatization 2, 13, 23, 45
strict scrutiny test 16, 17, 18
strip clubs 18, 20, 61, 245, 246
subjectivist approach 88(n238), 90
substantial/unjustifiable risk 121–122, 123, 123(n119)
sufficient condition requirement 25, 39, 67, 68, 73(n172), 74, 75, 142(n4)
suicide 184, 188
Sullivan, Graham R. 177

tangible harm 27
Tasioulas, John 69–70
taxation 137(n165), 214
tax evasion 39, 65(n138), 66, 75, 92, 93–94
terrorism 21, 55, 127(n130)
theft/robbery 112, 114, 144, 154–155
   see also burglary; shoplifting; tax evasion
three strikes and you're out 4, 98, 208(n63)
   see also Solem v. Helm
Timmons, M. 157(n75)
toleration principle 211, 237, 238, 240(n193), 245–254
torts 25, 72–74, 142
   see also civil wrongs/injunctions
torture 20, 206, 220, 235
   of animals 58, 59, 60, 161
trans fats, ingesting 20, 245, 246
trespass 32, 33, 141, 143, 166–168, 169–270
trivial wrongs 24, 89, 124
   and Categorical Imperative 157

criminalized 4, 39, 67, 70–71, 91–92(*n*246), 94, 98, 142
  see also false promising; littering

ulterior aims 42–43, 224, 226
umbrage 2, 9, 12, 34, 242, 256, 257
unfair advantage test 93(*n*254)
unfairness 48
United States (U.S.)
  begging criminalized in *see* begging
  Bill of Rights *see* United States Constitution
  criminalizing non-objective harm in 61, 63–64, 247
  disproportionate punishment in 12, 18–19, 76, 85–87
  firearm deaths/injuries in 105–106, 129
  firearm possession in *see* firearm possession
  freedom of speech in 11
  Harm Principle in 27
  human rights abuses in 12
  number/legitimacy of offences in 6, 208
  oblique intention in 121, 123
  personal autonomy/privacy right in 14–17, 76
  recklessness/negligence in 123–124
  Supreme Court 17, 19, 68, 78, 95, 98, 133, 245, 246, 246–247
United States Constitution 1, 9, 99
  Due Process Clause 10, 71, 78, 80
  Eighth Amendment *see* Eighth Amendment of U.S. Constitution
  human rights in 76, 77(*n*187), 78–79
  privacy interests in 14, 76, 79
  Second Amendment 86, 87, 101, 136–137
universal law 146, 164
Universal Principle of Right (Kant) 143, 164–165, 186
unprincipled criminalization 2–9, 204, 217
  and Categorical Imperative 157
  and populism 4, 6–7
urinating/defecating in public 110, 248, 250, 251, 252–254

utilitarian approach 21, 129, 130, 160

vagrancy 202
vandalism 20, 26–27
vice 27
victim's rights 71, 74(*n*175)
victimless crimes 3
violence 90, 187, 191
Vizard case (2005) 66
volenti non fit injuria 143, 178–179, 190
von Hirsch, Andrew 44, 44(*n*46), 69–70, 73, 93(*n*254), 120, 225(*nn*131, 136), 228–229, 233
  mediating principle of 247, 249, 250

Waldron, Jeremy 239, 251–252
Weait, Matthew 187–188
wealth/poverty discrimination 64–67
Weeks v. United Kingdom (1988) 19
welfare interests 42, 43, 49(*n*61), 51, 56(*n*87), 166, 223–224
well-being 9(*n*38), 45, 56(*n*87), 60(*n*106)
Wellman, Carl 186–187
Wells, C. 40(*n*18)
White, Justice 87–88
Wiggins, David 59
Williams, Glanville 72, 123(*n*119), 125, 126, 138
Williams v. Pryor (2001) 18
Wilson, James Q. 7, 110–111, 115
Wisconsin v. Yoder 15
witchcraft 215–216
Wolfenden Committee 27, 176–177(*n*12)
Wood, Allen W. 159–160
wrongful consequences 55
wrongful harm 37–42, 49, 56, 78, 141, 142, 158, 178–179, 212
  and hidden harms 32, 153–155
  and Offense Principle 195, 196–197
  see also under harmless wrongs
  and sovereignty principle 166

zero tolerance 7–8, 28
  initiatives 109–113
Zimring, Franklin E. 105–106(*n*23)